W9-BVZ-260

Current Biography®

Cumulated Index 1940–2005

Current Biography
Cumulated Index 1940–2005

The H.W. Wilson Company
New York • Dublin
2006

PRINTED IN THE UNITED STATES OF AMERICA

International Standard Book No. 0-8242-1054-9

Library of Congress Catalog Card No. (40-27432)

Copyright © 2006 by The H.W.Wilson Company. All rights reserved. No part of this Work may be reproduced or copied in any form or by any means, including but not restricted to graphic, electronic, and mechanical – for example, photocopying, recording, taping, or information and retrieval systems – without the express written permission of the publisher, except that a reviewer may quote and a magazine or newspaper may print brief passages as part of a review written specifically for inclusion in that magazine or newspaper.

PREFATORY NOTE

This index, covering the years from 1940 through 2005, cumulates and supersedes the *Current Biography Cumulated Index, 1940–2000*. The reader will need to consult only this index in order to locate a name.

The dates after the names indicate the monthly issue(s) and yearbooks containing the biographies and obituaries. If a subject was covered under a different name than the one listed here or in a joint article, the name that the biography appears under is listed in brackets after the date:

Ali, Muhammad Sep 63 [Clay, Cassius] Nov 78
Abbott, Bud Oct 41 [Abbott, Bud; and Costello, Lou] obit Jun 74
Costello, Lou Oct 41 [Abbott, Bud; and Costello, Lou] obit May 59

When two subjects have exactly the same name, their occupations are listed in brackets after their names in order to distinguish between them:

Segal, George [actor] Nov 75
Segal, George [artist] Jan 72

We hope that readers will appreciate the convenience of this index to the first sixty-six volumes of *Current Biography*.

Current Biography

Cumulated Index 1940–2005

3D see Massive Attack

Aalto, Alvar Apr 48 obit Jul 76

Aaltonen, Wäinö Jun 54 obit Jul 66

Aandahl, Fred G. Sep 58 obit May 66

Aaron, Hank May 58

Aaron, Henry see Aaron, Hank

Abacha, Sani Sep 96 obit Aug 98

Abakanowicz, Magdalena Jan 2001

Abbado, Claudio May 73

Abbas, Ferhat Mar 61 obit Feb 86

Abbas, Mahmoud Jun 99

Abbell, Maxwell Jul 51 obit Sep 57

Abbot, Anthony see Oursler, Fulton

Abbott, Berenice Jul 42 obit Feb 92

Abbott, Bud Oct 41 [Abbott, Bud; and Costello, Lou] obit Jun 74

Abbott, Douglas Jun 49

Abbott, Edith Sep 41 obit Oct 57

Abbott, Edwin Milton obit Jan 41

Abbott, George Apr 40 Oct 65 obit Apr 95

Abbott, Jim Sep 95

Abbott, Robert Sengstacke obit Mar 40

Abdel Rahman al Saud, Abdel Aziz see Ibn Saud, King of Saudi Arabia

Abdul Aziz Ibn Sa'ud see Ibn Saud, King of Saudi Arabia

Abdul Rahman see Rahman, Abdul

Abdul, Paula Sep 91

Abdul-Jabbar, Kareem Jul 67 [Alcindor, Lew] Feb 97

Abdullah bin Hussein Jan 2000

Abdullah Ibn Hussein, King of Jordan Jun 48 obit Sep 51

Abdullah, Achmed obit Jun 45

Abdullah, Al-Salim Al Sabah, Sheikh of Kuwait Jul 57 obit Jan 66

Abdullah, Mohammad Nov 52 obit Jan 83

Abdullah, Seif-ul-Islam, Prince see Seif-Ul-Islam Abdullah, Prince

Abé, Kobo Jul 89 obit Mar 93

Abel, I. W. Nov 65 obit Sep 87

Abelson, Nat Nov 57

Abelson, Philip H. Oct 65 obit Yrbk 2004

Abend, Hallett Sep 42 obit Feb 56

Abercrombie, Patrick Apr 46 obit Jun 57

Aberhart, William C. obit Jul 43

Abernathy, Ralph Jul 68 obit Jun 90

Abetz, Otto Feb 41

Abiola, Moshood Kashimawa Sep 98 obit Nov 98

Abizaid, John Oct 2003

Abraham, F. Murray Jan 91

Abraham, Spencer May 2001

Abrahams, Peter (WLB) Yrbk 57

Abram, Morris B. Oct 65 obit Jul 2000

Abrams, Benjamin Sep 54 obit Oct 67

Abrams, Charles Feb 69 obit Apr 70

Abrams, Creighton W. Oct 68 obit Oct 74

Abrams, Elliott Aug 88

Abrams, Floyd Jul 99

Abrams, Harry N. Jun 58 obit Jan 80

Abramson, Leslie Jun 99

Abs, Hermann J. Oct 70 obit May 94

Abu Ammar see Arafat, Yasir

Abul Kalam Azad, Maulana Jul 42 obit May 58

Abzug, Bella Jul 71 obit Jun 98

AC/DC Mar 2005

Ace, Goodman May 48 [Ace, Goodman; and Ace, Jane] obit May 82

Ace, Jane May 48 [Ace, Goodman; and Ace, Jane] obit Jan 75

Achebe, Chinua Jan 92

Achelis, Elisabeth Jun 54

Acheson, Albert R. obit Apr 41

Acheson, Dean Mar 41 Feb 49

obit Nov 71

Acker, Achille Van May 58 obit Sep 75

Ackerman, Carl W. Oct 45 obit Dec 70

Ackerman, Diane Jun 97

Ackley, H. Gardner Apr 68 obit May 98

Ackroyd, Peter May 93

Acland, Richard Aug 44

Acuff, Roy Jun 76 obit Jan 93

Adair, Frank E. May 46 obit Feb 82

Adamic, Louis Yrbk 40 obit Oct 51

Adamowski, Timothée obit May 43

Adams, Alice Aug 89 obit Aug 99

Adams, Alva B. obit Jan 42

Adams, Ansel May 77 obit Jun 84

Adams, Arthur S. Jan 51

Adams, Brock Jul 77 obit Yrbk 2004

Adams, Diana Apr 54 obit Mar 93

Adams, Douglas Jul 93 obit Sep 2001

Adams, Edith Feb 54

Adams, Eva Bertrand Sep 62 obit Oct 91

Adams, Franklin P. Jul 41 obit May 60

Adams, Gerry Sep 94

Adams, Grantley Herbert Sep 58 obit Jan 72

Adams, Herbert obit Jun 45

Adams, James Truslow Nov 41 obit Jul 49

Adams, John Cranford Sep 58 obit Jan 87

Adams, John May 88

Adams, Joseph H. obit Apr 41

Adams, Joseph Quincy obit Dec 46

Adams, Randolph G. Aug 43

Adams, Richard Oct 78

Adams, Roger Jun 47 obit Sep 71

Adams, Sherman Nov 52 obit

Jan 87

Adams, Stanley Feb 54 obit Mar 94

Adams, Thomas obit Apr 40

Adams, Yolanda Mar 2002

Adamson, Joy Oct 72 obit Feb 80

Addams, Charles Jan 54 obit Nov 88

Addams, Clifford Isaac obit Jan 43

Adderley, Cannonball see Adderley, Julian E.

Adderley, Julian E. Jul 61 obit Oct 75

Addington, Sarah obit Yrbk 40

Additon, Henrietta Silvis Sep 40

Ade, George obit Jul 44

Adé, King Sunny Nov 94

Adelman, Kenneth L. Jul 85

Adenauer, Konrad Jul 49 Apr 58 obit Jun 67

Adjani, Isabelle Jan 90

Adkins, Bertha S. May 53 obit Mar 83

Adkins, Charles obit May 41

Adkinson, Burton W. Jun 59

Adler, Cyrus obit May 40

Adler, Guido obit May 41

Adler, Harry Clay obit Apr 40

Adler, Julius Ochs Jun 48 obit Dec 55 Yrbk 56

Adler, Kurt Herbert Mar 79 obit Apr 88

Adler, Larry Feb 44 obit Oct 2001

Adler, Mortimer J. Apr 40 Sep 52 obit Sep 2001

Adler, Renata Jun 84

Adler, Stella Aug 85 obit Feb 93

Adolfo Nov 72

Adoula, Cyrille Mar 62

Adrian Feb 41 obit Nov 59

Adrian, E. D. Feb 55 obit Oct 77

Adzhubei, Aleksei I. Sep 64

obit May 93

Aerosmith Jul 2004

Affleck, Ben Mar 98 [Affleck, Ben; and Damon, Matt]

Afro Nov 58

Aga Khan IV, The Mar 60

Aga Khan, The May 46 obit Sep 57

Agam, Yaacov Apr 81

Agar, Herbert Mar 44 obit Jan 81

Agar, William May 49 obit Jul 72

Agassi, Andre Oct 89

Agnelli, Giovanni Jan 72 obit Jun 2003

Agnew, Spiro T. Dec 68 obit Nov 96

Agnon, Shmuel Yosef Mar 67 obit Apr 70

Aguilera, Christina Aug 2000

Aguirre Cerda, Pedro Jan 41 obit Jan 41

Ahern, Bertie Jul 98

Aherne, Brian Feb 60 obit Apr 86

Ahlgren, Mildred Carlson Jul 52

Ahmad, Imam of Yemen Mar 56 obit Nov 62

Ahmadu, Alhaji, Sardauna of Sokoto Jul 57 [Ahmadu, Al-haji, Sardauna of Sokoto; Awolowo, Obafemi; and Azikiwe, Nnamdi]

Ahmed II, Sidi obit Aug 42

Aichi, Kiichi Jul 71 obit Jan 74

Aiello, Danny Jun 92

Aigner-Clark, Julie Jan 2002

Aiken, Conrad May 70 obit Oct 73

Aiken, George D. Jun 47 obit Feb 85

Aiken, Howard Mar 47 obit May 73

Aiken, Loretta Mary see Mabley, Moms

Aikman, Troy May 95

Ailes, Roger E. Jan 89

Ailes, Stephen Jan 65 obit Oct

2001

Ailey, Alvin Mar 68 obit Jan 90

Ainsworth, William Newman, Bishop obit Aug 42

Aitken, William Maxwell Jul 40 obit Sep 64

Akalaitis, Joanne Feb 93

Akebono Aug 99

Aked, Charles F., Rev. obit Oct 41

Akers, John F. May 88

Akers, Michelle Nov 2004

Akihito, Emperor of Japan Apr 59 Aug 91

Aksyonov, Vassily Jan 90

Al Kuwatly, Shukri see Kuwatly, Shukri Al

Ala, Hussein May 51 obit Sep 64

Alagna, Roberto Jul 97

Alaïa, Azzedine Oct 92

Alain Sep 41

Alajalov, Constantin Jan 42 obit Jan 88

Alanis see Morissette, Alanis

Albanese, Licia Mar 46

Albarn, Damon see Blur

Albee, Edward Feb 63 Apr 96

Albee, Fred H. May 43 obit Apr 45

Alberghetti, Anna Maria Jan 55

Albers, Josef Jun 62 obit May 76

Albert, Arthur William Patrick obit Mar 42

Albert, Carl Jun 57 obit Jun 2000

Albert, Eddie Jan 54 obit Yrbk 2005

Alberti, Jules Jul 59

Alberto, Alvaro Mar 47

Albertson, Jack Mar 76 obit Jan 82

Albion, Robert Greenhalgh May 54 obit Oct 83

Albright, Ivan Feb 44 Dec 69 obit Jan 84

Albright, Madeleine Korbel

May 95 Apr 2000

Albright, Tenley Sep 56

Albright, William F. Sep 55

Alcayaga, Lucila Godoy see Mistral, Gabriela

Alcindor, Lew see Abdul-Jabbar, Kareem

Alcock, Norman Z. Mar 63

Alcorn, Hugh Meade, Jr. May 57 obit Mar 92

Alda, Alan Jan 77

Aldredge, Theoni Feb 94

Aldrich, Chester Holmes obit Feb 41

Aldrich, Richard Jun 55 obit Jun 86

Aldrich, Richard S. obit Feb 42

Aldrich, Winthrop W. Oct 40 Mar 53 obit Apr 74

Aldridge, James Mar 43

Aldridge, John W. (WLB) Yrbk 58

Aldrin, Buzz Sep 93

Aldrin, Edwin E. Jr. see Aldrin, Buzz

Alechinsky, Pierre Sep 88

Alegría, Ciro Dec 41

Aleixandre, Vicente Mar 78 obit Mar 85

Alekhine, Alexander obit May 46

Alemán, Miguel Sep 46 obit Jul 83

Alepoudelis, Odysseus see Elytis, Odysseus

Alessandri, Jorge May 59 obit Oct 86

Alexander of Hillsborough, Albert Victor Alexander, 1st Earl see Alexander, Albert Victor

Alexander of Tunis, Harold R. L. G. Alexander, 1st E see Alexander, Harold R. L. G.

Alexander, Albert Victor Yrbk 40 obit Feb 65

Alexander, Archie A. Jun 55 obit Mar 58

Alexander, Christopher Oct

2003

Alexander, Clifford L., Jr. Sep 77

Alexander, Donald C. Dec 74

Alexander, Franz Aug 42 Sep 60 obit Apr 64

Alexander, Harold R. L. G. Oct 42 obit Sep 69 [Alexander of Tunis, Harold R. L. G. Alexander, 1st Earl]

Alexander, Harry Held obit Feb 41

Alexander, Holmes Sep 56

Alexander, Jane Feb 77

Alexander, Jason Jan 98

Alexander, Lamar Jul 91

Alexander, Madame Sep 57

Alexander, Margaret Walker see Walker, Margaret

Alexander, Ruth Mar 43

Alexander, Willis W. Jul 69 obit Jan 86

Alexanderson, Ernst F. W. Sep 55 obit Aug 75

Alexei, Patriarch of Russia Mar 53 obit Jun 70

Alexie, Sherman Oct 98

Alfonsín, Raúl Jul 84

Alfonso XIII obit Apr 41

Alfrink, Bernard May 66 obit Feb 88

Alger, Ellice M. obit Apr 45

Al-Hassan, Prince of The Yemen Feb 57

Al-Husseini, Faisal Jan 98

Ali, Asaf see Asaf Ali

Ali, Chaudhri Mohamad Feb 56

Ali, Mohammed Oct 52 obit Mar 63

Ali, Muhammad Sep 63 [Clay, Cassius] Nov 78

Alia, Ramiz Jan 91

Alibek, Ken Jun 2002

Alibekov, Kanatjan see Alibek, Ken

Alice, Mary see Mary Alice

Alinsky, Saul Nov 68 obit Jul 72

Alioto, Joseph L. Sep 69 obit

Apr 98

Aliyev, Heydar Sep 99 obit Jul 2004

Allan, John J. Jan 50 obit Jan 61

Allee, Marjorie obit Jun 45

Allegro, John Dec 70 obit Apr 88

Allen, Arthur A. Jan 61 obit Mar 64

Allen, Betsy *see* Cavanna, Betty

Allen, Betsy *see* Cavanna, Betty

Allen, Betty Nov 90

Allen, Debbie Feb 87

Allen, Dick May 73

Allen, Edgar obit Mar 43

Allen, Ethan Mar 54 obit Nov 93

Allen, Florence E. Feb 41 Jul 63 obit Nov 66

Allen, Frank A. Mar 45 obit Jan 80

Allen, Fred Feb 41 obit May 56

Allen, George E. Mar 46 obit Jun 73

Allen, George Jan 75 obit Mar 91

Allen, George V. Nov 48 obit Oct 70

Allen, Gracie Jul 40 [Burns, George; and Allen, Gracie] Mar 51 obit Oct 64

Allen, Helen Howe *see* Howe, Helen

Allen, James E., Jr. Jun 69 obit Dec 71

Allen, Jay Oct 41 obit Feb 73

Allen, Joel Nott obit Mar 40

Allen, Larry Jul 42

Allen, Leo E. Jun 48 obit Mar 73

Allen, Marcus Oct 86

Allen, Marion obit Feb 42

Allen, Martha F. Oct 59

Allen, Mel Oct 50 obit Aug 96

Allen, Paul Jul 98

Allen, Peter Mar 83 obit Aug

92

Allen, Ralph Jul 58 obit Feb 67

Allen, Raymond B. Mar 52 obit May 86

Allen, Rick *see* Def Leppard

Allen, Robert May 41 [Pearson, Drew; and Allen, Robert]

Allen, Steve Jul 51 Mar 82 obit Jan 2001

Allen, Terry Nov 43 obit Nov 69

Allen, Tim May 95

Allen, William L. Sep 53

Allen, William M. Mar 53 obit Jan 86

Allen, Woody Dec 66 Sep 79

Allende, Isabel Feb 88

Allende, Salvador Sep 71 obit Nov 73

Alley, Kirstie Jul 94

Alley, Rewi Oct 43 obit Feb 88

Alliluyeva, Svetlana Oct 68

Allison, John M. Mar 56 obit Feb 79

Allman, David B. Feb 58 obit May 71

Allon, Yigal Sep 75 obit Apr 80

Allott, Gordon May 55 obit Apr 89

Allport, Gordon Sep 60 obit Dec 67

Allsburg, Chris Van Sep 96

Allyn, Lewis B. obit Jan 40

Allyn, Stanley C. Mar 56 obit Dec 70

Allyson, June Jan 52

Almazan, Juan Andreu May 40 obit Dec 65

Almendros, Nestor Nov 89 obit May 92

Almirante, Giorgio Jan 74 obit Jul 88

Almodóvar, Pedro Sep 90

Almond, Edward M. Mar 51 obit Aug 79

Almond, J. Lindsay, Jr. Mar

58 obit Jun 86

Alonso, Alicia Jul 55 Jun 77

Alou, Felipe Jun 99

Alou, Moises Apr 99

Alpert, George Sep 61 obit Oct 88

Alpert, Herb Jan 67

Alphand, Hervé Nov 51 obit Mar 94

Al-Sabah, Jaber al-Ahmad al-Jaber *see* Sabah, Jaber Al-Ahmad Al-Jaber Al-, Sheik

Alsberg, Carl Lucas obit Yrbk 40

Al-Shabandar, Moussa *see* Shabandar, Moussa

Alsop Sture-Vasa, Mary O'Hara *see* O'Hara, Mary

Alsop, Joseph Oct 52 [Alsop, Joseph W., Jr.; and Alsop, Stewart] obit Oct 89

Alsop, Stewart Oct 52 [Alsop, Joseph W., Jr.; and Alsop, Stewart] obit Jul 74

Alstadt, W. R. Jul 58

Alston, Walter Jun 54 obit Nov 84

Altenburg, Alexander obit Mar 40

Alter, George Elias obit Oct 40

Altizer, Thomas J. J. Jun 67

Altman, Robert Feb 74

Altmeyer, Arthur J. Nov 46 obit Dec 72

Al-Turabi, Hassan *see* Turabi, Hassan al-

Alvarez Bravo, Manuel Jan 99 obit Jan 2003

Alvarez Quintero, Joaquin obit Aug 44

Alvarez, Luis W. May 47 obit Oct 88

Alvarez, Walter C. Sep 53 obit Aug 78

Aly Khan, Prince May 60

Amado, Jorge Mar 86 obit Oct 2001

Amalrik, Andrei Apr 74 obit

Carías Andino, Tiburcio Dec 67

Ando, Tadao Jan 2000

Andrade, Victor Feb 53

Andre 3000 *see* OutKast

Andre, Carl May 86

Andreadis, Christina *see* Onassis, Christina

Andreas, Dwayne O. Mar 92

Andreessen, Marc Jun 97 [Andreessen, Marc; and Clark, James H.]

Andreotti, Giulio Feb 77

Andresen, August H. Feb 56 obit Mar 58

Andretti, Mario Jul 68

Andrew, Duke of York Mar 87

Andrewes, William Sep 52 obit Jan 75

Andrews, Anthony Jun 91

Andrews, Bert Sep 48 obit Oct 53

Andrews, C. M. obit Oct 43

Andrews, Charles O. obit Nov 46

Andrews, Cicily Isabel *see* West, Rebecca

Andrews, Dana Oct 59 obit Feb 93

Andrews, Frank M. Feb 42 obit Jun 43

Andrews, John B. obit Feb 43

Andrews, Julie Jul 56 Apr 94

Andrews, Roy Chapman Jan 41 Jul 53 obit May 60

Andrews, Stanley Jun 52

Andrews, T. Coleman Apr 54

Andric, Ivo Feb 62 obit May 75

Andropov, Yuri May 83 obit Apr 84

Andrus, Cecil D. Aug 77

Angarita, Isaías Medina *see* Medina Angarita, Isaías

Angeles, Victoria de los Feb 55 obit Aug 2005

Angell, James Rowland Yrbk 40 obit Mar 49

Angell, Marcia Nov 2005

Angell, Norman May 48 obit Dec 67

Angelou, Maya Jun 74 Feb 94

Angier, Natalie Aug 99

Angle, Paul McClelland Jul 55 obit Aug 75

Angoff, Charles (WLB) Yrbk 55 obit Jul 79

Anise *see* Strong, Anna Louise

Anka, Paul Feb 64

Annan, Kofi Mar 2000

Anne, Princess of Great Britain Oct 73

Annenberg, Walter H. Jan 70 obit Jan 2003

Annis, Edward R. Apr 64

Ann-Margret Sep 75

Anouilh, Jean Apr 54 obit Nov 87

Ansermet, Ernest Jul 49 obit Apr 69

Anslinger, H. J. May 48 obit Jan 76

Anspach, Charles L. Sep 56

Antall, József, Jr. Sep 90 obit Feb 94

Antes, Horst Feb 86

Antheil, George Jul 54 obit Apr 59

Anthony, Carmelo Jun 2005

Anthony, John J. Jan 42 obit Oct 70

Antoine Jun 55 obit Sep 76

Antoine, Josephine Aug 44

Antonescu, Ion Oct 40 obit Jul 46

Antonioni, Michelangelo Dec 64 May 93

Anuszkiewicz, Richard Oct 78

Aoki, Rocky Jun 2005

Aouita, Said May 90

Aoun, Michel Mar 90

Apgar, Virginia Feb 68 obit Oct 74

Appel, James Z. Mar 66 obit Oct 81

Appel, Karel Mar 61

Appiah, Kwame Anthony Jun 2002

Apple, R. W., Jr. Apr 93

Applebaum, Anne Aug 2004

Appleton, Edward Dale obit Mar 42

Appleton, Edward Victor Sep 45 obit Jun 65

Appleton, Robert obit Mar 45

Appley, Lawrence A. Jul 50 obit Jun 97

Appleyard, Rollo obit Apr 43

Apted, Michael Feb 2000

Aquino, Corazon Aug 86

Arafat, Yasir Mar 71 Nov 94 obit Feb 2005

Araki, Eikichi Oct 52 obit Apr 59

Aramburu, Pedro Eugenio Jan 57 obit Oct 70

Aranha, Oswaldo Mar 42 obit Apr 60

Arantes do Nascimento, Edson *see* Pelé

Aras, Tevfik Rüstü Jun 42

Araskog, Rand V. Nov 91

Arbenz Guzman, Jacobo Sep 53 obit Mar 71

Arcand, Denys Oct 90

Arcaro, Eddie Sep 58 obit Jan 98

Arcaro, George Edward *see* Arcaro, Eddie

Arce, José Nov 47 obit Oct 68

Archambault, Louis Sep 59

Archer, Dennis W. Feb 97

Archer, Glenn Leroy May 49

Archer, Jeffrey Sep 88

Archer, Lane *see* Hauck, Louise Platt

Archer, Michael D'Angelo *see* D'Angelo

Archipenko, Alexander Sep 53 obit Apr 64

Arciniegas, Germán May 54 obit Jun 2000

Arco, Georg Wilhelm Alexander Hans Graf Von obit Jan 40

Ardalan, Ali Gholi Apr 54

Arden, Elizabeth Jul 57 obit

obit Sep 65

Asaf Ali Jun 47 obit May 53

Asakai, Koichiro Sep 57

Ascher, Leo obit Apr 42

Ascoli, Max Feb 54 obit Mar 78

Asgeirsson, Asgeir Sep 52

Ash, Mary Kay May 95 obit Feb 2002

Ash, Peter see Hauck, Louise Platt

Ash, Roy Jul 68

Ashanti Jan 2003

Ashbery, John Aug 76

Ashbrook, John M. Oct 73 obit Jun 82

Ashcroft, John Sep 99

Ashcroft, Peggy Sep 63 Jan 87 obit Aug 91

Ashdown, Jeremy John Durham see Ashdown, Paddy

Ashdown, Paddy Oct 92

Ashe, Arthur Nov 66 obit Mar 93

Ashford and Simpson see Ashford, Nickolas; Simpson, Valerie

Ashford, Nickolas Apr 97 [Ashford, Nickolas; and Simpson, Valerie]

Ashida, Hitoshi Jun 48 obit Sep 59

Ashkenazy, Vladimir Jul 67

Ashley, Elizabeth Mar 78

Ashley, Maurice Sep 99

Ashley, Merrill Nov 81

Ashley, Thomas Ludlow May 79

Ashmore, Harry S. Sep 58 obit Apr 98

Ashmun, Margaret Eliza obit Apr 40

Ashrawi, Hanan Mar 92

Ashton, Frederick May 51 obit Sep 88

Ashwell, Rachel Oct 2004

Asimov, Isaac (WLB) Yrbk 53 Oct 68 obit May 92

Askew, Reubin Apr 73

Askey, E. Vincent Feb 61 obit

Feb 75

Askwith, George Ranken Askwith, 1st Baron obit Jul 42

Asner, Edward Aug 78

Aspin, Les Feb 86 obit Jul 95

Aspinall, Wayne N. Apr 68 obit Nov 83

Asquith, Margot obit Sep 45

Assad, Hafez Al- Jul 75 Apr 92 obit Aug 2000

Assis Chateaubriand Jun 57

Astaire, Fred Sep 45 Apr 64 obit Aug 87

Astin, Allen V. May 56 obit Apr 84

Astin, Patty Duke see Duke, Patty

Aston, Francis William obit Jan 46

Astor, Brooke Jan 87

Astor, John Jacob, 1st Baron of Hever May 54 obit Sep 71

Astor, Mary Nov 61 obit Nov 87

Astor, Nancy Witcher, Viscountess Nov 40 obit Jul 64

Asturias, Miguel Angel Oct 68 obit Jul 74

Aswell, James (WLB) Yrbk 51 obit Apr 55

Atalena see Jabotinsky, Vladimir Evgenevich

Atashin, Faegheh see Googoosh

Atcheson, George, Jr. Sep 46 obit Oct 47

Athenagoras I, Patriarch Mar 49 obit Sep 72

Atherton, Gertrude Franklin Horn Nov 40 obit Sep 48

Atherton, Warren H. Dec 43 obit May 76

Atkins, Chet Jan 75 obit Sep 2001

Atkins, Jeffrey see Ja Rule

Atkinson, Brooks Apr 42 Feb 61 obit Mar 84

Atkinson, Eleanor obit Jan 43

Atkinson, Joseph Hampton

May 56

Atkinson, Oriana (WLB) Yrbk 53 obit Oct 89

Atoll, John George Stewart-Murray, 8th Duke of obit May 42

Attaway, William Dec 41

Attenborough, David Apr 83

Attenborough, Richard May 84

Attlee, Clement Richard Attlee, 1st Earl May 40 Feb 47 obit Dec 67

Attwood, William Jan 68 obit Jul 89

Atwater, Lee Jun 89 obit May 91

Atwell, Wayne J. obit May 41

Atwill, Lionel obit Jun 46

Atwood, Donna May 54

Atwood, Margaret May 84

Aubrey, James T., Jr. Mar 72 obit Nov 94

Auchincloss, Louis (WLB) Yrbk 54 Aug 78

Auchinleck, Claude John Eyre Feb 42 obit May 81

Auden, W. H. Sep 71 obit Nov 73

Auel, Jean M. Feb 91

Auerbach, Arnold see Auerbach, Red'

Auerbach, Red' Feb 69

Auerbach-Levy, William Feb 48 obit Sep 64

Augér, Arleen Feb 89 obit Aug 93

Aughinbaugh, William obit Feb 41

Augstein, Rudolf Jun 66 obit Jan 2003

August, John see De Voto, Bernard

Augustine, Norman R. Jun 98

Aulaire, Edgar Parin d' Aug 40 [Aulaire, Ingri d'; and Aulaire, Edgar Parin d']

Aulaire, Ingri d' Aug 40 [Aulaire, Ingri d'; and Aulaire,

Edgar Parin d']

Aulenti, Gae Sep 99

Aung San Suu Kyi Feb 92

Auriol, Jacqueline Sep 53 obit Jun 2000

Auriol, Vincent Mar 47 obit Feb 66

Auster, Paul Mar 96

Austerlitz, Fred *see* Astaire, Fred

Austin, "Stone Cold" Steve Nov 2001

Austin, F. Britten obit May 41

Austin, Herbert Austin, 1st Baron obit Jul 41

Austin, Margretta Feb 54

Austin, Tracy May 81

Austin, Warren R. Jan 44 obit Feb 63

Austin, William Lane Apr 40

Autry, Gene Dec 47 obit Jan 99

Avedon, Richard Feb 75 obit Mar 2005

Avenol, Joseph Jan-Feb 40 obit Oct 52

Averoff-Tossiza, Evangelos May 57 obit Mar 90

Avery, Milton Jun 58 obit Feb 65

Avery, Sewell Jun 44 obit Jan 61

Avila Camacho, Manuel Sep 40 obit Yrbk 56

Avon, Anthony Eden, 1st Earl of *see* Eden, Anthony

Awolowo, Obafemi Jul 57 [Ahmadu, Alhaji, Sardauna of Sokoto; Awolowo, Obafemi; and Azikiwe, Nnamdi] obit Jul 87

Ax, Emanuel Mar 84

Ayala, Eusebio obit Jul 42

Ayala, Julio César Turbay *see* Turbay Ayala, Julio César

Ayckbourn, Alan Jan 80

Aydelotte, Frank Oct 41 Apr 52 obit Feb 57

Ayer, A. J. May 64 obit Aug 89

Aykroyd, Dan Jan 92

Aylwin, Patricio Aug 90

Ayres, Agnes obit Feb 41

Ayres, Leonard Porter May 40 obit Dec 46

Ayub Khan, Mohammad Apr 59 obit Jun 74

Azad, Abul Kalam, Maulana *see* Abul Kalam Azad, Maulana

Azana, Manuel obit Yrbk 40

Azcona Hoyo, José Feb 88

Azikiwe, Nnamdi Jul 57 [Ahmadu, Alhaji, Sardauna of Sokoto; Awolowo, Obafemi; and Azikiwe, Nnamdi] obit Aug 96

Aziz, Tariq May 91

Aznavour, Charles Feb 68

Azuma IV, Tokuho Apr 54

Azzam, Abdul Rahman Apr 47

Babangida, Ibrahim Sep 90

Babb, James T. Jul 55 obit Oct 68

Babbitt, Bruce E. Apr 87

Babbitt, Milton Sep 62

Babcock, Edward Chester *see* Van Heusen, Jimmy

Babson, Naomi Lane (WLB) Yrbk 52

Babson, Roger W. Feb 45 obit May 67

Babyface Jul 98

Baca-Flor, Carlos obit Jul 41

Bacall, Lauren Mar 70

Baccaloni, Salvatore Oct 44 obit Feb 70

Bach, P. D. Q. *see* Schickele, Peter

Bach, Reginald obit Feb 41

Bach, Richard Oct 73

Bacharach, Burt Dec 57 Oct 70

Bachauer, Gina Jun 54 obit Sep 77

Bache, Harold L. May 59

Bache, Jules S. obit May 44

Bacher, Robert F. Feb 47 obit

Yrbk 2005

Bachman, Richard *see* King, Stephen

Bachrach, Elise Wald obit Mar 40

Backe, John D. Apr 78

Backman, Jules Apr 52 obit Jun 82

Backstrand, C. J. Feb 54 obit Dec 68

Backstreet Boys May 2000

Bacon, Charles L. May 62

Bacon, Charles R. obit Jun 43

Bacon, Francis Feb 57 Aug 85 obit Jun 92

Bacon, George P. obit Nov 41

Bacon, Leonard Jun 41 obit Mar 54

Bacon, Peggy Jan-Feb 40 obit Mar 87

Bacon, Selden D. May 52 obit Feb 93

Bada, Angelo obit May 41

Baden-Powell, Lady May 46

Badger, Oscar C. May 49 obit Feb 59

Badillo, Herman May 71

Badoglio, Pietro Oct 40 obit Jan 57

Badu, Erykah Apr 98

Baehr, George May 42

Baekeland, Leo H. obit Apr 44

Baer, William J. obit Nov 41

Baez, Joan Nov 63

Bagley, William Chandler obit Jul 46

Bagnold, Enid Jun 64 obit May 81

Bagramyan, Ivan C. Dec 44 obit Jan 83

Bagwell, Jeff Aug 2000

Bahcall, John N. Apr 2000

Bailar, Benjamin F. Jul 76

Bailar, John C., Jr. Jul 59

Bailey, Abe obit Sep 40

Bailey, Carolyn Sherwin (WLB) Yrbk 48

Bailey, Consuelo Northrop Jun 54

Bailey, Donald Coleman Oct

45 obit Jul 85

Bailey, F. Lee Dec 67

Bailey, Glenda Oct 2001

Bailey, Guy Winfred obit Yrbk 40

Bailey, John M. Jun 62 obit Jun 75

Bailey, Josiah W. Apr 45 obit Jan 47

Bailey, L. H. Jun 48 obit Mar 55

Bailey, Pearl Jun 55 Oct 69 obit Oct 90

Bailey, Thomas L. obit Dec 46

Bailey, Vernon obit Jun 42

Baillie, Hugh Feb 46 obit Mar 66

Bainton, Roland H. Jun 62 obit Jun 84

Baird, Bil Mar 54 [Baird, Bil; and Baird, Cora] obit May 87

Baird, Cora Mar 54 [Baird, Bil; and Baird, Cora] obit Feb 68

Baird, John Lawrence obit Oct 41

Baitz, Jon Robin Aug 2004

Baker, Anita Apr 89

Baker, Asa George obit Oct 40

Baker, Charles Whiting obit Aug 41

Baker, Dorothy Dec 43 obit Sep 68

Baker, Dusty Apr 2001

Baker, Frank (WLB) Yrbk 48

Baker, George Nov 44 obit Aug 75

Baker, George T. Jun 53 obit Jan 64

Baker, Howard H. Mar 74 Aug 87

Baker, James A., 3d Feb 82

Baker, Janet Jun 71

Baker, John H. May 49

Baker, Josephine Jul 64 obit Jun 75

Baker, Louise (WLB) Yrbk

54

Baker, Melvin H. Feb 60

Baker, Mrs. Sydney J. *see* Baker, Nina Brown

Baker, Nicholson Aug 94

Baker, Nina Brown (WLB) Yrbk 47 obit Nov 57

Baker, Norma Jean *see* Monroe, Marilyn

Baker, Phil Nov 46 obit Jan 64

Baker, Ray Stannard Jan-Feb 40 obit Sep 46

Baker, Richard A. *see* Baker, Rick

Baker, Rick Mar 97

Baker, Roy G. Nov 48

Baker, Russell Mar 80

Baker, S. Josephine obit Apr 45

Bakke, E. Wight Sep 53 obit Jan 72

Bakker, Robert T. Aug 95

Bakshi, Ghulam Mohammad Jun 56 obit Sep 72

Bakshi, Ralph Mar 79

Bakula, Scott Feb 2002

Balaban, Barney Oct 46 obit Apr 71

Balaguer, Joaquín Nov 66 obit Yrbk 2002

Balanchine, George Nov 42 Jun 54 obit Jun 83

Balbo, Italo obit Aug 40

Balch, Emily Greene Jan 47 obit Mar 61

Balchen, Bernt Jan 49 obit Dec 73

Balderston, William Sep 49 obit Oct 83

Baldessari, John Jun 91

Baldomir, Alfredo Jun 42 obit Mar 48

Baldrige, Letitia Feb 88

Baldrige, Malcolm Aug 82 obit Sep 87

Baldwin, Alec Jul 92

Baldwin, C. B. Nov 43

Baldwin, Hanson W. Aug 42 obit Jan 92

Baldwin, James (WLB) Yrbk

59 Jul 64 obit Jan 88

Baldwin, Raymond E. Jul 46 obit Nov 86

Baldwin, Roger Nash Jan-Feb 40 obit Oct 81

Baldwin, Tammy Jun 2005

Baldwin, William H. Nov 45

Balenciaga May 54 obit May 72

Balewa, Abubakar Tafawa Sep 61 obit Feb 66

Baline, Israel *see* Berlin, Irving

Ball, George W. Feb 62 obit Jul 94

Ball, Joseph H. Oct 43 obit Feb 94

Ball, Lucille Sep 52 [Ball, Lucille; and Arnaz, Desi] Jan 78 obit Jun 89

Ball, Robert M. Jan 68

Ball, Stuart S. Jul 52

Ball, William May 74 obit Oct 91

Ball, Zachary (WLB) Yrbk 53

Balladur, Edouard Feb 94

Ballantine, Ian May 54 obit May 95

Ballantine, Stuart obit Jun 44

Ballard, J. G. May 88

Ballard, Kaye Sep 69

Ballard, Robert D. Jun 86

Ballesterios, Seve *see* Ballesteros, Severiano

Ballesteros, Severiano Sep 80

Balmain, Pierre Jul 54 obit Aug 82

Balthus Nov 79 obit May 2001

Baltimore, David Jul 83

Bampton, Rose Mar 40

Bancroft, Ann Jul 2000

Bancroft, Anne Jun 60

Banda, Hastings Jan 63 obit Feb 98

Bandaranaike, S. W. R. D. Sep 56 obit Nov 59

Bandaranaike, Sirimavo May

61 obit Jan 2001

Banderas, Antonio Mar 97

Banfield, Ashleigh Jul 2002

Banfield, Edward C. May 72 obit Feb 2000

Banfield, Jillian Feb 2000

Bani-Sadr, Abolhassan Feb 81

Bankhead, John H. May 43 obit Jul 46

Bankhead, Tallulah Jul 41 Jan 53 obit Feb 69

Bankhead, William Brockman Oct 40 obit Oct 40

Banks, Dennis Jun 92

Banks, Ernie May 59

Banks, Russell Jan 92

Banning, Kendall obit Feb 45

Banning, Margaret Culkin May 40 obit Feb 82

Bannister, Constance Jul 55 obit Yrbk 2005

Bannister, Roger Apr 56

Bannow, Rudolph F. Dec 60 obit Sep 62

Banting, Frederick Grant obit Apr 41

Bantock, Granville obit Dec 46

Banville, John May 92

Banzer Suárez, Hugo Sep 73 obit Yrbk 2002

Banzhaf, John F., 3d Dec 73

Bao Dai Nov 49 obit Oct 97

Barad, Jill E. Sep 95

Baragwanath, Mrs. John Gordon see McMein, Neysa

Barak, Ehud Aug 97

Baraka, Amiri see Jones, Leroi

Barber, Anthony Jan 71

Barber, Carl Jerome see Barber, Jerry

Barber, Jerry Apr 62 obit Nov 94

Barber, Mary I. Jul 41 obit Apr 63

Barber, Red Jul 43 obit Jan 93

Barber, Ronde see Barber, Tiki and Barber, Ronde

Barber, Samuel Sep 44 Sep 63

obit Mar 81

Barber, Tiki and Barber, Ronde Oct 2003

Barber, Tiki see Barber, Tiki and Barber, Ronde

Barber, Walter Lanier see Barber, Red

Barbey, Daniel E. Jan 45 obit Jun 69

Barbier, George W. obit Aug 45

Barbieri, Fedora Feb 57 obit Aug 2003

Barbirolli, John Yrbk 40 obit Oct 70

Barbour, Haley Nov 96

Barbour, Henry Gray obit Nov 43

Barbour, Ralph Henry obit Apr 44

Barbour, W. Warren obit Jan 44

Barclay, McClelland Sep 40 obit Yrbk 46

Barco Vargas, Virgilio Feb 90 obit Aug 97

Bard, Mary (WLB) Yrbk 56

Bardeen, John Sep 57 obit Apr 91

Barden, Graham A. Sep 49 obit Mar 67

Bardot, Brigitte Jan 60

Barenboim, Daniel Apr 69

Bari, Joe see Bennett, Tony

Baring, George Rowland Stanley May 71 obit May 91

Barker, Bob Nov 99

Barker, Lewellys Franklin obit Sep 43

Barker, Travis see blink-182

Barkley, Alben W. May 41 Jan 49 obit Jul 56

Barkley, Charles Oct 91

Barlow, Howard Jan-Feb 40 Jul 54 obit Mar 72

Barlow, Reginald obit Aug 43

Barnard, Chester I. Mar 45 obit Sep 61

Barnard, Christiaan N. May 68 obit Nov 2001

Barnard, Elinor M. obit Apr

42

Barnard, James Lynn obit Oct 41

Barnes, Albert Coombs Mar 45 obit Sep 51

Barnes, Clifford W. obit Nov 44

Barnes, Clive Mar 72

Barnes, Henry A. Jun 55 obit Nov 68

Barnes, Julian Mar 88

Barnes, Margaret Campbell (WLB) Yrbk 53

Barnes, Roy Jan 2000

Barnes, Stanley N. Sep 53

Barnes, Wendell B. Jun 57 obit Aug 85

Barnes, William R. obit Mar 45

Barnet, Will Jun 85

Barnett, Etta Moten Feb 2002

Barnett, Eugene E. May 41

Barnett, M. Robert Jan 50

Barnett, Ross Sep 61 obit Jan 88

Barney, Matthew Aug 2003

Barney, Samuel E. obit Mar 40

Barnhart, Clarence L. Sep 54 obit Jan 94

Barnouw, Erik Nov 40 obit Oct 2001

Barnsley, Alan Gabriel see Fielding, Gabriel

Baron Franks of Headington see Franks, Oliver Shewell

Barr, Alfred H., Jr. Jan 61 obit Oct 81

Barr, John A. Jan 61 obit Mar 79

Barr, Joseph W. Jan 68 obit May 96

Barr, Norman B., Rev. obit May 43

Barr, Roseanne May 89

Barr, Stringfellow Aug 40 obit Apr 82

Barr, William P. Jun 92

Barratt, Arthur Sheridan Jan 41

Barrault, Jean-Louis Mar 53

[Barrault, Jean-Louis; and Renaud, Madeleine] obit Mar 94

Barre, Raymond Jul 77

Barrere, Camille Eugene Pierre obit Yrbk 40

Barrère, Georges obit Aug 44

Barrett, C. Waller Mar 65

Barrett, Craig Mar 99

Barrett, Edward W. Feb 47 obit Feb 90

Barrett, Frank A. Jul 56 obit Jul 62

Barrett, William Aug 82 obit Nov 92

Barrett, Wilton Agnew obit Mar 40

Barrette, Antonio Jul 60 obit Feb 69

Barringer, Emily Dunning Mar 40 obit Jun 61

Barringer, Paul Brandon obit Mar 41

Barris, Chuck Mar 2005

Barros Hurtado, César Jan 59

Barrow, Errol W. Sep 68 obit Jul 87

Barrow, Joseph Louis *see* Louis, Joe

Barry, Dave May 98

Barry, John Mar 2000

Barry, Lynda Nov 94

Barry, Marion May 87

Barry, Patrick Frank, Bishop obit Sep 40

Barry, Rick Mar 71

Barry, William Bernard obit Dec 46

Barrymore, Drew Oct 98

Barrymore, Ethel Mar 41 obit Sep 59

Barrymore, John obit Jul 42

Barrymore, Lionel Jul 43 obit Jan 55

Barshefsky, Charlene Feb 2000

Barth, John May 69

Barth, Karl Nov 62 obit Feb 69

Barthé, Richmond Jul 40 obit

May 89

Barthelme, Donald Mar 76 obit Sep 89

Barthes, Roland Feb 79 obit May 80

Bartiromo, Maria Nov 2003

Bartlett, E. L. Jun 51 obit Mar 69

Bartlett, Jennifer Nov 85

Bartlett, Robert A. obit Jun 46

Bartók, Béla Sep 40 obit Oct 45

Bartol, William Cyrus obit Yrbk 40

Bartoli, Cecilia Jun 92

Barton, Bruce Feb 61 obit Oct 67

Barton, George A. May 53

Barton, George obit Apr 40

Barton, Robert B. M. Apr 59 obit Apr 95

Barton, William H., Jr. obit Aug 44

Bartz, Carol Jul 99

Baruch, Bernard M. Aug 41 Jul 50 obit Sep 65

Baryshnikov, Mikhail Feb 75

Barzel, Rainer May 67

Barzin, Leon May 51 obit Aug 99

Barzini, Luigi Jul 72 obit May 84

Barzun, Jacques Sep 64

Basaldella, Afro *see* Afro

Basdevant, Jules Feb 50 obit Mar 68

Basie, Count Jun 42 obit Jun 84

Basie, William *see* Basie, Count

Basinger, Kim Feb 90

Baskin, Leonard May 64 obit Aug 2000

Basoalto, Ricardo Elizier Neftali Reyes *see* Neruda, Pablo

Bass, George Mar 2000

Bass, Lance *see* 'N Sync

Bass, Robert M. Jul 89

Bassett, Angela May 96

Bassett, Sara Ware (WLB)

YRBK 56

Bassler, Bonnie Apr 2003

Batcheller, Hiland G. Apr 49 obit Jul 61

Bateman, Jason Oct 2005

Bates, Alan Mar 69 obit Yrbk 2004

Bates, Blanche obit Feb 42

Bates, Ernest Sutherland obit Jan 40

Bates, Granville obit Sep 40

Bates, H. E. Sep 44 obit Mar 74

Bates, Kathy Sep 91

Bates, Marston Apr 56 obit May 74

Bates, Sanford Jan 61 obit Nov 72

Bateson, Mrs. Gregory *see* Mead, Margaret

Bathgate, Andy Feb 64

Batista, Fulgencio Sep 40 Apr 52 obit Oct 73

Batt, William L. Feb 42 obit Mar 65

Batt, William L., Jr. Sep 62

Battle, John S. Nov 50 obit Jun 72

Battle, Kathleen Nov 84

Baudouin Sep 50 obit Oct 93

Baudrillard, Jean Jun 93

Baudrillart, Henri Marie Alfred, Cardinal obit Jul 42

Bauer, Erwin A. Feb 93 [Bauer, Erwin A.; and Bauer, Peggy]

Bauer, Gary L. Jan 99

Bauer, Hank Feb 67

Bauer, Louis Hopewell Oct 48 obit Mar 64

Bauer, Peggy Feb 93 [Bauer, Erwin A.; and Bauer, Peggy]

Baulieu, Etienne-Emile Nov 95

Baum, Kurt Sep 56 obit Feb 90

Baum, William Cardinal Oct 76

Baumer, Marie (WLB) Yrbk

58

Baumgartner, Leona Jan 50 obit Mar 91

Baur, Bertha obit Nov 40

Baur, Harry obit May 43

Baur, John I. H. Dec 69 obit Jul 87

Bausch, Edward obit Sep 44

Bausch, Pina Sep 86

Bausch, William obit Dec 44

Bausher, Mrs J. Lee *see* Jordan, Mildred

Bax, Arnold Sep 43 obit Jan 54

Baxter, Anne May 72 obit Feb 86

Baxter, Frank C. Mar 55

Baxter, James P., 3d Jul 47 obit Aug 75

Bay, Mrs. Charles Ulrick Jun 57

Bayar, Celal Jul 50 obit Oct 86

Bayard, Thomas F. obit Sep 42

Bayh, Birch E., Jr. Jun 65

Bayh, Evan Nov 98

Bayne, Stephen F., Jr. Jan 64 obit Mar 74

Bazelon, David L. Jan 71 obit Apr 93

Bazin, Germain Jan 59 obit Jul 90

Bea, Augustin, Cardinal Sep 64 obit Jan 69

Beach, Amy Marcy *see* Beach, Mrs. H. H. A.

Beach, Edward Oct 60 obit May 2003

Beach, Mrs. H. H. A. obit Feb 45

Beadle, George W. Apr 56 obit Aug 89

Beale, Howard Mar 59

Beall, J. Glenn Apr 55 obit Mar 71

Beall, Lester Nov 49 obit Sep 69

Beals, Carleton Jun 41 Yrbk 42 obit Aug 79

Beals, Ralph A. Feb 47 obit

Dec 54

Beam, Jacob D. Jul 59 obit Oct 93

Beame, Abraham D. Jul 74 obit Apr 2001

Bean, Louis H. Nov 48 obit Oct 94

Bean, Orson Feb 67

Beane, Billy Jul 2005

Beard, Charles A. Mar 41 [Beard, Charles A.; and Beard, Mary] obit Oct 48

Beard, Charles E. Jul 56 obit Oct 82

Beard, Daniel Carter obit Aug 41

Beard, Frank May 70

Beard, James Dec 64 obit Mar 85

Beard, James Thom obit Yrbk 42

Beard, Mary Ritter Mar 41 [Beard, Charles A; and Beard, Mary] obit Yrbk 59

Bearden, Bessye J. obit Nov 43

Bearden, Romare Jan 72 obit May 88

Beardsley, William S. Jun 50 obit Jan 55

Beaton, Cecil Oct 44 Jul 62 obit Mar 80

Beatrice, Marie Victoria Feodora obit Dec 44

Beatrix, Queen of The Netherlands May 81

Beattie, Ann Oct 85

Beatty, Arthur obit Apr 43

Beatty, Bessie Jan 44 obit Apr 47

Beatty, Jim Jan 63

Beatty, Warren May 62 May 88

Beaty, Shirley MacLean *see* Maclaine, Shirley

Beau, Lucas Victor Jun 54 obit Jan 87

Beauchamp, Mary Annette *see* Russell, Mary Annette Russell

Beauchamp, Mrs. Antony *see*

Churchill, Sarah

Beaulac, Willard L. Sep 58 obit Oct 90

Beauvoir, Simone De Jan 73 obit Jun 86

Beaux, Cecilia obit Nov 42

Beaverbrook, William Maxwell Aitken, 1st Baron *see* Aitken, William Maxwell

Beban, Gary May 70

Bebey, Francis Apr 94 obit Sep 2001

Bebler, Ales Apr 50

Bech, Joseph Feb 50 obit May 75

Bechtel, Stephen Davison Apr 57 obit May 89

Beck, Bertram M. May 61 obit Sep 2000

Beck, Dave May 49 obit Feb 94

Beck, Jozef obit Jul 44

Beck, Martin obit Jan 41

Beck, Mildred Buchwalder Jun 50

Beck, Mrs. Francis Carl *see* Beck, Mildred Buchwalder

Becker, Boris Feb 87

Becker, Gary S. Sep 93

Becker, May Lamberton May 41 obit Jul 58

Becker, Ralph E. Nov 48 obit Oct 94

Becker, William Dee obit Sep 43

Beckett, Samuel Feb 70 obit Feb 90

Beckett, Wendy Jan 98

Beckinsale, Kate Aug 2001

Beckman, Arnold O. Jan 2002 obit Yrbk 2004

Bedaux, Charles E. obit Apr 44

Bede, J. Adam obit Jun 42

Bedford, Sybille Feb 90

Beebe, Lucius Sep 40 obit Mar 66

Beebe, William Jul 41 obit Sep 62

Beech, Mrs. Walter H. *see*

Beech, Olive Ann

Beech, Olive Ann Jun 56 obit Sep 93

Beecham, Thomas Dec 41 Jan 51 obit May 61

Beeching, Richard Sep 63

Beecroft, John Mar 54 obit Dec 66

Beeding, Francis *see* Palmer, John Leslie

Beedle, William Franklin *see* Holden, William

Beene, Geoffrey Apr 78 obit Mar 2005

Beer, Thomas obit May 40

Beers, Charlotte Jun 98

Beers, Clifford W. obit Aug 43

Beers, Rand Oct 2004

Begaye, Kelsey Jan 2000

Begg, Alexander Swanson obit Nov 40

Begg, Colin Luke obit Mar 41

Begin, Menachem Oct 77 obit Apr 92

Begley, Ed Mar 56 obit Jun 70

Begtrup, Bodil Sep 46

Behan, Brendan Mar 61 obit May 64

Behar, Ruth May 2005

Behn, Sosthenes Jan 47 obit Sep 57

Behrens, Hildegard Jan 85

Behrman, Mrs. Philip *see* Alexander, Madame

Behrman, S. N. Feb 43 obit Nov 73

Beinum, Eduard van Apr 55 obit Jun 59

Beirne, J. A. Mar 46 obit Oct 74

Beitz, Berthold Feb 73

Bejart, Maurice Mar 71

Bekessy, Jean *see* Habe, Hans

Békésy, Georg von Dec 62 obit Sep 72

Bel Geddes, Barbara Yrbk 48 obit Yrbk 2005

Bel Geddes, Norman *see* Ged-

des, Norman Bel

Belafonte, Harry Jan 56

Belaúnde Terry, Fernando Jul 65 obit Yrbk 2002

Belaúnde, Víctor Andrés Feb 60 obit Feb 67

Belichick, Bill Sep 2002

Belkin, Samuel Nov 52 obit Jun 76

Bell Burnell, Jocelyn May 95

Bell, Art Apr 2000

Bell, Bernard Iddings Apr 53 obit Dec 58 Yrbk 59

Bell, Bert Sep 50 obit Dec 59

Bell, Daniel Dec 73

Bell, Daniel W. Oct 46 obit Nov 71

Bell, David E. Jun 61 obit Yrbk 2000

Bell, Derrick A. Feb 93

Bell, Edward Price obit Nov 43

Bell, Elliott V. Mar 53 obit Mar 83

Bell, Griffin B. Jun 77

Bell, Joshua Jul 2000

Bell, Lawrence D. Jul 42 obit Jan 57

Bell, Margaret Elizabeth (WLB) Yrbk 52

Bell, Marilyn Sep 56

Bell, S. J. *see* Bell Burnell, Jocelyn

Bell, T. H. May 76 obit Sep 96

Bell, Thomas M. obit May 41

Bellamann, Henry Sep 42 obit Jul 45

Bellamy, Carol Oct 99

Bellamy, Ralph Nov 51 obit Jan 92

Belli, Melvin M. Jul 79 obit Sep 96

Bellmon, Henry Jul 63

Bellow, Saul Feb 65 Nov 88 obit Aug 2005

Belluschi, Pietro Feb 59 obit Apr 94

Belmondo, Jean-Paul Dec 65

Belmont, Eleanor Robson Jul

44 obit Jan 80

Belmore, Alice obit Sep 43

Belt, Guillermo Nov 47 obit Sep 89

Beltrán, Pedro G. Apr 67 obit Apr 79

Belushi, James Jan 95

Belushi, John Jan 80 obit Apr 82

Belyayev, Pavel Jul 65 obit Mar 70

Bemelmans, Ludwig Apr 41 obit Dec 62

Bemis, Samuel Flagg Jun 50 obit Nov 73

Ben and Jerry *see* Cohen, Ben; Greenfield, Jerry

Ben Bella, Ahmed Feb 63

Benavente, Jacinto Jun 53 obit Sep 54

Benavides, Oscar obit Aug 45

Bench, Johnny Oct 71

Benchley, Belle Jennings Oct 40

Benchley, Nathaniel Sep 53 obit Feb 82

Benchley, Peter Jul 76

Benchley, Robert Sep 41 obit Jan 46

Bender, George H. Jan 52 obit Sep 61

Bender, James F. May 49 obit Mar 98

Bendetsen, Karl R. May 52 obit Sep 89

Bendix, Vincent obit May 45

Bendix, William Sep 48 obit Feb 65

Benedict XVI Sep 2005

Benedict, Ruth May 41 obit Nov 48

Benelli, Cardinal *see* Benelli, Giovanni

Benelli, Giovanni Sep 77 obit Jan 83

Benes, Eduard Jan 42 obit Oct 48

Benesh, Joan Jul 57 [Benesh, Rudolf; and Benesh, Joan]

Benesh, Rudolf Jul 57 [Benesh, Rudolf; and Benesh,

Joan]

Benét, Stephen Vincent obit Apr 43

Bengough, Percy R. Apr 51

Ben-Gurion, David Oct 47 Jan 57 obit Jan 74

Benigni, Roberto Jun 99

Benjamin, Andre *see* OutKast

Benjamin, William Evarts obit Mar 40

Benn, Tony Jun 65 Nov 82

Bennett, H. Stanley Apr 66 obit Oct 92

Bennett, Henry G. Feb 51 obit Feb 52

Bennett, Henry Gordon Mar 42 obit Oct 62

Bennett, Hugh Hammond Dec 46 obit Oct 60

Bennett, Ivan L. Nov 52 obit Aug 80

Bennett, James O'Donnell obit Mar 40

Bennett, James V. Apr 49 obit Feb 79

Bennett, John C. Jan 61 obit Jul 95

Bennett, John W. F. obit Oct 43

Bennett, Lerone Jan 2001

Bennett, Michael Mar 81 obit Aug 87

Bennett, Rawson, 2d Sep 58 obit Feb 68

Bennett, Richard obit Dec 44

Bennett, Richard Rodney Mar 92

Bennett, Robert L. Sep 67

Bennett, Robert Russell Apr 42 May 62 obit Oct 81

Bennett, Tony Mar 65 Jun 95

Bennett, W. A. C. May 53 obit May 79

Bennett, W. J. Jun 54

Bennett, Wallace F. Feb 49 obit Feb 94

Bennett, William J. Sep 85

Bennington, Chester *see* Linkin Park

Benny, Jack Aug 41 Nov 63

obit Feb 75

Benoit-Lévy, Jean Oct 47 obit Nov 59

Benrimo, J. Harry obit May 42

Bensin, Basil M. Jul 48

Benson, Allan Louis obit Oct 40

Benson, Edward Frederic obit Mar 40

Benson, Ezra Taft Feb 53 obit Aug 94

Benson, Francis Colgate, Jr. obit Apr 41

Benson, John Apr 40 obit Nov 62

Benson, Sally Aug 41 obit Sep 72

Bentley, Helen Delich Dec 71

Bentley, Irene obit Jul 40

Benton, Thomas Hart Oct 40 obit Mar 75

Benton, William Dec 45 obit May 73

Bentsen, Lloyd Sep 73 Apr 93

Benzer, Seymour May 2001

Ben-Zvi, Isaac Apr 53 obit Jun 63

Beranek, Leo L. Mar 63

Berding, Andrew H. Apr 60

Bérégovoy, Pierre Feb 93 obit Feb 93

Berelson, Bernard Jul 61 obit Nov 79

Berendsen, Carl August Oct 48 obit Dec 73

Berendt, John Apr 98

Beresford, Bruce Mar 93

Berg, Elizabeth Nov 99

Berg, Ernst J. obit Nov 41

Berg, Gertrude Jul 41 Sep 60 obit Nov 66

Berg, Hart O. obit Feb 42

Berg, Irving H. obit Nov 41

Berg, Patricia Jane Sep 40

Berganza, Teresa Jan 79

Bergé, Pierre Jan 90

Berge, Wendell Feb 46 obit Dec 55 Yrbk 56

Bergen, Candice Aug 76

Bergen, Edgar May 45 obit

Nov 78

Bergen, John J. Jun 61 obit Feb 81

Bergen, Polly Sep 58

Berger, Meyer Jan 43 obit Apr 59

Berger, Peter L. Mar 83

Berger, Sandy Feb 98

Berger, Thomas Jun 88

Berggrav, Eivind Oct 50 obit Mar 59

Bergland, Bob Sep 77

Bergman, Ingmar Apr 60 Oct 81

Bergman, Ingrid Jan-Feb 40 Sep 65 obit Oct 82

Bergonzi, Carlo Nov 92

Bergquist, Kenneth P. Mar 61

Bergson, Henri obit Feb 41

Bergson, Herbert A. Sep 50

Beria, Lavrenti P. Dec 42 obit Sep 54

Berigan, Bunny obit Jul 42

Berio, Luciano Mar 71 obit Yrbk 2003

Beriosova, Svetlana Sep 60 obit Feb 99

Berkeley, Busby Apr 71 obit May 76

Berkner, Lloyd V. Sep 49 obit Oct 67

Berkson, Seymour Oct 49 obit Mar 59

Berle, Adolf A., Jr. Jul 40 Jun 61 obit Apr 71

Berle, Milton Jun 49 obit Yrbk 2002

Berlin, Ellin Aug 44 obit Sep 88

Berlin, Irving May 42 May 63 obit Nov 89

Berlin, Isaiah Jul 64 obit Jan 98

Berlin, Steve *see* Los Lobos

Berlinguer, Enrico Jul 76 obit Aug 84

Berlitz, Charles F. Feb 57 obit Yrbk 2004

Berlosconi, Silvio Aug 94

Berman, Chris Aug 98

Berman, Emile Zola Jun 72

obit Aug 81

Berman, Eugene Jun 65 obit Feb 73

Berman, Lazar Sep 77 obit Yrbk 2005

Bernadotte, Folke, Count May 45 obit Nov 48

Bernard, Émile obit Jun 41

Bernardin, Joseph L. Oct 82 obit Jan 97

Bernardino, Minerva Mar 50 obit Nov 98

Bernays, Edward L. Feb 42 Sep 60 obit May 95

Bernbach, William Mar 67 obit Nov 82

Bernhard, Prince of The Netherlands Jun 50 obit Mar 2005

Bernhard, Sandra Sep 90

Bernheim, Bertram M. Sep 43

Bernie, Ben Dec 41 obit Dec 43

Bernier, Rosamond Feb 88

Bernstein, Carl Oct 76

Bernstein, Elmer Jun 2003

Bernstein, Leonard Feb 44 Feb 60 obit Nov 90

Bernstein, Philip S. Nov 51 obit Feb 86

Bernstein, Robert L. Jul 87

Berra, Lawrence May 52

Berra, Yogi see Berra, Lawrence

Berri, Claude Mar 89

Berri, Nabih Nov 85

Berrigan, Daniel Sep 70

Berrigan, Philip Feb 76 obit Mar 2003

Berry, Charles A. Apr 69

Berry, Chuck Apr 77

Berry, Edward Wilber obit Oct 45

Berry, George L. Jan 48 obit Jan 49

Berry, Halle May 99

Berry, James Gomer Jan 51 obit Mar 68

Berry, Martha McChesney

Apr 40 obit Apr 42

Berry, Mary Frances Jun 99

Berry, Wendell May 86

Berry, William Ewert Oct 41 obit Sep 54

Berryman, Guy see Coldplay

Berryman, James Thomas Jul 50 obit Oct 71

Berryman, John May 69 obit Feb 72

Bertolucci, Bernardo Jul 74

Berton, Pierre Oct 91 obit Yrbk 2005

Bertozzi, Carolyn R. Jul 2003

Bertram, Adolf, Cardinal obit Aug 45

Bertrand, Louis obit Feb 42

Bess, Demaree Jan 43 obit Sep 62

Bessmertnova, Natalya Jan 88

Bessmertnykh, Aleksandr A. Jun 91

Best, Charles H. Jun 57 obit May 78

Best, Edna Jul 54 obit Nov 74

Besteiro Y Fernandez, Julian obit Nov 40

Bestor, Arthur E. obit Mar 44

Bestor, Arthur Sep 58 obit Feb 95

Betancourt, Romulo May 60 obit Nov 81

Betancur, Belisario Apr 85

Bethe, Hans A. Jan-Feb 40 Apr 50 obit Aug 2005

Bethune, Gordon M. Jun 2001

Bethune, Mary McLeod Jan 42 obit Jul 55

Betjeman, John Mar 73 obit Jul 84

Bettelheim, Bruno Jul 61 obit May 90

Betteridge, Don see Newman, Bernard

Bettis, Valerie May 53 obit Nov 82

Bettman, Gary B. Mar 99

Bettmann, Otto L. Nov 61 obit Jul 98

Betts, Rome A. Mar 49

Beuys, Joseph Jul 80 obit Mar

86

Bevan, Aneurin May 43 obit Oct 60

Bevan, Arthur D. obit Aug 43

Bevan, Mrs. Aneurin see Lee, Jennie

Beveridge, William Henry Jan 43 obit May 63

Bevier, Isabel obit May 42

Bevin, Ernest Sep 40 Jun 49 obit May 51

Bevis, Howard L. Jan-Feb 40 Nov 50 obit Jun 68

Bevis, Palmer Apr 53

Beyen, J. W. Feb 53 obit Jun 76

Bezos, Jeff Jun 98

Bhabha, Homi J. Sep 56 obit Feb 66

Bhave, Vinoba Sep 53 obit Jan 83

Bhumibol Adulyadej see Rama IX, King of Thailand

Bhutto, Benazir Jul 86

Bhutto, Zulfikar Ali Apr 72 obit May 79

Biaggi, Mario Jan 86

Bialk, Elisa (WLB) Yrbk 54 obit May 90

Bible, Alan Feb 57 obit Oct 88

Bible, Geoffrey C. Feb 2002

Bickel, George L. obit Aug 41

Bidault, Georges May 45 obit Mar 83

Biddle, Anthony J. Drexel Mar 41 obit Jan 62

Biddle, Francis Sep 41 obit Dec 68

Biddle, George Feb 42 obit Jan 74

Biddle, Katherine Garrison Chapin Oct 43 obit Jan 84

Biden, Joseph R., Jr. Jan 87

Bieber, Owen F. Apr 86

Bierut, Boleslaw Sep 49 obit May 56

Biffle, Leslie L. Sep 46 obit May 66

Big Boi see OutKast

Bigart, Homer Jun 51 obit Jul

91

Bigelow, Karl W. Feb 49 obit Jun 80

Bigelow, William obit May 41

Biggers, John D. Sep 41 obit Feb 74

Biggs, E. Power Nov 50 obit May 77

Bikel, Theodore Mar 60

Bilandic, Michael A. Feb 79 obit Apr 2002

Bilbo, Theodore G. Apr 43 obit Oct 47

Bildt, Carl Jan 93

Biller, Moe Jun 87 obit Yrbk 2004

Billingsley, Sherman Feb 46 obit Dec 66

Billington, James H. May 89

Billwiller, Henrietta Hudson *see* Hudson, Henrietta

Bimson, Carl A. Mar 61

Binchy, Maeve Nov 95

Binder, Carroll May 51 obit Jul 56

Binder, Theodor Sep 64

Binet-Valmer, Jean obit Sep 40

Bing, Rudolf Feb 50 obit Nov 97

Bingham, Barry Sep 49 obit Sep 88

Bingham, Hiram Mar 51 obit Sep 56

Bingham, Jonathan B. Jul 54 obit Aug 86

Bingham, Millicent Todd Jun 61 obit Jan 69

Binh, Nguyen Thi *see* Nguyen Thi Binh

Binkley, Robert Cedric obit May 40

Binns, Joseph Patterson Jun 54 obit Mar 81

Binyon, Laurence obit Apr 43

Birch, Reginald B. obit Aug 43

Bird, Caroline Jul 76

Bird, Larry Jun 82

Bird, Rose E. May 84 obit

May 2000

Bird, Will R. Sep 54

Birdseye, Clarence Mar 46 obit Dec 56 Yrbk 57

Birdseye, Claude Hale obit Jul 41

Birdwell, Russell Jul 46 obit Mar 78

Birendra Bir Bikram Shah Dev, King of Nepal Aug 75 obit Sep 2001

Birge, Raymond Thayer Mar 40

Birmingham, Stephen May 74

Birnbaum, Nathan *see* Burns, George

Birnie, William A. H. Sep 52 obit Oct 79

Birren, Faber May 56 obit Feb 89

Bishop, André Jul 99

Bishop, Elizabeth Sep 77 obit Nov 79

Bishop, Eric *see* Foxx, Jamie

Bishop, Hazel Sep 57 obit Feb 99

Bishop, Isabel Oct 77 obit Apr 88

Bishop, Jim Jun 69 obit Sep 87

Bishop, Joey Apr 62

Bishop, William Avery Sep 41

Bissell, Claude T. May 59

Bissell, Clayton L. Feb 43

Bisset, Jacqueline May 77

Bisset, James G. P. Dec 46

Bitar, Salah Eddin Feb 58 obit Sep 80

Bittman, Mark Feb 2005

Bittner, Van A. Mar 47 obit Sep 49

Bjoerling, Jussi Sep 47 obit Nov 60

Björk Jul 2001

Björnsson, Sveinn Aug 44

obit Mar 52

Black, Alexander obit Jan 40

Black, Cathleen P. Jan 98

Black, Clint Aug 94

Black, Conrad M. Aug 92

Black, Eugene R. Jan 50 obit Apr 92

Black, Hugo LaFayette Sep 41 May 64 obit Nov 71

Black, Jack Feb 2002

Black, Karen Mar 76

Black, Shirley Temple Oct 45 Apr 70

Black, William Jul 64 obit May 83

Blackall, Frederick S., Jr. Jan 53

Blackburn, Elizabeth H. Jul 2001

Blackett, Patrick M. S. Feb 49 obit Sep 74

Blackfan, K. D. obit Jan 42

Blackie, Ernest Morell, Bishop obit Apr 43

Blackmun, Harry A. Oct 70 obit May 99

Blackton, J. Stuart obit Oct 41

Blackwell, Betsy Talbot Jun 54 obit Apr 85

Blackwell, Earl, Jr. Nov 60 obit May 95

Blades, Joan and Boyd, Wes Aug 2004

Blades, Joan *see* Blades, Joan and Boyd, Wes

Blades, Rubén May 86

Blaese, R. Michael Mar 2000

Blagonravov, A. A. Feb 58 obit Apr 75

Blaik, Earl H. Jan 45 obit Jul 89

Blain, Daniel Sep 47

Blaine, David Apr 2001

Blair, Bonnie Jul 92

Blair, David H. obit Nov 44

Blair, David Jan 61 obit May 76

Blair, James T., Jr. Apr 58 obit Sep 62

Blair, Tony Aug 96

Blaisdell, Thomas C. Jul 49

obit Feb 89

Blake, Doris Nov 41

Blake, Edgar, Bishop obit Jul 43

Blake, Eubie Apr 74 obit Apr 83

Blake, Eugene Carson Sep 55 obit Oct 85

Blake, Francis G. Jan 43 obit Mar 52

Blake, Nicholas *see* Day-Lewis, C.

Blake, Robert Oct 75

Blake, Tiffany obit Nov 43

Blakemore, Michael May 2001

Blaker, Richard obit Mar 40

Blakeslee, A. F. Oct 41 obit Jan 55

Blakeslee, Francis D. obit Nov 42

Blakey, Art Sep 88 obit Jan 91

Blakey, Michael L. Sep 2000

Blalock, Alfred Sep 46 [Blalock, Alfred; and Taussig, Helen B.] obit Nov 64

Blalock, Mrs. Richard W. May 50

Blamauer, Karoline *see* Lenya, Lotte

Blamey, Thomas Albert Jun 42 obit Jul 51

Blanc, Mel Jun 76 obit Sep 89

Blanch, Arnold May 40 Jan 54 obit Dec 68

Blanch, Mrs. Arnold (Alder) *see* Lee, Doris

Blanchard, Doc *see* Blanchard, Felix A.

Blanchard, Felix A. Mar 46

Blanchard, Hazel A. Jun 63

Blanche, Jacques obit Nov 42

Blanchett, Cate Aug 99

Blanchfield, Florence A. Sep 43 obit Jun 71

Blancke, Harold Jun 57

Blanco Galindo, Carlos obit Nov 43

Blanco, Kathleen Jun 2004

Blanda, George Sep 72

Blandford, John B., Jr. May

42 obit Mar 72

Blanding, Don Jan 57

Blanding, Sarah Gibson Jun 46 obit Apr 85

Blandy, W. H. P. Nov 42 obit Mar 54

Blank, Theodor Sep 52 obit Jul 72

Blankenhorn, Herbert Apr 56

Blanton, Smiley Jun 56 obit Jan 67

Blass, Bill Sep 66 obit Nov 2002

Blatch, Harriot Stanton obit Jan 41

Blatchford, Joseph H. Mar 71

Blatchley, Willis Stanley obit Jul 40

Blatnik, John A. Feb 58 obit Feb 92

Blattenberger, Raymond Mar 58 obit Jun 71

Blatty, William Peter Jun 74

Blau, Bela obit Yrbk 40

Blaustein, Jacob Apr 49 obit Jan 71

Blease, Cole L. obit Mar 42

Bledsoe, Jules obit Sep 43

Blegen, Judith Jun 77

Blier, Bertrand Oct 88

Blind Boys of Alabama Oct 2001

blink-182 Aug 2002

Bliss, A. Richard, Jr. obit Oct 41

Bliss, Anthony A. Apr 79 obit Nov 91

Bliss, Henry Evelyn Sep 53 obit Oct 55

Bliss, Ray C. Jan 66 obit Oct 81

Bliss, Raymond W. Jan 51 obit Jan 66

Blitch, Iris F. Apr 56 obit Oct 93

Blitzstein, Marc Jul 40 obit Mar 64

Bliven, Bruce Dec 41 obit Jul 77

Bloch, Charles Edward obit

Oct 40

Bloch, Claude C. Feb 42 obit Dec 67

Bloch, Ernest Sep 53 obit Oct 59

Bloch, Felix Sep 54 obit Nov 83

Block, Herbert L. Jul 54 obit Jan 2002

Block, John R. Apr 82

Block, Joseph L. Jun 61 obit Feb 93

Block, Paul obit Aug 41

Block, Rudolph *see* Lessing, Bruno

Blodgett, Katharine Burr Jan-Feb 40 May 52 obit Jan 80

Blomfield, Reginald obit Feb 43

Bloodworth-Thomason, Linda Feb 93

Bloom, Allan David Mar 88 obit Nov 92

Bloom, Claire May 56

Bloom, Harold Apr 87

Bloom, Sol May 43 obit Mar 49

Bloomberg, Michael Jun 96

Bloomberg, Michael R. Mar 2002

Bloomgarden, Kermit Dec 58 obit Nov 76

Blough, Roger M. Jul 55 obit Jan 86

Blough, Roy Jul 50 obit Sep 2000

Blount, Winton Malcolm Apr 69 obit Jan 2003

Bloustein, Edward J. Nov 65 obit Feb 90

Blücher, Franz Jan 56 obit Jun 59

Blue, Robert D. Dec 48 obit Feb 90

Blue, Vida Mar 72

Bluford, Guion S., Jr. Sep 84

Blum, Léon Nov 40 obit May 50

Blumberg, Baruch S. Nov 77

Blume, Judy Apr 80

Blume, Peter Mar 56 obit Jan

98

Bonomi, Ivanoe Aug 44 obit May 51

Bonomi, Maria Jul 60

Bonsal, Philip Wilson Jun 59 obit Sep 95

Bonsal, Stephen Aug 45 obit Jul 51

Bontecou, Lee Mar 2004

Bontemps, Arna (WLB) Yrbk 46 obit Jul 73

Bonynge, Richard Feb 81

Booker, Edna Lee Apr 40

Boone, J. T. Mar 51 obit Jun 74

Boone, Pat Jul 59

Boone, Richard Feb 64 obit Mar 81

Boorman, John Jun 88

Boorstin, Daniel J. Sep 68 Jan 84 obit Yrbk 2004

Boosler, Elayne May 93

Booth, Arch N. Dec 61

Booth, Ballington obit Nov 40

Booth, Evangeline Feb 41 obit Sep 50

Booth, Shirley Nov 42 Apr 53 obit Jan 93

Borah, William Edgar obit Jan 40

Borberg, William Nov 52 obit Sep 58

Borch, Fred J. Oct 71

Borcherds, Richard Feb 99

Bordaberry, Juan M. Apr 75

Borde, Jean de la see De La Borde, Jean

Borden, Neil H. May 54

Bordes, Pierre-Louis obit Sep 43

Boren, David L. Nov 89

Borg, Björn Dec 74

Borge, Victor Mar 46 May 93 obit Mar 2001

Borges, Jorge Luis Jan 70 obit Aug 86

Borgese, G. A. Dec 47 obit Jan 53

Borglum, Gutzon obit Apr 41

Borgnine, Ernest Apr 56

Boring, Edwin G. Mar 62 obit

Sep 68

Boris III, King of Bulgaria Feb 41 obit Yrbk 91 (died Aug 43)

Boris Vladimirovitch, Grand Duke of Russia obit Dec 43

Borlaug, Norman E. Jul 71

Borman, Frank Mar 69 Apr 80

Born, Max May 55 obit Feb 70

Borne, Mortimer Apr 54

Bornó, Louis obit Sep 42

Borodina, Olga Feb 2002

Borofsky, Jonathan Jul 85

Boros, Julius Nov 68 obit Aug 94

Borst, Lyle B. Jul 54 obit Yrbk 2002

Bortz, Edward Leroy Sep 47 obit Apr 70

Borysenko, Joan Oct 96

Borzage, Frank Dec 46 obit Sep 62

Bosch, Carl obit Jan 40

Bosch, Juan Jun 63 obit Feb 2002

Bosch, Robert obit Apr 42

Bose, Subhas Chandra Jun 44 obit Dec 45

Boskin, Michael J. Sep 89

Bosone, Reva Beck Jan 49

Bossy, Mike Jun 81

Bostwick, Arthur E. obit Apr 42

Bosustow, Stephen Jun 58

Bosworth, Hobart obit Feb 44

Botero, Fernando Mar 80

Botha Pik see Botha, Roelof F.

Botha, P. W. Sep 79

Botha, Roelof F. May 84

Bothe, Walther May 55 obit Apr 57

Bothwell, Jean (WLB) Yrbk 46

Botstein, Leon Aug 96

Botvinnik, Mikhail Jun 65 obit Jul 95

Bouchard, Lucien Apr 99

Boucher, Anthony Jun 62 obit

Jun 68

Bouchles, Olympia Jean see Snowe, Olympia J.

Boudreau, Lou Aug 42 obit Oct 2001

Boulanger, Nadia May 62 obit Jan 80

Boulding, Kenneth E. Mar 65 obit May 93

Boulez, Pierre Mar 69

Boult, Adrian Cedric Mar 46 obit Apr 83

Boulud, Daniel Jan 2005

Boumedienne, Houari Jan 71 obit Feb 79

Bourassa, Robert Sep 76 obit Jan 97

Bourdon, Rob see Linkin Park

Bourgeois, Louise Oct 83

Bourgès-Maunoury, Maurice Jul 57

Bourguiba, Habib ben Ali Sep 55 obit Aug 2000

Bourke-White, Margaret Jan 40 [White, Margaret Bourke] obit Oct 71

Bourne, Jonathan Jr. obit Oct 40

Bourne, St. Clair Jun 2000

Bourtzev, Vladimir L. obit Dec 42

Bouteflika, Abdelaziz Feb 76

Boutell, Clarence B. Jul 46

Boutell, Clip see Boutell, Clarence B.

Boutelle, Richard S. Sep 51

Bouton, Jim Oct 71

Boutros-Ghali, Boutros Apr 92

Bovet, Daniele Jan 58 obit Jun 92

Bowater, Eric Sep 56 obit Nov 62

Bowden, Bobby Nov 96

Bowden, Mark Jan 2002

Bowditch, Richard L. Jul 53 obit Nov 59

Bowe, Riddick Jun 96

Bowen, Catherine Drinker Jul 44 obit Dec 73

Bowen, Ira Sprague Jun 51

obit Apr 73

Bowen, Otis R. Nov 86

Bowen, William G. May 73

Bower, Bertha Muzzy obit Sep 40

Bowers, Claude Gernade Sep 41 obit Mar 58

Bowers, Faubion Sep 59 obit May 2000

Bowes, Edward Mar 41 obit Jul 46

Bowes-Lyon, Claud George obit Dec 44

Bowie, David Oct 76 Nov 94

Bowie, Edward Hall obit Sep 43

Bowker, Albert H. Jan 66

Bowles, Chester Sep 43 Jan 57 obit Jul 86

Bowles, Erskine Aug 98

Bowles, Paul Oct 90 obit Feb 2000

Bowman, George E. obit Nov 41

Bowman, Isaiah Jan 45 obit Feb 50

Bowman, Scotty Jan 99

Bowron, Fletcher Feb 50 obit Nov 68

Boxer, Barbara Apr 94

Boy George Oct 85

Boyce, Westray Battle Sep 45 obit Mar 72

Boyd of Merton, Viscount *see* Lennox-Boyd, Alan Tindal

Boyd, Alan S. Mar 65

Boyd, Bill Mar 50 obit Nov 72

Boyd, James [geophysicist] Mar 49

Boyd, James [historical novelist] obit Apr 44

Boyd, John W. Feb 2001

Boyd, Julian P. Jun 76 obit Aug 80

Boyd, Louise A. Sep 60 obit Nov 72

Boyd, Malcolm Mar 68

Boyd, Stephen Dec 61 obit Aug 77

Boyd, Wes *see* Blades, Joan and Boyd, Wes

Boyd, William *see* Boyd, Bill

Boyd-Orr, John Boyd Orr Jun 46 obit Sep 71

Boyer, Charles Feb 43 obit Oct 78

Boyer, Ernest L. Jan 88 obit Feb 96

Boyer, Harold Raymond Feb 52

Boyer, Ken Mar 66 obit Oct 82

Boyer, Lucien obit Aug 42

Boyer, Marion W. Jan 51 obit Jan 83

Boylan, Robert P. Apr 50

Boyle, Hal Jun 45 obit May 74

Boyle, Kay Jun 42 obit Feb 93

Boyle, T. Coraghessan Jan 91

Boyle, Tony *see* Boyle, W. A.

Boyle, W. A. Jul 70 obit Jul 85

Boyle, William M., Jr. Jun 49 obit Nov 61

Boylston, Helen Dore Jul 42 obit Nov 84

Bracco, Roberto obit Jun 43

Brace, Gerald Warner (WLB) Yrbk 47 obit Sep 78

Bracken, Brendan Dec 41

Bracken, Eddie Oct 44 obit Feb 2003

Brackett, Charles Feb 51 obit Apr 69

Brackman, Robert Jul 53 obit Sep 80

Bradbury, James H. obit Yrbk 40

Bradbury, Norris E. Apr 49 obit Nov 97

Bradbury, Ray Jun 53 Jul 82

Braddock, Bessie *see* Braddock, E. M.

Braddock, E. M. Jul 57 obit Jan 71

Brademas, John May 77

Braden, Spruille Sep 45 obit Mar 78

Bradford, Barbara Taylor Oct 91

Bradford, Robert F. Dec 48

obit May 83

Bradlee, Benjamin C. Sep 75

Bradley, Bill Jul 65 Sep 82

Bradley, David Apr 49

Bradley, Ed May 88

Bradley, Omar Nelson Jul 43 obit May 81

Bradley, Pat Feb 94

Bradley, Preston Mar 56

Bradley, Tom Nov 73 Oct 92 obit Jan 99

Bradshaw, John E. Apr 93

Bradshaw, Lillian Moore Jun 70

Bradshaw, Terry Apr 79

Bradshaw, Thornton F. Jun 82 obit Feb 89

Brady, James S. Oct 91

Brady, Nicholas F. Nov 88

Brady, Sarah Oct 96

Brady, Tom Aug 2004

Brady, William T. Jan 61 obit Jul 84

Bragdon, Claude obit Oct 46

Bragdon, Helen D. Feb 51

Bragg, Rick Apr 2002

Bragg, William Henry obit Apr 42

Brahdy, Mrs. Leopold *see* Rees, Mina S.

Brailowsky, Alexander Jun 56 obit Jun 76

Brainered, Norman *see* Fuller, S. R., Jr.

Bramah, Ernest obit Sep 42

Brameld, Theodore Jun 67 obit Jan 88

Bramuglia, Juan A. May 49 obit Nov 62

Branagh, Kenneth Apr 97

Branch, Michelle May 2005

Brancusi, Constantin Sep 55 obit Jun 57

Brand, Max *see* Faust, Frederick

Brand, Oscar Jun 62

Brandauer, Klaus Maria Jul 90

Brandeis, Louis D. obit Nov 41

Brandenburg, William A. obit

Yrbk 40

Brando, Marlon Apr 52 Mar 74 obit Yrbk 2004

Brandt, Bill Aug 81 obit Feb 84

Brandt, Willy Jun 58 Dec 73 obit Nov 92

Braniff, T. E. Apr 52 obit Mar 54

Branly, Edouard obit Apr 40

Brannaman, Ray H. Nov 47

Brannan, Charles F. Sep 48

Bransome, Edwin D. Apr 52

Branson, Richard Feb 95

Branzell, Karin Feb 46 obit Feb 75

Braque, Georges Nov 49 obit Oct 63

Brattain, Walter Sep 57 obit Nov 87

Brauchitsch, Heinrich Alfred Hermann Walther Von Mar 40 obit Dec 48

Braudel, Fernand Apr 85 obit Jan 86

Braun, Werner Jun 57 obit Jan 73

Bravo, Ellen Aug 97

Bravo, Rose Marie Jun 2004

Braxton, Toni Sep 2000

Bray, Robert S. Feb 66 obit Feb 75

Brazelton, T. Berry Oct 93

Brazzi, Rossano May 61 obit Mar 95

Bream, Julian Mar 68

Breathitt, Edward T. Jul 64 obit Sep 2004

Breathitt, Edward T. obit Sep 2004

Breckenridge, Lester Paige obit Oct 40

Breckinridge, Aida De Acosta Jun 54 obit Jul 62

Breech, Ernest R. Sep 55 obit Aug 78

Breedlove, Craig Sep 66

Breen, Edward D. Jul 2004

Breen, Joseph I. Jul 50 obit

Jan 66

Breitmeyer, Philip obit Jan 42

Brel, Jacques Mar 71 obit Nov 78

Brenan, Gerald Jul 86 obit Mar 87

Brendel, Alfred Jul 77

Brenly, Bob Apr 2002

Brennan, Edward A. Nov 90

Brennan, Francis, Cardinal Oct 67 obit Sep 68

Brennan, Peter J. Apr 73 obit Jan 97

Brennan, Walter May 41 obit Nov 74

Brennan, William J. Jun 57 obit Oct 97

Brenner, Charles H. Oct 2000

Brenner, David Mar 87

Brentano, Arthur obit Mar 44

Brentano, Heinrich Von Feb 55 obit Jan 65

Brenton, W. Harold Jan 53

Brereton, Lewis H. Dec 43 obit Oct 67

Breslin, Howard (WLB) Yrbk 58 obit Jul 64

Breslin, Jimmy Dec 73

Bresson, Robert Jan 71 obit Jun 2000

Brett, George H. Jun 42

Brett, George Jul 81

Brett, George P., Jr. Dec 48 obit May 84

Breuer, Lee Oct 99

Breuer, Marcel Sep 41 Jun 60 obit Aug 81

Brewer, Roy M. Sep 53

Brewster, Benjamin, Bishop obit Mar 41

Brewster, Chauncey Bunce, Bishop obit Jun 41

Brewster, Kingman, Jr. May 64 Sep 79 obit Jan 89

Brewster, Owen May 47 obit Feb 62

Breyer, Stephen G. Jun 96

Breytenbach, Breyten Jun 86

Brezhnev, Leonid I. Jan 63 Nov 78 obit Jan 83

Brice, Fanny Jun 46 obit Jul

51

Brick, John (WLB) Yrbk 53 obit Dec 73

Brickell, Herschel Nov 45 obit Jul 52

Bricker, John W. Apr 43 Jul 56 obit May 86

Brickner, Richard M. Sep 43

Brico, Antonia Sep 48 obit Oct 89

Bridge, Frank obit Mar 41

Bridges, Alfred Bryant Renton see Bridges, Harry

Bridges, Harry Nov 40 May 50 obit May 90

Bridges, Jeff Mar 91

Bridges, Lloyd Jul 90 obit May 98

Bridges, Robert obit Nov 41

Bridges, Styles Mar 48 obit Jan 62

Bridgman, P. W. Apr 55 obit Nov 61

Brier, Bob Sep 2002

Brier, Howard M. (WLB) Yrbk 51

Brier, Robert see Brier, Bob

Briggs, Ellis O. Apr 65 obit Apr 76

Briggs, Eugene S. Oct 48

Briggs, James E. Jun 57 obit Aug 79

Brigham, Carl Campbell obit Mar 43

Brigham, Clarence S. Jul 59 obit Oct 63

Brill, Steven Nov 97

Brimmer, Andrew Jul 68

Brin, Sergey and Page, Larry Oct 2001

Brind, Patrick Nov 52 obit Jan 64

Briney, Nancy Jan 54

Brink, Carol (WLB) Yrbk 46

Brinkley, Christie Feb 94

Brinkley, David Mar 60 Sep 87 obit Sep 2003

Brinkley, John R. obit Jul 42

Brinkley, Nell obit Dec 44

Brinton, Crane Jun 59 obit

Nov 68

Brinton, Howard H. Jul 49 obit Yrbk 84 (died Apr 73)

Briscoe, Connie Jan 2000

Briscoe, Robert May 57 obit Jul 69

Bristol, Arthur Leroy obit Jun 42

Bristol, Lee H. Sep 62

Bristow, Gwen Yrbk 40 obit Yrbk 84 (died Aug 80)

Bristow, Joseph Little obit Sep 44

Brittan, Leon Aug 94

Britten, Benjamin Oct 42 Apr 61 obit Feb 77

Britton, Edgar C. Apr 52 obit Oct 62

Bro, Margueritte Harmon (WLB) Yrbk 52

Broad, William Michael Albert see Idol, Billy

Broadbent, John Edward May 88

Broadhurst, Harry May 43

Brock, Lou Jun 75

Brock, William Emerson, 3d May 71

Brode, Mildred H. Sep 63

Brode, Wallace Jun 58 obit Oct 74

Broder, Samuel Aug 92

Broderick, Matthew May 87

Brodeur, Martin Nov 2002

Brodie, Bernard B. Sep 69 obit May 89

Brodkey, Harold Apr 89 obit Apr 96

Brodsky, Joseph Jul 82 obit Apr 96

Brody, Adrien Jul 2003

Brody, Jane E. Feb 86

Broeg, Bob May 2002

Brogan, Denis William (WLB) Yrbk 47 obit Feb 74

Broglie, Louis De Sep 55 obit May 87

Brokaw, Tom May 81 Nov 2002

Brokenshire, Norman May 50

obit Jun 65

Bromfield, Louis Jul 44 obit May 56

Bromley, Dorothy Dunbar Apr 46 obit Feb 86

Bronfman, Edgar M. Jul 74

Bronfman, Edgar M., Jr. Oct 95

Bronk, Detlev W. Oct 49 obit Jan 76

Bronowski, J. Sep 58 obit Oct 74

Bronson, Charles Mar 75 obit Mar 2004

Bronstein, Lev Davidovich see Trotsky, Leon

Brook, Alexander Apr 41 obit Apr 80

Brook, Peter May 61

Brooke, Alan Jan 41 obit Sep 63

Brooke, Basil Stanlake Jun 48 obit Oct 73

Brooke, Edward William, III Apr 67

Brookeborough, Basil Stanlake Brooke, 1st Viscount see Brooke, Basil Stanlake

Brooke-Popham, Robert Oct 41 obit Jan 54

Brookes, George S., Rev. Aug 40

Brookhart, Smith W. obit Jan 45

Brookner, Anita Feb 89

Brooks and Dunn Sep 2004

Brooks, Albert Apr 97

Brooks, Angie Mar 70

Brooks, C. Wayland Sep 47 obit Mar 57

Brooks, D. W. Jun 51

Brooks, David Apr 2004

Brooks, Diana D. Jun 98

Brooks, Donald Mar 72 obit Yrbk 2005

Brooks, Garth Mar 92

Brooks, Gwendolyn Jun 50 Jul 77 obit Feb 2001

Brooks, Jack Jun 92

Brooks, James Feb 59 obit

May 92

Brooks, James L. Apr 98

Brooks, Kix see Brooks and Dunn

Brooks, Louise Apr 84 obit Oct 85

Brooks, Matilda M. Nov 41

Brooks, Mel Sep 74

Brooks, Overton Jun 57 obit Dec 61

Brooks, Robert C. obit Apr 41

Brooks, Van Wyck Jun 41 Sep 60 obit Jun 63

Brooks, Vincent Jun 2003

Brophy, Thomas D'arcy Sep 52 obit Oct 67

Brosio, Manlio Sep 55 obit May 80

Brosnan, Jim Nov 64

Brosnan, Pierce Jan 97

Brossard, Edgar B. Jul 54

Brothers, Joyce Apr 71

Brough, Louise Jun 48

Broun, Heywood obit Jan 40

Brouwer, Dirk Mar 51 obit Mar 66

Browder, Earl Oct 44 obit Sep 73

Browdy, Benjamin G. Jul 51

Brower, Charles Feb 65 obit Nov 84

Brower, David Jun 73 obit Feb 2001

Brown, A. Ten Eyck obit Jul 40

Brown, Aaron Mar 2003

Brown, Albert Eger Jan 48

Brown, Alberta L. May 58

Brown, Angeline see Dickinson, Angie

Brown, Bobby Apr 91

Brown, Carleton obit Aug 41

Brown, Cecil Mar 42 obit Jan 88

Brown, Charles H. Aug 41 obit Mar 60

Brown, Charles L. Sep 81 obit Sep 2004

Brown, Charles R. Jul 58

Brown, Clarence J. Feb 47

obit Nov 65

Brown, Claude Nov 67 obit Apr 2002

Brown, Dan May 2004

Brown, David M. Jun 50

Brown, Dee Aug 79 obit Mar 2003

Brown, Edmund G. Mar 60 obit Apr 96

Brown, Edmund G., Jr. Apr 75

Brown, Francis Shunk obit Jan 40

Brown, George Dec 63 obit Jul 85

Brown, George H. Jan 71

Brown, George S. Oct 75 obit Feb 79

Brown, Gilmor Jul 44

Brown, Harold Sep 61 Oct 77

Brown, Harrison Jul 55 obit Feb 87

Brown, Helen Dawes obit Nov 41

Brown, Helen Gurley Nov 69

Brown, Helen Hayes *see* Hayes, Helen

Brown, Irving Jul 51 obit May 89

Brown, J. Carter Apr 76 obit Yrbk 2002

Brown, James Mar 92

Brown, Jerry *see* Brown, Edmund G., Jr.

Brown, Jesse Nov 93 obit Yrbk 2002

Brown, Jim Sep 64

Brown, Joe E. Feb 45 obit Sep 73

Brown, John Franklin obit Mar 40

Brown, John Mason Apr 42 obit May 69

Brown, Junior Nov 2004

Brown, Kwame Feb 2002

Brown, Larry [basketball coach] Apr 96

Brown, Larry [football play-er] Mar 73

Brown, Lee P. Sep 2002

Brown, Lester R. Jan 93

Brown, Lewis H. Oct 47 obit Mar 51

Brown, Newell Sep 59 obit Sep 2000

Brown, Pat *see* Brown, Edmund G.

Brown, Perry *see* Brown, Sanford Perry

Brown, Prentiss M. Jan 43 obit Feb 74

Brown, Rita Mae Sep 86

Brown, Robert McAfee May 65 obit Nov 2001

Brown, Ron Jul 89 obit Jun 96

Brown, Ronald K. May 2002

Brown, Sanford Perry Apr 49

Brown, Sterling Aug 82 obit Apr 89

Brown, Tina Feb 90

Brown, Tony Feb 97

Brown, Trisha Apr 97

Brown, Virginia Mae Jul 70 obit May 91

Brown, Willie Apr 97

Browne, Coral Dec 59 obit Jul 91

Browne, Edward E. obit Jan 46

Browne, George Elmer obit Sep 46

Browne, Jackson Oct 89

Browne, Mary Mumpere Shaver *see* Shaver, Mary

Browne, Sidney Jane obit Oct 41

Brownell, Herbert, Jr. Aug 44 Feb 54 obit Aug 96

Brownell, Samuel Miller Feb 54 obit Jan 91

Browner, Carol M. May 94

Browning, Frederick A. M. Jun 43 obit Apr 65

Browning, Jean *see* Madeira, Jean

Browning, John May 69 obit Jun 2003

Browning, Webster E. obit

Jun 42

Brownlow, Kevin Mar 92

Brownmiller, Susan Jan 78

Brownson, Charles B. Jul 55

Brownson, Josephine Mar 40

Broyhill, Joel T. May 74

Broz, Joseph *see* Broz, Tito Josip

Broz, Tito Josip Nov 43 Mar 55 obit Jun 80

Brozovich, Josip *see* Broz, Tito Josip

Brubeck, Dave Mar 56 Apr 93

Bruce, David K. E. Jun 49 Sep 61 obit Feb 78

Bruce, Howard Sep 48 obit Sep 61

Bruce, James Jan 49 obit Sep 80

Bruce, Louis R., Jr. May 72 obit Jul 89

Bruce, Robert Randolph obit Apr 42

Bruce, William Cabell obit Jun 46

Brucker, Wilbur M. Sep 55 obit Dec 68

Bruckheimer, Jerry Mar 99

Bruckner, Henry obit Jun 42

Brueggemann, Ingar Nov 2001

Bruhn, Erik Apr 59 obit May 86

Brumel, Valery Apr 63 obit Jun 2003

Brunauer, Esther C. Nov 47 obit Sep 59

Brundage, Avery Jan 48 obit Aug 75

Brundage, Percival F. Apr 57

Brundtland, Gro Harlem Nov 81

Bruner, Jerome Seymour Oct 84

Brunner, Edmund De S. Sep 58 obit Feb 74

Brunner, Jean Adam Sep 45 obit Jun 51

Bruns, Franklin R., Jr. May 54

Brunsdale, Norman Sep 54

Brush, George De Forest obit

Jun 41

Brustein, Robert Aug 75

Bruton, John Nov 96

Bryan, Charles W. obit Apr 45

Bryan, Ernest R. Jul 50 obit Feb 55

Bryan, George Sands obit Feb 44

Bryan, James E. Jun 62

Bryan, Julien Jul 40 obit Jan 75

Bryant, Anita Nov 75

Bryant, Bear *see* Bryant, Paul W.

Bryant, Benjamin Nov 43

Bryant, C. Farris Sep 61 obit Yrbk 2002

Bryant, Paul W. Jun 80 obit Mar 83

Bryce, Elizabeth Marion, Viscountess obit Jan 40

Brynner, Rock Mar 2005

Brynner, Yul Sep 56 obit Nov 85

Bryson, David *see* Counting Crows

Bryson, Lyman Sep 40 Sep 51 obit Feb 60

Brzezinski, Zbigniew Apr 70

Buatta, Mario May 91

Buber, Martin Jun 53 obit Jul 65

Bubka, Sergei Jul 96

Buchan, John Jan 40

Buchanan, Edna Sep 97

Buchanan, Frank Feb 51

Buchanan, Patrick J. Aug 85

Buchanan, Scott Sep 62 obit May 68

Buchanan, Thomas Drysdale obit Apr 40

Buchanan, Wiley T., Jr. Nov 57 obit Mar 86

Bucher, Walter H. Feb 57 obit Apr 65

Buchholz, Horst Mar 60 obit Aug 2003

Buchinsky, Charles *see* Bronson, Charles

Buchman, Frank N. D. Oct 40

obit Nov 61

Buchwald, Art Jan 60

Buck, Dorothea Dutcher *see* Buck, Mrs. J. L. Blair

Buck, Frank Jun 43 obit Apr 50

Buck, Gene Feb 41 obit May 57

Buck, Mrs. J. L. Blair Sep 47

Buck, Paul Herman Jul 55 obit Apr 89

Buck, Pearl Jul 56 obit Apr 73

Buck, Solon J. May 47 obit Jul 62

Buckland, Jon *see* Coldplay

Buckley, Christopher Apr 97

Buckley, James L. Oct 71

Buckley, Priscilla L. Apr 2002

Buckley, William F., Jr. Jun 62 Oct 82

Buckmaster, Henrietta (WLB) Yrbk 46 obit Jun 83

Buckner, Emory R. obit May 41

Buckner, Simon Bolivar, Jr. Oct 42 obit Jul 45

Budd, Edward G., Jr. Jul 49 obit Jul 71

Budd, Ralph Jul 40 obit Mar 62

Budenny, Semyon M. Sep 41 obit Dec 73

Budenz, Louis F. Jun 51 obit Jun 72

Budge, Donald Jun 41 obit Jun 2000

Budge, Hamer H. Dec 70 obit Yrbk 2003

Budington, William S. Jun 64

Buechner, Frederick (WLB) Yrbk 59

Buechner, Thomas S. Feb 61

Buell, Raymond Leslie obit Apr 46

Bueno, Maria Apr 65

Buetow, Herbert P. Mar 60 obit Mar 72

Buffet, Bernard Apr 59 obit

Feb 2000

Buffett, Jimmy Mar 99

Buffett, Warren E. Nov 87

Buffum, Charles A. obit Sep 41

Buford, John Lester Apr 56

Bugas, John S. Dec 47 obit Feb 83

Bugher, John C. Apr 53

Buitoni, Giovanni Jun 62 obit Mar 79

Bujones, Fernando Jan 76

Bukovsky, Vladimir Mar 78

Bukovsky, Volodya *see* Bukovsky, Vladimir

Bukowski, Charles Apr 94 obit Apr 94

Buley, R. Carlyle Jul 51 obit Jun 68

Bulgakov, Mikhail Afanasievich obit Mar 40

Bulganin, Nikolai A. Feb 55 obit Apr 75

Bull, Johan obit Oct 45

Bull, Odd Nov 68

Bullard, Edward Crisp Sep 54 obit May 80

Bullins, Ed May 77

Bullis, Harry A. Oct 46 obit Jan 64

Bullitt, William Christian Jul 40 obit Apr 67

Bullock, Sandra Aug 97

Bulosan, Carlos (WLB) Yrbk 46 obit Nov 56

Bultmann, Rudolf Jan 72 obit Sep 76

Bumbry, Grace Mar 64

Bumgarner, James *see* Garner, James

Bumpers, Dale Aug 79

Bunau-Varilla, Philippe obit Jul 40

Bunche, Ralph J. Feb 48 obit Jan 72

Bundesen, Herman Niels Oct 48 obit Nov 60

Bundy, McGeorge Mar 62 obit Jan 97

Bundy, William P. Jun 64 obit

Feb 2001

Bunge, Alejandro E. obit Jul 43

Bunim, Mary-Ellis obit Yrbk 2004

Bunim, Mary-Ellis *see* Bunim, Mary-Ellis, and Murray, Jonathan

Bunim, Mary-Ellis, and Murray, Jonathan May 2002

Bunker, Ellsworth Apr 54 Mar 78 obit Nov 84

Bunker, George M. Apr 57

Bunshaft, Gordon Mar 89 obit Oct 90

Bunting, Earl Feb 47

Bunting, Mary I. Jun 67 obit Apr 98

Bunting-Smith, Mary Ingraham *see* Bunting, Mary I.

Buñuel, Luis Mar 65 obit Sep 83

Burbidge, E. Margaret Nov 2000

Burchard, John E. Apr 58 obit Mar 76

Burchfield, Charles May 42 May 61 obit Mar 67

Burdell, Edwin S. Feb 52

Burdett, Winston Oct 43 obit Jul 93

Burdick, Charles Kellogg obit Aug 40

Burdick, Quentin N. May 63 obit Nov 92

Burdick, Usher L. Apr 52 obit Nov 60

Burford, Anne Gorsuch *see* Gorsuch, Anne

Burford, Anne McGill *see* Gorsuch, Anne

Burger, Warren E. Nov 69 obit Aug 95

Burgess, Anthony May 72 obit Jan 94

Burgess, Carter L. Apr 57 obit Yrbk 2002

Burgess, Robert W. Jul 60 obit Jul 69

Burgess, W. Randolph Jun 49

obit Nov 78

Burghley, David George Brownlow Cecil, Lord Jan 56

Burgin, William O. obit May 46

Burke, Arleigh A. Sep 55 obit Aug 96

Burke, Charles H. obit May 44

Burke, Edmund J., Father obit Feb 41

Burke, Edward Raymond Sep 40 obit Dec 68

Burke, Michael Apr 72 obit Mar 87

Burke, Thomas A. Jul 54 obit Jan 72

Burke, Thomas obit Oct 45

Burke, William R. Jul 61

Burke, Yvonne Brathwaite Oct 75

Burleigh, George William obit Apr 40

Burleigh, Harry T. Aug 41 obit Oct 49

Burliuk, David Apr 40 obit Mar 67

Burnet, Macfarlane May 54 obit Oct 85

Burnett, Carol Jan 62 Nov 90

Burnett, Charles Sep 95

Burnett, Hallie Southgate (WLB) Yrbk 54 obit Nov 91

Burnett, Mark May 2001

Burnett, Whit Apr 41 [Foley, Martha; and Burnett, Whit] obit Jun 73

Burney, Leroy E. Jul 57 obit Oct 98

Burnham, Donald C. Nov 68

Burnham, Forbes Nov 66 obit Oct 85

Burnham, James Nov 41 obit Jan 88

Burns, Alan Sep 53

Burns, Arthur F. Sep 53 Aug 76 obit Aug 87

Burns, Cecil Delisle obit Mar

42

Burns, E. L. M. Feb 55

Burns, Edward McN Feb 54

Burns, Eveline Mabel Nov 60 obit Jan 86

Burns, George Mar 51 [Burns, George; and Allen, Gracie] Jul 76 obit Nov 96

Burns, H. S. M. May 54 obit Dec 71

Burns, James Aloysius, Father obit Oct 40

Burns, James Mac Gregor Dec 62

Burns, John A. Feb 72 obit Jun 75

Burns, John L. Apr 60 obit Aug 96

Burns, Ken May 92

Burnseig, Arthur Frank *see* Burns, Arthur F.

Burpee, David Mar 55 obit Aug 80

Burr, Donald C. Sep 86

Burr, Henry obit May 41

Burr, Raymond Sep 61 obit Nov 93

Burrell, Stanley Kirk *see* Hammer

Burroughs, Augusten Apr 2004

Burroughs, William S. Nov 71 obit Nov 97

Burrows, Abe Nov 51 obit Jul 85

Burrows, Millar Jul 56 obit Jul 80

Burrows, Stephen Nov 2003

Burstyn, Ellen Jun 75

Burstyn, Mike May 2005

Burton, Alan C. Sep 56

Burton, Charles Emerson, Rev. obit Oct 40

Burton, Dan Sep 98

Burton, Harold H. Apr 45 obit Jan 65

Burton, Jean (WLB) Yrbk 48

Burton, LeVar Mar 2000

Burton, Lewis William, Bishop obit Yrbk 40

Burton, Richard [actor] Dec

60 obit Sep 84

Burton, Richard [writer] obit May 40

Burton, Tim Jul 91

Burton, Virginia Lee Sep 43 obit Dec 68

Burtt, Ben May 2003

Burwash, Lachlin Taylor obit Feb 41

Buscaglia, Leo Oct 83 obit Aug 98

Buscemi, Steve Apr 99

Busch, August A. Jul 73 obit Nov 89

Busch, Carl obit Feb 44

Busch, Charles Jun 95

Busch, Fritz Jan 46 obit Oct 51

Bush, Barbara Oct 89

Bush, George Jan 72 Sep 83

Bush, George W. Apr 97 Aug 2001

Bush, Jeb Feb 99

Bush, John Ellis see Bush, Jeb

Bush, Kate Mar 95

Bush, Laura Jun 2001

Bush, Prescott S. May 42 Jan 54 obit Dec 72

Bush, Vannevar Sep 40 May 47 obit Sep 74

Bush, Wendell T. obit Mar 41

Bushnell, Asa S. Jul 52 obit May 75

Bushnell, Candace Nov 2003

Busiek, Kurt Sep 2005

Bustamante, Alexander May 65 obit Sep 77

Butcher, Susan Jun 91

Butcher, Willard C. Jul 80

Buthelezi, Gatsha see Buthelezi, Mangosuthu G.

Buthelezi, Mangosuthu G. Oct 86

Butler of Saffron Walden, Richard Austen Butler, Baron see Butler, Richard Austen

Butler, Hugh Feb 50 obit Sep 54

Butler, John Jun 55 obit Nov 93

Butler, John M. May 54 obit

May 78

Butler, Nevile Apr 41

Butler, Nicholas Murray Nov 40 obit Dec 47

Butler, Paul M. May 55 obit Feb 62

Butler, R. Paul see Marcy, Geoffrey W., and Butler, R. Paul

Butler, Reg Sep 56

Butler, Richard Austen May 44 Sep 64 obit May 82

Butler, Robert N. Jan 97

Butler, Sally Dec 46

Butler, Smedley Darlington obit Aug 40

Buttenwieser, Benjamin J. Nov 50 obit Mar 92

Butterfield, Roger Place Mar 48 obit Yrbk 91 (died Jan 81)

Butterfly, Julia see Hill, Julia "Butterfly"

Butterworth, Charles obit Jul 46

Button, Richard Mar 49

Buttons, Red Sep 58

Butts, Alfred M. Jul 54 obit Jun 93

Butts, Calvin O. Feb 99

Butz, Earl L. Jul 72

Buzzi-Peccia, Arturo obit Oct 43

Byas, Hugh Mar 43 obit Apr 45

Byatt, A. S. Sep 91

Byers, Margaretta Sep 41

Byington, Spring Sep 56 obit Oct 71

Bykovsky, Valery Jan 65

Byrd, Charlie Oct 67 obit Mar 2000

Byrd, Harry F. Apr 42 Sep 55 obit Dec 66

Byrd, Richard E. Oct 42 May 56 obit May 57

Byrd, Robert C. Mar 60 Feb

78

Byrd, Sam Nov 42 obit Jan 56

Byrne, Brendan T. May 74

Byrne, Gabriel May 99

Byrne, Jane Jan 80

Byrne, John Keyes see Leonard, Hugh

Byrne, John Oct 2000

Byrnes, James F. Jun 41 Oct 51 obit Jun 72

Byrnes, John W. Oct 60 obit Mar 85

Byroade, Henry A. Feb 52 obit Mar 94

Byron, Arthur W. obit Sep 43

Byron, Don Sep 2000

Byron, William D. obit Apr 41

C. R. see Rajagopalachari, Chakravarti

Caan, James May 76

Caballé, Montserrat Jun 67

Caballero, Linda see La India

Cabot, John M. Sep 53 obit Apr 81

Cabot, Thomas D. Jun 51 obit Aug 95

Caccia, Harold Anthony Feb 57 obit Jan 91

Cacoyannis, Michael May 66

Cactus Jack see Foley, Mick

Caddell, Patrick H. Nov 79

Cadell, Elizabeth (WLB) Yrbk 51

Cadle, E. Howard obit Feb 43

Cadmus, Paul Jul 42 obit Mar 2000

Cadogan, Alexander Oct 44 obit Sep 68

Caesar, Sid Apr 51

Caetano, Marcello Mar 70 obit Jan 81

Café Filho, Joao Jan 55 obit Apr 70

Caffery, Jefferson Nov 43 obit Jun 74

Caffrey, James J. Jun 47 obit May 61

Cage, John Sep 61 obit Sep 92

Cage, Nicolas Apr 94

Cagney, James Dec 42 obit

May 86

Cahill, Michael Harrison obit Apr 40

Cahill, William T. Jun 70 obit Sep 96

Cahn, Sammy Nov 74 obit Mar 93

Cai Yuanpei obit Mar 40

Caillaux, Joseph obit Jan 45

Cain, Harry P. Apr 49 obit May 79

Cain, James M. Dec 47 obit Jan 78

Caine, Michael May 68 Jan 88

Cairns, Huntington Nov 40

Calatrava, Santiago Aug 97

Calder, A. Stirling obit Feb 45

Calder, Alexander Apr 46 Jul 66 obit Jan 77

Calder, Nigel Jun 86

Calder, Ritchie Apr 63 obit May 86

Calder, William M. obit Apr 45

Caldera, Rafael Jul 69

Calderón Guardia, Rafael Ángel Jun 42 obit Sep 70

Calderón, Sila M. Nov 2001

Calderone, Frank A. Jul 52 obit Apr 87

Calderone, Mary S. Nov 67 obit Jan 99

Caldicott, Helen Oct 83

Caldwell, Erskine Oct 40 obit May 87

Caldwell, Millard F. Nov 48 obit Feb 85

Caldwell, Mrs. Leslie Godfrey see Caldwell, Sarah C.

Caldwell, Sarah C. Jan 53

Caldwell, Sarah Oct 73

Caldwell, Taylor Jan-Feb 40 obit Oct 85

Caldwell, William E. obit May 43

Caldwell, Zoe Dec 70

Calero, Adolfo Oct 87

Calfee, John Edward obit Jan 41

Calhern, Louis Jul 51 obit Jul

56

Califano, Joseph A., Jr. Jun 77

Calisher, Hortense Nov 73

Calkins, Robert D. Oct 52 obit Sep 92

Callaghan, Daniel J. obit Jan 43

Callaghan, James Feb 68 obit Yrbk 2005

Callahan, Harry M. Nov 84 obit Jul 99

Callahan, John Sep 98

Callander, W. F. Oct 48

Callas, Maria Sep 56 obit Nov 77

Calle, Sophie May 2001

Callender, John Hancock Sep 55 obit Jun 95

Callery, Mary Jul 55

Calles, Plutarco Ellias obit Nov 45

Callow, John Michael obit Sep 40

Calloway, Cab Nov 45 obit Jan 95

Calvé, Emma obit Mar 42

Calverton, V. F. obit Jan 41

Calvin, Melvin Apr 62 obit Mar 97

Calvino, Italo Feb 84 obit Nov 85

Calvo Sotelo, Leopoldo Aug 81

Calwell, Arthur A. Oct 47

Cam, Helen M. Sep 48 obit Apr 68

Camac, Charles Nicoll Bancker obit Nov 40

Camacho, Manuel Avila see Avila Camacho, Manuel

Câmara, Helder Pessora Jul 71 obit Jan 2000

Camargo, Alberto Lleras see Lleras Camargo, Alberto

Cambridge, Godfrey Mar 69 obit Feb 77

Camby, Marcus Jan 2000

Camden, Harry P., Jr. obit Sep

43

Cameron, Basil Apr 43

Cameron, Charles S. Sep 54

Cameron, Hugh obit Jan 42

Cameron, James Jan 98

Camm, Sydney Apr 42 obit Apr 66

Cammerer, Arno B. obit Jun 41

Camp, John see Sandford, John

Campa, Miguel Angel Sep 57 obit Nov 65

Campanella, Roy Jun 53 obit Aug 93

Campbell, Bebe Moore Apr 2000

Campbell, Ben Nighthorse Oct 94

Campbell, Bill Jul 96

Campbell, Boyd May 56

Campbell, Donald Feb 64 obit Feb 67

Campbell, Douglas Jun 58

Campbell, E. Simms Jan 41 obit Mar 71

Campbell, Earl Apr 83

Campbell, Gerald Mar 41 obit Sep 64

Campbell, Glen Jul 69

Campbell, Grace (WLB) Yrbk 48 obit Jul 63

Campbell, Harold G. obit Aug 42

Campbell, Joseph Jun 84 obit Jan 88

Campbell, Malcolm Sep 47 obit Feb 49

Campbell, Mrs. Harvey see Campbell, Grace

Campbell, Mrs. Patrick obit May 40

Campbell, Mrs. W. E. Burton see Campbell, Patricia

Campbell, Naomi Feb 97

Campbell, Neve Jan 2000

Campbell, Patricia (WLB) Yrbk 57

Campbell, Philip P. obit Jul 41

Campbell, Viv see Def Leppard

Campbell, Willis C. obit Jun 41

Campeau, Robert Mar 89

Campinchi, César obit Apr 41

Campion, Jane Apr 94

Campney, Ralph Osborne Sep 55 obit Dec 67

Campora, Giuseppe Jul 57

Cámpora, Héctor José Oct 73 obit Feb 81

Camrose, William Ewert Berry, 1st Viscount *see* Berry, William Ewert

Canada, Geoffrey Feb 2005

Canaday, John May 62 obit Sep 85

Canaday, Ward M. Mar 51 obit Apr 76

Canady, Alexa Aug 2000

Canavan, Joseph J. obit Yrbk 40

Canby, Al H. obit Yrbk 40

Canby, Henry Seidel Sep 42 obit Jun 61

Candau, Marcolino G. Sep 54

Candee, Robert C. May 44

Candela, Félix Jul 60

Candia, Alfredo Ovanda *see* Ovanda Candia, Alfredo

Candler, Warren A. obit Nov 41

Candy, John Feb 90 obit May 94

Canegata, Leonard Lionel Cornelius *see* Lee, Canada

Canetti, Elias Jan 83 obit Oct 94

Canfield, Cass Apr 54 obit May 86

Canham, Erwin D. Jul 45 Jan 60 obit Feb 82

Caniff, Milton A. Jan 44 obit May 88

Canin, Ethan Aug 2001

Cannon, Annie J. obit Jun 41

Cannon, Cavendish W. Jul 57 obit Dec 62

Cannon, Clarence Nov 49 obit Jul 64

Cannon, Howard W. Feb 60

obit Yrbk 2002

Cannon, James, Jr., Bishop obit Nov 44

Cannon, Legrand, Jr. Mar 43

Cannon, Sarah Ophelia Colley *see* Pearl, Minnie

Cannon, Walter Bradford obit Nov 45

Canseco, José Nov 91

Canterbury, Hewlett Johnson, Dean of *see* Johnson, Hewlett

Cantinflas Jun 53 obit Jun 93

Canton, Allen A. obit Apr 40

Cantor, Eddie Nov 41 May 54 obit Jan 65

Cantu, Giuseppe obit Yrbk 40

Cantwell, Maria Feb 2005

Canty, Brendan *see* Fugazi

Capa, Cornell Jul 2005

Capehart, Homer E. Apr 47 obit Oct 79

Caperton, William B. obit Feb 42

Caplin, Mortimer M. Sep 61

Capogrossi, Giuseppe Dec 57

Capote, Truman Sep 51 Mar 68 obit Oct 84

Capp, Al May 47 obit Jan 80

Capper, Arthur Sep 46 obit Feb 52

Capra, Frank Apr 48 obit Oct 91

Capriati, Jennifer Nov 2001

Caputo, Philip Apr 96

Caradon, Hugh Foot *see* Foot, Hugh

Caramanlis, Constantine May 56 Apr 76 obit Jul 98

Caras, Roger A. Apr 88 obit Jul 2001

Caraway, Hattie W. Mar 45 obit Jan 51

Card, Andrew H. Jr. Nov 2003

Cardin, Pierre Mar 65

Cardon, P. V. May 54 obit Dec 65

Cardoso, Fernando Henrique

Oct 96

Carew, Rod Jan 78

Carewe, Edwin obit Jan 40

Carey, Charles Henry obit Oct 41

Carey, Drew Mar 98

Carey, Ernestine Gilbreth May 49 [Gilbreth, Frank B.; and Carey, Ernestine Gilbreth]

Carey, George Aug 91

Carey, Hugh L. Sep 65

Carey, James B. Nov 41 Jul 51 obit Nov 73

Carey, Mariah Jul 92

Carey, Ron May 92

Carey, Walter F. Feb 65

Carías Andino, Tiburcio Jun 42 obit Feb 70

Carl XVI Gustaf, King of Sweden Feb 74

Carle, Richard obit Aug 41

Carlin, George Oct 76

Carlino, Lewis John May 83

Carlisle, Kitty *see* Hart, Kitty Carlisle

Carlos, Juan Oct 51 obit Jun 93

Carlos, Prince Juan Oct 64

Carlson, A. J. Jan 48 obit Nov 56

Carlson, Evans F. Oct 43 obit Jun 47

Carlson, Frank Apr 49 obit Jul 87

Carlson, John F. obit May 45

Carlson, John Roy Oct 43

Carlson, Margaret Nov 2003

Carlson, William S. Jul 52 obit Jul 94

Carlsson, Ingvar Feb 88

Carlton, William Newnham Chattin obit Mar 43

Carlucci, Frank Oct 81

Carlyle, Alexander James, Rev. obit Jul 43

Carmack, John Mar 2000

Carmichael, Hoagy May 41 obit Feb 82

Carmichael, Oliver C. Jan 46

obit Dec 66

Carmichael, Stokely Apr 70 obit Feb 99

Carmines, Al Sep 72 obit Yrbk 2005

Carmody, John Michael May 40 obit Jan 64

Carmona, Antonio Oscar De Fragoso Nov 50 obit May 51

Carmona, Richard Jan 2003

Carnarvon, Countess of *see* Losch, Tilly

Carnegie, Dale Dec 41 Sep 55

Carnegie, Dorothy Sep 55 obit Jan 99

Carnegie, Hattie Oct 42 obit May 56

Carney, Art Apr 58 obit Yrbk 2004

Carney, Robert B. Oct 51 obit Aug 90

Carnovsky, Morris Jan 91

Caro, Anthony Nov 81

Caro, Robert A. Jan 84

Carol II, King of Romania Aug 40 obit May 53

Caroline, Princess of Monaco Nov 89

Caron, Leslie Sep 54

Carpenter, George L. Jan 43 obit May 48

Carpenter, Henry Cort Harold obit Nov 40

Carpenter, J. Henry Feb 43 obit Sep 54

Carpenter, John Alden May 47 obit May 51

Carpenter, Lewis Van obit Jul 40

Carpenter, Malcolm Scott Sep 62

Carpenter, Mary Chapin Feb 94

Carpentier, Marcel-Maurice

Apr 51

Carr, Alexander obit Dec 46

Carr, Emma Perry Apr 59

Carr, Robert Jan 73

Carr, Robert K. Apr 61

Carr, Wilbur J. obit Aug 42

Carr, William G. Sep 52 obit May 96

Carradine, Keith Aug 91

Carraway, Gertrude S. Jan 54

Carrel, Alexis Mar 40 obit Dec 44

Carreras, José Jun 79

Carrero Blanco, Luis Oct 73 obit Feb 74

Carrey, Jim Feb 96

Carrillo, Santiago Jun 77

Carrington, 6th Baron Jun 71

Carrington, Elaine Feb 44 obit Jul 58

Carroll, Diahann Sep 62

Carroll, James May 97

Carroll, Jim Oct 95

Carroll, John A. May 58 obit Oct 83

Carroll, John Jul 55 obit Jan 60

Carroll, Joseph F. Apr 62 obit Mar 91

Carroll, Madeleine Apr 49 obit Nov 87

Carroll, Pat Aug 80

Carroll, Thomas H. Jul 62 obit Oct 64

Carroll, Vinnette Sep 83 obit Feb 2003

Carroll-Abbing, J. Patrick Jul 67 obit Nov 2001

Carruth, Hayden Apr 92

Carsey, Marcy Jan 97

Carson, Benjamin S., Sr. May 97

Carson, John Renshaw obit Yrbk 40

Carson, Johnny Jan 64 Apr 82 obit Jul 2005

Carson, Rachel Nov 51 obit Jun 64

Carstens, Karl Apr 80 obit Aug 92

Cartas, María Estela Martínez

see Perón, Isabel

Carter, Benny Jul 87 obit Oct 2003

Carter, Betty Mar 82 obit Jan 99

Carter, Boake Jan 42 obit Yrbk 47

Carter, Don Mar 63

Carter, Elliott Nov 60

Carter, Hodding, 3rd Aug 81

Carter, Huntly obit May 42

Carter, James Earl, Jr. *see* Carter, Jimmy

Carter, James Feb 97

Carter, Jimmy [singer] *see* Blind Boys of Alabama

Carter, Jimmy [U.S. president] Sep 71 Nov 77

Carter, John Franklin *see* Franklin, Jay

Carter, John May 59 obit May 75

Carter, John Ridgely obit Jul 44

Carter, Lillian Jan 78 obit Jan 84

Carter, Nick *see* Backstreet Boys

Carter, Regina Oct 2003

Carter, Rosalynn Mar 78

Carter, Rubin May 2000

Carter, Shawn *see* Jay-Z

Carter, Stephen L. Jul 97

Carter, Vince Apr 2002

Carter, William Hodding, Jr. Jul 46 obit May 72

Cartier, Baron obit Jul 46

Cartier-Bresson, Henri Mar 47 May 76 obit Yrbk 2004

Cartland, Barbara Aug 79 obit Aug 2000

Carton De Wiart, Adrian May 40 obit Jul 63

Cartotto, Ercole obit Nov 46

Cartwright, Morse A. Sep 47 obit Jun 74

Carusi, Ugo Oct 48 obit Sep 94

Carvel, Elbert N. Jun 63

Carver, George Washington

Nov 40 obit Feb 43

Carver, Raymond Feb 84 obit Sep 88

Carvey, Dana Jun 92

Carville, James Mar 93

Cary, Frank T. Jan 80

Cary, Joyce (WLB) Yrbk 49 obit Jun 57

Cary, William L. Jan 63 obit Apr 83

Casa, Lisa Della see Della Casa, Lisa

Casadesus, Robert Jan 45 obit Nov 72

Casals, Pablo Nov 50 Nov 64 obit Dec 73

Casals, Rosemary Feb 74

Case, Clifford P. Mar 55 obit Apr 82

Case, Francis May 46 obit Sep 62

Case, Frank obit Jul 46

Case, Steve Oct 96

Casey, Bernie Jul 99

Casey, Edward Pearce obit Jan 40

Casey, Ralph E. Feb 66

Casey, Richard Gardiner Jan-Feb 40 obit Aug 76 [Casey, Lord]

Casey, Robert J. Mar 43 obit Jan 63

Casey, William J. Mar 72 obit Jun 87

Cash, Johnny Sep 69 obit Jan 2004

Cash, Rosanne Oct 91

Cashin, Bonnie May 70 obit Jun 2000

Cashman, Robert Nov 52

Caspary, Vera (WLB) Yrbk 47 obit Aug 87

Casper, Billy Jul 66

Cassady, John H. Oct 52 obit Mar 69

Cassavetes, John Jul 69 obit Mar 89

Cassel, Karl Gustav obit Mar 45

Cassidy, Claudia Sep 55 obit

Oct 96

Cassidy, Henry C. Sep 43

Cassini, Oleg Jul 61

Cassius see Foot, Michael

Castagna, Edwin Jun 64

Castagnetta, Grace Feb 54

Castaneda, Jorge Ubico see Ubico, Jorge

Castelli, Leo Aug 84 obit Jan 2000

Castelnau, Edouard De Curieres De obit May 44

Castelo Branco, Humberto de Alencar Feb 65 obit Oct 67

Castiella, Fernando María May 58 obit Feb 77

Castillo Armas, Carlos Jan 55 obit Sep 57

Castillo Nájera, Francisco May 46 obit Feb 55

Castillo, Antonio Sep 62

Castillo, Ramon S. Jul 41 obit Dec 44

Castle, Barbara Jan 67 obit Yrbk 2002

Castle, Lewis G. Jul 58 obit Sep 60

Castro E Silva, José Machado De obit Aug 43

Castro, Fidel Jul 58 Jul 70 Jun 2001

Castro, Raúl Feb 77

Caswell, Hollis L. Jul 56 obit Sep 89

Cates, Clifton B. Nov 50 obit Sep 70

Cates, Gilbert Mar 97

Catledge, Turner Jul 75 obit Jul 83

Catlett, Elizabeth May 98

Catroux, Georges May 43 obit Feb 70

Catt, Carrie Chapman Oct 40 obit Apr 47

Cattani-Amadori, Federico, Cardinal obit May 43

Cattell, J. McKeen obit Mar 44

Catto, Thomas Sivewright Catto, 1st Baron Nov 44

Catton, Bruce (WLB) Yrbk 54

obit Oct 78

Cattrall, Kim Jan 2003

Caturani, Michele Gaetano obit Mar 40

Caudill, Rebecca (WLB) Yrbk 50 obit Jan 86

Cauldwell, Leslie Giffen obit Jul 41

Caulfield, Joan May 54 obit Aug 91

Cauthen, Steve Jul 77

Cavaco Silva, Aníbal Mar 91

Cavallero, Ugo obit Oct 43

Cavalli-Sforza, Luigi Luca Aug 97

Cavallo, Evelyn see Spark, Muriel

Cavanagh, Jerome P. Apr 68 obit Jan 80

Cavanagh, Tom Jun 2003

Cavanah, Frances (WLB) Yrbk 54

Cavanaugh, John J. Mar 47 obit Feb 80

Cavanna, Betty (WLB) Yrbk 50 obit Oct 2001

Cavazos, Lauro F. Apr 89

Cave, Nick Jun 2005

Cavero, Salvador obit Mar 40

Cavert, Samuel McCrea Jan 51 obit Mar 77

Cavett, Dick Oct 70

Cawley, Evonne Goolagong see Goolagong, Evonne

Cayton, Horace R. Jan 46 [Cayton, Horace R; and Drake, St. Clair] obit Mar 70

Cazalet, Victor Alexander obit Aug 43

Ceausescu, Nicolae Nov 67 obit Feb 90

Cecil, Mary obit Feb 41

Cecil, Robert Arthur Nov 41 [Cecil of Essendon, Robert Arthur James Cecil, 1st Baron] obit Apr 72

Cédras, Raoul Jul 95

Cedric the Entertainer Feb 2004

Cela, Camilo José Jun 90 obit

Apr 2002

Celebrezze, Anthony J. Jan 63 obit Jan 99

Celler, Emanuel Oct 49 Nov 66 obit Mar 81

Celmins, Vija Jan 2005

Cenerazzo, Walter W. Sep 55

Cepeda, Orlando Oct 68

Ceram, C.W. see Marek, Kurt W.

Cerda, Pedro Aguirre see Aguirre Cerda, Pedro

Cerezo Arévalo, Vinicio see Cerezo, Marco Vinicio

Cerezo, Marco Vinicio Mar 87

Cerf, Bennett Nov 41 Sep 58 obit Oct 71

Cerf, Vinton G. Sep 98

Cernan, Eugene A. May 73

Ch'ing, Chiang see Jiang Qing

Chaban-Delmas, Jacques Jul 58 obit Feb 2001

Chabrol, Claude Jan 75

Chaddock, Robert Emmet obit Yrbk 40

Chadli, Bendjedid Apr 91

Chadourne, Marc obit Feb 41

Chadwick, Florence Oct 50 obit May 95

Chadwick, Helene obit Oct 40

Chadwick, James Nov 45 obit Oct 74

Chafee, John H. Nov 69 obit Jan 2000

Chafee, Lincoln Jan 2004

Chafee, Zechariah, Jr. Aug 42 obit Apr 57

Chagall, Marc Nov 43 Nov 60 obit May 85

Chagla, Mahomed Ali Currim Jun 59 obit Jan 84

Chaikin, Joseph Jul 81 obit Yrbk 2003

Chaikin, Sol C. Apr 79 obit Jun 91

Chailly, Riccardo Jun 91

Chain, Ernst Boris Nov 65 obit Oct 79

Chalk, O. Roy Nov 71 obit

Feb 96

Challans, Mary see Renault, Mary

Chalmers, Philip O. obit Mar 46

Chamberlain, Francis L. Jul 59

Chamberlain, John Rensselaer Apr 40 obit Jun 95

Chamberlain, Neville obit Yrbk 40

Chamberlain, Owen Mar 60

Chamberlain, Paul Mellen obit Jul 40

Chamberlain, Richard Jul 63 Nov 87

Chamberlain, Samuel Sep 54 obit Mar 75

Chamberlain, Wilt Jun 60 obit Jan 2000

Chamberlin, Georgia Louise obit Oct 43

Chambers, Raymond Wilson obit Jun 42

Chaminade, Cecile obit Jun 44

Chamorro, Violeta Barrios De Jun 90

Chamoun, Camille N. Jul 56 obit Sep 87

Champion, George Apr 61 obit Jan 98

Champion, Gower Sep 53 [Champion, Marge; and Champion, Gower] obit Oct 80

Champion, Marge Sep 53 [Champion, Marge; and Champion, Gower]

Champion, Pierre Honoré Jean Baptiste obit Aug 42

Champion, Will see Coldplay

Chan, Jackie Nov 97

Chan, Kong Sun see Chan, Jackie

Chance, Dean Jul 69

Chancellor, John Jan 62 Nov 88 obit Sep 96

Chandler, Albert Benjamin see Chandler, Happy

Chandler, Dorothy Buffum

Jul 57 [Chandler, Dorothy Buffum; and Chandler, Norman] obit Sep 97

Chandler, Happy Aug 43 Sep 56 obit Aug 91

Chandler, Norman Jul 57 [Chandler, Dorothy Buffum; and Chandler, Norman] obit Dec 73

Chandler, Otis Nov 68

Chandler, Raymond (WLB) Yrbk 46 obit Jun 59

Chandos, Oliver Lyttelton, 1st Viscount see Lyttelton, Oliver

Chandrasekhar, Sripati Oct 69 obit Sep 2001

Chandrasekhar, Subrahmanyan Mar 86 obit Oct 95

Chandy, Anna Apr 60

Chanel, Coco Sep 54 obit Feb 71

Chaney, John Mar 99

Chang Shan-Tze obit Yrbk 40

Chang, John M. Jun 49 obit Jul 66

Chang, Michael Jul 97

Channing, Carol Sep 64

Channing, Stockard Apr 91

Chao, Elaine L. May 2001

Chapin, Charles Value obit Mar 41

Chapin, James Mar 40 obit Sep 75

Chapin, Katherine Garrison see Biddle, Katherine Garrison Chapin

Chapin, Schuyler G. Feb 74

Chaplin, Charlie Yrbk 40 Mar 61 obit Feb 78

Chaplin, Geraldine Jul 79

Chapman, Albert K. Sep 52 obit Yrbk 84

Chapman, Blanche obit Aug 41

Chapman, Charles F. May 58 obit Yrbk 84 (died Mar 76)

Chapman, Daniel A. Apr 59

Chapman, Duane Mar 2005

Chapman, Frank Michler obit

Jan 46

Chapman, Gilbert W. Jun 57 obit Feb 80

Chapman, Helen Louise Busch *see* Chapman, Mrs. Theodore S.

Chapman, Leonard F. Jr. Jul 68 obit Sep 2000

Chapman, Mrs. Theodore S. Apr 55

Chapman, Oscar L. Feb 49 obit Apr 78

Chapman, Steven Curtis Oct 2004

Chapman, Sydney Jul 57 obit Sep 70

Chapman, Tracy Aug 89

Chappedelaine, Louis De obit Jan 40

Chappell, Tom May 94

Chappelle, Dave Jun 2004

Charisse, Cyd Jan 54

Charles, Eugenia Oct 86

Charles, Ezzard Jun 49 obit Aug 75

Charles, Michael Ray Oct 2005

Charles, Prince of Belgium May 46 obit Jul 83

Charles, Prince of Wales Nov 69

Charles, Ray Apr 65 Jun 92 obit Yrbk 2004

Charles-Roux, François

Charlesworth, James C. Sep 54 obit Mar 74

Charlot, Jean Sep 45 obit Yrbk 84 (died Mar 79)

Charlotte, Grand Duchess of Luxembourg Apr 49 obit Aug 85

Charnwood, Godfrey Rathbone Benson, Ist Baron obit Mar 45

Charques, Dorothy (WLB) Yrbk 58

Charques, Mrs. Robert Denis

see Charques, Dorothy

Charters, Spencer obit Mar 43

Charyk, Joseph V. Dec 70

Chase, Charley obit Aug 40

Chase, Chevy Mar 79

Chase, David Mar 2001

Chase, Edna Woolman Nov 40 obit Jun 57

Chase, Harry Woodburn Jun 48 obit Jun 55

Chase, Ilka May 42 obit Apr 78

Chase, Joseph Cummings May 55

Chase, Lucia Jul 47 Aug 75 obit Mar 86

Chase, Mary Ellen May 40 obit Oct 73

Chase, Mary Oct 45 obit Jan 82

Chase, Mrs. Hamilton *see* Seton, Anya

Chase, Stuart Oct 40 obit Jan 86

Chase, William C. Nov 52

Chase, William Sheafe, Rev. obit Sep 40

Chasez, JC *see* 'N Sync

Chasins, Abram Feb 60 obit Aug 87

Chast, Roz Jul 97

Chastain, Madye Lee (WLB) Yrbk 58

Chateaubriand, Assis *see* Assis Chateaubriand

Chatel, Yves obit Dec 44

Chatwin, Bruce Jan 88 obit Mar 89

Chauncey, Henry Jul 51 obit Mar 2003

Chauvel, Jean Oct 50 obit Jul 79

Chavan, Y. B. Apr 63

Chavarri, Emperatriz *see* Sumac, Yma

Chavchavadze, George Mar 43 obit Apr 62

Chávez, Carlos May 49 obit Sep 78

Chavez, Cesar Feb 69 obit Jun

93

Chavez, Dennis Mar 46 obit Jan 63

Chávez, Hugo May 2000

Chávez, Julio César Apr 99

Chavez, Linda Nov 99

Chavez-Thompson, Linda Mar 2000

Chavis, Benjamin F. Jan 94

Chayefsky, Paddy Sep 57 obit Sep 81

Chayefsky, Sidney *see* Chayefsky, Paddy

Cheadle, Don Sep 99

Cheatham, Kitty obit Feb 46

Cheeks, Maurice Feb 2004

Cheever, John Sep 75 obit Aug 82

Chelf, Frank L. Jun 52

Chen Cheng Sep 41 obit Apr 65

Chen Ning Yang *see* Yang, Chen Ning

Chen Shui-bian Sep 2000

Chen Yi Oct 59 obit Feb 72

Chen, Eugene obit Jul 44

Chen, Joan Sep 99

Chenault, Kenneth I. Jun 98

Cheney, Brainard (WLB) Yrbk 59 obit Mar 90

Cheney, Lynne V. Oct 92

Cheney, Richard B. Aug 89 Jan 2002

Cheney, Russell obit Aug 45

Chennault, Claire Lee Oct 42 obit Oct 58

Cher Jan 74 Jun 91

Chéreau, Patrice Jan 90

Cherkassky, Shura Oct 90 obit Mar 96

Cherne, Leo M. Yrbk 40 obit Mar 99

Chernenko, Konstantin U. Aug 84 obit May 85

Chernomyrdin, Viktor Aug 98

Chernyakhovsky, Ivan D. Oct 44 obit Apr 45

Cherry, Addie obit Dec 42

Cherry, Francis A. Jul 54 obit

Sep 65

Chertoff, Michael Oct 2005

Cherwell, Frederick Alexander Lindemann, 1st Baron *see* Lindemann, Frederick Alexander

Cheshire, Leonard Jan 62 obit Sep 92

Chesney, Kenny May 2004

Chesser, Elizabeth Sloan obit Mar 40

Chester, Edmund Mar 41

Chevalier, Elizabeth Pickett Jan 43

Chevalier, Maurice Jan 48 Mar 69 obit Feb 72

Chevrier, Lionel Jun 52

Chevrolet, Louis obit Aug 41

Chia, Sandro Jun 90

Chiang Ching-Kuo Sep 54 obit Mar 88

Chiang Kai-Shek Jan-Jun 40 May 53 obit May 75

Chiang Kai-shek, Mme. *see* Chiang Mei-Ling

Chiang Mei-Ling May 40 obit Mar 2004

Chiang T'ing-fu *see* Tsiang, T. F.

Chiang Tso-Pin obit Feb 43

Chiappe, Jean obit Jan 41

Chiari, Roberto F. Feb 61

Chicago, Judy Feb 81

Chichester, Francis Dec 67 obit Oct 72

Chidlaw, Benjamin W. Mar 55

Chieftains Mar 2004

Chifley, Joseph B. Aug 45 obit Jul 51

Chihuly, Dale Aug 95

Chih-Yuan Yang *see* Yang, Jerry

Child, Julia Feb 67 obit Nov 2004

Childs, Lucinda Apr 84

Childs, Marquis William Jan 43 obit Sep 90

Childs, Richard Spencer Sep

55 obit Jan 79

Chiles, Lawton Sep 71 obit Mar 99

Chillida, Eduardo Sep 85 obit Yrbk 2002

Chiluba, Frederick May 92

Chin, Frank Mar 99

Ching, Cyrus S. Jan 48 obit Feb 68

Ching-Kuo, Chiang *see* Chiang Ching-Kuo

Chinmoy, Sri Apr 76

Chiperfield, Robert B. Sep 56 obit May 71

Chipp, Mrs. Rodney Duane *see* Hicks, Beatrice A.

Chirac, Jacques Jun 75 Apr 93

Chirico, Giorgio de *see* De Chirico, Giorgio

Chisholm, Brock Jul 48 obit Mar 71

Chisholm, Shirley Oct 69 obit Apr 2005

Chissano, Joaquim Alberto Nov 90

Chi-tien, Mao *see* Yoshida, Shigeru

Cho, Margaret Oct 2000

Chodorov, Edward Apr 44 obit Nov 88

Chomsky, Noam Oct 70 Aug 95

Chopra, Deepak Oct 95

Chotzinoff, Samuel Apr 40 obit Apr 64

Chou En-Lai Sep 46 Jul 57 obit Feb 76

Chouinard, Yvon Jun 98

Chow Yun-Fat May 98

Chrebet, Wayne Feb 99

Chrétien, Jean Apr 90

Christenberry, Robert K. Mar 52 obit Jun 73

Christian X, King of Denmark Nov 43 obit May 47

Christians, Mady May 45 obit Dec 51

Christie, Agatha Sep 40 Jul 64 obit Mar 76

Christie, John Walter obit Feb

44

Christie, Julie Sep 66

Christie, William Jan 92

Christison, Philip Nov 45 obit Feb 94

Christman, Elisabeth Jan 47

Christo Mar 77

Christofilos, Nicholas C. Nov 65 obit Nov 72

Christopher, George Feb 58 obit Yrbk 2000

Christopher, George T. Nov 47 obit Jul 54

Christopher, Warren M. Jun 81 Nov 95

Chrysler, Walter Percy obit Oct 40

Chryssa Nov 78

Chu Shen obit Aug 43

Chu Teh Nov 42 obit Aug 76

Chuan Leekpai Nov 98

Chubb, L. Warrington Feb 47 obit May 52

Chuikov, Vasili May 43 obit May 82

Chun Doo Hwan Mar 81

Chung, Connie Jul 89

Chung, Myung-Whun Aug 90

Church, Frank Mar 58 Mar 78 obit May 84

Church, Marguerite Stitt Feb 51 obit Jul 90

Church, Sam, Jr. Oct 81

Church, Samuel Harden obit Nov 43

Churchill, Berton obit Yrbk 40

Churchill, Caryl Jun 85

Churchill, Edward D. Feb 63

Churchill, Gordon Sep 58

Churchill, Lady *see* Spencer-Churchill, Clementine Ogilvy Hozier

Churchill, Randolph Oct 47 obit Sep 68

Churchill, Sarah May 55 obit Jan 83

Churchill, Winston Jul 40 Mar 42 Jul 53 obit Mar 65

Churchland, Patricia S. May

2003

Chute, B. J. (WLB) Yrbk 50 obit Oct 87

Chute, Charles Lionel Sep 49 obit Jan 54

Chute, Joy *see* Chute, B. J.

Chute, Marchette Gaylord (WLB) Yrbk 50 obit Jul 94

Chwast, Seymour Sep 95

Chwatt, Aaron *see* Buttons, Red

Ciano, Galeazzo, Conte Jul 40 obit Feb 44

Ciardi, John Oct 67 obit May 86

Cicognani, Amleto Giovanni Cardinal Jul 51 obit Feb 74

Çiller, Tansu Sep 94

Cimino, Michael Jan 81

Cisler, Walker Sep 55 obit Jan 95

Cisneros, Henry Aug 87

Citrine, Walter McLennan Citrine Feb 41 obit Apr 83

Civiletti, Benjamin R. Feb 80

Clague, Ewan Jul 47 obit Jun 87

Claiborne, Craig Sep 69 obit Apr 2000

Claiborne, Liz Jun 89

Claiborne, Loretta Jul 96

Clair, René Nov 41 obit May 81

Claire, Ina May 54 obit Apr 85

Clampitt, Amy Feb 92 obit Nov 94

Clancy, Mrs. Carl Stearns *see* Lownsbery, Eloise

Clancy, Tom Apr 88

Clapp, Gordon R. Feb 47 obit Jun 63

Clapp, Margaret Jun 48 obit Jun 74

Clapp, Verner W. Mar 59 obit Sep 72

Clapper, Mrs. Raymond *see* Clapper, Olive Ewing

Clapper, Olive Ewing Sep 46 obit Jan 69

Clapper, Raymond Mar 40

obit Mar 44

Clapton, Eric Jun 87

Claremont, Chris Sep 2003

Clark, Bennett Champ Nov 41 obit Sep 54

Clark, Bobby May 49 obit Apr 60

Clark, Charles E. Jul 59 obit Mar 64

Clark, Dick May 59 Jan 87

Clark, Dorothy Park (WLB) Yrbk 57 [McMeekin, Isabel McLennan; and Clark, Dorothy Park]

Clark, Eleanor May 78 obit Apr 96

Clark, Eugenie Sep 53

Clark, Evans Sep 47 obit Nov 70

Clark, Fred G. Oct 49

Clark, Georgia Neese Sep 49 obit Feb 96

Clark, Helen Nov 2000

Clark, J. J. Jan 54 obit Sep 71

Clark, James H. Jun 97 [Andreessen, Marc; and Clark, James H.]

Clark, James Nov 65 obit Jun 68

Clark, Joe Oct 76

Clark, John Apr 52

Clark, John D. Jan 47

Clark, Joseph S. Jun 52 obit Mar 90

Clark, Kenneth B. Sep 64 obit Sep 2005

Clark, Kenneth Sep 63 obit Jul 83

Clark, Leonard Jan 56 obit Sep 57

Clark, Marguerite obit Nov 40

Clark, Mark W. Nov 42 obit Jun 84

Clark, Mary Higgins Jan 94

Clark, Paul F. Apr 55 obit Mar 73

Clark, Petula Feb 70

Clark, Ramsey Oct 67

Clark, Richard Wagstaff *see*

Clark, Dick

Clark, Robert L. Nov 52

Clark, Roy Jun 78

Clark, Sydney Sep 56

Clark, Tom C. Jul 45 obit Aug 77

Clark, Wesley K. Jul 99

Clark, William P. Jul 82

Clarke, Arthur C. Oct 66

Clarke, John Hessin obit May 45

Clarke, Martha Jan 89

Clarke, Robert *see* Indiana, Robert

Clarke, Ron May 71

Clarke, Walter May 47 obit Jan 65

Clarkson, Patricia Aug 2005

Clash, Kevin Jun 2000

Clausen, A. W. Nov 81

Claussen, Julia obit Jun 41

Clavell, James Oct 81 obit Nov 94

Claxton, Brooke Dec 47 obit Sep 60

Clay, Cassius *see* Ali, Muhammad

Clay, Laura obit Aug 41

Clay, Lucius D. May 45 Jun 63 obit Jun 78

Clayburgh, Jill Sep 79

Clayton, Eva McPherson Jun 2000

Clayton, Mrs. Joseph E. *see* Sampson, Edith S.

Clayton, P. B. May 55 obit Mar 73

Clayton, William L. Apr 44 obit Mar 66

Claytor, W. Graham, Jr. May 79 obit Jul 94

Cleaver, Eldridge Mar 70 obit Jul 98

Cleese, John Jan 84

Cleland, Max Feb 78

Clemens, Roger Aug 2003 Nov 88

Clemensen, Erik Christian obit Jul 41

Clement, Frank G. Jul 55 obit

Dec 69

Clement, M. W. Nov 46 obit Nov 66

Clement, Rufus E. Jun 46 obit Jan 68

Clemente, Roberto Feb 72 obit Feb 73

Clements, Earle C. Sep 55 obit May 85

Clendening, Logan obit Mar 45

Cleveland, Harlan Sep 61

Cleveland, James Aug 85 obit Apr 91

Cliburn, Van Sep 58

Clifford, Clark Mar 47 Sep 68 obit Jan 99

Clifford, John Nov 72

Clift, David H. Jun 52 obit Dec 73

Clift, Montgomery Jul 54 obit Sep 66

Clinchy, Everett R. Apr 41 obit Mar 86

Cline, John Wesley Jun 51 obit Sep 74

Clinton, Bill Apr 88 Nov 94

Clinton, George Jul 93

Clinton, Hillary Rodham Nov 93

Clinton, William Jefferson *see* Clinton, Bill

Clive, Edward E. obit Jul 40

Clooney, Rosemary Feb 57 obit Nov 2002

Close, Chuck Jul 83

Close, Glenn Nov 84

Close, Upton Dec 44 obit Jan 61

Clowes, Daniel Jan 2002

Clurman, Harold Feb 59 obit Nov 80

Clyburn, James E. Oct 2001

Clyde, George D. Jul 58 obit May 72

Coaldigger, Adam *see* Ameringer, Oscar

Coanda, Henri Jul 56 obit Feb 73

Coates, John obit Oct 41

Coates, Joseph Gordon obit Jul 43

Cobb, Geraldyn M. *see* Cobb, Jerrie

Cobb, Irvin S. obit Apr 44

Cobb, Jerrie Feb 61

Cobb, Lee J. Feb 60 obit Apr 76

Cobb, Ty Sep 51 obit Oct 61

Cobham, Charles John Lyttelton, 10th Viscount Apr 62

Coblentz, Stanton A. Jun 54

Coblentz, W. W. Mar 54 obit Nov 62

Cobo, Albert E. Nov 51 obit Dec 57 Yrbk 58

Coburn, Charles Jun 44 obit Nov 61

Coburn, James Jun 99 obit Feb 2003

Coca, Imogene Apr 51 obit Sep 2001

Cochran, Charles Blake Oct 40 obit Mar 51

Cochran, H. Merle Feb 50 obit Nov 73

Cochran, Jacqueline Sep 40 Jun 63 obit Oct 80

Cochran, Johnnie L. Jr. Jun 99 obit Oct 2005

Cochran, Thad Apr 2002

Cochrane, Edward L. Mar 51 obit Jan 60

Cockcroft, John Nov 48 obit Nov 67

Cocke, C. Francis Mar 52

Cocke, Erle, Jr. Jan 51 obit Sep 2000

Cocker, Jarvis Nov 98

Cockrell, Ewing May 51 obit Apr 62

Coco, James May 74 obit Apr 87

Coddington, Grace Apr 2005

Cody, John Patrick Cardinal Nov 65 obit Jun 82

Coe, Fred Jan 59 obit Jun 79

Coe, Sebastian Nov 80

Coe, Sue Aug 97

Coen, Ethan Sep 94 [Coen, Ethan; and Coen, Joel]

Coen, Joel Sep 94 [Coen, Ethan; and Coen, Joel]

Coetzee, J. M. Jan 87

Coffee, John M. Oct 46

Coffin, Frank M. Apr 59

Coffin, Haskell obit Jul 41

Coffin, Henry Sloane, Rev. Dr Apr 44 obit Jan 55

Coffin, William Sloane, Jr. Jul 68 Apr 80

Coggan, F. Donald Jul 74 obit Sep 2000

Coggeshall, Lowell T. Sep 63 obit Jan 88

Cogswell, Charles N. obit Feb 42

Cohan, George M. obit Jan 43

Cohen, Abby Joseph Jun 98

Cohen, Alexander H. Jun 65 obit Aug 2000

Cohen, Arthur A. Sep 60 obit Jan 87

Cohen, Barbara May 57 [Cohen, Barbara; and Roney, Marianne]

Cohen, Ben Apr 94 [Cohen, Ben; and Greenfield, Jerry]

Cohen, Benjamin A. May 48 obit May 60

Cohen, Benjamin V. Apr 41 obit Oct 83

Cohen, Howard William *see* Cosell, Howard

Cohen, Judy *see* Chicago, Judy

Cohen, Leonard Jun 69

Cohen, Manuel F. Apr 67 obit Aug 77

Cohen, Rob Nov 2002

Cohen, Wilbur J. Sep 68 obit Jul 87

Cohen, William S. Apr 82 Jan 98

Cohn, Linda Aug 2002

Cohu, La Motte T. Apr 51 obit Nov 68

Coit, Margaret Louise Jun 51

Coker, Elizabeth Boatwright (WLB) Yrbk 59 obit Nov 93

Colbert, Claudette Jan 45 May 64 obit Oct 96

Colbert, Edwin H. Sep 65 obit

Feb 2002

Colbert, Gregory Sep 2005

Colbert, Lester L. Apr 51 obit Nov 95

Colby, Charles Dewitt obit Nov 41

Colby, Nathalie S. obit Jul 42

Colby, William E. Jan 75 obit Jul 96

Coldplay May 2004

Coldwell, M. J. Sep 43 obit Oct 74

Cole, Albert M. Jan 54

Cole, David L. Jan 49 obit Mar 78

Cole, Edward N. Jul 72 obit Jul 77

Cole, Janet *see* Hunter, Kim

Cole, Jessie Duncan Savage obit Yrbk 40

Cole, Johnnetta B. Aug 94

Cole, Nat King Feb 56 obit Mar 65

Cole, Natalie Nov 91

Cole, W. Sterling Mar 54 obit May 87

Cole-Hamilton, J. B. obit Sep 45

Coleman, Cy Aug 90 obit Feb 2005

Coleman, Georgia obit Nov 40

Coleman, J. P. Sep 56 obit Nov 91

Coleman, James S. Oct 70 obit Jun 95

Coleman, John R. Oct 74

Coleman, John S. Apr 53 obit Jul 58

Coleman, Lonnie (WLB) Yrbk 58 obit Oct 82

Coleman, Norman Sep 2004

Coleman, Ornette Jun 61

Coleman, Steve Jul 2004

Coleman, William T., Jr. Mar 76

Coles, Nathaniel Adams *see*

Cole, Nat King

Coles, Robert Nov 69

Colijn, Hendricus obit Jan 45

Colina, Rafael De La Jan 51

Collen, Phil *see* Def Leppard

Coller, Taube *see* Davis, Tobé Coller

Colles, Henry Cope obit Apr 43

Collet, John C. Feb 46 obit Feb 56

Collier, Constance Jul 54 obit Jun 55

Collier, John Mar 41 obit Jul 68

Collier, Sophia Jul 2002

Collier, William, Sr. obit Mar 44

Collingwood, Charles Jun 43 obit Nov 85

Collingwood, R. G. obit Mar 43

Collins, Cardiss Feb 97

Collins, Eddie obit Oct 40

Collins, Edward Day obit Jan 40

Collins, Francis S. Jun 94

Collins, Gail Mar 99

Collins, George Lewis obit Aug 40

Collins, Hunt *see* Hunter, Evan

Collins, J. Lawton Nov 49 obit Oct 87

Collins, Jackie Jul 2000

Collins, James Dec 63

Collins, James J. obit Apr 43

Collins, Jim Aug 2003

Collins, Joan Jan 84

Collins, John F. Jan 65 obit Feb 96

Collins, Judy Apr 69

Collins, LeRoy Jun 56 Apr 65 obit May 91

Collins, Lorin Cone obit Yrbk 40

Collins, Martha Layne Jan 86

Collins, Marva Nov 86

Collins, Michael May 75

Collins, Patricia Hill Mar

2003

Collins, Phil Nov 86

Collins, Seaborn P. Apr 55

Collins, Susan May 2000

Collison, Wilson obit Jul 41

Collor De Mello, Fernando Mar 90

Collyer, John L. Mar 47

Colman, Ronald Jul 43 obit Sep 58

Colombo, Emilio Apr 71

Colonna, Simonetta *see* Simonetta

Colquitt, Oscar Branch obit Mar 40

Columbus, Chris Nov 2001

Colville, Alex Mar 85

Colvin, Mamie White Dec 44 obit Jan 56

Colvin, Mrs. D. Leigh *see* Colvin, Mamie White

Colvin, Shawn Mar 99

Colwell, Eileen Jul 63

Colwell, Rita R. May 99

Comaneci, Nadia Feb 77

Comber, Elizabeth *see* Han Suyin

Combs, Bert Thomas Jun 60 obit Feb 92

Combs, Sean *see* Puff Daddy

Comden, Betty Mar 45 [Comden, Betty; and Green, Adolph]

Comer, James P. Aug 91

Cometbus, Aaron Mar 2005

Comfort, Alex Sep 74 obit Aug 2000

Commager, Henry Steele Jan 46 obit May 98

Commoner, Barry Sep 70

Como, Perry Apr 47 obit Jul 2001

Companys, Luis obit Yrbk 40

Compton, Arthur H. Aug 40 Sep 58 obit May 62

Compton, Karl T. Mar 41 obit Sep 54

Compton, Wilson Apr 52 obit May 67

Conable, Barber B. Jul 84 obit

Sep 2004

Conant, James Bryant Mar 41 Feb 51 obit Apr 78

Concheso, Aurelio Fernández May 42 obit Jan 56

Condon, E. U. Apr 46 obit May 74

Condon, Eddie Oct 44 obit Oct 73

Condon, Frank obit Feb 41

Condon, Richard Feb 89 obit Jun 96

Cone, David Feb 98

Cone, Fairfax M. Jul 66 obit Aug 77

Conerly, Charles Apr 60 obit Apr 96

Congdon, William May 67 obit Jul 98

Conigliaro, Tony Feb 71 obit Apr 90

Coningham, Arthur Nov 44 obit Feb 48

Conley, Eugene Jul 54 obit Feb 82

Conley, William Gustavus obit Yrbk 40

Conn, Billy Aug 41 obit Aug 93

Connah, Douglas John obit Oct 41

Connally, John B. Jul 61 obit Aug 93

Connally, Tom Dec 41 Apr 49 obit Jan 64

Connaught, Arthur William Patrick Albert, Duke of *see* Albert, Arthur William Patrick

Conneff, Kevin *see* Chieftains

Connell, Arthur J. Feb 54

Connell, Karl obit Dec 41

Connelly, Jennifer Jun 2002

Connelly, Marc Nov 69 obit Feb 81

Conner, Dennis Nov 87

Conner, Nadine Jan 55 obit Aug 2003

Connerly, Ward Nov 2000

Connery, Lawrence J. obit

Dec 41

Connery, Sean Jan 66 Jun 93

Conness, Robert obit Mar 41

Connick, Harry, Jr. Nov 90

Connolly, Cyril (WLB) Yrbk 47

Connolly, Maureen Nov 51 obit Sep 69

Connolly, Paul *see* Wicker, Tom

Connolly, Walter obit Jul 40

Connor, John T. Apr 61 obit Feb 2001

Connors, Jimmy Sep 75

Conover, Harry Feb 49 obit Oct 65

Conrad, Barnaby, Jr. Sep 59

Conrad, Charles, Jr. Dec 65

Conroy, Pat [Canadian government official] Jul 54

Conroy, Pat [novelist] Jan 96

Considine, Robert Dec 47 obit Nov 75

Considine, Thomas Terry *see* Considine, Robert

Constantine II, King of The Hellenes Apr 67

Constanza, Midge *see* Costanza, Midge

Contadin, Fernand Joseph Desire *see* Fernandel

Conti, Tom Jun 85

Converse, Frederick Shepherd obit Aug 40

Conway, Gerry *see* Fairport Convention

Conway, Jill Ker Jun 91

Conway, John Horton Sep 2003

Conway, Thomas *see* Conway, Tim

Conway, Tim Apr 81

Conyers, John, Jr. Sep 70

Cook, Barbara Feb 63

Cook, Donald C. May 52 obit Feb 82

Cook, Donald Jul 54 obit Dec 61

Cook, Fannie (WLB) Yrbk 46 obit Oct 49

Cook, Frederick Albert obit

Sep 40

Cook, Marlow W. Jan 72

Cook, Mrs. Jerome E. *see* Cook, Fannie

Cook, Richard W. Jul 2003

Cook, W. W. obit Dec 43

Cooke, Alistair Jun 52 May 74 obit Oct 2004

Cooke, Cardinal *see* Cooke, Terence J.

Cooke, Hope *see* Hope Namgyal, Maharani of Sikkim

Cooke, Leslie E. Jun 62 obit Apr 67

Cooke, Morris Llewellyn May 50 obit May 60

Cooke, Terence J. Sep 68 obit Nov 83

Cooley, Denton A. Jan 76

Cooley, Harold D. Mar 51 obit Mar 74

Coolidge, Dane obit Sep 40

Coolidge, Elizabeth Sprague Aug 41 obit Jan 54

Coolidge, William David Jun 47 obit Mar 75

Coolio Aug 98

Coon, Carleton S. Sep 55 obit Jul 81

Cooney, Joan Ganz Jul 70

Coons, Albert H. Jun 60

Coontz, Stephanie Jul 2003

Cooper, Alfred Duff Aug 40 obit Mar 54 [Norwich, Alfred Duff Cooper, 1st Viscount]

Cooper, Chris Jul 2004

Cooper, Courtney Ryley obit Nov 40

Cooper, Cynthia Aug 98

Cooper, Edwin obit Aug 42

Cooper, Gary Dec 41 obit Jul 61

Cooper, Gladys Feb 56 obit Jan 72

Cooper, Irving S. Apr 74 obit Jan 86

Cooper, Jere Mar 55 obit Feb 58

Cooper, John Sherman Jun 50

obit Apr 91

Cooper, Joseph D. Feb 52

Cooper, Kent Oct 44 obit Mar 65

Cooper, Leroy Gordon, Jr. Sep 63

Cooper, Louise Field (WLB) Yrbk 50 obit Jan 93

Cooper, R. Conrad Jan 60

Coover, Robert Feb 91

Copeland, Benjamin, Rev. obit Jan 41

Copeland, Lammot Du Pont May 63

Copland, Aaron Sep 40 Mar 51 obit Jan 91

Copperfield, David Jul 92

Coppers, George H. May 52

Coppola, Francis Ford May 74 Jul 91

Coppola, Nicholas see Cage, Nicolas

Coppola, Sofia Nov 2003

Corbett, Jim May 46 obit Jun 55

Corbusier see Le Corbusier

Corcoran, Thomas Gardiner Mar 40 obit Feb 82

Cordero, Angel Oct 75

Cordier, Andrew W. Apr 50 obit Sep 75

Cordier, Constant obit Mar 40

Cordier, Gilbert see Rohmer, Eric

Cordiner, Ralph J. Jan 51 obit Jan 74

Cordon, Guy Apr 52 obit Jul 69

Corea, Chick Oct 88

Corea, Claude Mar 61 obit Nov 62

Corella, Angel Mar 99

Corelli, Franco Feb 64 obit Mar 2004

Corey, Paul Yrbk 40

Cori, Carl F. Dec 47 [Cori, Carl F; and Cori, Gerty T] obit Feb 85

Cori, Gerty T. Dec 47 [Cori, Carl F; and Cori, Gerty T]

obit Jan 58

Corigliano, John Jun 89

Corita see Kent, Corita

Corman, Roger Feb 83

Cornelius, John C. Jun 60

Cornell, Katharine May 41 Mar 52 obit Jul 74

Cornwell, David John Moore see Le Carré, John

Cornwell, Patricia May 97

Correll, Charles J. Dec 47 [Gosden, Freeman F.; and Correll, Charles J.] obit Nov 72

Corrigan, Joseph M., Bishop obit Aug 42

Corrigan, Mairead Apr 78

Corsaro, Frank Aug 75

Corson, Fred Pierce May 61 obit Apr 85

Cortázar, Julio Feb 74 obit Apr 84

Cortelyou, George Bruce obit Yrbk 40

Cortines, Adolfo Ruiz see Ruiz Cortines, Adolfo

Cortney, Philip Jan 58 obit Jul 71

Corwin, Norman Yrbk 40

Cory, John Mackenzie Sep 49 obit May 88

Cosby, Bill Apr 67 Oct 86

Cosell, Howard Nov 72 obit Jul 95

Cosgrave, Liam Jun 77

Cossiga, Francesco Jan 81

Cost, March Jan 58 obit Apr 73

Costa E Silva, Arthur Da Sep 67 obit Feb 70

Costa Gomes, Francisco Da May 76

Costa-Gavras Sep 72

Costain, Thomas B. May 53 obit Dec 65

Costanza, Midge Jun 78

Costas, Bob Jan 93

Costello, Elvis Sep 83

Costello, John A. Apr 48 obit Feb 76

Costello, Lou Oct 41 [Abbott,

Bud; and Costello, Lou] obit May 59

Costle, Douglas M. Jun 80

Costner, Kevin Jun 90

Cot, Pierre Jun 44 obit Oct 77

Cothran, James W. Sep 53

Cotnareanu, Philippe see Cortney, Philip

Cotrubas, Ileana Oct 81

Cotten, Joseph Jul 43 obit Apr 94

Cottenham, Mark Everard Pepys, 6th Earl of see Pepys, Mark Everard

Cotter, Audrey see Meadows, Audrey

Cotter, Jayne see Meadows, Jayne

Cotterell, Geoffrey (WLB) Yrbk 54

Cotton, Joseph Bell obit Sep 40

Cotton, Norris Feb 56 obit May 89

Cottrell, Dorothy (WLB) Yrbk 55 obit Sep 57

Coty, René Apr 54 obit Jan 63

Coudenhove-Kalergi, Richard N., Count Feb 48 obit Oct 72

Coudert, Frederic René, Jr. Jun 41 obit Jul 72

Cougar, John see Mellencamp, John

Coughlin, Charles Edward Sep 40 obit Jan 80

Coulter, Ann Sep 2003

Coulter, Calvin Brewster obit Jan 40

Coulter, John B. Jun 54

Counsell, Craig Sep 2002

Counting Crows Gillis, John see White Stripes

Counting Crows Mar 2003

Counts, George S. Dec 41 obit Jan 75

Couples, Fred Jul 93

Courant, Richard Sep 66 obit Mar 72

Couric, Katie Mar 93

Cournand, André F. Mar 57

obit Apr 88

Courrèges, André Jan 70

Court, Margaret Sep 73

Courtenay, Tom May 64

Cousins, Frank Feb 60 obit Jul 86

Cousins, Margaret Jun 54 obit Oct 96

Cousins, Norman Aug 43 Aug 77 obit Jan 91

Cousteau, Jacques-Yves Jun 53 Jan 76 obit Sep 97

Cousy, Bob Sep 58

Coutts, Frederick Mar 64

Couve de Murville, Maurice Apr 55 obit Jun 2000

Covarrubias, Miguel Jul 40 obit Apr 57

Covey, Stephen R. Jan 98

Cowan, Minna G. Feb 48

Coward, Noel Jan 41 Mar 62 obit May 73

Cowden, Howard A. Mar 52

Cowdry, E. V. Jan 48

Cowen, Joshua Lionel Sep 54 obit Nov 65

Cowles, Fleur Apr 52

Cowles, Gardner, Jr. Jun 43 obit Aug 85

Cowles, John Jun 54 obit Apr 83

Cowles, Mike see Cowles, Gardner, Jr.

Cowles, Virginia May 42 obit Nov 83

Cowley, Malcolm Jun 79 obit May 89

Cox, Allyn Jul 54 obit Jan 83

Cox, Archibald Jul 61 obit Yrbk 2004

Cox, Bobby Feb 98

Cox, Christopher Jul 99

Cox, E. Eugene Apr 43 obit Feb 53

Cox, Harvey Nov 68

Cox, Herald R. Apr 61

Cox, Lynne Sep 2004

Cox, Wally Feb 54 obit Apr 73

Cox, William Trevor see

Trevor, William

Coxe, Howard obit Jan 41

Coy, Wayne Mar 48 obit Dec 57 Yrbk 58

Coyne, James E. Jul 55

Coyne, Wayne see Flaming Lips

Cozzens, James Gould Jun 49 obit Oct 78

Crabtree, James W. obit Jul 45

Craft, Robert Mar 84

Craig, Cleo F. Sep 51 obit Jun 78

Craig, Elizabeth May Jun 49 obit Sep 75

Craig, George N. Feb 50 obit Feb 93

Craig, Lyman C. Apr 64 obit Sep 74

Craig, Malin Mar 44 obit Aug 45

Craig, Walter E. Jun 64 obit Sep 86

Craigavon, James Craig, 1st Viscount obit Jan 41

Craigie, Robert Jul 42 obit Jul 59

Crain, Jeanne Nov 51 obit Sep 2004

Cram, Ralph Adams Oct 42 obit Oct 42

Cramer, Stuart Warren obit Aug 40

Crandall, Robert L. Nov 92

Crane, Eva Aug 93

Crane, Philip M. May 80

Cranko, John Jul 70 obit Sep 73

Cranston, Alan Feb 50 Oct 69 obit Mar 2001

Cravath, Paul Drennan obit Aug 40

Craveiro Lopes, Francisco Higino Mar 56 obit Nov 64

Craven, Frank obit Oct 45

Craven, Thomas Apr 44 obit Apr 69

Crawford, Broderick Apr 50 obit Jun 86

Crawford, Cheryl Dec 45 obit

Nov 86

Crawford, Cindy Aug 93

Crawford, Frederick C. Feb 43 obit Feb 95

Crawford, Joan Jan 46 Sep 66 obit Jul 77

Crawford, Michael Jan 92

Crawford, Morris Barker obit Yrbk 40

Crawford, Phyllis Nov 40

Crawshaw, William Henry obit Aug 40

Craxi, Bettino Feb 84 obit Jun 2000

Crayencour, Marguerite de see Yourcenar, Marguerite

Cream, Arnola Raymond see Walcott, Joe

Creasey, John Sep 63 obit Jul 73

Creed May 2002

Creeft, José De see de Creeft, José

Creel, George Jun 44 obit Jan 54

Creeley, Robert Oct 88 obit Yrbk 2005

Cregar, Laird obit Jan 45

Crenshaw, Ben Sep 85

Crerar, H. D. G. Nov 44 obit May 65

Cresap, Mark W., Jr. Oct 59 obit Sep 63

Crespin, Régine Sep 79

Cresson, Edith Sep 91

Cresswell, Robert obit Nov 43

Cret, Paul Philippe Nov 42 obit Nov 45

Crewe, Albert V. Feb 64

Crewe, Robert Offley Ashburton Crewe-Milnes, 1st Marquis of obit Jul 45

Crews, Laura Hope obit Jan 43

Crichton, Michael Apr 76 Nov 93

Crick, Francis Mar 83 obit Yrbk 2004

Crider, John H. Jun 49 obit

Sep 66

Crile, George obit Feb 43

Cripps, Stafford Jul 40 Apr 48 obit Jun 52

Crisler, Fritz *see* Crisler, Herbert Orin

Crisler, Herbert Orin Feb 48 obit Oct 82

Crispin, Edmund (WLB) Yrbk 49

Criss, Peter *see* Kiss

Crist, William E. Nov 45

Cristiani, Alfredo Jan 90

Crittenden, Danielle Jul 2003

Croce, Benedetto Jan 44 obit Jan 53

Crocetti, Dino *see* Martin, Dean

Crocker, Chester A. Jul 90

Crockett, Lucy Herndon (WLB) Yrbk 53

Croft, Arthur C. Jun 52

Cromer, 3d Earl of *see* Baring, George Rowland Stanley

Crompton, Rookes Evelyn Bell obit Mar 40

Cromwell, James Aug 2005

Cromwell, James H. R. Mar 40 obit May 90

Cronenberg, David May 92

Cronin, A. J. Jul 42 obit Mar 81

Cronin, Joe Mar 65 obit Nov 84

Cronkite, Walter Jan 56 Nov 75

Cronyn, Hume Mar 56 Jun 88 obit Yrbk 2003

Croom, Sylvester Aug 2004

Crosbie, John Carnell Jan 90

Crosby, Bing Sep 41 Jun 53 obit Jan 78

Crosby, John C. Jun 53

Crosby, John Nov 81 obit Yrbk 2003

Crosby, Robert Jun 54

Crosland, Anthony Sep 63 obit Apr 77

Crosley, Powel, Jr. Jun 47 obit Jun 61

Cross, Amanda *see* Heilbrun,

Carolyn G.

Cross, Ben Aug 84

Cross, Burton M. Apr 54 obit Jan 99

Cross, Milton John Jan-Feb 40 obit Feb 75

Cross, Ronald H. Jun 41

Crosser, Robert Mar 53 obit Sep 57

Crossfield, A. Scott Oct 69

Crossley, Archibald M. Dec 41 obit Jul 85

Crossman, R. H. S. May 47 obit Jun 74

Crouch, Stanley Mar 94

Crouse, Russel Jun 41 obit May 66

Crow, Carl Oct 41 obit Jul 45

Crow, John O. Mar 69

Crow, Sheryl May 98

Crowe, Cameron Mar 96

Crowe, Russell May 2000

Crowe, William J., Jr. Jul 88

Crowell, T. Irving obit Mar 42

Crowley, John J., Father obit Apr 40

Crowley, Leo T. Jun 43 obit Jun 72

Crown, Henry Jan 72 obit Oct 90

Crownfield, Gertrude obit Jul 45

Crowther, Bosley Jul 57 obit Apr 81

Cruise, Tom Apr 87

Crum, Bartley C. May 47 obit Feb 60

Crumb, George Dec 74

Crumb, R. Apr 95

Crumit, Frank obit Oct 43

Crump, N. R. Sep 57

Cruyff, Johan Nov 81

Cruz, Celia Jul 83 obit Nov 2003

Cruz, Hernan Santa *see* Santa Cruz, Hernan

Cruz, Penelope Jul 2001

Cruze, James obit Sep 42

Cruzen, Richard H. Mar 47

obit Jun 70

Crystal, Billy Feb 87

Csáky, Stephen obit Mar 41

Csermanck, János *see* Kádár, János

Csonka, Larry Feb 77

Cuban, Mark Mar 2001

Cubberley, Ellwood P. obit Nov 41

Cudahy, John C. obit Oct 43

Cuevas, José Luis Jan 68

Cugat, Xavier May 42 obit Jan 91

Cukor, George Apr 43 obit Mar 83

Culbertson, Ely May 40 obit Mar 56

Culkin, Francis D. obit Sep 43

Cullberg, Birgit Nov 82 obit Nov 99

Cullen, Bill Jan 60 obit Sep 90

Cullen, Countee obit Mar 46

Cullen, Glenn Ernest obit May 40

Cullen, Hugh Roy Jul 55 obit Sep 57

Cullen, Thomas H. obit Apr 44

Cullis, Winifred C. Nov 43 obit Jan 57

Cullman, Howard S. Jun 51 obit Sep 72

Culshaw, John Jun 68 obit Jun 80

Culver, Essae Martha Sep 40

Culver, John C. Nov 79

Cummings, Elijah E. Feb 2004

Cummings, Robert Jan 56 obit Feb 91

Cuneo, John F. Jun 50

Cunhal, Álvaro Sep 75 obit Yrbk 2005

Cunningham, Alan Jun 46 obit Apr 83

Cunningham, Andrew Browne, 1st Viscount Cunningham May 41 obit Sep

2000

Damaskinos, Archbishop Nov 45 obit Jul 49

Damerel, Donna obit Apr 41

Damon, Lindsay Todd obit Jan 40

Damon, Matt Mar 98 [Affleck, Ben; and Damon, Matt]

Damon, Ralph S. Jul 49 obit Mar 56

Damrosch, Walter Mar 44 obit Jan 51

Dancer, Stanley Jun 73 obit Yrbk 2005

Dandurand, Raoul obit Apr 42

Dandy, Walter E. obit May 46

Danforth, John C. Jan 92

Danforth, William obit Jun 41

D'Angelo May 2001

Dangerfield, George Sep 53 obit Mar 87

Dangerfield, Rodney obit Feb 2005

Daniel, Clifton Mar 66 obit Jul 2000

Daniel, Price Jan 56 obit Oct 88

Daniel, Robert Prentiss May 52 obit Mar 68

Daniel, W. C. Dan Jun 57

Daniell, Raymond Mar 44 obit Jun 69

Danielovitch, Issur see Douglas, Kirk

Daniel-Rops, Henry Mar 57 obit Oct 65

Daniels, Arthur Hill obit Apr 40

Daniels, Charles N. obit Mar 43

Daniels, Farrington Jul 65 obit Sep 72

Daniels, Grace B. Sep 59

Daniels, Jonathan Apr 42 obit Jan 82

Daniels, Josephus Oct 44 obit Feb 48

Däniken, Erich Von see Von Däniken, Erich

Danilova, Alexandra Jul 87

obit Sep 97

Dannay, Frederic Jul 40 [Dannay, Frederic; and Lee, Manfred B.] obit Oct 82

Danner, Blythe Jan 81

Danner, Louise Rutledge obit Nov 43

Danson, Ted Oct 90

Dantchenko, Vladimir Nemirovich- see Nemirovich-Dantchenko, Vladimir (Ivanovich)

Danto, Arthur C. Apr 95

Dardel, Nils Von obit Jul 43

Darden, Christopher A. Feb 97

Darden, Colgate W., Jr. Sep 48

Dargan, E. Preston obit Feb 41

Darin, Bobby Mar 63 obit Feb 74

Daringer, Helen Fern (WLB) Yrbk 51

Dark, Alvin Mar 75

Darlan, Jean Mar 41 obit Feb 43

Darling, Jay Norwood Jul 42 obit Mar 62

Darling, Sharon May 2003

Darman, Richard G. May 89

Darré, R. Walther Nov 41 obit Jan 57 (died Sep 53)

Darrell, R. D. Sep 55 obit Jun 88

Darrow, Whitney, Jr. Dec 58 obit Oct 99

Dart, Justin W. Nov 46 obit Mar 84

Dart, Raymond A. Sep 66 obit Jan 89

Darwell, Jane Jun 41 obit Oct 67

Darwin, Leonard obit May 43

Daschle, Tom Oct 95

Dashiell, Willard obit Jun 43

Dashwood, Elizabeth Monica see Delafield, E. M.

Dassault, Marcel Jun 70 obit

Jun 86

Dassin, Jules Mar 71

Daud Khan, Sardar Mohammed Mar 57

Daudet, León obit Aug 42

Daugherty, Carroll Roop Oct 49 obit Jun 88

Daugherty, Harry M. obit Dec 41

Daugherty, James Jul 40 obit Apr 74

Dauser, Sue S. Aug 44

Dausset, Jean May 81

Davenport, Charles B. obit Apr 44

Davenport, Eugene obit May 41

Davenport, Marcia Jan 44 obit Mar 96

Davenport, Russell W. Jan 44 obit Jun 54

Davey, Jocelyn see Raphael, Chaim

Davey, Martin L. obit May 46

David, Donald K. Feb 48 obit Jun 79

David, Edward E., Jr. May 74

David, Hal Sep 80

David, Julian see Mackaye, David L.; Mackaye, Julia Gunther

David, Larry Aug 98

Davidovich, Bella May 89

Davidovitch, Ljuba obit Mar 40

Davidson, Garrison Holt Jun 57 obit Feb 93

Davidson, Gordon Apr 2005

Davidson, Irwin D. Jan 56

Davidson, Jo Apr 45 obit Feb 52

Davidson, John F. Nov 60 obit Apr 89

Davidson, John Sep 76

Davidson, Richard J. Aug 2004

Davidson, Roy E. Sep 63 obit Sep 64

Davidson, William L. Jul 52

Davies, Clement Oct 50 obit

May 62

Davies, Dennis Russell May 93

Davies, Ernest May 51

Davies, Joseph E. Apr 42 obit Jul 58

Davies, Peter Maxwell Mar 80

Davies, Robertson Jun 75 obit Mar 96

Davies, Ronald N. Sep 58 obit Jun 96

Davies, Walford obit May 41

Davies, William Henry obit Nov 40

Davis, Adelle Jan 73 obit Jul 74

Davis, Al Jul 85

Davis, Andrew May 83

Davis, Angela Yvonne Nov 72

Davis, Anthony May 90

Davis, Archie K. May 66

Davis, Benjamin O. Jr. Sep 55 obit Yrbk 2002

Davis, Benjamin O. Sr. Dec 42 obit Jan 71

Davis, Bette Oct 41 Mar 53 obit Nov 89

Davis, Chester Charles Jul 40 obit Nov 75

Davis, Clive Jul 2000

Davis, Colin Nov 68

Davis, Edward W. Sep 55 obit Feb 74

Davis, Elmer May 40 obit Sep 58

Davis, Geena Oct 91

Davis, Gladys Rockmore Sep 53 obit Apr 67

Davis, Glenn Dec 46 obit Yrbk 2005

Davis, Gray Jun 99

Davis, Harvey N. Jul 47 obit Jan 53

Davis, Herbert John Jan-Feb 40 obit May 67

Davis, J. Frank obit May 42

Davis, James C. Apr 57 obit

Feb 82

Davis, Jess H. Jan 56

Davis, Joan Jun 45 obit Sep 61

Davis, John William Mar 53 obit May 55

Davis, Jonathan M. obit Aug 43

Davis, Joseph Graham Jr. *see* Davis, Gray

Davis, Joseph S. Jul 47 obit Jun 75

Davis, Judy Nov 93

Davis, Mac Aug 80

Davis, Martin S. Nov 89 obit Jan 2000

Davis, Meyer Jun 61 obit Jun 76

Davis, Miles Jun 62 obit Nov 91

Davis, Mrs. Floyd (MacMillan) *see* Davis, Gladys Rockmore

Davis, Nathanael V. Jan 59 obit Yrbk 2005

Davis, Norman H. Jan-Feb 40 obit Aug 44

Davis, Ossie Oct 69 obit Yrbk 2005

Davis, Patti Nov 86

Davis, Peter Feb 83

Davis, Robert (WLB) Yrbk 49

Davis, Robert C. obit Oct 44

Davis, Robert H. obit Dec 42

Davis, Roy H. Feb 55 obit Sep 56

Davis, Sammy, Jr. Sep 56 Jul 78 obit Jul 90

Davis, Stuart Aug 40 Jul 64

Davis, Tobé Coller Dec 59 obit Feb 63

Davis, Wade Jan 2003

Davis, Watson Dec 45 obit Oct 67

Davis, Westmoreland obit Oct 42

Davis, William Ellsworth Apr 40

Davis, William H. Jun 41 obit Oct 64

Davis, William May 73

Davis, William Rhodes Mar

41 obit Mar 41

Davison, F. Trubee Dec 45

Davison, Frederic E. Feb 74

Dawes, Rufus Cutler obit Jan 40

Dawkins, Richard Aug 97

Dawson of Penn, Bertrand Dawson, 1st Viscount obit Apr 45

Dawson, Bertrand, 1st Viscount Dawson of Penn *see* Dawson of Penn, Bertrand Dawson, 1st Viscount

Dawson, John A. Sep 52

Dawson, William Apr 41 obit Sep 72

Dawson, William Levi Apr 45 obit Dec 70

Day, Albert M. Dec 48

Day, Doris Apr 54

Day, Dorothy May 62 obit Jan 81

Day, Edmund Ezra Sep 46 obit Apr 51

Day, J. Edward May 62 obit Jan 97

Day, Laraine Sep 53

Day, Pat Oct 97

Dayal, Rajeshwar Feb 61

Dayan, Moshe Mar 57 obit Jan 82

Dayan, Yaël Apr 97

Day-Lewis, C. Jan-Feb 40 Jul 69 obit Jul 72

Day-Lewis, Daniel Jul 90

De Alvear, Marcelo T. obit May 42

de Angeli, Marguerite (WLB) Yrbk 47

De Angeli, Mrs. John *see* de Angeli, Marguerite

De Bakey, Michael E. Mar 64

De Beck, William Morgan obit Jan 43

De Benedetti, Carlo May 90

De Bono, Emilio (Giuseppe Gaspare Giovanni) obit Feb 44

de Branges, Louis Nov 2005

De Broglie, Louis, Prince *see*

obit Aug 2001

de Varona, Donna Aug 2003

De Voto, Bernard Sep 43 obit Jan 56

De Vries, Peter (WLB) Yrbk 59 obit Jan 94

De Vry, Herman A. obit May 41

de Waart, Edo Mar 90

De Wiart, Adrian Carton see Carton De Wiart, Adrian

De Witt, John L. Jul 42

De Wohl, Louis (WLB) Yrbk 55 obit Oct 61

De Wolfe, James P. Aug 42 obit Mar 66

Deakin, Arthur Jan 48 obit Jun 55

Deakins, Roger May 2001

Dean, Arthur Hobson Mar 54 obit Jan 88

Dean, Dizzy Sep 51 obit Sep 74

Dean, Erica see Burstyn, Ellen

Dean, Gordon Sep 50 obit Nov 58

Dean, H. Trendley Jun 57 obit Jul 62

Dean, Howard Oct 2002

Dean, Jay Hanna see Dean, Dizzy

Dean, Jerome Herman see Dean, Dizzy

Dean, Jimmy Dec 65

Dean, Laura Oct 88

Dean, Patrick May 61 obit Jan 95

Dean, Vera Micheles May 43 obit Dec 72

Dean, William F. Sep 54 obit Oct 81

Deane, Martha [radio personality, 1889-1976] see McBride, Mary Margaret

Deane, Martha [radio personality, 1909-73] see Young, Marian

Deane, Sidney N. obit Jun 43

Dearborn, Ned H. Jan 47 obit

Oct 62

Dearden, John Jul 69 obit Sep 88

Dearie, Blossom Feb 89

Deasy, Luere B. obit Apr 40

Deasy, Mary (WLB) Yrbk 58

Déat, Marcel Jan 42 obit May 55

Debray, Régis Jun 82

Debre, Michel May 59 obit Oct 96

Debus, Kurt H. Nov 73 obit Nov 83

DeBusschere, Dave Oct 73 obit Yrbk 2003

Debutts, Harry A. Apr 53

Debye, Peter J. W. Jul 63 obit Jan 67

DeCarlo, Dan Aug 2001 obit Mar 2002

Decker, George H. Jan 61

Decker, Karl obit Feb 42

Decker, Mary Oct 83

Deconcini, Dennis Feb 92

Decoursey, Elbert Sep 54

Decter, Midge Apr 82

Dee, Ruby Nov 70

Deep Throat see Felt, W. Mark

Deer, Ada E. Sep 94

Dees, Morris S., Jr. Jan 95

Def Leppard Jan 2003

Defauw, Désiré Jan-Feb 40 obit Oct 60

Defferre, Gaston Sep 67 obit Jun 86

Deford, Frank Aug 96

DeGaetani, Jan Oct 77

Degeneres, Ellen Apr 96

Dehler, Thomas Jul 55 obit Oct 67

Dehn, Adolf Apr 41 obit Jul 68

Deighton, Len Sep 84

Dejong, David C. Jul 44 obit Nov 67

Dejong, Meindert (WLB) Yrbk 52 obit Sep 91

Del Castillo, Antonio see Castillo, Antonio

Del Monaco, Mario Feb 57

obit Jan 83

del Naja, Robert see Massive Attack

Del Toro, Benicio Sep 2001

Del Tredici, David Mar 83

Delacorte, George T. Nov 65 obit Jul 91

Delafield, E. M. obit Jan 44

Deland, Margaret Wade obit Mar 45

Delaney, Shelagh Apr 62

Delany, Annie Elizabeth see Delany, Bessie

Delany, Bessie Nov 95 [Delany, Sadie; and Delany, Bessie] obit Jan 96

Delany, Sadie Nov 95 [Delany, Sadie; and Delany, Bessie] obit Apr 99

Delany, Sarah see Delany, Sadie

Delany, Walter S. Dec 52

Delaunay, Sonia Aug 77 obit Feb 80

DeLauro, Rosa Mar 2000

Delay, Tom May 99

Delgado, José Feb 76

Delilah Apr 2005

Delillo, Don Jan 89

Dell, Michael Jun 98

Dell, Robert Edward obit Sep 40

Della Casa, Lisa Jul 56

Della Chiesa, Vivian Nov 43

Della Femina, Jerry Nov 79

Dellinger, David Aug 76 obit Yrbk 2004

Dello Joio, Norman Sep 57

Dellums, Ronald V. Sep 72 Sep 93

Delon, Alain Apr 64

Deloncle, Eugene obit Feb 44

DeLonge, Tom see blink-182

DeLorean, John Z. Mar 76 obit Yrbk 2005

Deloria, Vine, Jr. Sep 74

Delors, Jacques Jun 89

Delson, Brad see Linkin Park

DeMarcus, Jay see Rascal Flatts

Demikhov, Vladimir P. Jun

60 obit Feb 99

DeMille, Nelson Oct 2002

Deming, Dorothy May 43

Deming, Edwin W. obit Dec 42

Deming, W. Edwards Sep 93 obit Mar 94

Demirel, Süleyman Feb 80

Demme, Jonathan Apr 85

Demott, Richard H. Feb 51 obit Nov 68

Dempsey, Jack Feb 45 obit Jul 83

Dempsey, John Jun 61 obit Sep 89

Dempsey, Miles Christopher Oct 44 obit Jul 69

Dempsey, William Harrison see Dempsey, Jack

Dench, Judi Jan 99

Dendramis, Vassili Jun 47 obit Jul 56

Denebrink, Francis C. Feb 56 obit Jun 87

Denenberg, Herbert S. Dec 72

Deneuve, Catherine Feb 78

Denfeld, Louis E. Dec 47 obit May 72

Deng Xiaoping May 76 Jun 94 obit Apr 97

Denham, R. N. Oct 47 obit Sep 54

Deniel, Enrique, Pla y see Pla Y Deniel, Enrique

Dennehy, Brian Jul 91

Denning, Alfred Thompson Jul 65 obit Jun 99

Dennis, Charles Henry obit Nov 43

Dennis, Eugene May 49 obit Mar 61

Dennis, Felix Apr 2000

Dennis, Lawrence Mar 41 obit Oct 77

Dennis, Olive Wetzel Jun 41

Dennis, Patrick see Tanner, Edward Everett, 3d

Dennis, Sandy Jan 69 obit May 92

Dennison, Robert Lee Apr 60

obit May 80

Denniston, Reynolds obit Mar 43

Denny, Charles R., Jr. May 47

Denny, Collins, Bishop obit Jul 43

Denny, George V., Jr. Sep 50 obit Jan 60

Denny, George Vernon Jr. Sep 40

Densen-Gerber, Judianne Nov 83 obit Jul 2003

Densford, Katharine J. Feb 47

Dent, Allie Beth see Martin, Allie Beth

Dent, Frederick B. Apr 74

Denton, Jeremiah A., Jr. May 82

Denver, John Jan 75 obit Jan 98

DePaola, Tomie Feb 99

Depardieu, Gérard Oct 87

Depinet, Ned E. Jun 50

Depp, Johnny May 91

Depreist, James Oct 90

Der Harootian, Koren Jan 55

Dermot, Jessie see Elliott, Maxine

Dern, Bruce Oct 78

Dern, Laura Oct 92

Derrida, Jacques Jul 93 obit Mar 2005

Dershowitz, Alan M. Sep 86

Derthick, Lawrence Gridley Apr 57 obit Mar 93

Derwent, Clarence Nov 47 obit Nov 59

Derwinski, Edward J. Aug 91

Des Graz, Charles Louis obit Yrbk 40

Des Portes, Fay Allen obit Nov 44

Desai, Morarji Sep 58 Jan 78 obit Jun 95

Dessès, Jean Jan 56 obit Oct 70

Destiny's Child Aug 2001

Dett, R. Nathaniel obit Nov 43

Deuel, Wallace R. Aug 42

Deukmejian, George Jun 83

Deupree, Richard R. Apr 46

obit May 74

Deutsch, Julius Nov 44 obit Mar 68

Deutschendorf, Henry John, Jr. see Denver, John

Devaney, John Patrick obit Nov 41

Dever, Paul A. May 49 obit Jul 58

Devereaux, William Charles obit Sep 41

Devers, Gail Jul 96

Devers, Jacob Loucks Sep 42 obit Jan 80

Devi, Gayatri see Jaipur, Maharani of

Devine, John M. Jan 48

Deviny, John J. Sep 48 obit Apr 55

Devito, Danny Feb 88

Devlin, Bernadette Jan 70

Devoe, Ralph G. Oct 44 obit Nov 66

Devries, William C. Jan 85

Dewart, William T. obit Mar 44

Dewey, Charles S. Jan 49 obit Feb 81

Dewey, John Aug 44 obit Jul 52

Dewey, Thomas E. Jul 40 Sep 44 obit Apr 71

Dewhurst, Colleen Jul 74 obit Oct 91

Dewhurst, J. Frederic Jan 48 obit Jul 67

Dexheimer, W. A. Feb 55

Dexter, John Jul 76 obit May 90

Dhaliwal, Daljit Nov 2000

Dhebar, U. N. Jun 55

Di Suvero, Mark Nov 79

Dial, Morse G. Mar 56 obit Jan 83

Diamant, Gertrude Nov 42

Diamond, David Nov 66 obit Yrbk 2005

Diamond, Neil May 81

Diana, Princess of Wales Jan 83 obit Nov 97

Díaz Ordaz, Gustavo May 65

obit Sep 79

Diaz, Cameron Apr 2005

Dibelius, Otto May 53 obit Mar 67

DiCaprio, Leonardo Mar 97

Dichter, Ernest Jan 61 obit Jan 92

Dick, Charles obit May 45

Dickerson, Debra Apr 2004

Dickerson, Ernest Jul 2000

Dickerson, Nancy Hanschman Sep 62 obit Jan 98

Dickerson, Roy E. obit Apr 44

Dickey, James Apr 68 obit Mar 97

Dickey, John Sloan Apr 55 obit Apr 91

Dickinson, Amy Apr 2004

Dickinson, Angie Feb 81

Dickinson, Edwin Sep 63 obit Feb 79

Dickinson, Lucy Jennings Nov 45

Dickinson, Luren D. obit Jun 43

Dickinson, Mrs. LaFell see Dickinson, Lucy Jennings

Dickinson, Robert L. Mar 50 obit Jan 51

Dickinson, Willoughby Hyett Dickinson, 1st Baron obit Jul 43

Dickson, Lovat Sep 62

Dickson, Marguerite (WLB) Yrbk 52 obit Jan 54

Diddley, Bo Jun 89

Didion, Joan Sep 78

Didrikson, Babe see Zaharias, Babe Didrikson

Diebenkorn, Richard Dec 71 obit May 93

Diebold, John Mar 67

Diefenbaker, John George May 57 obit Oct 79

Diefendorf, Allen Ross obit Sep 43

Diehl, Frances White Oct 47

Diehl, Mrs. Ambrose N. see Diehl, Frances White

Diem, Ngo Dinh see Ngo

Dinh Diem

Dies, Martin Apr 40 obit Jan 73

Dieterich, William H. obit Yrbk 40

Dieterle, William Sep 43 obit Feb 73

Dietrich, Marlene Jun 53 Feb 68 obit Jun 92

Dietz, David Oct 40 obit Apr 85

Dietz, Howard Oct 65 obit Sep 83

DiFiglia, Michael Bennett see Bennett, Michael

Difranco, Ani Aug 97

Diggs, Charles C., Jr. Jul 57 obit Nov 98

Dike, Phil Dec 42

Dill, John Greer Feb 41 obit Dec 44

Dillard, Annie Jan 83

Dillard, James Hardy obit Sep 40

Diller, Barry Apr 86

Diller, Phyllis Jul 67

Dillman, Bradford Jan 60

Dillon, C. Douglas Apr 53 obit May 2003

Dillon, Matt May 85

DiMaggio, Joe Jun 41 Jul 51 obit May 99

DiMaggio, Joseph Paul see DiMaggio, Joe

Dimechkie, Nadim Feb 60

Dimitrov, Georgi May 49

Dimon, James Jun 2004

Dine, Jim Jun 69

Dinehart, Alan obit Sep 44

Ding, J. N. see Darling, Jay Norwood

Dingell, John D. Mar 49 obit Nov 55 Yrbk 56

Dingell, John D., Jr. Aug 83

Dinkins, David Mar 90

Dinsmore, Charles Allen obit Oct 41

Dior, Christian Oct 48 obit Jan 58

Dirksen, Everett McKinley

Apr 41 Sep 57 obit Nov 69

Dirnt, Mike see Green Day

Disalle, Michael V. Jan 51 obit Nov 81

Disney, Anthea Jun 98

Disney, Doris Miles (WLB) Yrbk 54

Disney, Walt Aug 40 Apr 52 obit Feb 67

Ditchy, Clair W. Mar 54 obit Oct 67

Dith Pran Oct 96

Ditka, Mike Oct 87

Ditmars, Raymond Lee Sep 40 obit Jul 42

Ditter, J. William obit Jan 44

Divine, Frank H. obit May 41

Dix, Dorothy Jan-Jun 40 obit Feb 52

Dix, William S. Jun 69 obit Apr 78

Dixey, Henry E. obit Apr 43

Dixie Chicks July 2000

Dixon, Dean Apr 43 obit Jan 77

Dixon, Jeane Feb 73 obit Mar 97

Dixon, Owen Aug 42

Dixon, Paul Rand Jan 68

Dixon, Pierson Sep 54 obit Jun 65

Dixon, Thomas obit May 46

Dixon, Willie May 89 obit Apr 92

Djanira Jan 61

Djerassi, Carl Oct 2001

Djilas, Milovan Sep 58 obit Jul 95

Djuanda Apr 58 obit Jan 64

Djukanovic, Milo Aug 2001

Dmitri, Ivan see West, Levon

DMX Aug 2003

Doan, Leland I. Oct 52 obit May 74

Dobbie, William Jul 45

Dobbs, Mattiwilda Sep 55

Dobie, J. Frank Dec 45 obit Nov 64

Dobnievski, David see Dubinsky, David

Dobrynin, Anatoly F. Sep 62

Dobson, James C. Aug 98

Dobson, William Alexander obit Jul 43

Dobzhansky, Theodosius Sep 62 obit Feb 76

Docking, George Jun 58 obit Mar 64

Doctorow, E. L. Jul 76

Dodd, Alvin E. Nov 47 obit Jul 51

Dodd, Christopher J. Oct 89

Dodd, Martha (WLB) Yrbk 46 obit Jan 91

Dodd, Norris E. Feb 49 obit Sep 68

Dodd, Thomas J. Sep 59 obit Jul 71

Dodd, William Edward obit Mar 40

Dodds, Gil Jun 47 obit Apr 77

Dodds, Harold W. Dec 45 obit Jan 81

Dodge, Bayard Feb 48 obit Jul 72

Dodge, Cleveland E. Mar 54 obit Feb 83

Dodge, David (WLB) Yrbk 56

Dodge, John V. Jul 60

Dodge, Joseph Morrell Nov 47 obit Jan 65

Dodge, Raymond obit May 42

Doe, Samuel Kanyon May 81 obit Nov 90

Doenitz, Karl Nov 42 obit Feb 81

Doherty, Henry Latham obit Jan 40

Doherty, Robert E. Sep 49 obit Dec 50

Dohnányi, Christoph von Oct 85

Doi, Peter Tatsuo Nov 60

Doi, Takako Jul 92

Doihara, Kenji Mar 42 obit Feb 49

Doisy, Edward A. Mar 49 obit

Jan 87

Dolan, D. Leo Sep 56

Dolbier, Maurice (WLB) Yrbk 56 obit Jan 94

Dolci, Danilo Sep 61 obit Mar 98

Dole, Elizabeth Hanford Jun 83 Jan 97

Dole, Robert J. Apr 72 Oct 87

Dolin, Anton Jan 46 obit Jan 84

Dollard, Charles Dec 48 obit Apr 77

Dolly, Jenny obit Jul 41

Domagk, Gerhard Mar 58 obit Jun 64

Domenici, Pete V. Jun 82

Domingo, Placido Mar 72

Dominguín, Luis Miguel Mar 72 obit Jul 96

Domini, Amy Nov 2005

Doms, Keith Jun 71

Donahey, Vic obit May 46

Donahue, Phil May 80

Donald, Arnold W. Nov 2005

Donald, David Sep 61

Donald, W. H. Jul 46

Donaldson, Jesse M. Jan 48 obit May 70

Donaldson, Sam Sep 87

Donaldson, William Jun 2003

Donegan, Horace W. B. Jul 54 obit Jan 92

Dongen, Cornélius Théodorus Marie van *see* Dongen, Kees Van

Dongen, Kees Van Sep 60 obit Jul 68

Donleavy, J. P. Jul 79

Donlon, Mary Jul 49 obit May 77

Donnadieu, Marguerite *see* Duras, Marguerite

Donnell, Forrest C. Sep 49

Donnelly, Antoinette *see* Blake, Doris

Donnelly, Phil M. Jun 56 obit Nov 61

Donnelly, Walter J. Sep 52 obit Jan 71

Donner, Frederic G. Jan 59

obit Apr 87

Donoso, José Feb 78 obit Feb 97

Donovan, Carrie Sep 99 obit Feb 2002

Donovan, Hedley Sep 99 May 65 obit Oct 90

Donovan, James B. Jun 61 obit Mar 70

Donovan, Raymond J. Jan 82

Donovan, William J. Mar 41 Sep 54 obit Apr 59

Dooley, Thomas A. Jul 57 obit Mar 61

Doolittle, James H. Aug 42 Mar 57 obit Jan 94

Dooyeweerd, H. Sep 58

Dorati, Antal Jul 48 obit Jan 89

Doriot, Jacques Nov 40

Dorman, Gerald D. Jun 70

Dornay, Louis obit Sep 40

Dornberger, Walter R. Feb 65 obit Sep 80

Dorough, Howie D. *see* Backstreet Boys

Dorpfeld, Wilhelm obit Jan 40

Dorris, Michael Mar 95 obit Jun 97

Dorsett, Tony Apr 80

Dorsey, Jimmy Apr 42 [Dorsey, Jimmy; and Dorsey, Tommy] obit Sep 57

Dorsey, Tommy Apr 42 [Dorsey, Jimmy; and Dorsey, Tommy] obit Feb 57

Dorticós, Osvaldo Feb 63 obit Aug 83

Dos Passos, John Aug 40 obit Nov 70

dos Santos, José Eduardo *see* Santos, José Edwardo Dos

Doster, James J. obit Dec 42

Doten, Carroll Warren obit Aug 42

Doubilet, David Mar 2003

Doubleday, Nelson May 87

Doudna, Jennifer Feb 2005

Dougherty, Dora Mar 63

Doughton, Robert L. Jul 42

obit Dec 54 Yrbk 55

Douglas of Kirtleside, William Sholto Douglas, 1st Baron *see* Douglas, Sholto

Douglas, Arthur F. Nov 50 obit May 56

Douglas, Ashanti *see* Ashanti

Douglas, Donald W. Nov 41 Dec 50 obit Mar 81

Douglas, Emily Taft Apr 45 obit Mar 94

Douglas, Helen Gahagan Sep 44 obit Aug 80

Douglas, James H. Sep 57 obit Apr 88

Douglas, Jerry Aug 2004

Douglas, John E. Jul 2001

Douglas, Kirk Mar 52

Douglas, Lewis W. Mar 47 obit May 74

Douglas, Marjory Stoneman Jul 53 obit Jul 98

Douglas, Melvyn May 42 obit Sep 81

Douglas, Michael *see* Crichton, Michael Apr 87

Douglas, Mike May 68

Douglas, Paul H. Apr 49 obit Nov 76

Douglas, Sholto Jun 43 obit Dec 69

Douglas, T. C. *see* Thompson, William

Douglas, Walter J. obit Sep 41

Douglas, William O. Oct 41 Nov 50 obit Mar 80

Douglas-Home, Alexander Frederick Feb 58 obit Jan 96 [Home, Alexander Frederick Douglas-Home, 14th Earl of]

Dove, Rita May 94

Dover, Elmer obit Nov 40

Dow, Willard H. Feb 44 obit May 49

Dowd, Maureen Sep 96

Dowding, Hugh Caswell Tremenheere, 1st Baron Nov 40 obit Apr 70

Dowell, Anthony May 71

Dowling, Eddie Feb 46 obit Apr 76

Dowling, Robert W. Oct 52 obit Nov 73

Dowling, Walter C. Mar 63 obit Sep 77

Downes, Olin Mar 43 obit Oct 55

Downey, Fairfax (WLB) Yrbk 49 obit Aug 90

Downey, Morton Jul 49 obit Jan 86

Downey, Robert Jr. Aug 98

Downey, Sheridan Oct 49 obit Jan 62

Downs, Hugh Mar 65

Downs, Robert B. Jan 41 Jun 52 obit Apr 91

Doxiadis, Constantinos A. Sep 64 obit Sep 75

Doyle, Adrian Conan Sep 54

Doyle, Roddy Oct 97

Dr. Seuss *see* Geisel, Theodor Seuss

Drabble, Margaret May 81

Drabinsky, Garth Oct 97

Drake, Alfred Apr 44 obit Sep 92

Drake, Frank Donald Jan 63

Drake, James Jul 2005

Drake, St. Clair Jan 46 [Cayton, Horace R; and Drake, St. Clair] obit Aug 90

Drapeau, Jean Dec 67 obit Oct 99

Draper, Charles Stark Dec 65 obit Sep 87

Draper, Dorothy May 41 obit Apr 69

Draper, Paul Feb 44 obit Jan 97

Draper, William H., Jr. Mar 52 obit Feb 75

Dream Froese, Jerome *see* Tangerine Dream

Drees, Willem Jan 49 obit Jul 88

Dreiser, Theodore obit Feb 46

Drescher, Fran Apr 98

Dressen, Chuck Jul 51 obit Nov 66

Drew, Charles R. May 44 obit May 50

Drew, Elizabeth Oct 79

Drew, George A. Dec 48 obit May 84

Drexler, Clyde Jan 96

Drexler, Millard S. Jan 93

Dreyfus, Camille May 55 obit Dec 56 Yrbk 57

Dreyfus, Pierre Jul 58 obit Mar 95

Dreyfuss, Henry May 48 Oct 59 obit Dec 72

Dreyfuss, Richard Jan 76

Dridzo, Solomon Abramovichch *see* Lozovsky, S. A.

Driesch, Hans obit Jun 41

Drinan, Robert F. Jun 71

Driscoll, Alfred E. Jan 49 obit May 75

Driskell, David C. Aug 2000

Droch *see* Bridges, Robert

Drossaerts, Arthur Jerome obit Oct 40

Drouet, Bessie Clarke obit Oct 40

Drozd, Steven *see* Flaming Lips

Drozniak, Edward Jul 62 obit Jan 67

Drucker, Eugene *see* Emerson String Quartet

Drucker, Peter F. May 64

Druckman, Jacob May 81 obit Aug 96

Drum, Hugh A. Jul 41 obit Nov 51

Drummond, Roscoe Nov 49 obit Nov 83

Dryden, Hugh L. Apr 59 obit Jan 66

Dryden, Lennox *see* Steen, Marguerite

Dryfoos, Orvil E. Jan 62 obit Jul 63

Drysdale, Don Feb 65 obit Sep 93

Du Bois, Guy Pène Oct 46 obit Oct 58

Du Bois, Shirley Graham Oct 46 [Graham, Shirley] obit

Jun 77

Du Bois, W. E. B. Jan-Jun 40 obit Oct 63

Du Bose, Horace Mellard obit Mar 41

Du Fournet, Louis Rene Marie Charles Dartige obit Mar 40

Du Jardin, Rosamond (WLB) Yrbk 53

Du Maurier, Daphne May 40 obit Jun 89

Du Mont, Allen B. Jun 46 obit Jan 66

Du Pont, Francis Irénée obit May 42

Du Pont, Pierre Samuel Sep 40 obit May 54

Du Pré, Jacqueline May 70 obit Nov 87

Du Puy, William Atherton obit Oct 41

Du Vigneaud, Vincent Jan 56 obit Feb 79

Duarte, José Napoleón Sep 81 obit Apr 90

Dubcek, Alexander Nov 68

Dubilier, William Sep 57 obit Oct 69

Dubinsky, David Dec 42 Jun 57 obit Jan 83

Dublin, Louis Israel Oct 42 obit Yrbk 91 (died Mar 69)

Dubois, Eugéne obit May 41

Dubos, René J. Oct 52 Jan 73 obit Apr 82

Dubridge, L. A. Jun 48 obit Mar 94

Dubuffet, Jean Jul 62 obit Jul 85

Duc Tho, Le see Le Duc Tho

Duchamp, Gaston Emile see Villon, Jacques

Duchamp, Marcel Jun 60 obit Dec 68

Duchin, Eddy Jan 47 obit Mar 51

Duchin, Peter Jan 77

Duclos, Jacques Feb 46 obit

Jun 75

Dude Love see Foley, Mick

Dudley, Bide obit Feb 44

Dudley, Walter Bronson see Dudley, Bide

Duerk, Alene Sep 73

Duesberg, Peter H. Jun 2004

Dufek, George J. Mar 57

Duff, James H. Apr 48 obit Feb 70

Duffey, Joseph D. Mar 71

Duffy, Bernard C. Jul 52 obit Nov 72

Duffy, Edmund Jan-Jun 40 obit Nov 62

Duffy, James J. obit Feb 42

Dufy, Raoul Mar 51 obit May 53

Dugan, Alan Nov 90 obit Oct 2004

Dugan, Alan obit Oct 2004

Dugan, Raymond Smith obit Oct 40

Duggan, Ervin S. Oct 98

Duggan, Laurence May 47 obit Jan 49

Duggar, Benjamin Minge Nov 52 obit Nov 56

Dukakis, Michael S. Feb 78

Dukakis, Olympia Jul 91

Duke, Angier Biddle Feb 62 obit Jul 95

Duke, Patty Sep 63

Duke, Vernon Jun 41 obit Mar 69

Dukelsky, Vladimir see Duke, Vernon

Dullea, Keir Jun 70

Dulles, Allen W. Mar 49 obit Mar 69

Dulles, Eleanor Lansing Sep 62 obit Jan 97

Dulles, John Foster Aug 44 Sep 53 obit Jul 59

Dumas, Roland Oct 90

Dunaway, Faye Feb 72

Dunbar, Paul B. Jul 49 obit Nov 68

Dunbar, Rudolph Oct 46

Duncan, Andrew Rae Jul 41

obit May 52

Duncan, Charles W. Apr 80

Duncan, David Douglas Nov 68

Duncan, Malcolm obit Jun 42

Duncan, Michael Clarke Aug 2000

Duncan, Patrick obit Sep 43

Duncan, Sandy Jan 80

Duncan, Thomas W. Dec 47

Duncan, Tim Nov 99

Duncan, Todd Jul 42 obit May 98

Dunham, Charles L. Mar 66

Dunham, Franklin Jan 42 obit Jan 62

Dunham, Katherine Mar 41

Dunkerley, William Arthur see Oxenham, John

Dunlap, John B. Dec 51 obit Feb 65

Dunlop, John T. Apr 51 obit Sep 2004

Dunlop, John T. obit Sep 2004

Dunn, Gordon E. May 66

Dunn, J. Allan obit May 41

Dunn, James Clement May 43 obit Jun 79

Dunn, Jennifer Mar 99

Dunn, Loula F. Mar 51

Dunn, Ronnie see Brooks and Dunn

Dunne, Dominick May 99

Dunne, Irene Aug 45 obit Nov 90

Dunne, John Gregory Jun 83 obit Yrbk 2004

Dunning, John R. May 48 obit Oct 75

Dunninger, Joseph Sep 44 obit May 75

Dunnock, Mildred Sep 55 obit Sep 91

Dunrossil, William Shepherd Morrison, 1st Viscount see Morrison, William Shepherd

Dunst, Kirsten Oct 2001

Dunton, A. Davidson Jan 59 obit Apr 87

Duplessis, Maurice Oct 48

obit Nov 59

Durán, Roberto Sep 80

Durang, Christopher Jun 87

Durant, Will Sep 64 obit Jan 82

Durante, Jimmy Sep 46 obit Mar 80

Duranty, Walter Jan 43 obit Dec 57 Yrbk 58

Duras, Marguerite Nov 85 obit May 96

Durbin, Deanna Jun 41

Durenberger, David F. Oct 88

Durgin, C. T. Sep 54 obit May 65

Durham, Carl Jul 57 obit Jun 74

Duritz, Adam *see* Counting Crows

Durkin, Martin P. Feb 53 obit Jan 56

Durning, Charles Sep 97

Durocher, Leo Sep 40 Jul 50 obit Nov 91

Durocher, Mrs. Leo *see* Day, Laraine

Durrell, Gerald May 85 obit Apr 95

Durrell, Lawrence Jul 63 obit Jan 91

Dürrenmatt, Friedrich Feb 59 obit Apr 91

Dusser De Barenne, Joannes Gregorius obit Aug 40

Dutoit, Charles Feb 87

Dutra, Eurico Gaspar Mar 46 obit Sep 74

Dutton, Charles S. Oct 2000

Dutton, Lawrence *see* Emerson String Quartet

Duva, Lou Nov 99

Duval, David Oct 99

Duvalier, François

Duvalier, Jean-Claude Jun 72

Duvall, Evelyn Millis Oct 47

Duvall, Mrs. Sylvanus Milne *see* Duvall, Evelyn Millis

Duvall, Robert Jul 77

Duvieusart, Jean Sep 50

Duvivier, Julien Jul 43 obit

Jan 68

Dwight, Reginald Kenneth *see* John, Elton

Dwinell, Lane Jun 56 obit Jun 97

Dworkin, Andrea Oct 94 obit Yrbk 2005

Dworshak, Henry C. Jan 50 obit Oct 62

Dye, Marie Dec 48

Dyer-Bennet, Richard Jun 44 obit Feb 92

Dyhrenfurth, Norman G. Apr 65

Dyke, Cornelius G. obit Jun 43

Dykstra, Clarence A. Jan 41 obit Jun 50

Dykstra, John Apr 63 obit May 72

Dylan, Bob May 65 Oct 91

Dyson, Esther Aug 97

Dyson, Freeman J. Jan 80

Dyson, Michael Eric Oct 97

Dzhugashvili, Iosif Vissarionovich *see* Stalin, Joseph

Eady, Wilfrid Oct 47 obit Feb 62

Eagleburger, Lawrence S. Nov 92

Eagleton, Thomas Nov 73

Eaker, Ira Clarence Oct 42 obit Sep 87

Eames, Charles Jan 65 obit Oct 78

Eanes, António Ramalho Apr 79

Earle, Steve Oct 98

Earle, Sylvia A. May 92

Early, Gerald May 95

Early, Stephen T. Jul 41 Dec 49 obit Sep 51

Early, William Ashby Mar 54

Easley, Claudius M. obit Jul 45

Eastland, James O. Jan 49 obit Apr 86

Eastman, Joseph B. Jul 42 obit May 44

Eastman, Max Apr 69 obit

Apr 69

Eastwood, Clint Oct 71 Mar 89

Eaton, Charles A. May 45 obit Mar 53

Eaton, Cyrus S. Jul 48 obit Jul 79

Eban, Abba Oct 48 May 57 obit Mar 2003

Ebbers, Bernard J. Feb 98

Ebbott, Percy J. Oct 54

Eberhart, Richard Jan 61 obit Yrbk 2005

Eberle, Irmengarde (WLB) Yrbk 46

Ebersol, Dick Jul 96

Eberstadt, Ferdinand Dec 42 obit Jan 70

Ebert, Roger Mar 97

Eboue, Felix Adolphe obit Jul 44

Ebsen, Buddy Jan 77 obit Yrbk 2003

Ebsen, Christian Rudolph, Jr. *see* Ebsen, Buddy

Eccles, David Jan 52 obit May 99

Eccles, John C. Oct 72 obit Jul 97

Eccles, Marriner S. Apr 41 obit Feb 78

Ecevit, Bülent Jan 75

Echeverría Álvarez, Luis Nov 72

Echols, Oliver P. Dec 47 obit Jul 54

Eckardt, Felix Von Jan 56

Ecker, Frederick H. Jun 48 obit May 64

Eckert, Robert A. Mar 2003

Eckstein, Gustav May 42 obit Nov 81

Eckstein, Otto Feb 67 obit May 84

Eckstine, Billy Jul 52 obit Apr 93

Eco, Umberto Apr 85

Edberg, Stefan Jan 94

Eddington, Arthur Stanley Apr 41 obit Yrbk 91 (died

Nov 44)

Eddins, William Feb 2002

Eddy, Manton S. Feb 51 obit Jun 62

Eddy, Nelson Feb 43 obit May 67

Ede, James Chuter May 46 obit Jan 66

Edel, Leon Jul 63 obit Nov 97

Edelman, Gerald M. Apr 95

Edelman, Marian Wright Sep 92

Edelman, Maurice Jan 54 obit Feb 76

Eden, Anthony Yrbk 40 Apr 51 obit Mar 77

Edey, Birdsall Otis obit Aug 40

Edge, Walter Evans Jun 45 obit Jan 57

Edgerton, Harold E. Nov 66 obit Mar 90

Edinburgh, Philip, 3d Duke of see Mountbatten, Philip

Edison, Charles Jul 40 obit Oct 69

Edman, Irwin Jul 53 obit Oct 54

Edmonds, Walter Dumaux Sep 42

Edwards, Blake Jan 83

Edwards, Bob Sep 2001

Edwards, Charles C. Oct 73

Edwards, Don Mar 83

Edwards, Douglas Aug 88 obit Jan 91

Edwards, Gus obit Dec 45

Edwards, India Sep 49 obit Mar 90

Edwards, James B. Nov 82

Edwards, Joan Oct 53 obit Oct 81

Edwards, John H. obit Yrbk 45

Edwards, John Oct 2004

Edwards, Ralph L. Jul 43

Edwards, Teresa Mar 98

Edwards, Vincent Oct 62 obit May 96

Edwards, Waldo B. Jun 43 [Hingson, Robert A.; Ed-

wards, Waldo B.; and Southworth, James L.]

Egan, Edward M. Jul 2001

Egan, Jennifer Mar 2002

Egan, William Allen Sep 59 obit Jul 84

Egbert, Sherwood H. Jun 63 obit Oct 69

Egeberg, Roger O. Jan 70 obit Nov 97

Eger, Ernst Oct 42

Eggers, Dave Jul 2000

Eggerth, Marta Nov 43

Eggleston, Edward Mason obit Mar 41

Eggleston, William Feb 2002

Eghbal, Manouchehr May 59 obit Feb 78

Eglevsky, Andre Feb 53 obit Feb 78

Egloff, Gustav Sep 40

Egorov, Boris (Borisovitch) see Yegorov, Boris

Egoyan, Atom May 94

Ehlers, Vernon J. Jan 2005

Ehrenburg, Ilya Jun 66 obit Nov 67

Ehrenreich, Barbara Mar 95

Ehricke, Krafft A. Jun 58 obit Feb 85

Ehrlich, Paul R. Sep 70

Ehrlichman, John D. Oct 79 obit Apr 99

Eichelberger, Clark M. Jan 47 obit Mar 80

Eichelberger, Robert L. Jan 43 obit Dec 61

Eicher, Edward C. May 41 obit Jan 45

Eichheim, Henry obit Oct 42

Eidmann, Frank Lewis obit Nov 41

Eiko and Koma May 2003

Eiko see Eiko and Koma

Eilshemius, Louis Michel Apr 40 obit Feb 42

Einaudi, Luigi Jul 48 obit Jan 62

Einem, Gottfried Von Jul 53 obit Sep 96

Einstein, Albert Nov 41 May

53 obit Jun 55

Eiseley, Loren Jun 60 obit Sep 77

Eisen, Gustav obit Yrbk 40

Eisendrath, Maurice N. May 50 obit Jan 74

Eisenhower, Dwight D. Aug 42 Feb 48 Sep 57 obit May 69

Eisenhower, John S. D. Jul 69

Eisenhower, Mamie May 53 obit Jan 80

Eisenhower, Milton S. Dec 46 obit Jul 85

Eisenhower, Mrs. Dwight D. see Eisenhower, Mamie

Eisenman, Peter Oct 97

Eisenschiml, Otto Oct 63 obit Jan 64

Eisenstaedt, Alfred Jan 75 obit Oct 95

Eisenstein, Sergei May 46 obit Mar 48

Eisler, Hanns May 42 obit Nov 62

Eisner, Michael D. Nov 87

Eisner, Will Oct 94 obit May 2005

Eklund, John M. Dec 49 obit Mar 97

Eklund, Sigvard Jul 62

Ekman, Carl Gustaf obit Jul 45

El Cordobés Jan 66

El Mallakh, Kamal Oct 54 obit Jan 88

Elath, Eliahu see Epstein, Eliahu

El-Bitar, Salah see Bitar, Salah Eddin

Elder, Albert L. Sep 60

Elder, Lee Aug 76

Elders, Joycelyn Mar 94

Eldridge, Edward H. obit Jun 41

Eldridge, Florence Mar 43 [March, Fredric; and Eldridge, Florence] obit Sep 88

Eldridge, Roy Mar 87 obit Apr 89

El-Glaoui, Thami El-Mezouari, Pasha of Marrakech Sep 54 obit Mar 56

Eliade, Mircea Nov 85 obit Jun 86

Elias, Leona Baumgartner *see* Baumgartner, Leona

Elias, Rosalind Jan 67

Elion, Gertrude B. Mar 95 obit May 99

Eliot, George Fielding Jan-Feb 40 obit Jun 71

Eliot, Martha May Oct 48 obit Apr 78

Eliot, T. S. Oct 62 obit Feb 65

Eliot, Thomas H. May 42 obit Jan 92

Elisofon, Eliot Jan 72 obit May 73

Elizabeth II, Queen of Great Britain Jun 44 Jun 55

Elizabeth, Princess of Great Britain *see* Elizabeth II, Queen of Great Britain

Elizabeth, Queen Mother of Great Britain Aug 81 obit Jun 2002

Elizalde, Joaquin M. Feb 48 obit Mar 65

Elizondo, Hector Jan 92

El-Khoury, Bechara *see* Khoury, Bechara El-

Elkin, Stanley Jul 87 obit Aug 95

Ellender, Allen J. Jul 46 obit Oct 72

Ellerbee, Linda Oct 86

Ellerman, Ferdinand obit Apr 40

Elling, Kurt Jan 2005

Ellingson, Mark Sep 57 obit Apr 93

Ellington, Buford Sep 60 obit May 72

Ellington, Duke Mar 41 Jan 70 obit Jul 74

Elliot, Kathleen Morrow Mar 40

Elliott, Bob Oct 57 [Elliott, Bob; and Goulding, Ray]

Elliott, Harriet Wiseman Jul 40 obit Sep 47

Elliott, Herbert Jul 60

Elliott, Joe *see* Def Leppard

Elliott, John Lovejoy obit Jun 42

Elliott, Maxine Mar 40

Elliott, Osborn Jan 78

Elliott, Sean Apr 2001

Elliott, William Thompson obit Aug 40

Ellis, Albert Jul 94

Ellis, Bret Easton Nov 94

Ellis, Carleton obit Mar 41

Ellis, Elmer Jul 62

Ellis, John Tracy Mar 90 obit Jan 93

Ellis, Perry Jan 86 obit Jan 86

Ellis, Ruth Sep 2000

Ellison, Lawrence J. Jan 98

Ellison, Ralph Oct 68 Jun 93 obit Jun 94

Elliston, Herbert Jun 49 obit Mar 57

Ellroy, James Apr 98

Ellroy, Lee Earle *see* Ellroy, James

Ellsberg, Daniel Dec 73

Ellsberg, Edward Nov 42 obit Yrbk 91 (died Jan 83)

Elman, Mischa Oct 45 obit Jun 67

El-Solh, Sami *see* Solh, Sami

Elson, Arthur Mar 40

Elson, Edward L. R. Nov 67 obit Nov 93

Eltinge, Julian obit Apr 41

Elvehjem, C. A. May 48 obit Oct 62

Elway, John Nov 90

Ely, Paul Oct 54 obit Mar 75

Ely, Richard Theodore obit Nov 43

El-Yafi, Abdullah *see* Yafi, Abdullah El-

Elytis, Odysseus Sep 80 obit Jun 96

Elzy, Ruby obit Aug 43

Emanuel, Rahm Apr 98

Emanuel, Victor May 51 obit Jan 61

Embree, Edwin R. Dec 48 obit

Mar 50

Emeny, Brooks Nov 47

Emerson String Quartet Jul 2002

Emerson, Faye Sep 51 obit May 83

Emerson, Lee E. Oct 53

Emerson, Roy Jun 65

Emerson, Victor Lee obit Jul 41

Emery, Ann (WLB) Yrbk 52

Emery, Dewitt Oct 46 obit Oct 55

Eminem Jan 2001

Emmerich, Roland Nov 2000

Emmerson, Louis Lincoln obit Mar 41

Emmet, Evelyn Mar 53

Emmet, Mrs. Thomas Addis *see* Emmet, Evelyn

Emmet, William L. obit Nov 41

Emmons, Delos C. Mar 42 obit Dec 65

Emmons, Glenn L. Oct 54

Empie, Paul C. Oct 58

Emrich, Duncan Mar 55

Enckell, Carl J. A. Apr 50 obit Jun 59

Endara, Guillermo Feb 91

Endeley, E. M. L. Jul 59

Enders, John F. Jun 55 [Enders, John F.; Robbins, Frederick C.; and Weller, Thomas H.] obit Jan 86

Engel, Carl obit Jun 44

Engel, Kurt obit Mar 42

Engelbreit, Mary Oct 99

Engibous, Thomas J. Oct 2003

Engle, Clair Mar 57 obit Oct 64

Engle, Paul Jun 42 obit May 91

Englebright, Harry L. obit Jul 43

Engleman, James Ozro obit Nov 43

English, Diane Jun 93

English, Mrs. William D. *see*

Kelly, Judith

Englund, Robert Mar 90

Engstrom, E. W. Dec 51 obit Feb 85

En-lai, Chou *see* Chou En-Lai

Enright, Elizabeth (WLB) Yrbk 47 obit Sep 68

Enrique Tarancón, Vicente Oct 72 obit Feb 95

Ensler, Eve Aug 2002

Ensor, James, Baron obit Feb 43

Enters, Angna Jan-Feb 40 Jun 52 obit Apr 89

Entezam, Nasrollah Dec 50

Entremont, Philippe Mar 77

Ephron, Nora Jan 90

Epstein, Abraham obit Jun 42

Epstein, Eliahu Dec 48 obit Aug 90

Epstein, Jacob Jul 45 obit Nov 59

Epstein, Jason Aug 90

Epstein, Joseph Mar 90

Epstein, Samuel S. Aug 2001

Epstein, Theo May 2004

Ercoli, Ercole *see* Togliatti, Palmiro

Erdman, Jean Sep 71

Erdrich, Louise Apr 89

Erhard, Ludwig Jan 50 Jun 64 obit Jul 77

Erhard, Werner Apr 77

Erickson, John Edward obit Jun 46

Ericsson-Jackson, Aprille J. Mar 2001

Erikson, Erik H. *see* Erikson, Erik H. May 71 obit Jul 94

Erikson, Leonard F. Oct 53

Erkin, Feridun C. Jan 52

Erlander, Tage Oct 47 obit Aug 85

Erlanger, Mitchell Louis obit Oct 40

Ernst, Jimmy Mar 66 obit Apr 84

Ernst, Max Dec 42 Oct 61 obit May 76

Ernst, Morris L. Aug 40 Feb

61 obit Jul 76

Ershad, Hussain Mohammad Nov 84

Erskine, G. B. Jul 46 obit Jul 73

Erskine, George Jan 52 obit Nov 65

Erté Nov 80 obit Jun 90

Ertegun, Mehmet Munir obit Jan 45

Ervin, Sam J., Jr. Jan 55 Oct 73 obit Jun 85

Erving, Julius May 75

Esch, John J. obit Jun 41

Eschenbach, Christoph Aug 89

Escobar, Marisol *see* Marisol

Eshelman, W. W. May 60

Eshkol, Levi Oct 63 obit Apr 69

Esiason, Boomer Nov 95

Esiason, Norman Julius *see* Esiason, Boomer

Esposito, Phil May 73

Espy, A. Michael "Mike" Oct 93

Estefan, Gloria Oct 95

Estenssoro, Victor Paz *see* Paz Estenssoro, Victor

Estenssoro, Victor Paz *see* Paz Estenssoro, Victor

Estes, Eleanor (WLB) Yrbk 46 obit Sep 88

Estes, Elliott M. Jan 79 obit May 88

Estes, Harlow Mar 41

Estes, Mrs. Rice *see* Estes, Eleanor

Estes, Richard Nov 95

Estes, Simon Aug 86

Esteven, John *see* Shellabarger, Samuel

Estevez, Ramon *see* Sheen, Martin

Estigarribia, Jose Felix Mar 40 obit Mar 40

Estrada, Joseph Feb 2000

Eszterhas, Joe Apr 98

Etheridge, Melissa May 95

Etherington, Edwin D. Apr 66

obit Apr 2001

Ethridge, Mark Jan 46 obit Jun 81

Ettinger, Richard P. Dec 51 obit Apr 71

Ettinghausen, Walter *see* Eytan, Walter

Ettl, John obit Feb 41

Etzel, Franz Sep 57 [Armand, Louis; Etzel, Franz; and Giordani, Francesco]

Etzioni, Amitai Mar 80

Eugenides, Jeffrey Oct 2003

Eurich, Alvin C. Jun 49 obit Aug 87

Eustis, Helen (WLB) Yrbk 55

Eustis, Oskar Oct 2002

Eustis, Paul Jefferson *see* Eustis, Oskar

Evanovich, Janet Apr 2001

Evans, Alice Catherine Oct 43 obit Oct 75

Evans, Anne obit Feb 41

Evans, Arthur obit Sep 41

Evans, Bergen (WLB) Yrbk 55 obit Apr 78

Evans, Dale *see* Rogers, Dale Evans

Evans, Daniel Aug 75

Evans, Donald L. Nov 2001

Evans, Edith Jun 56 obit Jan 77

Evans, Edward R. G. R. May 41 obit Nov 57 [Mountevans, Edward R. G. R. Evans, 1st Baron]

Evans, Faith Feb 99

Evans, Harold Apr 85

Evans, Herbert M. Jul 59 obit Apr 71

Evans, Hugh Ivan Nov 50 obit Jul 58

Evans, Janet Jul 96

Evans, Linda Mar 86

Evans, Luther H. Aug 45 obit Feb 82

Evans, Maurice May 40 Jun 61 obit May 89

Evans, Nancy Mar 2000

Evans, Poncé Cruse *see* Heloise

Evans, Walker Sep 71 obit Jun 75

Evarts, Esther *see* Benson, Sally

Evatt, Harriet (WLB) Yrbk 59

Evatt, Herbert V. May 42 obit Jan 66

Evatt, Mrs. William S. *see* Evatt, Harriet

Eve Jul 2003

Everett, Percival Sep 2004

Everett, Rupert Jan 2005

Evergood, Philip Oct 44 Oct 60 obit Apr 73

Evers, James Charles Apr 69

Evers-Williams, Myrlie Aug 95

Evert, Chris Apr 73

Eves, Reginald Grenville Sep 40 obit Aug 41

Evren, Kenan Apr 84

Ewbank, Weeb Jun 69 obit Feb 99

Ewell, Tom May 61 obit Nov 94

Ewing, James obit Jul 43

Ewing, Maria Apr 90

Ewing, Maurice Jan 53 obit Jun 74

Ewing, Oscar R. Jul 48 obit Mar 80

Ewing, Patrick May 91

Exeter, David George Brownlow Cecil, 6th Marquis of *see* Burghley, David George Brownlow Cecil, Lord

Exley, Frederick Oct 89 obit Aug 92

Exner, Max J. obit Nov 43

Exon, J. James Nov 96 obit Yrbk 2005

Eyadéma, Etienne Gnassingbé Apr 2002 obit Yrbk 2005

Eyde, Samuel obit Aug 40

Eyler, John Aug 2000

Eyre, Chris May 2003

Eyre, Katherine Wigmore (WLB) Yrbk 49 (WLB) Yrbk 57

Eyre, Mrs. Dean Atherton *see*

Eyre, Katherine Wigmore

Eyring, Henry Oct 61

Eysenck, Hans J. Nov 72 obit Nov 97

Eyskens, Gaston Nov 49 obit Feb 88

Eytan, Walter Oct 58 obit Oct 2001

Eyüboglu, Bedri Rahmi Sep 54

F. P. A. *see* Adams, Franklin P.

Fabares, Nanette *see* Fabray, Nanette

Faber, Sandra Apr 2002

Fabian, Robert Apr 54 obit Aug 78

Fabius, Laurent Feb 85

Fabray, Nanette Jan 56

Fackenthal, Frank D. Feb 49 obit Nov 68

Fadiman, Anne Aug 2005

Fadiman, Clifton May 41 Oct 55 obit Sep 99

Fagan, Garth Aug 98

Fagerholm, Karl August Oct 48 obit Jul 84

Fagg, Fred D., Jr. Feb 56 obit Jan 82

Fagnani, Charles P. obit Mar 41

Fahd, Crown Prince of Saudi Arabia May 79 obit Yrbk 2005

Fahd, King of Saudi Arabia *see* Fahd, Crown Prince of Saudi Arabia

Fahy, Charles Jan 42 obit Nov 79

Fair, A. A. *see* Gardner, Erle Stanley

Fairbank, John King Oct 66 obit Nov 91

Fairbanks, Douglas Jan 40

Fairbanks, Douglas Jr. Nov 41 Feb 56 obit Aug 2000 obit Aug 20000

Fairchild, Benjamin Lewis obit Dec 46

Fairchild, David Jul 53 obit

Oct 54

Fairchild, Henry Pratt Dec 42 obit Dec 56 Yrbk 57

Fairchild, John B. Jun 71

Fairclough, Ellen Oct 57 obit Yrbk 2005

Fairclough, Mrs. Gordon *see* Fairclough, Ellen

Fairfax, Beatrice Aug 44 obit Jan 46

Fairfield, Cecily Isabel *see* West, Rebecca

Fairless, Benjamin F. Jun 42 May 57 obit Feb 62

Fairport Convention Sep 2005

Faisal Ibn Abdul-Aziz Al Saud, Prince Jan 48

Faisal II, King of Iraq *see* Feisal II, King of Iraq

Faisal, King of Saudi Arabia May 66 obit May 75

Faldo, Nick Sep 92

Falk, Maurice obit Apr 46

Falk, Peter Jul 72

Falkner, Roland Post obit Jan 41

Fall, Albert B. obit Jan 45

Falla, Manuel de obit Dec 46

Fallaci, Oriana Feb 77

Fälldin, Thorbjörn May 78

Fallon, Jimmy Jul 2002

Fallows, James Nov 96

Falls, Robert Jan 2004

Faludi, Susan Feb 93

Falwell, Jerry Jan 81

Fanfani, Amintore Oct 58 obit Mar 2000

Fang Lizhi Nov 89

Fangmeier, Stefen Aug 2004

Fanning, Shawn Sep 2000

Farah Diba Pahlevi Mar 76

Farber, Sidney Sep 67 obit May 73

Farhi, Nicole Nov 2001

Faricy, William T. Jun 48

Farish, William S. obit Jan 43

Farley, James A. Sep 44 obit Aug 76

Farley, Walter (WLB) Yrbk

49 obit Feb 90

Farmer, Guy Feb 55

Farmer, James Feb 64 obit Sep 99

Farmer, Paul Feb 2004

Farmer-Paellmann, Deadria Mar 2004

Farnsworth, Arthur obit Oct 43

Farnsworth, Jerry Oct 54

Farnsworth, Mrs. Jerry *see* Sawyer, Helen

Farny, George W. obit Oct 41

Farouk Oct 42 obit May 65

Farrakhan, Louis Apr 92

Farrar, John Jun 54 obit Jan 75

Farrar, Margaret Jul 55 obit Aug 84

Farrell, Dave *see* Linkin Park

Farrell, Eileen Feb 61 obit Jun 2002

Farrell, James T. Sep 42 obit Oct 79

Farrell, Suzanne Sep 67

Farrelly, Bobby *see* Farrelly, Peter and Bobby

Farrelly, Peter and Bobby Sep 2001

Farrington, Joseph R. May 48 obit Sep 54

Farrington, Mary Elizabeth Pruett Jun 55 obit Sep 84

Farrington, Mrs. Joseph R *see* Farrington, Mary Elizabeth Pruett

Farrow, Mia Apr 70

Fasanella, Ralph Jun 75 obit Mar 98

Fascell, Dante B. Apr 60 obit Feb 99

Fassbaender, Brigitte Jun 94

Fassbinder, Rainer Werner May 77 obit Aug 82

Fassett, Kaffe Jun 95

Fast, Howard Apr 43 Apr 91 obit Jul 2003

Fatemi, Hossein May 53 obit Jan 55

Fath, Jacques Apr 51 obit Jan

55

Fatone, Joey *see* 'N Sync

Fattah, Chaka Sep 2003

Faubus, Orval E. Oct 56 obit Feb 95

Fauci, Anthony S. Aug 88

Fauley, Wilbur F. obit Feb 43

Faulk, Marshall Jan 2003

Faulkner, Brian Feb 72 obit May 77

Faulkner, Nancy (WLB) Yrbk 56

Faulkner, William Jan 51 obit Sep 62

Fauntroy, Walter E. Feb 79

Faure, Edgar Feb 52 obit May 88

Faurot, Joseph A. obit Jan 43

Faust, Clarence H. Mar 52 obit Aug 75

Faust, Frederick obit Jul 44

Fausto-Sterling, Anne Sep 2005

Faversham, William obit May 40

Favre, Brett Nov 96

Fawcett, Edward obit Nov 42

Fawcett, Farrah *see* Fawcett-Majors, Farrah

Fawcett, Joy May 2004

Fawcett, Sherwood L. Dec 72

Fawcett-Majors, Farrah Feb 78

Fawley, Wilbur *see* Fauley, Wilbur F.

Fawzi, Mahmoud Dec 51

Fay, Frank Aug 45 obit Dec 61

Fay, J. Michael Sep 2001

Fay, Martin *see* Chieftains

Feather, Vic Mar 73 obit Sep 76

Fechteler, William M. Sep 51 obit Oct 67

Fedorenko, Nikolai T. Dec 67

Fedorova, Nina Nov 40

Feifel, Herman Aug 94 obit Yrbk 2005

Feiffer, Jules Oct 61

Feikema, Feike (WLB) Yrbk

50

Feingold, Russell D. Jul 98

Feininger, Andreas Oct 57 obit May 99

Feininger, Lyonel Jul 55 obit Mar 56

Feinsinger, Nathan P. May 52 obit Jan 84

Feinstein, Dianne Jun 79 Aug 95

Feinstein, Isidor *see* Stone, I. F.

Feinstein, John Jul 98

Feinstein, Michael Apr 88

Feis, Herbert Oct 61 obit May 72

Feisal II, King of Iraq Jul 55 obit Oct 58

Feld, Eliot Oct 71

Feld, Irvin Feb 79 obit Nov 84

Feldmann, Markus Jun 56 obit Jan 59

Feldstein, Martin May 83

Feldt, Gloria Jul 2000

Feliciano, José Jul 69

Felix, Robert H. Apr 57 obit May 90

Felker, Clay S. Feb 75

Feller, Abraham H. Nov 46 obit Jan 53

Feller, Bob Aug 41

Fellini, Federico Jun 57 Oct 80 obit Jan 94

Fellows, George Emory obit Mar 42

Fellows, Harold E. Feb 52 obit May 60

Fels, William C. Apr 59 obit Jan 65

Felt, Harry D. Mar 59

Felt, W. Mark Sep 2005

Feltin, Maurice Cardinal May 54 obit Nov 75

Felton, Ralph A. Sep 57

Feltsman, Vladimir Apr 88

Fenimore-Cooper, Susan De Lancey obit Mar 40

Fenwick, Millicent Apr 77 obit Nov 92

Feoktistov, Konstantin Nov

67

Ferber, Herbert Nov 60 obit Oct 91

Ferguson, Elsie Feb 44 obit Jan 62

Ferguson, Garland S. Jul 49 obit Jun 63

Ferguson, Harriet Jan 47 obit Feb 66

Ferguson, Harry Mar 56 obit Jan 61

Ferguson, Homer May 43 obit Mar 83

Ferguson, Howard obit Apr 46

Ferguson, James Edward obit Nov 44

Ferguson, Malcolm P. May 57

Ferguson, Maynard Feb 80

Fergusson, Erna (WLB) Yrbk 55

Ferlinghetti, Lawrence Jun 91

Fermi, Enrico Oct 45 obit Jan 55

Fermi, Laura May 58

Fermi, Mrs. Enrico see Fermi, Laura

Fermor, Patrick Leigh (WLB) Yrbk 55

Fernandel Oct 55 obit Apr 71

Fernandes, L. Esteves Oct 50

Fernandez Concheso, Aurelio see Concheso, Aurelio Fernández

Ferrari, Enzo May 67 obit Sep 88

Ferraro, Geraldine A. Sep 84

Ferré, Gianfranco Jul 91

Ferré, Luis A. Mar 70 obit Mar 2004

Ferrell, Will Feb 2003

Ferren, John Jul 58 obit Oct 70

Ferrer, José Figueres see Figueres Ferrer, José

Ferrer, José May 44 [Ferrer, José; and Hagen, Uta] obit Mar 92

Ferrer, Rafael Jul 2001

Ferrero, Gina L. obit May 44

Ferrero, Guglielmo obit Sep 42

Ferrier, Kathleen Oct 51 obit Dec 53

Ferris, Harry Burr obit Yrbk 40

Ferris, Scott obit Jul 45

Ferris, Timothy Jan 2001

Ferriss, Hugh Jul 45 obit Mar 62

Festing, Francis W. Feb 45

Feuermann, Emanuel obit Jul 42

Few, William Preston obit Yrbk 40

Fey, Tina Apr 2002

Feynman, Richard P. Oct 55 Nov 86 obit Apr 88

Fichandler, Zelda Jun 87

Fidrych, Mark Mar 78

Fiedler, Arthur Sep 45 May 77 obit Sep 79

Fiedler, Leslie A. Dec 70 obit Yrbk 2003

Field, Betty Sep 59 obit Nov 73

Field, Frederick Laurence obit Dec 45

Field, Henry Mar 55 obit Mar 86

Field, Marshall, 3d Apr 41 Mar 52 obit Jan 57

Field, Rachel Lyman obit May 42

Field, Sally Oct 79

Fielding, Gabriel Feb 62 obit Apr 87

Fielding, Mantle obit May 41

Fielding, Temple Apr 69 obit Jul 83

Fields, Dorothy Feb 58 [Fields, Herbert; and Fields, Dorothy] obit May 74

Fields, Gracie Apr 41 obit Nov 79

Fields, Herbert Feb 58 [Fields, Herbert; and Fields, Dorothy]

Fields, Lew obit Sep 41

Fields, Mark Apr 2005

Fields, Stanley obit Jun 41

Fiene, Ernest Aug 41

Fiennes, Ralph Sep 96

Fierstein, Harvey Feb 84

Figgis, D. W. Nov 48 obit Jan 65

Figl, Leopold Apr 48 obit Jun 65

Figueiredo, João Baptista Jan 80 obit May 2000

Figueres Ferrer, José Oct 53 obit Aug 90

Figueroa, Ana Feb 52

Filho, Joao Cafe see Café Filho, Joao

Fili-Krushel, Patricia Nov 99

Filmus, Tully Apr 64 obit Jun 98

Filo, David Oct 97 [Yang, Jerry; and Filo, David]

Filov, Bogdan Dimitrov see Philoff, Bogdan

Finch, Caleb E. Sep 2004

Finch, Flora obit Jan 40

Finch, Jennie Oct 2004

Finch, Peter Sep 72 obit Mar 77

Finch, Robert H. Mar 69 obit Jan 96

Fincher, David May 2000

Finckel, David see Emerson

Fine, Benjamin Mar 61

Fine, John S. Sep 51 obit Jul 78

Finet, Paul Sep 51

Finger, Charles Joseph obit Mar 41

Fingesten, Peter Oct 54 obit Oct 87

Finkelstein, Arthur J. Nov 99

Finkelstein, Louis Nov 40 Mar 52 obit Jan 92

Finklea, Tula Ellice see Charisse, Cyd

Finletter, Thomas K. Jan 48 obit Jun 80

Finley, Charles O. Jun 74 obit

Apr 96

Finley, David E. Feb 51 obit Apr 77

Finley, John Huston Mar 40

Finley, Karen Sep 98

Finn, William Joseph Jul 40

Finnbogadóttir, Vigdis May 87

Finnegan, Joseph F. Apr 59 obit Apr 64

Finney, Albert Oct 63

Finney, Gertrude E. (WLB) Yrbk 57

Finney, Mrs. John Montfort *see* Finney, Gertrude E.

Finnie, Mrs. Haldeman *see* Holt, Isabella

Fiorina, Carleton Jan 2000

Fireman, Paul Mar 92

Firestone, Harvey S., Jr. Jul 44 obit Jul 73

Firkusny, Rudolf Oct 79 obit Sep 94

Firth, Colin Mar 2004

Fischbacher, Siegfried *see* Siegfried

Fischer, Bobby Oct 63 May 94

Fischer, Carlos L. Feb 59

Fischer, Hans obit May 45

Fischer, Israel Frederick obit Apr 40

Fischer, John H. Jul 60

Fischer, John May 53 obit Oct 78

Fischer, Louis May 40 obit Mar 70

Fischer-Dieskau, Dietrich Feb 67

Fischl, Eric Jun 86

Fish, Bert obit Sep 43

Fish, Hamilton Jan 41 obit Mar 91

Fish, Marie Poland Oct 41 obit Apr 89

Fishback, Margaret Apr 41 obit Nov 85

Fishbein, Morris May 40 obit

Nov 76

Fishburne, Laurence Aug 96

Fisher, Carrie Feb 91

Fisher, Clarence S. obit Sep 41

Fisher, Eddie Oct 54

Fisher, Fred obit Mar 42

Fisher, Geoffrey Francis Mar 45 obit Nov 72

Fisher, Harry L. Oct 54

Fisher, John Stuchell obit Aug 40

Fisher, M. F. K. (WLB) Yrbk 48 Sep 83 obit Aug 92

Fisher, Sterling Yrbk 40

Fisher, Walter C. Jul 50

Fisher, Welthy Dec 69 obit Feb 81

Fisk, James Brown Jan 59 obit Oct 81

Fiske, Bradley Allen obit May 42

Fiske, Charles obit Mar 42

Fiske, James Porter obit Dec 41

Fisketjon, Gary cb

Fister, George M. Jun 63 obit Jul 76

Fitch, Aubrey Oct 45 obit Jul 78

Fitch, Robert Elliot Apr 62

Fittipaldi, Emerson Apr 92

Fitz Gerald, Leslie M. Sep 54

Fitzgerald, Albert J. Oct 48 obit Jul 82

Fitzgerald, Barry Feb 45 obit Feb 61

Fitzgerald, Cissy obit Jul 41

Fitzgerald, Ed Apr 47 [Fitzgerald, Ed; and Fitzgerald, Pegeen] obit Jun 82

Fitzgerald, Ella Oct 56 Jul 90 obit Aug 96

Fitzgerald, F. Scott obit Feb 41

Fitzgerald, Frances Jun 87

Fitzgerald, Garret Aug 84

Fitzgerald, Geraldine Oct 76 obit Yrbk 2005

Fitzgerald, Pegeen Apr 47

[Fitzgerald, Ed; and Fitzgerald, Pegeen] obit Apr 89

Fitzgerald, Robert Sep 76 obit Mar 85

Fitzgibbons, John obit Oct 41

Fitzmaurice, George obit Aug 40

Fitzpatrick, D. R. Jul 41 obit Jul 69

Fitzpatrick, George L. obit Jun 41

Fitzroy, Edward Algernon obit Apr 43

Fitzsimmons, Frank E. May 71 obit Jul 81

Fitzwater, Marlin May 88

Fivoosiovitch, Edith Gregor *see* Halpert, Edith Gregor

Flack, Roberta Nov 73

Flagg, James Montgomery Nov 40 obit Sep 60

Flagstad, Kirsten May 47 obit Jan 63

Flaherty, Robert Mar 49 obit Sep 51

Flair, Ric Mar 2000

Flaming Lips Oct 2002

Flanagan, Edward Joseph Sep 41 obit Jun 48

Flanagan, Tommy Apr 95 obit Mar 2002

Flanders, Michael Jan 70 obit Jun 75

Flanders, Ralph E. Jan 48 obit Apr 70

Flandin, Pierre-étienne Jan 41 obit Oct 58

Flannagan, John B. obit Mar 42

Flanner, Janet May 43 obit Jan 79

Flannery, Harry W. Oct 43

Flansburgh, John *see* They Might Be Giants

Flatts Rosas, Cesar *see* Los Lobos

Flavin, Martin Dec 43 obit Feb 68

Fleck, Alexander Fleck, 1st

Baron Apr 56 obit Oct 68

Fleck, Béla Nov 96

Fleck, Jack Sep 55

Fleeson, Doris May 59 obit Oct 70

Fleischman, Ruth Geri *see* Hagy, Ruth Geri

Fleischmann, Manly Jul 51

Fleisher, Leon Jan 71

Fleming, Alexander Apr 44 [Fleming, Alexander; and Florey, Howard W.] obit May 55

Fleming, Amalia Nov 72 obit Apr 86

Fleming, Ambrose obit May 45

Fleming, Arthur Henry obit Sep 40

Fleming, Berry (WLB) Yrbk 53 obit Nov 89

Fleming, Donald M. Feb 59 obit Mar 87

Fleming, Ian Jan 64

Fleming, John A. May 40 obit Oct 56

Fleming, Peggy Jul 68

Fleming, Philip Bracken Apr 40 obit Dec 55 Yrbk 56

Fleming, Renée May 97

Fleming, Robben W. Dec 70

Fleming, Sam M. Jun 62

Flemming, Arthur S. Jun 51 Apr 60 obit Nov 96

Flesch, Carl obit Jan 45

Flesch, Rudolf Apr 48 obit Nov 86

Fletcher, Angus Sep 46 obit Nov 60

Fletcher, Arthur Nov 71 obit Yrbk 2005

Fletcher, C. Scott Feb 53

Fletcher, Inglis (WLB) Yrbk 47 obit Jul 69

Fletcher, James May 72 obit Feb 92

Fletcher, Mrs. John George *see* Fletcher, Inglis

Flexner, Abraham Jun 41 obit Nov 59

Flexner, Bernard obit Jun 45

Flexner, Jennie M. obit Jan 45

Flexner, Simon obit Jun 46

Flickinger, Roy C. obit Aug 42

Flikke, Julia O. Jul 42

Flinders Petrie, William Matthew *see* Petrie, William Matthew Flinders

Flood, Daniel J. Aug 78 obit Aug 94

Flore, Edward F. obit Oct 45

Florence, Fred F. Jun 56 obit Feb 61

Florey, Howard Apr 44 [Fleming, Alexander; and Florey, Howard W.] obit Apr 68

Florinsky, Michael T. Oct 41 obit Jan 82

Florio, James J. May 90

Flory, Paul J. Mar 75 obit Nov 85

Floyd, Carlisle Jul 60

Floyd, William obit Jan 44

Flutie, Doug Oct 85

Fly, James Lawrence Sep 40 obit Feb 66

Flying Officer X *see* Bates, H. E.

Flynn, Edward J. Sep 40 obit Oct 53

Flynn, Elizabeth Gurley Oct 61 obit Nov 64

Flynn, Keri *see* Burstyn, Ellen

Flynn, Raymond Oct 93

Flynt, Larry Sep 99

Fo, Dario Nov 86

Fodor, Eugene Apr 76

Foer, Jonathan Safran Sep 2002

Foerster, Friedrich Wilhelm Jul 62 obit Feb 66

Fogarty, Anne Oct 58 obit Mar 80

Fogarty, John E. Apr 64 obit Mar 67

Fokine, Michel obit Oct 42

Foley, Martha Apr 41 [Foley, Martha; and Burnett, Whit] obit Oct 77

Foley, Mick Sep 2001

Foley, Raymond M. Oct 49 obit Apr 75

Foley, Thomas S. Sep 89

Folger, A. D. obit Jun 41

Folkers, Karl Oct 62

Folkman, Judah May 98

Folks, Homer Yrbk 40

Follett, Ken Jan 90

Folliard, Edward T. Nov 47 obit Feb 77

Folon, Jean-Michel Feb 81

Folsom, Frank M. Feb 49 obit Mar 70

Folsom, James Elisha Sep 49 obit Jan 88

Folsom, Marion B. Jan 50 obit Nov 76

Fonda, Bridget Jan 94

Fonda, Henry Dec 48 Nov 74 obit Sep 82

Fonda, Jane Jul 64 Jun 86

Fonda, Peter Mar 98

Foner, Eric Aug 2004

Fong, Hiram L. Feb 60 obit Yrbk 2004

Fong-Torres, Ben Aug 2001

Fontaine, Joan May 44 [Fontaine, Joan; and de Havilland, Olivia]

Fontana, Tom Aug 2000

Fontanne, Lynn Jun 41 [Lunt, Alfred; and Fontanne, Lynn] obit Sep 83

Fonteyn, Margot Dec 49 Mar 72 obit Apr 91

Foot, Hugh Oct 53 obit Nov 90

Foot, Michael Dec 50 May 81

Foote, H. W. obit Mar 42

Foote, Horton Aug 86

Foote, Shelby Apr 91 obit Yrbk 2005

Forand, Aime J. Jun 60 obit Mar 72

Forbes, B. C. Mar 50 obit Jul 54

Forbes, Guillaume, Archbishop obit Jul 40

Forbes, John J. Apr 52

Forbes, Kathryn Dec 44 obit Jun 66

Forbes, Malcolm S. Feb 75 obit Apr 90

Forbes, Steve May 96

Force, Juliana Mar 41 obit Oct 48

Ford, Benson Feb 52 obit Sep 78

Ford, Betty *see* Ford, Elizabeth

Ford, Blanche Chapman *see* Chapman, Blanche

Ford, Edsel obit Jul 43

Ford, Edward Charles *see* Ford, Whitey

Ford, Eileen Oct 71

Ford, Elizabeth Sep 75

Ford, Frederick W. Nov 60 obit Sep 86

Ford, Gerald R. Mar 61 Nov 75

Ford, Glenn Jun 59

Ford, Harold E. Jr. Nov 99

Ford, Harrison Sep 84

Ford, Henry Dec 44 obit May 47

Ford, Henry, II Apr 46 Jun 78 obit Nov 87

Ford, John Feb 41 obit Nov 73

Ford, Richard Sep 95

Ford, Tennessee Ernie Mar 58 obit Jan 92

Ford, Tom May 98

Ford, W. W. obit Aug 41

Ford, Whitey Apr 62

Ford, Worthington C. obit Apr 41

Foreman, Clark Oct 48 obit Aug 77

Foreman, George May 74 Aug 95

Foreman, Richard Jul 88

Forest, Lee de *see* De Forest, Lee

Forman, Milos Dec 71

Fornos, Werner H. Jul 93

Forrest, Allan obit Sep 41

Forrest, Vernon Jul 2002

Forrest, Wilbur S. May 48 obit May 77

Forrestal, James V. Feb 42 Jan 48 obit Jul 49

Forrester, Maureen Jul 62

Forsberg, Peter Nov 2005

Forsee, Gary D. Oct 2005

Forssmann, Werner Mar 57 obit Aug 79

Forster, E. M. Apr 64 obit Sep 70

Forster, Rudolph obit Aug 43

Forsyth, Bill Jan 89

Forsyth, Cecil obit Feb 42

Forsyth, Frederick May 86

Forsyth, W. D. Apr 52

Forsythe, John May 73

Forsythe, Robert S. obit Aug 41

Forsythe, William Feb 2003

Fortas, Abe Feb 66 obit May 82

Fortey, Richard Sep 2005

Fosdick, Harry Emerson Oct 40 obit Nov 69

Fosdick, Raymond B. Feb 45 obit Sep 72

Foss, Joe *see* Foss, Joseph Jacob

Foss, Joseph Jacob Oct 55 obit Yrbk 2003

Foss, Lukas Jun 66

Fosse, Bob Jun 72 obit Nov 87

Fossett, J. Stephen *see* Fossett, Steve

Fossett, Steve Apr 2005

Fossey, Dian May 85 obit Feb 86

Foster, Harry Hylton- *see* Hylton-Foster, Harry

Foster, Jodie Jun 81 Aug 92

Foster, John S., Jr. Dec 71

Foster, John *see* Furcolo, Foster

Foster, Maximilian obit Nov

43

Foster, Norman Sep 2000

Foster, Richard C. obit Jan 42

Foster, William C. Nov 50

Foster, William Zebulon Jul 45 obit Nov 61

Fougner, G. Selmer obit May 41

Fouilhoux, J. Andre obit Jul 45

Fountain, Clarence *see* Blind Boys of Alabama

Fournet, Louis Rene Marie Charles Dartige du *see* Du Fournet, Louis Rene Marie Charles Dartige

Fowler, Alfred obit Aug 40

Fowler, Gene Mar 44 obit Sep 60

Fowler, Henry H. Sep 52 obit May 2000

Fowler, Mark S. Mar 86

Fowler, R. M. Oct 54

Fowler, William A. Sep 74 obit May 95

Fowler-Billings, Katharine Jan 40

Fowles, John Mar 77

Fox Quesada, Vicente May 2001

Fox, Carol Jul 78 obit Sep 81

Fox, Genevieve (WLB) Yrbk 49 obit Dec 59

Fox, Jacob Nelson *see* Fox, Nellie

Fox, Jay *see* Carewe, Edwin

Fox, John McDill obit May 40

Fox, Michael Feb 77

Fox, Michael J. Nov 87

Fox, Nellie Mar 60 obit Feb 76

Fox, Robert J. May 70 obit Jun 84

Fox, Sidney obit Jan 43

Fox, Virgil Jan 64 obit Jan 81

Foxx, Jamie May 2005

Foxx, Redd Dec 72 obit Jan 92

Foyle, Gilbert Jun 54 [Foyle, Gilbert; and Foyle William

Alfred] obit Jan 72

Foyle, William Alfred Jun 54 [Foyle, Gilbert; and Foyle William Alfred] obit Jul 63

Foyt, A. J. Nov 67

Fracci, Carla Feb 75

Fraga Iribarne, Manuel May 65

Frager, Malcolm Apr 67 obit Aug 91

Frahm, Herbert *see* Brandt, Willy

Frakes, Jonathan Jul 99

Frampton, Peter May 78

Franca, Celia May 56

France, Pierre Mendès- *see* Mendès-France, Pierre

Francescatti, Zino Oct 47 obit Nov 91

Franciosa, Anthony Jul 61

Francis, Arlene May 56 obit Sep 2001

Francis, Clarence Feb 48 obit Mar 86

Francis, Connie Jul 62

Francis, Dick Aug 81

Francis, Emile Apr 68

Francis, Frank Jul 59 obit Apr 89

Francis, Sam Oct 73 obit Jan 95

Francisco, Don Feb 2001

Francis-Williams Mar 46 obit Sep 70

Franck, James May 57 obit Jul 64

Franco, Afranio de Mello *see* Mello Franco, Afranio De

Franco, Francisco Mar 42 Mar 54 obit Jan 76

Francois-Poncet, Andre Oct 49 obit Mar 78

Frank, Anthony M. Aug 91

Frank, Barney Apr 95

Frank, Glenn obit Nov 40

Frank, Hans Mar 41 obit Nov 46

Frank, Jerome N. Apr 41 obit Mar 57

Frank, Lawrence K. Jan 58 [Frank, Lawrence K; and

Frank, Mary] obit Nov 68

Frank, Louis obit May 41

Frank, Mary Jan 58 [Frank, Lawrence K.; and Frank, Mary]

Frank, Reuven Jun 73

Frank, Robert Aug 97

Frank, Waldo David Nov 40 obit Mar 67

Franke, William B. Sep 59 obit Aug 79

Frankel, Bernice *see* Arthur, Beatrice

Frankel, Charles Apr 66 obit Jul 79

Frankel, Felice Apr 98

Frankel, Max Apr 87

Franken, Al Jun 99

Franken, Rose Yrbk 41 (WLB) Yrbk 47 obit Aug 88

Frankenberg, Mrs. Lloyd *see* Maciver, Loren

Frankenheimer, John Oct 64 obit Oct 2002

Frankensteen, Richard T. Dec 45

Frankenthaler, Helen Apr 66

Frankfurter, Felix Jun 41 Jul 57 obit Apr 65

Frankl, Viktor E. Jul 97 obit Nov 97

Franklin, Aretha Dec 68 May 92

Franklin, Frederic Sep 43

Franklin, Irene obit Aug 41

Franklin, Jay Oct 41 obit Jan 68

Franklin, John Hope Oct 63

Franklin, John M. Sep 49 obit Aug 75

Franklin, Kirk Mar 2000

Franklin, Shirley C. Aug 2002

Franklin, Walter S. Feb 50 obit Oct 72

Franks, Oliver Shewell Mar 48 obit Jan 93

Franks, Tommy R. Jan 2002

Franz, Dennis Jul 95

Franzen, Jonathan Sep 2003

Fraser of North Cape, Bruce Austin Fraser, 1st Baron *see*

Fraser, Bruce

Fraser, Antonia Oct 74

Fraser, Brad Jul 95

Fraser, Brendan Feb 2001

Fraser, Bruce Jul 43 obit Apr 81

Fraser, Douglas Andrew Oct 77

Fraser, Hugh Russell Jun 43

Fraser, Ian Dec 47

Fraser, Ian Forbes Jun 54

Fraser, James Earle Jul 51 obit Jan 54

Fraser, Leon obit May 45

Fraser, Malcolm Mar 76

Fraser, Peter May 42 obit Jan 51

Fraser, Robert Oct 56

Fratellini, Paul obit Yrbk 40

Frayn, Michael Jan 85

Frazer, James obit Jul 41

Frazer, Joseph W. Mar 46 obit Sep 71

Frazer, Spaulding obit Apr 40

Frazier, Edward Franklin Jul 40

Frazier, Ian Aug 96

Frazier, Joe Apr 71

Frazier, Walt Feb 73

Frear, J. Allen, Jr. Oct 54

Frears, Stephen Apr 90

Fred, E. B. Dec 50

Fredenthal, David Sep 42 obit Jan 59

Frederick, John T. Jun 41

Frederick, Pauline Oct 54 obit Jul 90

Fredericks, Henry St. Clair *see* Mahal, Taj

Frederik IX, King of Denmark Nov 47 obit Mar 72

Frederika, Consort of Paul I, King of The Hellenes Jan 55 obit Apr 81

Fredman, Samuel, Rabbi obit Jun 41

Freed, James Ingo. Nov 94

Freedlander, Arthur R. obit Aug 40

Freedley, George Sep 47 obit

Nov 67

Freedman, Benedict Sep 47 [Freedman, Benedict; and Freedman, Nancy]

Freedman, Nancy Sep 47 [Freedman, Benedict; and Freedman, Nancy]

Freeh, Louis J. May 96

Freehafer, Edward G. Jun 55 obit Feb 86

Freeman, James Edward, Bishop obit Jul 43

Freeman, John Jun 69

Freeman, Lucy Oct 53 obit Yrbk 2005

Freeman, Morgan Feb 91

Freeman, Orville L. Jun 56 obit Yrbk 2003

Freeman, R. Austin obit Nov 43

Freeman-Thomas, Freeman, 1st Marquess of Willingdon see Willingdon, Freeman Freeman-Thomas, 1st Marquess of

Frehley, Ace see Kiss

Frehley, Paul see Frehley, Ace

Frei, Eduardo Apr 65 obit Mar 82

Freilicher, Jane Nov 89

Freitag, Walter Jan 54 obit Oct 58

Fremantle, Francis Edward obit Oct 43

French, Hollis obit Jan 41

French, Marilyn Sep 92

French, Paul Comly May 51 obit Sep 60

French, Paul see Asimov, Isaac

French, Robert W. Oct 59

Freni, Mirella Apr 77

Fresnay, Pierre Feb 59 obit Feb 75

Freston, Tom Aug 2003

Freud, Anna Apr 79 obit Mar 83

Freud, Lucian Jul 88

Freund, Philip (WLB) Yrbk 48

Freundlich, Herbert obit May 41

Freyberg, Bernard Cyril, 1st Baron Freyberg Oct 40 obit Sep 63

Frick, Ford May 45 obit Jun 78

Frick, Wilhelm Aug 42 obit Nov 46

Friday, William Apr 58

Friedan, Betty Nov 70 Mar 89

Friedkin, William Jun 87

Friedman, Bruce Jay Jun 72

Friedman, Herbert Sep 63 obit Nov 2000

Friedman, Jane Mar 2001

Friedman, Milton Oct 69

Friedman, Thomas L. Oct 95

Friel, Brian Jun 74

Friendly, Edwin S. Jul 49 obit Sep 70

Friendly, Fred W. Sep 57 Aug 87 obit May 98

Frings, Ketti Jan 60 obit Apr 81

Frisch, Karl Von Feb 74 obit Yrbk 83 (died Jun 82)

Frisch, Max Jan 65 obit Jun 91

Frische, Carl A. Oct 62

Frissell, Toni Jun 47 obit Jun 88

Frist, Bill Nov 2002

Froehlich, Jack E. Jul 59

Froese, Edgar see Tangerine

Frohman, Daniel obit Feb 41

Frohnmayer, John E. Apr 90

Fromm, Erich Apr 67 obit May 80

Frondizi, Arturo Oct 58 obit Jun 95

Frost, David Jul 69

Frost, Frances Mary (WLB) Yrbk 50 obit Apr 59

Frost, Jack see Erhard, Werner

Frost, Leslie M. Oct 53 obit Jul 73

Frost, Robert Sep 42 obit Mar 63

Frothingham, Channing Mar 48 obit Nov 59

Frowick, Roy Halston see Halston

Fruehauf, Roy Feb 53 obit Jan 66

Frum, David Jun 2004

Fry, Christopher Feb 51 obit Yrbk 2005

Fry, Franklin Clark Jun 46 obit Sep 68

Fry, Kenneth D. Apr 47

Fry, Stephen Sep 98

Frye, David Mar 75

Frye, Jack Apr 45 obit Apr 59

Frye, Northrop Aug 83 obit Mar 91

Fuchs, Joseph Oct 62 obit May 97

Fuchs, Michael J. Feb 96

Fuchs, Vivian E. Oct 58 obit Jan 2000

Fudge, Ann M. Jun 98

Fuentes, Carlos Oct 72

Fuentes, Miguel Ydígoras see Ydígoras Fuentes, Miguel

Fugard, Athol Jun 75

Fugazi Mar 2002

Fujimori, Alberto Nov 90

Fujiyama, Aiichiro Apr 58 obit May 85

Fukuda, Takeo Jun 74 obit Sep 95

Fukuyama, Francis Jun 2001

Fulani, Lenora Mar 2000

Fulbright, J. William Nov 43 Oct 55 obit Apr 95

Fulghum, Robert Jul 94

Fuller, Alfred C. Oct 50 obit Jan 74

Fuller, Bonnie May 2000

Fuller, Charles E. Dec 51 obit May 68

Fuller, Charles Jun 89

Fuller, Clara Cornelia obit Yrbk 40

Fuller, George Washington

obit Yrbk 40

Fuller, John L. Mar 59

Fuller, Kathryn S. Jan 94

Fuller, Margaret H. Jun 59

Fuller, Millard Apr 95

Fuller, Mrs. Raymond G. *see* Fox, Genevieve

Fuller, R. Buckminster Jan 60 Feb 76 obit Aug 83

Fuller, S. R., Jr. May 41 obit Mar 66

Fuller, Samuel Aug 92 obit Jan 98

Fuller, Walter Deane Mar 41 obit Jan 65

Fulmer, Hampton Pitts obit Dec 44

Fulton, E. D. Jan 59

Funk, Casimir May 45 obit Jan 68

Funk, Charles Earle Jun 47 obit Jul 57

Funk, Walther Oct 40 obit Sep 60

Funk, Wilfred Jan 55 obit Jul 65

Funston, Keith Jul 51 obit Jul 92

Funt, Allen Dec 66 obit Nov 99

Fuoss, Robert M. Feb 59 obit Mar 80

Fuqua, Stephen Ogden Feb 43

Furcolo, Foster Jan 58 obit Sep 95

Furey, Warren W. May 50 obit Jan 59

Furman, N. Howell Dec 51 obit Oct 65

Furnas, Clifford Cook Oct 56 obit Jun 69

Furness, Betty Feb 68 obit Jun 94

Furstenberg, Diane von *see* Von Fürstenberg, Diane

Furtseva, Ekaterina A. Jun 56 obit Dec 74

Futter, Ellen V. Oct 85

Fyan, Loleta D. Dec 51

Fyfe, H. Hamilton Yrbk 40

obit Jul 51

G, Kenny *see* Kenny G

Gabin, Jean Jun 41 obit Jan 77

Gable, Clark May 45 obit Jan 61

Gable, Dan Aug 97

Gabo, Naum Apr 72 obit Oct 77

Gabor, Dennis Oct 72 obit Apr 79

Gabor, Eva Jul 68 obit Sep 95

Gabor, Zsa Zsa Mar 88

Gabriel, Peter Jan 90

Gabriel, Roman Nov 75

Gabrielson, Guy Oct 49 obit Jun 76

Gaddafi, Moamar al- *see* Qaddafi, Muammar Al-

Gaddis, William Nov 87 obit Mar 99

Gades, Antonio Feb 73 obit Yrbk 2004

Gaer, Joseph (WLB) Yrbk 51

Gaffney, T. St. John obit Mar 45

Gág, Wanda obit Jul 46

Gagarin, Yuri Oct 61 obit May 68

Gage, Nicholas Mar 90

Gagne, Eric Jun 2004

Gahagan, Helen *see* Douglas, Helen Gahagan

Gaillard, Félix Feb 58 obit Oct 70

Gaines, Ernest J. Mar 94

Gainza Paz, Alberto Apr 51 obit Feb 78

Gaither, Frances (WLB) Yrbk 50 obit Jan 56

Gaither, H. Rowan, Jr. May 53 obit Jun 61

Gaitskell, Hugh Jun 50 obit Feb 63

Gajdusek, D. Carleton Jun 81

Galanos, James Sep 70

Galard Terraube, Geneviève De Oct 54

Galassi, Jonathan Sep 99

Galbraith, John Kenneth Mar

59 May 75

Galdikas, Biruté M. F. Mar 95

Gale, Henry Gordon obit Jan 43

Gale, Robert Jan 87

Galen, Clemens August Von obit Apr 46

Galindo, Carlos Blanco *see* Blanco Galindo, Carlos

Galinsky, Ellen Oct 2003

Gallagher, Buell Gordon May 53 obit Jan 79

Gallagher, William J. obit Oct 46

Gallagher, William M. Oct 53 obit Nov 75

Gallant, Mavis May 90

Gallegos Freire, Rómulo May 48 obit May 69

Gallery, Daniel V. Apr 66 obit Mar 77

Galli, Rosina obit Jan 40

Galliano, John Oct 96

Gallico, Paul Apr 46 obit Sep 76

Gallo, Fortune Oct 49 obit May 70

Gallo, Robert C. Oct 86

Galloway, Irene O. May 53 obit Feb 63

Galloway, Joseph L. Sep 2003

Gallup, George Mar 40 Dec 52 obit Sep 84

Galtieri, Leopoldo Aug 82 obit Yrbk 2003

Galvin, Robert W. Mar 60

Galway, James Jun 80

Gamble, Ralph A. Jan 53 obit May 59

Gambling, John B. Mar 50 obit Jan 75

Gambrell, E. Smythe Jun 56

Gamelin, Marie Gustave *see* Gamelin, Maurice Gustave

Gamelin, Maurice Gustave Jan-Jun 40 obit Jul 58

Gamow, George Oct 51 obit Oct 68

Gandhi, Indira Oct 59 Jun 66 obit Jan 85

Gandhi, Mohandas Dec 42

obit Feb 48

Gandhi, Rajiv Apr 85 obit Jul 91

Gandhi, Sonia May 98

Gandolfini, James Feb 2000

Gandy, Kim Oct 2001

Ganfield, William Arthur obit Yrbk 40

Gannett, Frank Ernest Mar 45 obit Feb 58

Gannett, Lewis Aug 41 obit Mar 66

Gannon, Robert I., Rev. Mar 45 obit May 78

Ganso, Emil obit Jun 41

Gaposchkin, Cecilia Payne- see Payne-Gaposchkin, Cecilia

Garagiola, Joe Jan 76

Garand, John C. Aug 45 obit Apr 74

Garbett, Cyril Forster, Archbishop of York Feb 51 obit Mar 56

Garbo, Greta Apr 55 obit Jun 90

Garbus, Martin Nov 2000

García Márquez, Gabriel Jul 73

García Pérez, Alan Nov 85

Garcia, Carlos P. Jun 57 obit Jul 71

Garcia, Cristina Aug 99

Garcia, Jerry May 90 obit Oct 95

Garcia, Sergio Mar 2001

Garciaparra, Nomar Jun 2000

Gardiner, James Garfield Jun 56 obit Mar 62

Gardiner, Robert K. Jul 75

Gardner, Arthur Jan 56 obit Jun 67

Gardner, Ava Mar 65 obit Mar 90

Gardner, Ed Sep 43 obit Oct 63

Gardner, Erle Stanley Jun 44 obit Apr 70

Gardner, Howard Oct 98

Gardner, John Oct 78 obit

Nov 82

Gardner, John W. Mar 56 Mar 76 obit May 2002

Gardner, Lester D. Sep 47 obit Feb 57

Gardner, Martin Sep 99

Gardner, Matthias B. Jun 52

Gardner, O. Max Jan 47

Gardner, Rulon Nov 2004

Garfield, Harry A. obit Feb 43

Garfield, Henry see Rollins,

Garfield, John Apr 48 obit Jul 52

Garfunkel, Art Jun 74

Gargan, William Jan 69 obit Apr 79

Garland, Hamlin Mar 40

Garland, Judy Nov 41 Dec 52 obit Sep 69

Garn, Edwin see Garn, Jake

Garn, Jake Aug 85

Garner, Erroll Sep 59 obit Mar 77

Garner, James Nov 66

Garnett, Kevin Sep 98

Garnsey, Elmer Ellsworth obit Dec 46

Garratt, Geoffrey Theodore obit Jun 42

Garreau, Roger Apr 50

Garrels, Anne Mar 2004

Garrels, Arthur obit Aug 43

Garrison, Deborah Jan 2001

Garrison, Lloyd K. Jun 47 obit Nov 91

Garroway, Dave May 52 obit Sep 82

Garson, Greer Sep 42 obit Jun 96

Garst, Jonathan Oct 64

Garst, Roswell Apr 64 obit Jan 78

Garst, Shannon (WLB) Yrbk 47

Garth, David [political consultant] Jan 81

Garth, David [writer] (WLB)

Yrbk 57

Gartner, Michael May 90

Garvey, Jane P. Sep 2000

Garvey, Marcus obit Aug 40

Garvin, Clifton Canter, Jr. Nov 80

Garwin, Richard L. Mar 89

Gary, John Jul 67 obit Mar 98

Gary, Raymond Oct 55 obit Feb 94

Gary, Willie E. Apr 2001

Garza, Ed Jun 2002

Garzarelli, Elaine Sep 95

Garzón, Baltasar Mar 2001

Gasch, Marie Manning see Fairfax, Beatrice

Gaselee, Stephen obit Aug 43

Gaskin, Ina May May 2001

Gasparotti, Mrs. John J. see Seifert, Elizabeth

Gasperi, Alcide De Dec 46 obit Oct 54

Gass, William H. Apr 86

Gasser, Herbert S. Oct 45 obit Jul 63

Gassman, Vittorio Oct 64 obit Oct 2000

Gassner, John Jan 47 obit Jun 67

Gaston, Cito Apr 93

Gaston, Clarence Edwin see Gaston, Cito

Gatch, Lee Mar 66 obit Jan 69

Gates, Bill May 91

Gates, Henry Louis Oct 92

Gates, Melinda Feb 2004

Gates, Ralph F. Sep 47

Gates, Robert M. Apr 92

Gates, Thomas S., Jr. Sep 57 obit May 83

Gates, William H. see Gates, Bill

Gates, William obit Jan 40

Gatti-Casazza, Giulio obit Oct 40

Gaubatz, Lynn Feb 2001

Gaud, William S. Jan 69 obit Feb 78

Gaulle, Charles De Sep 40 Jun

49 Apr 60 obit Dec 70

Gaultier, Jean-Paul Jan 99

Gaumont, Leon Ernest obit Sep 46

Gauss, Christian Apr 45 obit Dec 51

Gauss, Clarence E. Jan 41 obit Jun 60

Gauthier, Joseph Alexandre George, Archbishop obit Oct 40

Gautier, Felisa Rincón De Oct 56 obit Nov 94

Gaver, Mary Virginia Jun 66 obit Mar 92

Gavin, James M. Feb 45 Sep 61 obit Apr 90

Gavin, John Sep 62

Gavras, Costa *see* Costa-Gavras

Gavrilov, Andrei Oct 2000

Gavrilovic, Stoyan May 46 obit Mar 65

Gawande, Atul Mar 2005

Gay, Peter Feb 86

Gayda, Virginio Sep 40 obit Sep 43

Gayle, Crystal Mar 86

Gayle, Helene Jan 2002

Gaylord, Robert Mar 44

Gazzaniga, Michael S. Apr 99

Gazzara, Ben Nov 67

Gebel-Williams, Gunther Dec 71 obit Oct 2001

Gebrselassie, Haile Jul 99

Gedda, Nicolai Nov 65

Geddes, Barbara Bel *see* Bel Geddes, Barbara

Geddes, Norman Bel May 40 obit Jul 58

Geer, Alpheus obit Oct 41

Geffen, David Jan 92

Gehrig, Lou Jan-Jun 40 obit Jul 41

Gehrmann, Don Oct 52 (see also correction p. 664 YRBK 52)

Gehry, Frank Jun 87

Geiger, Roy S. Jul 45 obit Mar 47

Geijer, Arne Jul 64

Geis, Bernard Sep 60 obit Mar 2001

Geisel, Ernesto Aug 75 obit Nov 96

Geisel, Theodor Seuss Feb 68 obit Nov 91

Gelb, Leslie H. Jan 2003

Geldof, Bob Mar 86

Geldzahler, Henry Sep 78 obit Oct 94

Geller, Margaret J. Jun 97

Geller, Uri Sep 78

Gellhorn, Walter May 67 obit Feb 96

Gell-Mann, Murray Feb 66 Oct 98

Gemayel, Amin Mar 83

Geneen, Harold S. Feb 74 obit Jan 98

Genet *see* Flanner, Janet

Genet, Jean Apr 74 obit Jun 86

Gennaro, Peter Jun 64 obit Feb 2001

Genscher, Hans-Dietrich Jun 75

Gentele, Goeran Sep 72

Genthe, Arnold obit Oct 42

George II, King of Greece Dec 43 obit Apr 47

George Tupou, King of Tonga *see* Taufa'ahau Tupou IV

George VI, King of Great Britain Mar 42 obit Mar 52

George, Albert Bailey obit Apr 40

George, Boy *see* Boy George

George, David Lloyd Nov 44 obit May 45

George, Elizabeth Mar 2000

George, Harold L. Dec 42

George, Manfred Oct 65 obit Feb 66

George, Walter F. Jun 43 Jun 55 obit Oct 57

George, Zelma W. Oct 61 obit Sep 94

George-Brown, Baron *see*

Brown, George

Gephardt, Richard A. Oct 87

Gerard, Ralph W. May 65 obit Apr 74

Geraud, André Sep 40 obit Jan 75

Gerberding, Julie Louise Sep 2004

Gerbner, George Aug 83

Gere, Richard Aug 80

Gergen, David Feb 94

Gergiev, Valery Jan 98

Gerhardsen, Einar Mar 49 obit Nov 87

Germond, Jack W. Jul 2005

Gernreich, Rudi Dec 68 obit Jun 85

Gerow, Leonard Townsend Apr 45 obit Dec 72

Gerowitz, Judy *see* Chicago, Judy

Gershwin, Ira Jan 56 obit Oct 83

Gerson, Michael Feb 2002

Gerstacker, Carl A. Oct 61 obit Jul 95

Gerstenmaier, Eugen Feb 58 obit May 86

Gerstner, Louis V. Jun 91

Gerulaitis, Vitas Jun 79 obit Nov 94

Gervasi, Frank Jun 42 obit Mar 90

Gesell, Arnold L. Nov 40 obit Sep 61

Gest, Morris obit Jul 42

Getman, F. H. obit Jan 42

Getty, Estelle Mar 90

Getty, Gordon P. Feb 85

Getz, Stan Apr 71 obit Aug 91

Geyer, Georgie Anne Aug 86

Gheerbrant, Alain Feb 59

Gheorghiu-Dej, Gheorghe Oct 58 obit May 65

Ghezali, Salima May 98

Ghormley, Robert Lee Oct 42 obit Oct 58

Ghose, Sri Chinmoy Kumar *see* Chinmoy, Sri

Ghulam Mohammed *see* Mohammed, Ghulam

Giacometti, Alberto Feb 56 obit Feb 66

Giacomin, Edward Mar 68

Giamatti, A. Bartlett Apr 78 obit Oct 89

Giamatti, Paul Sep 2005

Giannini, A. P. Mar 47 obit Jul 49

Giannini, Giancarlo Jun 79

Giannini, L. M. Nov 50 obit Oct 52

Giannulli, Mossimo Feb 2003

Giap, Vo Nguyen see Vo Nguyen Giap

Giauque, William F. Jan 50 obit May 82

Gibb, Barry Sep 81

Gibbings, Robert (WLB) Yrbk 48 obit Mar 58

Gibbings, Terence Harold Robsjohn see Robsjohn-Gibbings, T. H.

Gibbs, Constance see Bannister, Constance

Gibbs, George obit Jul 40

Gibbs, Joe Apr 92

Gibbs, Lois Sep 99

Gibbs, William Francis Apr 44 obit Nov 67

Gibson, Althea Oct 57 obit Feb 2004

Gibson, Bob Dec 68

Gibson, Charles Dana obit Feb 45

Gibson, Charles Sep 2002

Gibson, Ernest W. Jul 49 obit Dec 69

Gibson, Ernest Willard obit Aug 40

Gibson, Hugh Jan 53 obit Feb 55

Gibson, John W. Oct 47

Gibson, Kenneth A. May 71

Gibson, Mel Apr 84 Aug 2003

Gibson, Robert W., Jr. May 69

Gibson, Virginia see Johnson, Virginia E.

Gibson, William Jul 83

Gibstein, Yaacov see Agam, Yaacov

Giddens, Anthony Apr 98

Gideonse, Harry D. May 40 obit May 85

Gidney, Ray M. Oct 53

Giegengack, A. E. Nov 44 obit Sep 74

Gielgud, John Apr 47 Feb 84 obit Aug 2000

Gierek, Edward May 71 obit Oct 2001

Gieseking, Walter Oct 56 obit Jan 57

Gifford, Chloe Mar 59

Gifford, Francis Newton see Gifford, Frank

Gifford, Frank May 64 Jan 95

Gifford, Kathie Lee Nov 94

Gifford, Sanford R. obit Apr 44

Gifford, Walter S. Jan 45 obit Jun 66

Gigli, Romeo Aug 98

Gil Fortoul, José obit Aug 43

Gilbert, George obit May 43

Gilbert, Martin Feb 91

Gilbert, Rod Jul 69

Gilbert, Walter Nov 92

Gilbreth, Frank B. Jr. May 49 obit Jul 2001 [Gilbreth, Frank B.; and Carey, Ernestine Gilbreth]

Gilbreth, Lillian M. May 40 Sep 51 obit Feb 72

Gilbreth, Mrs. Frank Bunker see Gilbreth, Lillian M.

Gilchrist, Brad Jan 99

Gilchrist, Guy Jan 99

Gilchrist, Huntington Apr 49 obit Mar 75

Gilder, George Oct 81

Gilder, Robert Fletcher obit Mar 40

Gilder, Rosamond Nov 45 obit Oct 86

Gildersleeve, Virginia C. Aug 41 obit Sep 65

Gilels, Emil Oct 56 obit Jan 86

Giles, Barney McKinney Jul

44 obit Aug 84

Giles, Janice Holt (WLB) Yrbk 58

Giles, Mrs. Henry Earl see Giles, Janice Holt

Gill, Eric obit Jan 41

Gillespie, Dizzy Apr 57 Jan 93 obit Jan 93

Gillespie, John Birks see Gillespie, Dizzy

Gillespie, Louis John obit Mar 41

Gillet, Louis obit Aug 43

Gillette, Guy M. Sep 46 obit Apr 73

Gillham, Mrs. Robert Marty see Enright, Elizabeth

Gilligan, Carol May 97

Gilligan, John J. May 72

Gillingham, Charles see

Gillis, James M., Rev. Jun 56 obit Jun 57

Gillmore, Frank obit May 43

Gillooly, Edna Rae see Burstyn, Ellen

Gilmer, Elizabeth Meriwether see Dix, Dorothy

Gilmore, Eddy Jun 47 obit Dec 67

Gilmore, James S. III Jun 2001

Gilmore, John Washington obit Aug 42

Gilmore, Melvin Randolph obit Sep 40

Gilmore, Voit Feb 62

Gilmour, John obit Apr 40

Gilpatric, Roswell L. Mar 64 obit May 96

Gilroy, Frank D. Oct 65

Gilruth, Robert R. Oct 63 obit Yrbk 2000

Gimbel, Bernard F. Mar 50 obit Dec 66

Gimbel, Peter Jan 82 obit Aug 87

Ginastera, Alberto Jan 71

Ginger, Lyman V. May 58

Gingold, Hermione Oct 58 obit Jul 87

Gingrich, Arnold Feb 61 obit

Sep 76

Gingrich, Newt Jul 89

Ginsberg, Allen Apr 70 Apr 87 obit Jun 97

Ginsberg, Mitchell I. Jun 71 obit May 96

Ginsberg, Samuel *see* Krivitsky, Walter G.

Ginsburg, Ruth Bader Feb 94

Ginzberg, Eli Mar 66 obit Yrbk 2003

Ginzburg, Natalia Jul 90 obit Nov 91

Giordani, Francesco Sep 57 [Armand, Louis; Etzel, Franz; and Giordani, Francesco] obit Mar 61

Giovanna, Ella Rosa *see* Grasso, Ella

Giovanni, Nikki Apr 73

Gipson, Fred (WLB) Yrbk 57

Gipson, Lawrence Henry Oct 54 obit Nov 71

Giral, Jose May 46

Giraud, Henri Honore Dec 42 obit Apr 49

Giraudoux, Jean obit Mar 44

Girdler, Tom M. Apr 44 obit Mar 65

Giri, V. V. Jan 70 obit Aug 80

Giroud, Françoise Apr 75 obit Jul 2003

Giroux, Robert Nov 82

Giscard D'estaing, Valéry Jul 67 Oct 74

Gish, Dorothy Aug 44 [Gish, Dorothy; and Gish, Lillian] obit Sep 68

Gish, Lillian Aug 44 [Gish, Dorothy; and Gish, Lillian] Aug 78 obit Apr 93

Giuliani, Rudolph W. Apr 88

Giulini, Carlo Maria Mar 78 obit Yrbk 2005

Givenchy, Hubert De May 55

Givens, Willard E. Sep 48 obit Jul 71

Gjesdal, Cornelia *see* Knutson, Coya

Gladwell, Malcolm Jun 2005

Glaoui, Thami el-Mezouari

el- *see* El-Glaoui, Thami El-Mezouari, Pasha of Marrakech

Glaser, Donald A. Mar 61

Glaser, Milton May 80

Glasgow, Ellen obit Jan 46

Glass, Carter Oct 41 obit Jun 46

Glass, H. Bentley Apr 66 obit Yrbk 2005

Glass, Philip Mar 81

Glasser, Ira Jan 86

Glazer, Nathan Dec 70

Gleason, C. W. obit Dec 42

Gleason, Herbert John *see* Gleason, Jackie

Gleason, Jackie Oct 55 obit Aug 87

Gleason, John S., Jr. Jun 58

Gleason, Thomas W. Oct 65 obit Mar 93

Glemp, Jozef Sep 82

Glenn, John H., Jr. Jun 62 Mar 76 Jan 99

Glenn, Mary Wilcox obit Yrbk 40

Glennan, T. Keith Oct 50 obit Jun 95

Glennie, Evelyn Jul 97

Glennon, John obit Apr 46

Glicenstein, Enrico obit Feb 43

Glicenstein, Henryk *see* Glicenstein, Enrico

Glick, Mrs. Frank *see* Kirkus, Virginia

Glintenkamp, H. obit May 46

Glover, Danny Apr 92

Glover, Savion Mar 96

Glubb, John Bagot Sep 51 obit May 86

Glueck, Eleanor Touroff Oct 57 [Glueck, Sheldon; and Glueck, Eleanor T.] obit Nov 72

Glueck, Nelson Oct 48 Jul 69 obit Mar 71

Glueck, Sheldon Oct 57 [Glueck, Sheldon; and Glueck, Eleanor T.] obit

May 80

Glyn, Elinor obit Nov 43

Gmeiner, Hermann May 63 obit Jun 86

Gobbi, Tito Jan 57 obit May 84

Gobel, George Mar 55 obit Apr 91

Godard, Jean-Luc May 69 Oct 93

Goddard, James L. Oct 68

Goddard, Paulette obit Jun 90

Goddard, Robert H. obit Sep 45

Godden, Rumer Aug 76

Godfrey, Arthur Jul 48 obit May 83

Godoy, Alcayaga Lucila *see* Mistral, Gabriela

Godunov, Alexander Feb 83 obit Jul 95

Godwin, Gail Oct 95

Goebbels, Joseph Sep 41 obit Yrbk 91 (died May 45)

Goedhart, G. J. van Heuven *see* Heuven Goedhart, G. J. Van

Goertz, Arthémise (WLB) Yrbk 53

Goetz, Delia (WLB) Yrbk 49 obit Sep 96

Goetz, George *see* Calverton, V. F.

Goff, M. Lee Jun 2001

Gogarty, Oliver St. John Jul 41 obit Dec 57

Goheen, Robert F. Jan 58

Goizueta, Roberto C. Aug 96 obit Jan 98

Gold, Herbert (WLB) Yrbk 55

Gold, Thomas Jun 66 obit Yrbk 2004

Goldberg, Arthur J. Jul 49 Jul 61 obit Mar 90

Goldberg, Bill Apr 2001

Goldberg, Emmanuel *see* Robinson, Edward G.

Goldberg, Reuben Lucius *see* Goldberg, Rube

Goldberg, Rube Sep 48 obit

Jan 71

Goldberg, Whoopi Mar 85

Goldblum, Jeff Jul 97

Goldbogen, Avrom Hirsch *see* Todd, Mike

Golden, Clinton S. Apr 48 obit Sep 61

Golden, Harry Jan 59 obit Nov 81

Golden, John Mar 44 obit Sep 55

Golden, Thelma Sep 2001

Goldenson, Leonard H. Sep 57 obit May 2000

Goldenweiser, Alexander A. obit Sep 40

Goldin, Daniel S. Jun 93

Golding, William Mar 64 obit Aug 93

Goldman, Edwin Franko Sep 42 obit May 56

Goldman, Emma obit Jan 40

Goldman, Eric F. Jul 64 obit Apr 89

Goldman, Frank Jan 53 obit Apr 65

Goldman, Mrs. Marcus Selden *see* Goldman, Mrs. Olive Remington

Goldman, Olive Remington Sep 50 [Goldman, Mrs. Marcus Selden]

Goldman, William Jan 95

Goldmann, Nahum May 57 obit Oct 82

Goldman-Rakic, Patricia Feb 2003

Goldmark, Henry obit Mar 41

Goldmark, Peter C. Nov 40 Dec 50 obit Feb 78

Goldovsky, Boris Dec 66 obit Aug 2001

Goldsborough, John Byron obit May 43

Goldsborough, Phillips Lee obit Dec 46

Goldsborough, T. Alan Jun 48 obit Jul 51

Goldschmidt, Neil Aug 80

Goldsman, Akiva Sep 2004

Goldsmith, James Feb 88 obit

Oct 97

Goldsmith, Jerry May 2001 obit Nov 2004

Goldsmith, Jimmy *see* Goldsmith, James

Goldsmith, Lester Morris Apr 40

Goldsmith, Peter *see* Priestley, J. B.

Goldstein, Betty Naomi *see* Friedan, Betty

Goldstein, Elliott *see* Gould, Elliott

Goldstein, Israel Jul 46 obit Jun 86

Goldstein, Joseph L. Jul 87

Goldstine, Herman Heine Nov 52

Goldstine, Herman Heine Nov 52 obit Yrbk 2004

Goldsworthy, Andy Oct 2000

Goldthwaite, Anne obit Mar 44

Goldwater, Barry M. May 55 Jun 78 obit Aug 98

Goldwater, S. S. obit Dec 42

Goldwyn, Samuel Jan 44 obit Mar 74

Golenor, John Anthony *see* Gavin, John

Goler, George Washington obit Nov 40

Golikov, Filip Apr 43 obit Sep 80

Gollancz, Victor Oct 63 obit Apr 67

Golschmann, Vladimir Apr 51 obit May 72

Golub, Leon Aug 84 obit Yrbk 2004

Goma Y Tomas, Isidoro obit Oct 40

Gomez, Laureano May 50 obit Sep 65

Gomulka, Wladyslaw Jan 57 obit Oct 82

Gong Li May 97

Gonzales, Alberto R. Apr 2002

Gonzales, Pancho Oct 49 obit

Sep 95

Gonzales, Richard *see* Gonzales, Pancho

Gonzalez Videla, Gabriel Jun 50

Gonzalez, Adolfo Suarez *see* Suárez González, Adolfo

González, César Oct 54

Gonzalez, Efren W. Jan 71

González, Felipe Jan 78

Gonzalez, Henry Jun 64 Feb 93 obit Feb 2001

Good, Mary L. Sep 2001

Good, Robert A. Mar 72 obit Yrbk 2003

Goodall, Jane Nov 67 Nov 91

Goode, Richard Nov 88

Goode, W. Wilson Oct 85

Goodell, Charles E. Dec 68 obit Mar 87

Gooden, Dwight Apr 86

Goodhart, Arthur Lehman Jul 64 obit Feb 79

Goodloe, John D. Apr 47

Goodman, Andrew Apr 75 obit Jun 93

Goodman, Benjamin David *see* Goodman, Benny

Goodman, Benny Jan 42 Oct 62 obit Aug 86

Goodman, Bertram May 54

Goodman, Julian Feb 67

Goodman, Paul Jun 68 obit Oct 72

Goodpaster, Andrew J. Jul 69 obit Yrbk 2005

Goodrich, Arthur obit Aug 41

Goodrich, Frances Oct 56 [Goodrich, Frances; and Hackett, Albert] obit Apr 84

Goodrich, James Putnam obit Oct 40

Goodrich, Lloyd May 67 obit May 87

Goodrich, Marcus Apr 41 obit Jan 92

Goodson, Mark May 78 obit Feb 93

Goodspeed, Edgar Johnson Nov 46 obit Mar 62

Goodwin, Doris Kearns Nov

Goodwin, Harry obit Dec 42

Goodwin, Richard N. Dec 68

Goodwin, Robert C. May 51

Googe, George L. Jul 47 obit Dec 61

Googoosh May 2001

Goolagong, Evonne Nov 71

Goossens, Eugene May 45 obit Sep 62

Gopnik, Adam Apr 2005

Gorbach, Alfons Oct 61 obit Oct 72

Gorbachev, Mikhail Aug 85

Gorbachev, Raisa May 88 obit Nov 99

Gordimer, Nadine (WLB) Yrbk 59 Jun 80

Gordon Walker, Patrick Jan 66

Gordon, Bruce S. Oct 2005

Gordon, C. Henry obit Jan 41

Gordon, Crawford, Jr. Mar 58 obit Mar 67

Gordon, Cyrus H. May 63 obit Aug 2001

Gordon, David Jun 94

Gordon, Donald Oct 50 obit Jun 69

Gordon, Dorothy Jan 55 obit Jul 70

Gordon, Ed Jul 2005

Gordon, Edmund W. Jun 2003

Gordon, Godfrey Jervis see Gordon, Jan

Gordon, Jan obit Mar 44

Gordon, Janet see Woodham-Smith, Cecil Blanche Fitzgerald

Gordon, Jeff Aug 2000

Gordon, John Sloan obit Yrbk 40

Gordon, Kermit Jul 63 obit Aug 76

Gordon, Leon obit Feb 44

Gordon, Lincoln Feb 62

Gordon, Mary Nov 81

Gordon, Max Oct 43 obit Jan 79

Gordon, Mike see Phish Gor-

man, R. C. Jan 2001

Gordon, Odetta Felious see Odetta

Gordon, Ruth Apr 43 Apr 72 obit Oct 85

Gordon, Thomas S. Apr 57 obit Apr 59

Gordy, Berry, Jr. Jul 75

Gore, Al see Gore, Albert Jr.

Gore, Albert Jan 52 obit Feb 99

Gore, Albert Jr. Jun 87

Gore, Mary Elizabeth Aitcheson see Gore, Tipper

Gore, Tipper Oct 2000

Górecki, Henryk May 94

Gorelick, Kenny see G, Kenny

Goren, Charles H. Mar 59 obit Jul 91

Gorey, Edward Nov 76 obit Aug 2000

Gorin, Igor Jul 42 obit Jun 82

Göring, Hermann Wilhelm Aug 41 obit Nov 46

Görk, Haydar Oct 56

Gorman, Herbert Sherman Mar 40 obit Jan 55

Gorman, Mike see Gorman, Thomas F. X.

Gorman, Thomas F. X. Oct 56 obit Jul 89

Gorme, Eydie Feb 65

Gorrie, Jack Mar 52

Gorsuch, Anne Sep 82 obit Yrbk 2004

Gort, Viscount Oct 40 obit May 46

Gorton, John Grey Jul 68 obit Yrbk 2002

Gorton, Slade Aug 93

Gosden, Freeman F. Dec 47 [Gosden, Freeman F.; and Correll, Charles J.] obit Feb 83

Goshorn, Clarence B. Mar 50 obit Jan 51

Goss, Albert S. Mar 45 obit Dec 50

Gossage, Goose see Gossage,

Rich

Gossage, Rich Aug 84

Gossett, Louis, Jr. Nov 90

Gossett, William T. Jul 69 obit Oct 98

Gott, J. Richard III Oct 99

Gott, William Henry Ewart obit Oct 42

Gottlieb, Adolph Jan 59 obit Apr 74

Gottlieb, Melvin B. Jan 74 obit Mar 2001

Gottlieb, Robert A. Sep 87

Gottwald, Klement Apr 48 obit Apr 53

Goudge, Elizabeth Sep 40 obit Aug 84

Goudsmit, Samuel A. Oct 54 obit Feb 79

Goudy, Frederic William Jun 41 obit Jun 47

Gough, Lewis K. Jan 53 obit Jan 68

Gouin, Felix Mar 46 obit Oct 79 (died Oct 77)

Goulart, Joao Sep 62 obit Feb 77

Gould, Arthur R. obit Sep 46

Gould, Beatrice Blackmar Nov 47 [Gould, Beatrice Blackmar; and Gould, Bruce] obit Apr 89

Gould, Bruce Nov 47 [Gould, Beatrice Blackmar; and Gould, Bruce] obit Oct 89

Gould, Chester Sep 71 obit Jul 85

Gould, Elliott Feb 71

Gould, Glenn Oct 60 obit Nov 82

Gould, Laurence M. Jan 78 obit Aug 95

Gould, Morton Sep 45 Jan 68 obit May 96

Gould, Ronald Nov 52

Gould, Samuel B. Jan 58 obit Sep 97

Gould, Stephen Jay Sep 82 obit Aug 2002

Goulding, Ray Oct 57 [Elliott, Bob; and Goulding, Ray]

obit May 90

Goulet, Robert Sep 62

Goulian, Mehran Jul 68

Gourdji, Françoise *see* Giroud, Françoise

Gourielli, Helena Rubinstein *see* Rubinstein, Helena

Gove, Philip B. Oct 62 obit Jan 73

Gow, James Mar 44 [Gow, James; and d'Usseau, Arnaud] obit Mar 52

Gowdy, Curt May 67

Gower, Pauline Aug 43 obit Mar 47

Gowers, Timothy Jan 2001

Gowers, William Timothy *see* Gowers, Timothy

Gowon, Yakubu Jun 70

Grace, Alonzo G. Jan 50 obit Dec 71

Grace, Eugene Gifford Apr 41 obit Oct 60

Grace, J. Peter, Jr. Mar 60 obit Jun 95

Grace, Princess of Monaco Mar 55 Oct 77 obit Nov 82

Grade, Lew Aug 79 obit Mar 99

Grady, Henry F. Jul 47 obit Nov 57

Graebner, Clark Feb 70

Graebner, Walter Aug 43

Graf, Herbert May 42 obit May 73

Graf, Steffi Feb 89

Graffman, Gary Jul 70

Grafton, Samuel Jan-Feb 40 obit Feb 98

Grafton, Sue Sep 95

Graham, Billy Apr 51 Jan 73

Graham, Bob Jul 86

Graham, Clarence R. Nov 50

Graham, Donald E. May 98

Graham, Elinor (WLB) Yrbk 52

Graham, Elizabeth N. *see* Arden, Elizabeth

Graham, Evarts A. Feb 52 obit

May 57

Graham, Florence Nightingale *see* Arden, Elizabeth

Graham, Frank P. May 41 Jul 51 obit Apr 72

Graham, Franklin May 2002

Graham, Gwethalyn Jan 45 obit Jan 66

Graham, Harry Chrysostom Apr 50

Graham, Horace F. obit Jan 42

Graham, John Oct 62 obit Apr 91

Graham, Jorie May 97

Graham, Katharine Jan 71 obit Oct 2001

Graham, Martha Feb 44 Jun 61 obit May 91

Graham, Philip L. Feb 48 obit Oct 63

Graham, Robert *see* Graham, Bob

Graham, Sheilah Oct 69 obit Jan 89

Graham, Susan Oct 2005

Graham, Virginia Oct 56 obit Mar 99

Graham, Wallace H. Feb 47 obit Mar 96

Graham, William Franklin *see* Graham, Billy

Graham, Winston (WLB) Yrbk 55 obit Yrbk 2003

Gramm, Donald Nov 75 obit Jul 83

Gramm, Phil May 86

Grammer, Kelsey May 96

Granahan, Kathryn E. Oct 59 obit Sep 79

Granato, Cammi Apr 98

Granato, Catherine Michelle *see* Granato, Cammi

Grand, Sarah obit Jul 43

Grandi, Dino Jul 43 obit Jul 88

Grandin, Temple Jul 94

Grandjany, Marcel May 43 obit Apr 75

Grandma Moses *see* Moses,

Grandma

Granger, Lester B. Apr 46 obit Mar 76

Granger, Walter obit Oct 41

Granholm, Jennifer M. Oct 2003

Granik, Theodore Dec 52 obit Nov 70

Grant, Cary Sep 41 Nov 65 obit Jan 87

Grant, Elihu obit Dec 42

Grant, Ethel Watts Mumford *see* Mumford, Ethel Watts

Grant, Gordon Jun 53 obit Jul 62

Grant, Heber J. obit Jun 45

Grant, Hilda Kay *see* Hilliard, Jan

Grant, Hugh Sep 95

Grant, Lee Mar 74

Grant, Margaret *see* Franken, Rose

Grant, Robert obit Jul 40

Grantham, Alexander May 54

Grantley, John Richard Brinsley Norton, 5th Baron obit Sep 43

Granville, William Spencer Leveson-Gower, 4th Earl *see* Leveson-Gower, William Spencer

Grappelli, Stéphane Aug 88 obit Feb 98

Graser, Earle W. obit Jun 41

Grass, Günter Oct 64 Jul 83

Grasso, Ella May 75 obit Mar 81

Grasso, Richard Oct 2002

Grau San Martin, Ramón Oct 44 obit Oct 69

Grau, Shirley Ann (WLB) Yrbk 59

Grauer, Ben Feb 41 Jul 59 obit Jul 77

Grauer, Mrs. Ben *see* Kahane, Melanie

Gravel, Maurice Robert *see* Gravel, Mike

Gravel, Mike Jan 72

Graves, Alvin C. Dec 52 obit

Oct 65

Graves, Bibb obit May 42

Graves, Earl G. Aug 97

Graves, Florence George May 2005

Graves, Frederick Rogers obit Jul 40

Graves, Michael Jan 89

Graves, Morris Jul 56 obit Sep 2001

Graves, Nancy May 81 obit Jan 96

Graves, Robert May 78 obit Feb 86

Graves, William Sidney obit Mar 40

Gray, C. Boyden Aug 89

Gray, Carl R., Jr. Mar 48 obit Feb 56

Gray, Elizabeth Janet Sep 43

Gray, Frizzell *see* Mfume, Kweisi

Gray, George, Kruger- *see* Kruger-Gray, George

Gray, Georgia Neese Clark *see* Clark, Georgia Neese

Gray, Gordon Sep 49 obit Feb 83

Gray, Hanna Holborn Mar 79

Gray, Harold E. Feb 69

Gray, L. Patrick Sep 72 obit Yrbk 2005

Gray, Macy May 2000

Gray, Simon Jun 83

Gray, Spalding Sep 86 obit Yrbk 2004

Gray, William H., 3d Feb 88

Grayson, C. Jackson, Jr. Sep 72

Grayson, David *see* Baker, Ray Stannard

Graziani, Rodolfo Apr 41 obit Mar 55

Grebe, John J. Oct 55

Grechko, Andrei A. Nov 68 obit Jun 76

Greco, José Mar 52 obit Mar 2001

Gréco, Juliette Jan 92

Grede, William J. Feb 52 obit

Aug 89

Greeley, Andrew M. Dec 72

Greeley, Dana McLean Mar 64 obit Aug 86

Green Day Aug 2005

Green, Adolph Mar 45 obit Mar 2003 [Comden, Betty; and Green, Adolph]

Green, Al Feb 96

Green, Constance McLaughlin Oct 63

Green, Darrell Jan 2001

Green, David *see* Ben-Gurion, David

Green, Dwight H. Apr 48 obit Apr 58

Green, Edith May 56 obit Jun 87

Green, Florence Topping obit Jun 45

Green, Howard Jan 60

Green, Julian Jan-Feb 40 obit Oct 98

Green, Mark J. Feb 88

Green, Martyn Jun 50 obit Apr 75

Green, Mrs. Howard *see* Green, Florence Topping

Green, Theodore Francis Feb 50 obit Jun 66

Green, Tim Aug 2000

Green, Tom Oct 2003

Green, William Mar 42 obit Jan 53

Greenaway, Emerson Jul 58 obit Jun 90

Greenaway, Peter Feb 91

Greenbaum, Lucy *see* Freeman, Lucy

Greenberg, Hank *see* Greenberg, Maurice R. Jun 47 obit Oct 86

Greenberg, Jack M. Nov 2001

Greenberg, Maurice R. Nov 2000

Greenberg, Noah May 64 obit Feb 66

Greenbie, Sydney Sep 41 obit Sep 60

Greene, Balcomb Nov 65 obit

Jan 91

Greene, Bob Jul 95

Greene, Brian Aug 2000

Greene, Frank Russell obit Jan 40

Greene, Graham Oct 69 obit May 91

Greene, Harold H. Aug 85 obit May 2000

Greene, Hugh Sep 63 obit Apr 87

Greene, Lorne Jan 67 obit Oct 87

Greene, Nancy Mar 69

Greene, Wallace M. Jun 65 obit Aug 2003

Greenebaum, Leon C. Jan 62 obit May 68

Greenewalt, C. H. Jan 49

Greenfield, Abraham Lincoln obit Sep 41

Greenfield, Jerry Apr 94 [Cohen, Ben; and Greenfield, Jerry]

Greenough, Carroll obit Oct 41

Greenspan, Alan Dec 74 Jan 89

Greenstein, Jesse L. Sep 63 obit Yrbk 2003

Greenstreet, Sydney May 43 obit Mar 54

Greenway, Walter Burton obit Feb 41

Greenwood, Allen obit Dec 42

Greenwood, Arthur Oct 40 obit Sep 54

Greenwood, Colin *see* Radiohead

Greenwood, Joan May 54 obit Apr 87

Greenwood, Jonny *see* Radiohead

Greer, Germaine Nov 71 Oct 88

Gregg, Alan *see* Mallette,

obit Jun 86

Gross, Robert E. Jan 56 obit Nov 61

Grossberg, Yitzroch Loiza *see* Rivers, Larry

Grossinger, Jennie Oct 56 obit Jan 73

Grosvenor, Gilbert Dec 46 obit Mar 66

Grosvenor, Graham Bethune obit Dec 43

Grosvenor, Melville Bell Apr 60 obit Jun 82

Grosz, George Apr 42 obit Oct 59

Grosz, Karoly Sep 88 obit Mar 96

Grotewohl, Otto Jul 50 obit Nov 64

Groth, John Feb 43 obit Aug 88

Grotowski, Jerzy Dec 70 obit Mar 99

Grouès, Henri Antoine *see* Pierre, Abbé

Grove, Andrew S. Mar 98

Groves, Ernest R. Jun 43 [Groves, Ernest R; and Groves, Gladys Hoagland] obit Oct 46

Groves, Gladys Hoagland Jun 43 [Groves, Ernest R; and Groves, Gladys Hoagland] obit Sep 80

Groves, Leslie R. Aug 45 obit Oct 70

Gruber, Frank Nov 41 obit Feb 70

Gruber, Karl Feb 47

Gruber, L. Franklin obit Feb 42

Gruber, Ruth Jun 2001

Gruber, Samuel H. Aug 2004

Grubin, David Aug 2002

Gruen, Victor Mar 59 obit Apr 80

Gruenbaum, Victor David *see* Gruen, Victor

Gruenberg, Sidonie Matsner May 40 obit May 74

Gruening, Ernest Dec 46 Jul

66 obit Sep 74

Gruenther, Alfred M. Dec 50 obit Jul 83

Grumman, Leroy R. Aug 45 obit Jan 83

Gruppe, Charles Paul obit Nov 40

Grzimek, Bernhard Mar 73 obit May 87

Guardia, Ernesto De La, Jr. Jan 57

Guardia, Rafael Angel Calderon *see* Calderón Guardia, Rafael Ángel

Guardia, Ricardo Adolfo de la *see* De La Guardia, Ricardo Adolfo

Guare, John Aug 82

Gubaidulina, Sofia Oct 99

Gubelman, Minei Izrailevich *see* Yaroslavsky, Emelyan

Gubitosi, Michael James Vijencio *see* Blake, Robert

Guccione, Bob Aug 94

Guccione, Kathy Keeton *see* Keeton, Kathy

Gudjonsson, Halldor *see* Laxness, Halldór

Gudmundsdottir, Björk *see* Björk

Guedalla, Philip obit Feb 45

Gueden, Hilde Apr 55

Guerard, Albert J. (WLB) Yrbk 46 obit Mar 2001

Guerrero, José Gustavo Jan 47 obit Jan 59

Guertner, Franz obit Mar 41

Guest, Edgar A. Sep 41 obit Nov 59

Guevara, Che *see* Guevara, Ernesto

Guevara, Ernesto Jun 63 obit Dec 67

Guffey, Joseph F. Mar 44 obit May 59

Guggenheim, Florence *see* Guggenheim, Mrs. Daniel

Guggenheim, Harry F. Oct 56 obit Mar 71

Guggenheim, Mrs. Daniel obit Jul 44 [Guggenheim,

Florence]

Guggenheim, Mrs. Harry F. *see* Patterson, Alicia

Guggenheim, Peggy Oct 62 obit Feb 80

Guggenheimer, Minnie Oct 62 obit Jun 66

Guggenheimer, Mrs. Charles S. *see* Guggenheimer, Minnie

Guidry, Ron May 79

Guillaumat, Marie Louis Adolphe obit Jul 40

Guillaume, Augustin Jan 52

Guillaume, Robert Apr 2000

Guillermoprieto, Alma Sep 2004

Guinan, Matthew Sep 74 obit May 95

Guinazu, Enrique Ruiz *see* Ruiz Guiñazú, Enrique

Guinier, Lani Jan 2004

Guinness, Alec Oct 50 Mar 81 obit Oct 2000

Guinness, Arthur Jun 48

Guinness, Walter Edward obit Dec 44

Guinzburg, Harold K. Jul 57 obit Jan 62

Guion, Connie M. Feb 62

Guise, Jean Pierre Clement Marie, Duc De obit Oct 40

Guisewite, Cathy Feb 89

Guiterman, Arthur obit Mar 43

Gulick, Luther Halsey Jun 45 obit Mar 93

Gullander, W. P. Oct 63

Gullion, Allen W. Feb 43 obit Jul 46

Gumbel, Bryant Jul 86

Gumbel, Greg Sep 96

Gumm, Frances *see* Garland, Judy

Gumm, Harry *see* Von Tilzer, Harry

Gumpert, Martin Dec 51

Gundersen, Gunnar Feb 59 obit Aug 79

Gunn, Selskar Michael obit

Sep 44

Gunn, Thom Nov 88 obit Yrbk 2004

Gunter, Julius Caldeen obit Yrbk 40

Gunter, Ray Jul 67 obit Jun 77

Gunther, Franklin Mott obit Feb 42

Gunther, John Nov 41 Feb 61 obit Jul 70

Guptill, Arthur L. Mar 55 obit May 56

Gurney, A. R. Jul 86

Gurney, Chan Oct 50

Gursky, Andreas Jul 2001

Gustaf V, King of Sweden Sep 42 obit Dec 50

Gustaf VI, King of Sweden Dec 50 obit Nov 73

Gustafsson, Greta Lovisa see Garbo, Greta

Gustavus V, King of Sweden see Gustaf V, King of Sweden

Gustavus VI, King of Sweden see Gustaf VI, King of Sweden

Guston, Philip Feb 71 obit Jul 80

Guth, Alan H. Sep 87

Guthman, Edwin O. Jun 50

Guthrie, A. B., Jr. Jul 50 obit Jul 91

Guthrie, Charles Ellsworth obit Sep 40

Guthrie, Janet Oct 78

Guthrie, Tyrone Jul 54 obit Jul 71

Guthrie, William Buck obit Yrbk 40

Guthrie, Woody May 63 obit Dec 67

Gutt, Camille Apr 48

Guttmacher, Alan F. Oct 65 obit May 74

Guy, Buddy Feb 2000

Guy, Raymond F. May 50

Guyer, Ulysses Samuel obit Jul 43

Guzman, Jacobo Arbenz see

Arbenz Guzman, Jacobo

Guzy, Carol Feb 2000

Gwathmey, Charles Jan 88

Gwathmey, James T. obit Apr 44

Gwathmey, Robert Dec 43 obit Nov 88

Gwenn, Edmund Sep 43 obit Nov 59

Gwynn, Tony Oct 96

Gyalpo Wangchuk see Wangchuk, Jigme Dorji, Druk Gyalpo of Bhutan

Györgyi, Albert Szent- see Szent-Györgyi, Albert

Haack, Robert W. Mar 69 obit Aug 92

Haacke, Hans Jul 87

Haagen-Smit, A. J. Mar 66 obit May 77

Haakon VII, King of Norway May 40 obit Dec 57

Haas, Arthur E. obit Apr 41

Haas, Francis J. Aug 43 obit Oct 53

Haas, Jonathan Jun 2003

Habash, George Mar 88

Habe, Hans Feb 43 obit Nov 77

Haber, Heinz Dec 52

Habib, Philip Charles Sep 81 obit Jul 92

Habibie, Bacharuddin Jusuf Oct 98

Habré, Hissène Aug 87

Hacha, Emil Dec 42 obit Sep 45

Hacker

Hacker see Hackett, Buddy

Hackett, Albert Oct 56 [Goodrich, Frances; and Hackett, Albert] obit May 95

Hackett, Buddy May 65 obit Oct 2003

Hackett, Charles obit Feb 42

Hackett, Horatio B. obit Nov 41

Hackett, Walter obit Mar 44

Hackman, Gene Jul 72

Hackworth, Green H. Jan 58

obit Sep 73

Hadas, Moses Mar 60 obit Nov 66

Haddon, Alfred Cort obit May 40

Haddon, William, Jr. Feb 69 obit Apr 85

Hadfield, Robert Abbott obit Nov 40

Hadley, Jerry Nov 91

Hafstad, Lawrence R. Oct 56 obit Jan 94

Hagegard, Hakan May 85

Hagel, Chuck Aug 2004

Hagen, John P. Oct 57 obit Nov 90

Hagen, Uta May 44 obit Yrbk 2004 [Ferrer, José; and Hagen, Uta] Oct 63

Hagen, Victor Wolfgang von see Von Hagen, Victor Wolfgang

Hagerty, James C. Mar 53 obit Jun 81

Haggard, Merle Jan 77

Haggard, William David obit Mar 40

Hagman, Larry Sep 80

Hagy, Ruth Geri Oct 57

Hahn, Emily Jul 42 obit Apr 97

Hahn, Hilary Sep 2002

Hahn, Joseph see Linkin Park

Hahn, Otto Mar 51 obit Oct 68

Haig, Alexander Meigs, Jr. Jan 73 Sep 87

Haig-Brown, Roderick (WLB) Yrbk 50

Haile Selassie I Apr 41 Oct 54 obit Oct 75

Hailey, Arthur Feb 72 obit Yrbk 2005

Hailsham of St. Marylebone, Quintin Hogg Jul 54 obit Feb 2002

Hailsham, Quintin McGarel Hogg, 2d Viscount see Hogg, Quintin McGarel

Hainisch, Michael obit Mar 40

Hair, Jay D. Nov 93 obit Jan

2003

Haitink, Bernard Nov 77

Halaby, Najeeb E. Oct 61 obit Yrbk 2003

Halasz, Laszlo Jan 49 obit Feb 2002

Halberstam, David Apr 73

Haldane, John Burdon Sanderson Nov 40 obit Jan 65

Haldeman, Bob see Haldeman, H. R.

Haldeman, H. R. Sep 78 obit Jan 94

Hale, Arthur obit Mar 40

Hale, Clara Jul 85 obit Feb 93

Hale, Richard W. obit Apr 43

Haley, Alex Jan 77 obit Mar 92

Haley, Andrew G. Oct 55 obit Nov 66

Haley, William J. Apr 48 obit Oct 87

Halfin, Diane Simone Michelle see Von Fürstenberg, Diane

Halifax, Edward Frederick Lindley Wood, 1st Earl of Sep 40 obit Feb 60

Halim, Mustafa Ben Sep 56

Hall, Arsenio Sep 89

Hall, Conrad L. Aug 2000 obit May 2003

Hall, Deidre Nov 2002

Hall, Donald May 84

Hall, Edward T. Feb 92

Hall, Florence Aug 43

Hall, Floyd D. Jun 70

Hall, Frank O. obit Dec 41

Hall, Fred Oct 55 obit May 70

Hall, George A. obit Nov 41

Hall, George W. obit Dec 41

Hall, Gus May 73 obit Jan 2001

Hall, James obit Jul 40

Hall, Josef Washington see Close, Upton

Hall, Joyce Clyde May 53 obit Jan 83

Hall, Leonard W. Jul 53 obit

Jul 79

Hall, Marjory (WLB) Yrbk 57

Hall, Paul Feb 66 obit Aug 80

Hall, Peter Feb 62

Hall, Radclyffe obit Nov 43

Hall, Raymond S. Oct 53

Hall, Richard Melville see Moby

Hall, Steffie see Evanovich, Janet

Hall, Tex G. May 2005

Hall, William Edwin Jan 54 obit Mar 61

Hallaren, Mary A. Mar 49 obit Yrbk 2005

Halleck, Charles A. Mar 47 obit Apr 86

Halley, Rudolph Jun 53 obit Jan 57

Halligan, William J. Oct 57

Hallinan, Vincent Oct 52 obit Nov 92

Halloran, Roy D. obit Dec 43

Hallstein, Walter Oct 53 obit May 82

Hallström, Lasse Feb 2005

Halpert, Edith Gregor Jul 55 obit Nov 70

Halprin, Mrs. Samuel W. see Halprin, Rose Luria

Halprin, Rose Luria Jun 50

Halsey, Edwin A. obit Mar 45

Halsey, Margaret Nov 44 obit Apr 97

Halsey, William F., Jr. Dec 42 obit Nov 59

Halsman, Philippe Mar 60 obit Aug 79

Halston Dec 72 obit May 90

Hamblet, Julia E. Oct 53

Hambro, Carl Joachim May 40 obit Feb 65

Hamed, Prince Naseem Oct 98

Hamer, Dean H. Jun 97

Hamill, Dorothy Jun 76

Hamill, Pete Feb 98

Hamilton, Alice May 46 obit Nov 70

Hamilton, Charles Jul 76 obit

Feb 97

Hamilton, Clayton obit Oct 46

Hamilton, Clive see Lewis, C. S.

Hamilton, Cosmo obit Dec 42

Hamilton, Edith Apr 63

Hamilton, George Livingston obit Nov 40

Hamilton, Hale obit Jul 42

Hamilton, Laird Aug 2005

Hamilton, Lee H. Mar 88

Hamilton, Margaret Apr 79 obit Jul 85

Hamilton, Scott Apr 85

Hamilton, Tom see Aerosmith

Hamlin, Clarence Clark obit Yrbk 40

Hamlin, Talbot Oct 54 obit Dec 56 Yrbk 57

Hamlisch, Marvin May 76

Hamm, Mia Sep 99

Hamm, Morgan see Hamm, Paul and Morgan

Hamm, Paul and Morgan Nov 2004

Hamm, Paul see Hamm, Paul and Morgan

Hammarskjöld, Dag May 53 obit Nov 61

Hammer Apr 91

Hammer, Armand Jun 73 obit Feb 91

Hammerstein, Oscar Feb 44 obit Nov 60

Hammerstein-Equord, Kurt Von obit Jun 43

Hammon, Becky Jan 2003

Hammon, William McDowell Sep 57 obit Nov 89

Hammond, Aubrey Lindsay obit Apr 40

Hammond, Caleb D., Jr. Apr 56

Hammond, E. Cuyler Jun 57 obit Jan 87

Hammond, Godfrey Oct 53 obit Oct 69

Hammond, Graeme M. obit Dec 44

Hammond, John Hays, Jr. Jul

62 obit Apr 65

Hammond, John Jul 79 obit Aug 87

Hampden, Walter May 53 obit Sep 55

Hampshire, Susan Jan 74

Hampson, Thomas Mar 91

Hampton, Lionel Oct 71 obit Yrbk 2002

Han Suyin (WLB) Yrbk 57

Hancher, Virgil M. Feb 57 obit Mar 65

Hancock, Florence Nov 48

Hancock, Graham Feb 2005

Hancock, John M. Apr 49 obit Dec 56 Yrbk 57

Hancock, Joy B. Feb 49 obit Oct 86

Hand, Learned Apr 50 obit Nov 61

Handke, Peter Apr 73

Handler, Philip Feb 64 obit Feb 82

Handley, Harold W. Jul 60 obit Nov 72

Handlin, Oscar Jul 52

Handy, Thomas T. Sep 51 obit Jun 82

Handy, W. C. Mar 41 obit Jun 58

Haney, Fred Jan 67

Hanfmann, George M. A. Oct 67 obit May 86

Hanks, Nancy Sep 71 obit Mar 83

Hanks, Tom Apr 89

Hanley, James obit Apr 42

Hanna, Edward Joseph obit Aug 44

Hanna, William Jul 83 obit Sep 2001

Hannagan, Steve Aug 44 obit Mar 53

Hannah, Daryl May 90

Hannah, John A. Oct 52 obit Apr 91

Hannan, Philip M. Jul 68

Hannegan, Robert E. Jun 44 obit Nov 49

Hannikainen, Tauno Jul 55

obit Dec 68

Hannity, Sean Apr 2005

Hansberry, Lorraine Sep 59 obit Feb 65

Hanschman, Nancy see Dickerson, Nancy Hanschman

Hansell, Haywood S. Jan 45 obit Jan 89

Hansen, Alvin H. Sep 45 obit Aug 75

Hansen, Carl F. Oct 62

Hansen, Fred Dec 65

Hansen, H. C. Mar 56 obit Apr 60

Hansen, Harry Dec 42 obit Yrbk 91 (died Jan 77)

Hansen, James E. May 96

Hansen, Liane May 2003

Hansenne, Marcel Apr 46

Hanson, Duane Oct 83 obit Mar 96

Hanson, Howard Oct 41 Sep 66 obit Apr 81

Hanson, Ole obit Sep 40

Hansson, Per Albin Oct 42 obit Nov 46

Hanus, Paul H. obit Feb 42

Harada, Tasuku obit Mar 40

Harbach, Otto Jul 50 obit Mar 63

Harber, W. Elmer Mar 51

Harberger, John, John Pico see Mr. John

Harbison, John Feb 93

Harbord, James G. Mar 45 obit Sep 47

Harburg, E. Y. Jul 80 obit Apr 81

Harcourt, Nic Oct 2005

Hard, Darlene Jul 64

Hardaway, Tim Jul 98

Harden, Arthur obit Aug 40

Harden, Cecil M. Feb 49 obit Feb 85

Harden, Marcia Gay Sep 2001

Harden, Mrs. Frost Revere see Harden, Cecil M.

Hardenbrook, Donald J. Jul

62 obit Aug 76

Hardie, S. J. L. Jul 51

Hardin, Clifford M. May 69

Hardin, Garrett Sep 74 obit Apr 2004

Harding, Allan Francis see Harding, John

Harding, John Oct 52

Harding, Margaret S. Apr 47

Harding, Nelson obit Feb 45

Hardwick, Elizabeth Feb 81

Hardwicke, Cedric Oct 49 obit Oct 64

Hardy, Ashley Kingsley obit Sep 40

Hardy, Porter, Jr. May 57 obit Jun 95

Hare, David Aug 83

Hare, Raymond A. Jul 57 obit May 94

Harewood, George Henry Hubert Lascelles, 7th Earl of see Lascelles, George Henry Hubert

Hargis, Billy James Mar 72 obit Yrbk 2005

Hargrave, Thomas J. Apr 49 obit Apr 62

Hargrove, Marion Jun 46 obit Yrbk 2004

Hargrove, Roy Apr 2000

Häring, Bernard Jun 69 obit Sep 98

Haring, Keith Aug 86 obit Apr 90

Harington, Charles obit Yrbk 40

Harjo, Joy Aug 2001

Harkin, Tom Jan 92

Harkins, Paul D. Apr 64

Harkness, Douglas S. Oct 61

Harkness, Edward Stephen Jan 40

Harkness, Georgia Nov 60

Harkness, Rebekah Apr 74 obit Sep 82

Harlan, John Marshall May 55 obit Feb 72

Harlan, Otis obit Jan 40

Harlech, William David Ormsby Gore see Ormsby-

Gore, David

Harmon, Ernest N. Nov 46 obit Jan 80

Harmon, Millard F. Dec 42 obit Apr 45

Harmsworth, Esmond Cecil Dec 48 obit Sep 78

Harmsworth, Harold Sidney obit Jan 41

Harnoncourt, Nikolaus Jan 91

Harnoncourt, René d' *see* D'harnoncourt, René

Harnwell, Gaylord P. Jun 56

Haroutunian, Khoren Der *see* Der Harootian, Koren

Harp, Edward B. Jr. Oct 53

Harper, Alexander James obit Nov 40

Harper, Ben Jan 2004

Harper, Marion, Jr. Mar 61 obit Feb 90

Harper, Samuel Northrup obit Mar 43

Harper, Theodore Acland obit Jun 42

Harper, Valerie Feb 75

Harrar, J. George Jan 64 obit Jun 82

Harrell, Lynn Feb 83

Harrelson, Ken Apr 70

Harrelson, Walter May 59

Harrelson, Woody Jan 97

Harrer, Heinrich Oct 54

Harridge, Will Sep 49 obit Jun 71

Harriman, Averill *see* Harriman, W. Averell

Harriman, E. Roland Mar 51 obit Apr 78

Harriman, Florence Jaffray Hurst Mar 40 obit Nov 67

Harriman, Mrs. J. Borden *see* Harriman, Florence Jaffray Hurst

Harriman, W. Averell Apr 41 Nov 46 obit Sep 86

Harrington, David Nov 98

Harrington, Francis Clark obit Mar 40

Harrington, Michael Jan 69

Oct 88 obit Sep 89

Harrington, Russell C. Apr 56 obit Oct 71

Harris, Arthur Travers Sep 42 obit May 84

Harris, Barbara Apr 68

Harris, Barbara C. Jun 89

Harris, Bernice Kelly (WLB) Yrbk 49

Harris, Bucky Jun 48 obit Jan 78

Harris, Cyril M. Feb 77

Harris, E. Lynn Jun 96

Harris, Emmylou Oct 94

Harris, Eva Mar 2004

Harris, Franco Jun 76

Harris, Fred R. Jan 68

Harris, Harwell Hamilton Jan 62 obit Jan 91

Harris, James Rendel obit Apr 41

Harris, Judith Rich Apr 99

Harris, Julie Feb 56 Aug 77

Harris, Louis May 66

Harris, Mark (WLB) Yrbk 59

Harris, Mrs. Herbert Kavanaugh *see* Harris, Bernice Kelly

Harris, Mrs. Irving Drought *see* McCardell, Claire

Harris, Oren May 56

Harris, Patricia Roberts Dec 65 obit May 85

Harris, Richard May 64 obit Yrbk 2003

Harris, Rosemary Sep 67

Harris, Roy Aug 40 obit Nov 79

Harris, Sam H. obit Aug 41

Harris, Seymour E. Feb 65 obit Dec 74

Harris, Stanley Raymond *see* Harris, Bucky

Harris, Walter Jun 55

Harris, William, Jr. obit Oct 46

Harrison, Earl G. Aug 43 obit Oct 55

Harrison, George M. Jan 49 obit Jan 69

Harrison, George Nov 66 Jan

89 obit Mar 2002

Harrison, Gilbert A. Mar 49

Harrison, James L. Oct 62

Harrison, Jim Jul 92

Harrison, Joan May 44 obit Oct 94

Harrison, Marvin Aug 2001

Harrison, Pat obit Aug 41

Harrison, Rex Jan 47 Feb 86 obit Jul 90

Harrison, Shelby M. Jan 43

Harrison, Wallace K. Mar 47 obit Jan 82

Harrison, William B. Jr. Mar 2002

Harrison, William H. Feb 49 obit Jul 56

Harrison, William K. Jul 52 obit Aug 87

Harron, Marion J. Dec 49

Harron, Mary Sep 2000

Harry, Debbie Nov 81

Harsanyi, Zsolt obit Apr 44

Harsch, Joseph C. Oct 44 obit Aug 98

Hart, Albert Bushnell obit Aug 43

Hart, Basil Henry Liddell *see* Liddell Hart, Basil Henry

Hart, Edward J. Feb 53 obit Jun 61

Hart, Gary May 76

Hart, Kitty Carlisle Oct 82

Hart, Lorenz May 40 [Rodgers, Richard; and Hart, Lorenz] obit Feb 44

Hart, Merwin K. Oct 41 obit Jan 63

Hart, Mickey Jan 94

Hart, Moss Jul 40 Nov 60 obit Feb 62

Hart, Philip A. Sep 59 obit Feb 77

Hart, Thomas C. Jan 42 obit Sep 71

Hart, William S. obit Jul 46

Hartford, Huntington, 2d Jun 59

Hartigan, Grace Sep 62

Hartke, Vance Mar 60 obit

Yrbk 2003

Hartle, Russell P. Jun 42 obit Jan 62

Hartley, Fred A., Jr. Jun 47 obit Jun 69

Hartley, Hal Aug 95

Hartley, Marsden obit Oct 43

Hartman, David Jun 81

Hartman, Grace Nov 42 [Hartman, Paul; and Hartman, Grace] obit Oct 55

Hartman, Louis F. Jan 53 obit Nov 70

Hartman, Paul Nov 42 [Hartman, Paul; and Hartman, Grace] obit Dec 73

Hartmann, Heidi I. Apr 2003

Hartnell, Norman May 53 obit Aug 79

Hartnett, Robert C. Dec 49

Hartung, Hans Jul 58 obit Feb 90

Hartwell, John A. obit Jan 41

Hartwell, Lee see Hartwell, Leland H.

Hartwell, Leland H. Nov 99

Hartwig, Walter obit Mar 41

Harty, Hamilton obit Apr 41

Hartzog, George B., Jr. Jul 70

Harvard, Beverly Sep 97

Harvey, E. Newton May 52

Harvey, Laurence May 61 obit Jan 74

Harvey, Paul Mar 86

Hasek, Dominik May 98

Haseltine, William A. Nov 98

Hashimoto, Ryutaro Feb 98

Haskell, Molly Nov 98

Haskell, William N. Feb 47 obit Sep 52

Haskin, Frederic J. obit Jun 44

Haskins, Caryl P. Feb 58 obit Feb 2002

Haslett, Caroline Oct 50 obit Mar 57

Hasluck, Paul Oct 46

Hass, Hans Feb 55

Hass, Henry B. Apr 56 obit

Apr 87

Hass, Robert Feb 2001

Hassan II Sep 64 obit Oct 99

Hassan, Mahmoud Jul 47

Hassanal Bolkiah see Bolkiah, Muda Hassanal

Hassel, Kai-Uwe Von May 63

Hassenfeld, Alan G. Jul 2003

Hastert, Dennis Apr 99

Hastie, William H. Mar 44 obit Jun 76

Hatch, Carl A. Dec 44 obit Nov 63

Hatch, Orrin G. Aug 82

Hatcher, Harlan Oct 55 obit May 98

Hatcher, Richard G. Feb 72

Hatfield, Mark O. Nov 59 Mar 84

Hatoyama, Ichiro May 55 obit May 59

Hatta, Mohammad Dec 49 obit Yrbk 91 (died Mar 80)

Hauck, Louise Platt obit Feb 44

Hauerwas, Stanley Jun 2003

Hauge, Gabriel Oct 53 obit Sep 81

Haughey, Charles J. Feb 81

Haughton, Daniel J. Sep 74 obit Aug 87

Hauptmann, Gerhart obit Jul 46

Hauser, Conrad Augustine obit Apr 43

Hauser, Gayelord Jun 55 obit Feb 85

Hauser, Helmut Eugene Benjamin Gellert see Hauser, Gayelord

Hauser, Philip M. Jul 69 obit Feb 95

Haushofer, Karl Apr 42 obit Sep 46

Havel, Václav Mar 85 Aug 95

Havill, Edward (WLB) Yrbk 52

Hawass, Zahi Apr 2000

Hawes, Elizabeth Oct 40 obit

Yrbk 91 (died Sep 71)

Hawk, Tony Jun 2000

Hawke, Bob Aug 83

Hawke, Ethan May 98

Hawkes, Anna L. Rose Oct 56

Hawkes, Herbert E. obit Jun 43

Hawking, Stephen W. May 84

Hawkins, Augustus Freeman Feb 83

Hawkins, Edler G. Jan 65

Hawkins, Erick Jan 74 obit Feb 95

Hawkins, Erskine Sep 41 obit Jan 94

Hawkins, Harry C. Apr 52

Hawkins, Jack Nov 59 obit Oct 73

Hawkins, Paula Sep 85

Hawkinson, Tim Aug 2005

Hawks, Howard May 72 obit Mar 80 (died Dec 77)

Hawley, Cameron (WLB) Yrbk 57

Hawley, H. Dudley obit May 41

Hawley, Paul R. Apr 46 obit Jan 66

Hawley, Willis C. obit Sep 41

Hawn, Goldie Dec 71

Haworth, Leland J. Dec 50 obit May 79

Hax, Carolyn Nov 2002

Hay, Charles M. obit Mar 45

Hay, Mrs. Dudley C. see Hay, Regina Deem

Hay, Regina Deem Jul 48

Haya De La Torre, Víctor Raúl Jun 42 obit Sep 79

Hayakawa, S. I. Nov 59 Jan 77 obit Apr 92

Hayakawa, Sessue Sep 62 obit Jan 74

Hayashi, Senjuro obit Mar 43

Haycraft, Howard Nov 41 Feb 54 obit Jan 92

Haydée, Marcia Oct 77

Hayden, Carl T. Jul 51 obit Mar 72

Hayden, Melissa May 55

Hayden, Sterling May 78 obit

Jul 86

Hayden, Tom Apr 76

Hayek, Friedrich A. Von Jun 45 obit May 92

Hayes, A. J. Oct 53

Hayes, Alfred Feb 66 obit Feb 90

Hayes, Anna Hansen Nov 49

Hayes, Bob obit Sep 66 Jan 2003

Hayes, Carlton Joseph Huntley Jun 42 obit Nov 64

Hayes, David V. Apr 66

Hayes, Denis Oct 97

Hayes, Helen Jan 42 Oct 56 May 93

Hayes, Isaac Oct 72

Hayes, Mrs. John E. *see* Hayes, Anna Hansen

Hayes, Peter Lind Mar 59 obit Jul 98

Hayes, Robert M. Apr 89

Hayes, Roland May 42 obit Mar 77

Hayes, Samuel P. Sep 54 obit Sep 58

Hayes, Samuel P., Jr. Sep 54

Hayes, Wayne Woodrow *see* Hayes, Woody

Hayes, Woody Feb 75 obit May 87

Haynes, Cornell Jr. *see* Nelly

Haynes, George Edmund Mar 46 obit Apr 60

Haynes, Roy Asa obit Yrbk 40

Haynes, Todd Jul 2003

Hays, Arthur Garfield Sep 42 obit Feb 55

Hays, Brooks Jan 58 obit Jan 82

Hays, Wayne L. Nov 74 obit Apr 89

Hays, Will H. Jul 43 obit Apr 54

Hayter, Stanley William Dec 45 obit Jun 88

Hayward, Leland Feb 49 obit Apr 71

Hayward, Susan May 53 obit

May 75

Haywood, Allan S. May 52 obit Apr 53

Hayworth, Rita May 60 obit Jul 87

Hazard, Paul Mar 41

Hazeltine, Alan Mar 48 obit Jul 64

Hazen, Charles D. obit Nov 41

Hazzard, Shirley Jan 91

Head, Edith May 45 obit Jan 82

Head, Henry obit Yrbk 40

Head, Matthew *see* Canaday, John

Head, Walter W. Apr 45 obit Jun 54

Headley, Elizabeth Cavanna *see* Cavanna, Betty

Headley, Elizabeth *see* Cavanna, Betty

Heald, Henry Townley Feb 52 obit Jan 76

Healey, Denis Dec 71

Healy, Bernadine P. Nov 92

Healy, Timothy S. Jan 93 obit Jan 93

Heaney, Seamus Jan 82

Heard, Alexander Nov 66

Hearne, John J. Jul 50 obit May 69

Hearnes, Warren E. Jun 68

Hearns, Thomas Mar 83

Hearst, Patricia Aug 82

Hearst, William Randolph, Jr. Oct 55 obit Jul 93

Heath, Edward Oct 62 obit Yrbk 2005

Heath, James R. Oct 2003

Heath, S. Burton Jan-Feb 40 obit Sep 49

Heathcoat-Amory, Derick *see* Amory, Derick Heathcoat

Heatter, Gabriel Apr 41 obit May 72

Hebert, F. Edward Nov 51 obit Feb 80

Heche, Anne Sep 98

Hecht, Anthony May 86 obit

Yrbk 2005

Hecht, Ben Feb 42 obit Jun 64

Hecht, George J. Oct 47 obit Jun 80

Heckart, Eileen Jun 58 obit Mar 2002

Heckerling, Amy Jul 99

Heckler, Margaret M. Aug 83

Heckscher, August [financier] obit Jun 41

Heckscher, August [foundation executive] Oct 58 obit Jun 97

Hedden, Worth Tuttle (WLB) Yrbk 57 obit Jan 86

Hedin, Sven Anders May 40 obit Jan 53

Hedtoft, Hans Mar 49 obit Mar 55

Heeney, A. D. P. Jun 53

Hees, George Oct 59

Heffner, Richard D. Oct 64

Heflin, Van Jul 43 obit Sep 71

Hefner, Christie Oct 86

Hefner, Hugh Sep 68

Hegan, Alice Caldwell *see* Rice, Alice Caldwell Hegan

Heidegger, Martin Jun 72 obit Jul 76

Heiden, Eric Jun 80

Heiden, Konrad Mar 44 obit Sep 75 (died Jul 66)

Heidenstam, Rolf Von Oct 51 obit Oct 58

Heidenstam, Verner Von obit Jul 40

Heifetz, Jascha Feb 44 obit Feb 88

Height, Dorothy I. Sep 72

Heilbroner, Robert L. Jun 75 obit Yrbk 2005

Heilbrun, Carolyn G. Jan 93 obit Feb 2004

Heimlich, Henry J. Oct 86

Heineman, Ben W. Jan 62

Heinemann, Gustav Jun 69 obit Aug 76

Heinlein, Robert A. Mar 55 obit Jun 88

Heinrichs, April May 2000

Heintzleman, B. Frank Jun 53

obit Sep 65

Heinz, H. J. 2d Jun 47 obit Apr 87

Heinz, John Apr 81 obit May 91

Heisenberg, Werner Apr 57 obit Mar 76

Heiser, Victor G. Apr 42 obit May 72

Heiskell, Andrew Mar 66 obit Yrbk 2003

Heiss, Carol E. Oct 59

Hektoen, Ludvig Dec 47 obit Sep 51

Helburn, Theresa Sep 44 [Langner, Lawrence; and Helburn, Theresa] obit Nov 59

Held, Al Jan 86 obit Yrbk 2005

Helfgott, David Mar 97

Heliker, John Jan 69 obit Jul 2000

Hélion, Jean Nov 43 obit Jan 88

Heller, John R., Jr. Feb 49 obit Jul 89

Heller, Joseph Jan 73 obit Mar 2000

Heller, Walter Wolfgang Sep 61 obit Aug 87

Hellinger, Mark Sep 47 obit Jul 48

Hellman, Lillian May 41 Jun 60 obit Aug 84

Hellyer, Paul Sep 69

Helms, Jesse A. Jul 79

Helms, Richard Oct 67 obit Yrbk 2003

Helmsley, Harry B. Jun 85 obit Mar 97

Heloise Jun 96

Helpern, Milton May 73 obit Jun 77

Helpmann, Robert Feb 50 obit Nov 86

Helprin, Mark Aug 91

Helstein, Ralph Jun 48 obit May 85

Heming, Arthur Henry

Howard obit Yrbk 40

Hemingway, Margaux Mar 78 obit Sep 96

Hemingway, Mary Sep 68 obit Jan 87

Hench, Philip S. Dec 50 obit May 65

Henderson, Donald A. Mar 2002

Henderson, E. L. Jun 50 obit Oct 53

Henderson, Florence Apr 71

Henderson, Hazel Nov 2003

Henderson, Joe Jun 96 obit Oct 2001

Henderson, Lawrence J. obit Apr 42

Henderson, Leon Jul 40 obit Jan 87

Henderson, Loy W. Mar 48 obit May 86

Henderson, Nevile Apr 40 obit Feb 43

Henderson, Rickey Sep 90

Henderson, Skitch Jul 66

Hendl, Walter Jun 55

Hendricks, Barbara Mar 89

Hendrickson, Robert C. Nov 52 obit Feb 65

Hendrickson, Sue Oct 2001

Henie, Sonja Sep 40 Jan 52 obit Nov 70

Henkle, Henrietta see Buckmaster, Henrietta

Henley, Beth Feb 83

Henner, Marilu Feb 99

Henning, Doug Aug 76 obit Apr 2000

Hennings, Thomas C., Jr. Oct 54 obit Nov 60

Hennock, Frieda B. Nov 48 obit Sep 60

Henreid, Paul Jul 43 obit Jun 92

Henriot, Philippe obit Aug 44

Henry Garofalo, Janeane Mar 2005

Henry, Brad Jan 2005

Henry, David D. Jun 66 obit

Nov 95

Henry, E. William Feb 64

Henry, John W. May 2005

Henry, Jules obit Aug 41

Henry, Marguerite (WLB) Yrbk 47

Henry, Mellinger Edward obit Mar 46

Henry, Mrs. Sidney Crocker see Henry, Marguerite

Henry-Haye, Gaston Nov 40

Hensel, H. Struve Dec 48 obit Jul 91

Henson, Jim Mar 77 obit Jul 90

Hentoff, Nat Aug 86

Henze, Hans Werner Apr 66

Hepburn, Audrey Mar 54 Mar 93

Hepburn, Katharine May 42 Nov 69 obit Nov 2003

Hepburn, Mitchell F. Dec 41 obit Feb 53

Heppner, Ben Jan 97

Hepworth, Barbara Feb 57 obit Aug 75

Herbert, Bob Oct 98

Herbert, Don Feb 56

Herbert, Elizabeth Sweeney Feb 54

Herbert, Mrs. Leo J. see Herbert, Elizabeth Sweeney

Herblock see Block, Herbert

Herblock see Block, Herbert L.

Herbrand Arthur Russell obit Oct 40

Herbster, Ben M. Jul 62 obit Mar 85

Hering, Hermann S. obit Jul 40

Herlihy, James Leo Sep 61 obit Jan 94

Herlin, Emil obit Feb 43

Herman, Alexis M. Jan 98

Herman, Jerry Jan 65

Herman, Mildred see Hayden, Melissa

Herman, Pee Wee see Reubens, Paul

Herman, Woody Apr 73 obit

Jan 88

Hernández Colón, Rafael May 73

Hernández Martínez, Maximiliano Jun 42 obit Jun 66

Hernandez, Aileen C. Jul 71

Hernandez, Keith Feb 88

Hernández, Livan Mar 98

Hernandez, Orlando Apr 2000

Herod, William Rogers Mar 51 obit Sep 74

Herold, J. Christopher (WLB) Yrbk 59 obit Feb 65

Herrera Campíns, Luis Jul 80

Herrera, Carolina Mar 96

Herrera, Felipe Mar 68

Herrera, Omar Torrijos *see* Torrijos Herrera, Omar

Herrera, Paloma Apr 2000

Herrick, Elinore Morehouse Apr 47 obit Jan 65

Herrick, Francis Hobart obit Nov 40

Herring, Clyde L. obit Nov 45

Herring, Pendleton Jul 50 obit Yrbk 2004

Herriot, Edouard Feb 46 obit Jun 57

Hersey, John Feb 44 obit May 93

Hersh, Seymour Mar 84

Hershey, Alfred D. Jul 70 obit Aug 97

Hershey, Barbara Aug 89

Hershey, Lewis B. Jun 41 Jun 51 obit Jul 77

Hershey, Milton S. obit Nov 45

Hershiser, Orel Feb 90

Hersholt, Jean Dec 44 obit Sep 56

Herskovits, Melville J. Nov 48 obit Apr 63

Herskovitz, Marshall Sep 2000

Herter, Christian A. Dec 47

Mar 58 obit Feb 67

Hertz, Alfred obit Jun 42

Hertz, Emanuel obit Jul 40

Hertzberg, Arthur Jun 75

Hertzler, Arthur E. obit Oct 46

Hertzog, James Barry Munnik obit Jan 43

Herzberg, Gerhard Feb 73 obit Jul 99

Herzog, Chaim Apr 88 obit Jun 97

Herzog, Isaac Halevi Apr 59

Herzog, Jacques *see* Herzog, Jacques, and de Meuron, Pierre

Herzog, Jacques, and de Meuron, Pierre Jun 2002

Herzog, Maurice Jul 53

Herzog, Paul M. Jul 45 obit Jan 87

Herzog, Werner Aug 78

Hesburgh, Theodore M. Jan 55 Jul 82

Heschel, Abraham Joshua Apr 70 obit Mar 73

Heseltine, Michael Jun 85

Hess, Dean E. Sep 57

Hess, Elmer Jan 56 obit Jun 61

Hess, Max Oct 61 obit Nov 68

Hess, Myra Sep 43 obit Jan 66

Hess, Rudolf Mar 41 obit Oct 87

Hess, Victor Francis Oct 63 obit Feb 65

Hesse, Hermann Oct 62

Hesselgren, Kerstin Jan 41 obit Oct 62

Hester, James M. Jun 62

Heston, Charlton May 57 Jul 86

Hetfield, James Jan 2000

Heusen, Jimmy Van *see* Van Heusen, Jimmy

Heusinger, Adolf Feb 56

Heuss, Theodor Nov 49 obit Jan 64

Heuven Goedhart, G. J. Van Oct 52 obit Sep 56

Hevesy, George De Apr 59

obit Sep 66

Heward, Leslie H. obit Jun 43

Hewart, Gordon obit Jun 43

Hewitt, Don Jun 88

Hewitt, Henry K. Apr 43 obit Nov 72

Hewitt, Lleyton Oct 2002

Hewlett, J. Monroe obit Dec 41

Hewlett, Sylvia Ann Sep 2002

Heydrich, Reinhard Jul 42 obit Jul 42

Heydt, Herman A. obit Oct 41

Heyerdahl, Thor Dec 47 Sep 72 obit Yrbk 2002

Heym, Stefan Mar 43 obit Mar 2002

Heyman, Mrs. Marcus A. *see* Komarovsky, Mirra

Heymann, David L. Jul 2004

Heymann, Lida Gustava obit Sep 43

Heyns, Roger W. Dec 68 obit Nov 95

Heyrovsk, Jaroslav Jul 61 obit May 67

Heyward, Du Bose obit Jul 40

Hiaasen, Carl Apr 97

Hibbard, Edna obit Feb 43

Hibbard, Frederick P. obit Oct 43

Hibbard, Henry D. obit Dec 42

Hibbs, Ben Jul 46 obit May 75

Hickam, Homer H. Jr. Oct 2000

Hickel, Walter J. May 69

Hickenlooper, Bourke B. May 47 obit Oct 71

Hickerson, John D. May 50 obit Apr 89

Hickey, Margaret A. Dec 44 obit Feb 95

Hickey, Thomas F. obit Feb 41

Hickman, Emily Jun 45 obit Jul 47

Hickman, Herman Nov 51

Sloane, Eric

Hinrichs, Gustav obit May 42

Hinshaw, Carl Jul 51 obit Oct 56

Hinshelwood, Cyril Norman Apr 57 obit Dec 67

Hinsley, Arthur obit Apr 43

Hinton, Christopher Jun 57

Hirohito, Emperor of Japan Jan 42 Mar 76 obit Feb 89

Hirsch, I. Seth obit May 42

Hirsch, John Apr 84 obit Oct 89

Hirsch, Judd Mar 84

Hirschfeld, Al Jan 71 obit Jul 2003

Hirschfelder, Joseph Oakland Dec 50 obit May 90

Hirshfield, Morris Sep 43

Hirshhorn, Joseph H. Nov 66 obit Oct 81

Hirst, Hugo Hirst, 1st Baron Nov 41 obit Mar 43

Hirt, Al Feb 67 obit Jul 99

Hiss, Alger Feb 47 obit Jan 97

Hitch, Charles J. Nov 70 obit Nov 95

Hitchcock, Alfred Mar 41 Jul 60 obit Jun 80

Hitchcock, Charles B. Oct 54 obit May 69

Hitchcock, Thomas obit Jun 44

Hitchens, Christopher Mar 99

Hite, Shere Feb 88

Hitler, Adolf Mar 42 obit Jan 57 (died Apr 45)

Hitti, Philip K. Jun 47 obit Feb 79

Hitz, Ralph obit Jan 40

Ho Chi Minh Nov 49 Oct 66 obit Nov 69

Ho Ying-Chin Oct 42 obit Jan 88

Ho, David D. Jun 97

Hoad, Lew Sep 56 obit Sep 94

Hoagland, Edward Sep 82

Hoare, Samuel John Gurney Oct 40 obit Jul 59 [Templewood, Samuel John Gurney

Hoare, 1st Viscount]

Hobbs, Leonard S. Oct 54 obit Jan 78

Hobby, Mrs. William *see* Hobby, Oveta Culp

Hobby, Oveta Culp Jul 42 Feb 53 obit Oct 95

Hobson Pilot, Ann May 2003

Hobson, John Atkinson obit Apr 40

Hobson, Laura Keane Zametkin Sep 47 obit Apr 86

Hobson, Mellody Aug 2005

Hoch, Danny Oct 99

Hochhuth, Rolf Oct 76

Hockenberry, John Oct 96

Hocking, William Ernest Mar 62 obit Jul 66

Hockney, David Jul 72

Hodel, Donald P. Jun 87

Hodes, Henry I. Feb 59 obit Apr 62

Hodge, John R. Jun 45 obit Jan 64

Hodges, Courtney H. May 41 obit Feb 66

Hodges, Gil Oct 62 obit May 72

Hodges, Luther H. Jul 56 obit Nov 74

Hodgkin, Howard May 91

Hodgson, J. D. Nov 70

Hodgson, Joseph V. Jun 45

Hodgson, W. R. May 46 obit Apr 58

Hodson, William obit Mar 43

Hodza, Milan obit Aug 44

Hoegh, Leo A. Jul 56 obit Yrbk 2000

Hoellering, Franz Oct 40

Hoey, Clyde R. Oct 49 obit Jul 54

Hoey, Jane M. Sep 50

Hoff, Philip H. Sep 63

Hoffa, James P. Jul 99

Hoffa, Jimmy May 72 obit Mar 83

Hoffer, Eric Mar 65 obit Jul 83

Hoffman, Abbie Apr 81 obit

Jun 89

Hoffman, Alice Sep 92

Hoffman, Anna Rosenberg Jan 43 Jan 51 obit Jul 83

Hoffman, Clare E. Mar 49 obit Jan 68

Hoffman, Dustin Dec 69 Jan 96

Hoffman, Johannes Apr 50

Hoffman, Joseph G. May 58 obit Jan 75

Hoffman, Malvina Yrbk 40 obit Sep 66

Hoffman, Paul G. Feb 46 obit Nov 74

Hoffman, Philip Seymour May 2001

Hofmann, Hans Oct 58 obit Mar 66

Hofmann, Klaus H. Apr 61

Hofstadter, Richard Oct 56 obit Dec 70

Hofstadter, Robert Oct 62 obit Jan 91

Hogan, Ben Oct 48 obit Oct 97

Hogan, Frank S. Sep 53 obit May 74

Hogan, Hulk Nov 98

Hogan, Paul Aug 87

Hogben, Lancelot Dec 41 obit Jan 84

Hoge, James F., Jr. Apr 98

Hogg, Quintin McGarel Sep 57

Hogg, Quintin *see* Hailsham of St. Marylebone, Quintin Hogg

Hoggart, Richard Oct 63

Hogwood, Christopher Jul 85

Hohenlohe-Waldenburg, Stefanie Richter, Princess Jan-Feb 40

Hohenzollern, Friedrich Wilhelm Victor Albert obit Jul 41 [Wilhelm II]

Hoiby, Lee Mar 87

Holaday, William M. May 58

Holaday, William Perry obit Mar 46

Holberg, Mrs. Richard A. *see*

Holberg, Ruth Langland

Holberg, Ruth Langland (WLB) Yrbk 49

Holbrook, Hal May 61

Holbrook, Sabra Nov 48

Holbrooke, Richard C. Oct 98

Holcomb, Thomas Jul 42 obit Jul 65

Holden, Betsy Jul 2003

Holden, Louis Edward obit Jun 42

Holden, William Jun 54 obit Jan 82

Holder, Geoffrey Oct 57

Holenstein, Thomas May 58 obit Jan 63

Holifield, Chet Oct 55 obit Apr 95

Holl, Steven Jul 2004

Holladay, Billie *see* Holladay, Wilhelmina

Holladay, Wilhelmina Oct 87

Holland, Agnieszka Jan 98

Holland, Charles Thurstan obit Mar 41

Holland, Dave Mar 2003

Holland, Kenneth Mar 52 obit Feb 78

Holland, Sidney Jan 50 obit Nov 61

Holland, Spessard L. Feb 50 obit Dec 71

Hollander, Jacob Harry obit Sep 40

Hollander, John Sep 91

Hollenbeck, Don Feb 51 obit Sep 54

Holley, Edward G. Jun 74

Holley, Robert W. Jan 67 obit Apr 93

Holliday, Jennifer Jun 83

Holliday, Judy Apr 51 obit Jul 65

Holliger, Heinz Jan 87

Hollings, Ernest F. Jul 82

Hollister, John B. Oct 55

Hollomon, J. Herbert Mar 64 obit Aug 85

Holloway, James L., Jr. Jan 47

Holloway, Stanley Feb 63 obit

Mar 82

Holm, Celeste Apr 44

Holm, Hanya Jul 54 obit Jan 93

Holm, Ian Mar 2002

Holman, Eugene May 48 obit Oct 62

Holmes, Burton May 44 obit Oct 58

Holmes, D. Brainerd Mar 63

Holmes, Jesse Herman obit Jul 42

Holmes, John Haynes Jan 41 obit May 64

Holmes, Julius C. Feb 45 obit Sep 68

Holmes, Larry Aug 81

Holmes, Phillips obit Oct 42

Holmes, Robert D. Jul 58

Holmgren, Mike Oct 2000

Holroyd, Michael Mar 89

Holsti, Rudolf obit Sep 45

Holt, Andrew David Nov 49 obit Sep 87

Holt, Arthur E. obit Mar 42

Holt, Cooper T. Jul 57

Holt, Hamilton Dec 47 obit May 51

Holt, Harold E. Oct 66 obit Feb 68

Holt, Isabella (WLB) Yrbk 56 obit May 62

Holt, John Jun 81 obit Nov 85

Holt, Rackham Apr 44

Holton, Linwood Feb 71

Holtz, Jackson J. Mar 50

Holtz, Lou Jun 89

Holtzman, Elizabeth Nov 73

Holyfield, Evander Aug 93

Holyoake, Keith Jacka Feb 63 obit Feb 84

Holzer, Jenny Jun 90

Home, Alexander Frederick Douglas-Home, 14th Earl of *see* Douglas-Home, Alexander Frederick

Homer, Arthur B. Jul 52 obit Sep 72

Hondros, Chris Nov 2004

Honecker, Erich Apr 72 obit

Jul 94

Honegger, Arthur Apr 41 obit Feb 56

Honeywell, Annette Jul 53

Honeywell, Harry E. obit Jan 40

Hong, Hei-Kyung Nov 2003

Honjo, Shigeru, Baron obit Jan 46

Hoo, Victor Mar 47 obit Jul 72

Hood, Clifford F. Apr 53 obit Jan 79

Hook, Sidney Oct 52 Apr 88 obit Sep 89

Hooker, John Lee Nov 92 obit Sep 2001

Hooks, Bell Apr 95

Hooks, Benjamin L. Apr 78

Hooks, Robert Mar 70

Hooper, C. E. Apr 47 obit Feb 55

Hooper, Franklin Henry obit Oct 40

Hoopes, Darlington Sep 52 obit Nov 89

Hooton, Earnest Albert Yrbk 40 obit Jun 54

Hoover, Herbert Mar 43 obit Jan 65

Hoover, Herbert, Jr. Oct 54 obit Sep 69

Hoover, J. Edgar Feb 40 May 50 obit Jun 72

Hoover, Lou Henry *see* Hoover, Mrs. Herbert

Hoover, Mrs. Herbert obit Feb 44

Hope Namgyal, Maharani of Sikkim Feb 67

Hope, Bob Jun 41 Oct 53 obit Yrbk 2003

Hope, Clifford R. May 53 obit Jul 70

Hope, Leslie Townes *see* Hope, Bob

Hope, Stanley C. May 59 obit Oct 82

Hope, Victor Alexander John

Jan 42 obit Feb 52

Hopkins, Alfred obit Jul 41

Hopkins, Arthur Jun 47 obit Apr 50

Hopkins, Bernard Apr 2002

Hopkins, Ernest Martin Oct 44 obit Oct 64

Hopkins, Harry Lloyd Feb 41 obit Mar 46

Hopkins, John Jay Mar 54 obit Jul 57

Hopkins, Louis Bertram obit Sep 40

Hopkins, Nancy May 2002

Hopkins, Nevil Monroe obit May 45

Hoppe, Willie Jun 47 obit Apr 59

Hoppenot, Henri Etienne Mar 44

Hopper, Dennis Aug 87

Hopper, Edward Dec 50 obit Jul 67

Hopper, Hedda Nov 42 obit Mar 66

Hoppus, Mark *see* blink-182

Horder, Thomas J. Horder, 1st Baron Jul 44 obit Oct 55

Hore-Belisha, Leslie Horebelisha, 1st Baron Jul 41 obit May 57

Horgan, Paul Feb 71 obit May 95

Horgan, Stephen H. obit Oct 41

Horlick, William Jr. obit Apr 40

Hormel, James Oct 99

Hormel, Jay C. Jul 46 obit Oct 54

Horn, Carl Von Nov 67

Horn, Roy Uwe Ludwig *see* Roy

Hornblow, Arthur, Sr. obit Jun 42

Hornby, Leslie *see* Twiggy

Horne, Charles F. obit Nov 42

Horne, John E. Dec 52 obit

Apr 85

Horne, Lena Jun 44 Nov 85

Horne, Marilyn Jul 67

Horner, H. Mansfield Oct 55 obit Jul 83

Horner, Henry obit Nov 40

Horner, James Mar 97

Horner, John R. Sep 92

Horner, Matina Souretis Jul 73

Horney, Karen Aug 41 obit Jan 53

Hornig, Donald F. May 64

Hornsby, Rogers Sep 52 obit Feb 63

Hornung, Paul Feb 63

Horowitz, Vladimir Sep 43 Mar 66 obit Jan 90

Horrocks, Brian Jan 45 obit Mar 85

Horsbrugh, Baroness Florence Feb 52 obit Mar 70

Horsfall, Frank L., Jr. Mar 41 Jan 61 obit Apr 71

Horst Jun 92 obit Mar 2000

Horthy De Nagybánya, Nicholas Oct 40 obit Apr 57

Horthy, Stephen obit Oct 42

Horton, Edward Everett Dec 46 obit Nov 70

Horton, Mildred McAfee *see* McAfee, Mildred H.

Horwich, Frances Oct 53 obit Oct 2001

Horwich, Mrs. Harvey L. *see* Horwich, Frances

Horwood, William T. F. obit Feb 44

Hoshino, Naoki Nov 40

Hoskins, Bob Sep 90

Hoskins, Lewis M. Sep 50

Hosmer, Craig May 58 obit Mar 83

Hosokawa, Morihiro May 94

Hottel, Althea Kratz Oct 48

Hou Hsiao-hsien Jul 99

Hough, Henry Hughes obit Oct 43

Houghton, Alanson B. obit Nov 41

Houghton, Amory Jan 47 obit

Apr 81

Houghton, Mrs. Hiram Cole Sep 50

Houk, Ralph Jul 62

Houle, Cyril O. May 62

Hounsfield, Godfrey Mar 80 obit Yrbk 2004

Hounsou, Djimon Aug 2004

Houphouët-Boigny, Félix Oct 58 Jul 91 obit Feb 94

Hours-Miédan, Magdeleine Apr 61

Houseman, John Jul 59 Apr 84 obit Jan 89

Houser, Theodore V. Mar 57 obit Feb 64

Houssay, Bernardo Alberto Jan 48 obit Nov 71

Houston, Allan Nov 2003

Houston, Andrew Jackson obit Aug 41

Houston, Charles H. Jul 48 obit Jun 50

Houston, David Franklin obit Oct 40

Houston, James A. Jul 87 obit Yrbk 2005

Houston, Robert Griffith obit Mar 46

Houston, Whitney Nov 86

Houtte, Jean Van Mar 52

Hovde, Bryn J. Jan 46 obit Oct 54

Hovey, Otis Ellis obit Jun 41

Hoveyda, Amir Abbas Oct 71 obit Jun 79

Hovhaness, Alan Apr 65 obit Oct 2000 obit oct 2000

Hovick, Rose Louise *see* Lee, Gypsy Rose

Hoving, Jane Pickens Langley *see* Pickens, Jane

Hoving, Thomas Apr 67

Hoving, Walter Sep 46 obit Feb 90

Howar, Barbara Aug 89

Howard, Alice Sturtevant obit Nov 45

Howard, Bart B. Jan-Jun 40 obit Apr 41

Howard, Cordelia *see* Macdonald, Cordelia Howard

Howard, Elizabeth (WLB) Yrbk 51

Howard, Elston Apr 64 obit Feb 81

Howard, Frank Jan 72

Howard, John Mar 99

Howard, Katherine G. Jul 53

Howard, Leslie obit Jul 43

Howard, Mrs. Charles P. *see* Howard, Katherine G.

Howard, Mrs. Henry *see* Howard, Alice Sturtevant

Howard, Ron Jan 79 Aug 95

Howard, Roy Wilson Nov 40 obit Jan 65

Howard, Tim Sep 2005

Howard, Trevor Jul 64 obit Feb 88

Howe, C. D. Sep 45 obit Feb 61

Howe, Frederic Clemson obit Sep 40

Howe, Geoffrey Oct 80

Howe, Gordie Mar 62

Howe, Gordon *see* Howe, Gordie

Howe, Harold II Nov 67 obit Yrbk 2003

Howe, Harrison E. obit Feb 43

Howe, Helen (WLB) Yrbk 54 obit Mar 75

Howe, Irving Apr 78 obit Jul 93

Howe, James Wong Feb 43 obit Sep 76

Howe, Quincy Nov 40 obit Apr 77

Howe, Samuel B. obit Apr 41

Howe, Tina Jan 90

Howell, Charles R. Feb 54 obit Sep 73

Howell, Wallace E. Jul 50 obit Sep 99

Howell, William H. obit Mar 45

Howley, Christine Wetherill *see* Leser, Tina

Howorth, Lucy Somerville Oct 51 obit Nov 97

Howorth, Mrs. Joseph Marion

see Howorth, Lucy Somerville

Howrey, Edward F. Jul 53

Hoxha, Enver Jan 50 obit Jun 85

Hoxie, Charles A. obit Dec 41

Hoyer, Steny Mar 2004

Hoyle, Fred Apr 60 obit Jan 2002

Hoyt, Palmer Sep 43 obit Aug 79

Hrawi, Elias Feb 92

Hrdlicka, Ales Nov 41 obit Oct 43

Hrdy, Sarah Blaffer Jun 2000

Hruska, Roman Lee Jul 56 obit Jul 99

Hsiao-ping, Teng *see* Deng Xiaoping

Hsiung, S.-F Jul 42

Hsiung, Shih-hui *see* Hsiung, S.-F

Hu Shih Feb 42 obit Apr 62

Hu Yaobang Nov 83 obit Jun 89

Hua Guofeng Mar 77

Hua Kuo-feng *see* Hua Guofeng

Hubbard, Bernard Jul 43 obit Jul 62

Hubbard, Margaret Ann (WLB) Yrbk 58

Hubeny, Maximilian J. obit Sep 42

Huberman, Bronislaw Jul 41 obit Jul 47

Huck, Arthur Feb 57 obit Mar 73

Huckabee, Mike Nov 2005

Huckel, Oliver, Rev. obit Jan 40

Huddleston, Trevor Oct 63 obit Jul 98

Hudleston, Edmund C. May 51

Hudlin, Reginald May 99

Hudlin, Warrington May 99

Hudson, C. W. obit Jun 43

Hudson, Charles L. Apr 67 obit Nov 92

Hudson, Harold W. obit Mar

43

Hudson, Henrietta obit May 42

Hudson, Jeffery *see* Crichton, Michael

Hudson, Manley O. Jun 44 obit Jun 60

Hudson, Robert S. Nov 42 obit Apr 57

Hudson, Rock Oct 61 obit Nov 85

Huebner, Clarence R. Oct 49 obit Nov 72

Huebner, Robert J. Sep 68 obit Nov 98

Huerta, Dolores Nov 97

Huffington, Arianna Stassinopoulos Jul 98

Hufstedler, Shirley M. May 80

Huggins, Charles B. Feb 65 obit Mar 97

Huggins, Godfrey Nov 56 obit Jun 71

Hughes, Barnard Sep 81

Hughes, Cathy Feb 2000

Hughes, Charles Evans Jul 41 obit Oct 48

Hughes, Edward Everett obit Jan 40

Hughes, Edward James *see* Hughes, Ted

Hughes, Emmet John Jan 64 obit Nov 82

Hughes, Harold E. Jun 63 obit Jan 97

Hughes, Hatcher obit Nov 45

Hughes, Howard Apr 41 obit May 76

Hughes, John Sep 91

Hughes, Karen Oct 2001

Hughes, Langston Oct 40 obit Jul 67

Hughes, Martha Groomes *see* Hughes, Toni

Hughes, Paul Dec 43

Hughes, R. O. Oct 50

Hughes, Richard J. Jul 62 obit Feb 93

Hughes, Robert May 87

Hughes, Rowland R. Feb 56

obit Jun 57

Hughes, Sarah T. Nov 50 obit Jul 85

Hughes, Ted Jun 79 obit Jan 99

Hughes, Toni May 41

Hughley, D. L. Mar 2000

Hugo, Chad *see* Neptunes

Huizenga, H. Wayne Jan 95

Hulcy, Dechard A. Sep 51

Hull, Bobby Oct 66

Hull, Brett Feb 92

Hull, Cordell Aug 40 obit Oct 55

Hull, Helen R. May 40 obit Sep 71

Hull, Jane Dee Feb 2002

Hull, John Adley obit Jun 44

Hull, John E. Apr 54

Hull, Josephine Oct 53 obit May 57

Hull, William Edward obit Jul 42

Humbard, Rex Sep 72

Humbert II, King of Italy *see* Umberto II, King of Italy

Hume, Edgar Erskine Aug 44 obit Mar 52

Hume, T. C. obit Dec 43

Humphrey, Doris Apr 42 [Humphrey, Doris; and Weidman, Charles] obit Mar 59

Humphrey, George M. Feb 53 obit Mar 70

Humphrey, Helen F. Nov 52 obit Oct 63

Humphrey, Hubert H. Jul 49 Apr 66 obit Mar 78

Humphreys, Harry E., Jr. Nov 49 obit Nov 67

Humphry, Derek Mar 95

Hun Sen Apr 90

Hun, John Gale obit Nov 45

Hung-chun, Yu *see* Yui, O. K.

Hunsaker, Jerome C. Oct 42 obit Nov 84

Hunt Lieberson, Lorraine Jul

2004

Hunt, Bunker Aug 80

Hunt, H. L. Jan 70 obit Jan 75

Hunt, Helen Nov 96

Hunt, Herold C. May 56 obit Jan 77

Hunt, James B., Jr. Jun 93

Hunt, John Oct 54 [Hunt, John; Hillary, Edmund; and Tenzing Norkey] obit Jan 99

Hunt, Lester C. Mar 51 obit Sep 54

Hunt, Linda Jan 88

Hunt, Mabel Leigh (WLB) Yrbk 51

Hunter, Alberta May 79 obit Jan 85

Hunter, Catfish May 75 obit Nov 99

Hunter, Croil Jul 51 obit Oct 70

Hunter, Dard Sep 60 obit Mar 66

Hunter, Evan (WLB) Yrbk 56 obit Yrbk 2005

Hunter, Glenn obit Mar 46

Hunter, Holly Jul 94

Hunter, Jim *see* Hunter, Catfish

Hunter, Kermit May 59 obit Sep 2001

Hunter, Kim May 52 obit Yrbk 2002

Hunter, Ross Dec 67 obit May 96

Hunter-Gault, Charlayne Apr 87

Hunthausen, Raymond G. Aug 87

Huntington, Anna Hyatt Oct 53 obit Dec 73

Huntley, Chester Robert *see* Huntley, Chet

Huntley, Chet Oct 56 obit May 74

Huntly, Frances E. *see* Mayne, Ethel C.

Huntziger, Charles Dec 41

obit Dec 41

Huppert, Isabelle Nov 81

Hurd, Douglas Feb 90

Hurd, Peter Oct 57 obit Sep 84

Hurley, Charles F. obit May 46

Hurley, Laurel Jun 57

Hurley, Patrick J. Nov 44 obit Sep 63

Hurley, Roy T. Jun 55 obit Dec 71

Hurok, Sol Sep 41 Apr 56 obit Apr 74

Hurston, Zora Neale May 42 obit Apr 60

Hurt, John Jan 82

Hurt, William May 86

Hurtado, Cesar Barros *see* Barros Hurtado, César

Hurtado, Miguel de la Madrid *see* De La Madrid, Miguel

Husak, Gustav Oct 71 obit Jan 92

Husing, Edward Britt *see* Husing, Ted

Husing, Ted Jun 42 obit Oct 62

Hussein I, King of Hashemite Jordan *see* Hussein, King of Jordan

Hussein Ibn Talal *see* Hussein, King of Jordan

Hussein, Ahmed Mar 56 obit Feb 85

Hussein, King of Jordan Jul 55 Apr 86 obit Apr 99

Hussein, Saddam Sep 81

Hussein, Taha Oct 53 obit Dec 73

Husseini, Faisal al- *see* Al-Husseini, Faisal

Husted, Marjorie Child Jun 49 obit Feb 87

Huston, Anjelica Jul 90

Huston, John Feb 49 Mar 81 obit Oct 87

Huston, Walter Feb 49 obit May 50

Hutcheson, William L. Sep 43 obit Jan 54

Hutchins, Robert Maynard

Yrbk 40 Feb 54 obit Jul 77

Hutchinson, Paul Dec 49 obit Jun 56

Hutchinson, Ray Coryton Nov 40

Hutchison, Bruce Oct 56

Hutchison, Kay Bailey Sep 97

Hutchison, Miller Reese obit Apr 44

Hutton, Betty Jun 50

Hutton, Lauren Jul 94

Hutton, Maurice obit May 40

Hutton, Mrs. Lee W. Feb 48

Huxley, Julian Aug 42 Oct 63 obit Apr 75

Huxtable, Ada Louise Mar 73

Hwang, David Henry May 89

Hy Yao-pang *see* Hu Yaobang

Hyatt, Anna *see* Huntington, Anna Hyatt

Hyde, H. Van Zile May 60

Hyde, Henry J. Oct 89

Hyderabad, Usman Ali, Nizam of *see* Usman Ali, Nizam of Hyderabad

Hylton-Foster, Harry Jan 61 obit Nov 65

Hymans, Paul obit Apr 41

Hynde, Chrissie Apr 93

Hynek, J. Allen Dec 68 obit Jun 86

Hyvernat, Henry, Mgr. obit Jul 41

Iacocca, Lee A. Oct 71 Oct 88

Iakovos, Archbishop Jul 60 obit Yrbk 2005

Ibáñez, Carlos Dec 52 obit Jul 60

Ibarra, Jose Maria Velasco *see* Velasco Ibarra, José María

Ibárruri, Dolores Jun 67 obit Jan 90

Ibn Saud, King of Saudi Arabia Feb 43 obit Jan 54

Icahn, Carl C. Apr 86

Ice-T Sep 94

Ickes, Harold L. Jul 41 obit Mar 52

Idei, Nobuyuki Mar 97

Idell, Albert E. Oct 43 obit Oct 58

Idleman, Finis Schuyler, Rev. obit May 41

Idol, Billy Jan 94

Idris al-Sanussi, Emir Muhammed *see* Idris I, King of Libya

Idris I, King of Libya Jan 56 obit Jul 83

Idris Senussi I *see* Idris I, King of Libya

Ifill, Gwen Sep 2005

Igleheart, Austin S. Oct 50

Iglesias, Enrique Apr 99

Iglesias, Julio Jun 84

Iglesias, Roberto Feb 60

Iglesias, Santiago Jan 40

Igoe, Herbert A. obit Apr 45

Ikeda, Hayato May 61 obit Oct 65

Il Sung, Kim *see* Kim Il Sung

Ilg, Frances L. Sep 56 [Ilg, Frances L; and Ames, Louise] obit Sep 81

Iliescu, Ion Jun 90

Ilitch, Michael Feb 2005

Illia, Arturo Jan 65 obit Mar 83

Illich, Ivan Dec 69 obit Yrbk 2003

Ilsley, J. L. Feb 48

Iman Jun 95

Imlay, L. E. obit Aug 41

Immelt, Jeffrey R. Feb 2004

Impellitteri, Vincent R. Feb 51 obit Mar 87

Imus, Don Feb 96

Ince, Godfrey Sep 43

India.Arie Feb 2002

Indiana, Robert Mar 73

Indigo Girls Aug 98

Infeld, Leopold May 41 Jul 63 obit Mar 68

Ingalls, Jeremy (WLB) Yrbk 54 obit Jul 2000

Ingalls, Mildred Dodge Jeremy *see* Ingalls, Jeremy

Inge, William Jun 53 obit Jul 73

Ingersoll, Ralph Jul 40 obit May 85

Ingersoll, Raymond Vail obit Mar 40

Ingersoll, Royal E. Oct 42 obit Jul 76

Ingles, Harry C. Nov 47

Inglis, John J. obit Oct 46

Ingram, Jonas H. Apr 47 obit Oct 52

Inkster, Juli Sep 2002

Innaurato, Albert Mar 88

Innes, Hammond (WLB) Yrbk 54

Innis, Roy May 69

Innocenti, Ferdinando Feb 59 obit Jul 66

Inonu, Ismet Mar 41 Oct 64 obit Feb 74

Inouye, Daniel K. May 60 Sep 87

Inverchapel of Loch Eck, Archibald John Kerr Clark Kerr, 1st Baron *see* Kerr, Archibald Clark

Ionesco, Eugène Oct 59 obit Jun 94

Ireland, Patricia Jun 92

Irene Jun 46 obit Jan 63

Irons, Ernest E. Oct 49 obit Apr 59

Irons, Jeremy Aug 84

Ironside, Edmund May 40

Ironside, Henry Allan Feb 45 obit Feb 51

Ironside, William Edmund Ironside, 1st Baron obit Nov 59

Irvan, Ernie Jul 98

Irvine, Alexander Fitzgerald, Rev. obit May 41

Irving, Frederick A. Mar 51

Irving, John Oct 79

Irving, Jules Jul 70 obit Sep 79

Irwin, Bill Oct 87

Irwin, Elisabeth obit Dec 42

Irwin, Helen G. Oct 52

Irwin, Margaret (WLB) Yrbk 46 obit Yrbk 91 (died Dec 67)

Irwin, Robert B. Mar 48 obit

Jan 52

Irwin, Robert Jan 93

Irwin, Steve Aug 2000

Isaacs, George Oct 45

Isaacs, Susan Oct 93

Isaak, Chris May 93

Isbin, Sharon Aug 2003

Iselin, Columbus O'D Nov 48 obit Feb 71

Isham, Norman obit Feb 43

Isherwood, Christopher Oct 72 obit Feb 86

Ishibashi, Tanzan Mar 57 obit Jun 73

Ishiguro, Kazuo Sep 90

Ishimoto, Tatsuo Apr 56

Ismay, Hastings Lionel Apr 43 obit Feb 66

Isozaki, Arata Apr 88

Israel, Edward L., Rabbi obit Dec 41

Istomin, Eugene Oct 77 obit Feb 2004

Italiaander, Rolf Jun 64

Italiano, Annemarie see Bancroft, Anne

Itami, Juzo May 90 obit Mar 98

Ittner, Martin H. Nov 42 obit May 45

Iturbi, José Sep 43 obit Aug 80

Iverson, Kenneth R. Apr 51

Ives, Burl Jan 46 May 60 obit Jun 95

Ives, Charles Jun 47 obit Jul 54

Ives, Irving M. Feb 48 obit Apr 62

Ives, James E. obit Feb 43

Ivey, John E., Jr. Jul 60 obit Aug 92

Ivey, Judith Jun 93

Ivins, Michael see Flaming Lips

Ivins, Molly Jun 2000

Ivory, James Jul 81

Izac, Edouard V. M. Dec 45 obit Mar 90

Izetbegovic, Alija Aug 93 obit

Jun 2004

J. S. of Dale see Stimson, Frederic Jesup

Ja Rule Jul 2002

Jabbar, Kareem Abdul see Abdul-Jabbar, Kareem

Jabotinsky, Vladimir Evgenevich obit Sep 40

Jacinto, Domenich Felipe see Dali, Salvador

Jack, Homer A. Jul 61 obit Oct 93

Jack, William S. Mar 44

Jackman, Hugh Oct 2003

Jackson, Alan Apr 2004

Jackson, Anne Sep 80

Jackson, Bo Jun 91

Jackson, C. D. Oct 51 obit Nov 64

Jackson, Charles May 44 obit Nov 68

Jackson, Chevalier Jul 40

Jackson, Daniel Dana obit Oct 41

Jackson, Eugene B. Jun 61

Jackson, F. J. F. obit Jan 42

Jackson, Glenda Dec 71

Jackson, Hal Oct 2002

Jackson, Henry M. Oct 53 Oct 79 obit Oct 83

Jackson, Janet Jun 91

Jackson, Jesse Dec 70 Jan 86

Jackson, Jesse L., Jr. May 98

Jackson, Joe [comedian] obit Jul 42

Jackson, Joe [musician] Feb 96

Jackson, Lady see Ward, Barbara

Jackson, Lauren Jun 2003

Jackson, Mahalia Oct 57 obit Mar 72

Jackson, Maynard H. Jr. Sep 76 obit Yrbk 2003

Jackson, Michael [beer connoisseur] Aug 2005

Jackson, Michael [singer]

Nov 83

Jackson, Peter Jan 2002

Jackson, Phil Jul 92

Jackson, Reggie Jan 74

Jackson, Robert H. Mar 40 Oct 50 obit Dec 54

Jackson, Samuel L. Nov 96

Jackson, Shirley Ann Jul 99

Jackson, Thomas Penfield Jun 2001

Jackson, William H. Mar 51 obit Nov 71

Jackson, William K. Jul 46 obit Dec 47

Jacob, François Dec 66

Jacob, John E. Feb 86

Jacobi, Derek May 81

Jacobi, Victor obit Nov 42

Jacobs, Amos see Thomas, Danny

Jacobs, Jane Mar 77

Jacobs, Joe obit Jan 40

Jacobs, Marc Feb 98

Jacobs, Philip Peter obit Aug 40

Jacobs, Randall Aug 42 obit Oct 67

Jacobs, W. W. obit Oct 43

Jacobson, Leon Oct 62 obit Feb 93

Jacobsson, Per Oct 58 obit Jun 63

Jacopi, Giulio Jan 59

Jaden, Donna Mae see Paige, Janis

Jaffe, Harold W. Sep 92

Jaffe, Susan Sep 97

Jagan, Cheddi Apr 63 obit May 97

Jagendorf, Moritz Adolf (WLB) Yrbk 52

Jagger, Bianca Apr 87

Jagger, Janine Apr 2004

Jagger, Mick Dec 72

Jagr, Jaromir Apr 97

Jahn, Helmut Feb 89

Jaipur, Maharani of Mar 68

Jakes, John Sep 88

Jakes, T.D. Jun 2001

Jakobovits, Immanuel Jun 88

obit Feb 2000

Jamali, Mohd F. Jan 54 obit Aug 97

James, Alex *see* Blur

James, Alexander R. obit Apr 46

James, Arthur Curtiss obit Jul 41

James, Arthur Horace Jul 40 obit Jun 73

James, Bill Jun 2004

James, Charles Jul 56

James, Clive Nov 84

James, Daniel, Jr. Mar 76 obit Apr 78

James, Edgerrin Jan 2002

James, F. Cyril Oct 56

James, Harry Sep 43 obit Aug 83

James, LeBron Nov 2005

James, P. D. Aug 80

James, W. Frank obit Jan 46

James, Will obit Nov 42

Jameson, William J. Jul 54

Jamieson, J. K. Jun 74

Jamieson, Leland obit Sep 41

Jamison, Judith Jan 73

Jan 2002

Janas, Sigmund Apr 50

Janeway, Eliot Sep 70 obit Apr 93

Janeway, Elizabeth Mar 44 obit Yrbk 2005

Janis, Byron Jun 66

Janis, Sidney Jul 70 obit Jan 90

Janney, Russell Mar 47 obit Sep 63

Janov, Arthur May 80

Janowitz, Tama Aug 89

Jansen, Dan Sep 94

Jansen, William Oct 51 obit Apr 68

Janson, Paul Emile obit Aug 44

Janssen, Charles L. obit Mar 41

Janssen, David Mar 67 obit Apr 80

Janssens, Jean Baptiste *see*

Janssens, John Baptist

Janssens, John Baptist Sep 59 obit Dec 64

Jarman, Sanderford Sep 42 obit Dec 54 Yrbk 55

Jarmusch, Jim Apr 90

Jarreau, Al Oct 92

Jarrett, Keith May 85

Jarring, Gunnar Oct 57 obit Yrbk 2002

Jaruzelski, Wojciech Mar 82

Järvi, Neeme Nov 93

Jarvik, Robert K. Jul 85

Jarvis, Erich D. May 2003

Jarvis, Howard Feb 79 obit Sep 86

Jarvis, Lucy Apr 72

Jarvis, Robert Y. obit Dec 43

Jastrow, Joseph obit Feb 44

Jastrow, Robert Jan 73

Javacheff, Christo Vladmirov *see* Christo

Javits, Jacob K. Jun 48 Oct 58 obit Apr 86

Jaworski, Leon Jun 74 obit Feb 83

Jay, Peter Oct 78

Jay, Ricky May 94

Jayewardene, J. R. Jan 84 obit Jan 97

Jayewardene, Junius Richard *see* Jayewardene, J. R.

Jaynes, Clare (WLB) Yrbk 54

Jay-Z Aug 2002

Jazy, Michel Apr 67

Jeanmaire, Renée Nov 52

Jeanneret-Gris, Charles-Edouard *see* Le Corbusier

Jeans, James Hopwood Apr 41 obit Oct 46

Jebb, Gladwyn Dec 48

Jeffers, Eve Jihan *see* Eve

Jeffers, William M. Nov 42 obit Apr 53

Jefferson, Margo L. Jun 99

Jeffords, James Sep 2001

Jelliffe, Smith Ely obit Oct 45

Jellinek, Elvin M. May 47 obit

Jan 64

Jemison, Mae C. Jul 93

Jencks, Christopher Apr 73

Jenkins, Hayes Alan May 56

Jenkins, Jerry B. *see* LaHaye, Tim and Jenkins, Jerry B.

Jenkins, Lew Jan 41 obit Yrbk 91 (died Oct 81)

Jenkins, Macgregor obit Apr 40

Jenkins, Ray H. Jun 54 obit Feb 81

Jenkins, Roy Mar 66 Oct 82 obit Yrbk 2003

Jenkins, Sara (WLB) Yrbk 53

Jenks, Leon E. obit Mar 40

Jenner, Bruce Aug 77

Jenner, William E. Jun 51 obit May 85

Jennings, B. Brewster May 51 obit Dec 68

Jennings, John (WLB) Yrbk 49

Jennings, Paul Dec 69 obit Oct 87

Jennings, Peter Nov 83 obit Sep 2005

Jennings, Waylon Apr 82 obit Apr 2002

Jensen, Arthur R. Jan 73

Jensen, Ben F. Feb 60 obit Apr 70

Jensen, Jack Eugene *see* Jensen, Jackie

Jensen, Jackie Jun 59 obit Oct 82

Jensen, Mrs. Clyde R. *see* Bard, Mary

Jensen, Mrs. Oliver *see* Stafford, Jean

Jensen, Oliver O. May 45 obit Yrbk 2005

Jernegan, John D. Nov 59

Jerusalem, Siegfried Sep 92

Jessel, George Mar 43 obit Jul 81

Jessup, Philip C. Apr 48 obit Mar 86

Jester, Beauford H. Jul 48 obit

Sep 49

Jet *see* Urquidez, Benny

Jett, Joan Sep 93

Jewett, Frank B. Dec 46 obit Jan 50

Jewett, James R. obit May 43

Jewison, Norman Jun 79

Jhabvala, Ruth Prawer Mar 77

Jiang Qing *see* Chiang Ching-Kuo Jun 75 obit Jan 92

Jiang Zemin May 95

Jillette, Penn Jun 2000 [Penn and Teller]

Jiménez, Juan Ramón Feb 57 obit Sep 58

Jimenez, Marcos Perez *see* Pérez Jiménez, Marcos

Jimenez, Marcos Perez *see* Pérez Jiménez, Marcos

Jimerson, Earl W. Sep 48 obit Dec 57 Yrbk 58

Jin, Deborah Apr 2004

Jingsheng, Wei *see* Wei Jingsheng

Jinnah, Mohammed Ali May 42 obit Oct 48

Jobert, Michel Feb 75 obit Yrbk 2002

Jobim, Antonio Carlos Jul 91 obit Feb 95

Jobs, Steven Mar 83 Sep 98

Jodl, Alfred obit Nov 46

Jodoin, Claude Mar 56

Joel, Billy Sep 79

Joesten, Joachim Jun 42

Joffrey, Robert Nov 67 obit Nov 88

Johannesen, Grant Jun 61 obit Yrbk 2005

Johanson, Donald C. Feb 84

Johansson, Ingemar Nov 59

Johansson, Scarlett Mar 2005

John Paul I, Pope Nov 78 obit Jan 79

John Paul II, Pope Nov 79 Mar 2000 obit Jun 2005

John XXIII, Pope Feb 59 obit Jul 63

John, Augustus Oct 41 obit

Jan 62

John, Elton Mar 75

John, Tommy Oct 81

Johns, Glynis Sep 73

Johns, Jasper May 67 May 87

Johnson, Alexander obit Jul 41

Johnson, Alvin Aug 42 obit Jul 71

Johnson, Amy obit Feb 41

Johnson, Arnold M. Oct 55 obit May 60

Johnson, Arthur Newhall obit Sep 40

Johnson, Ben Jun 88

Johnson, Bernice *see* Reagon, Bernice Johnson

Johnson, Betsey Jan 94

Johnson, Beverly Sep 94

Johnson, Brian *see* AC/DC

Johnson, C. Oscar Feb 48 obit Jan 66

Johnson, Charles Sep 91

Johnson, Charles Spurgeon Nov 46 obit Jan 57

Johnson, Clarence L. Oct 68 obit Mar 91

Johnson, Claudia Alta Oct 64

Johnson, Clifton obit Jan 40

Johnson, Crockett Dec 43 obit Jan 84

Johnson, Daniel Nov 67 obit Nov 68

Johnson, Davey Sep 99

Johnson, David M. Jul 52

Johnson, Don Apr 86

Johnson, Douglas Wilson obit Apr 44

Johnson, Dwayne "The Rock" Jul 2000

Johnson, Earvin Jan 82

Johnson, Ed Dec 46 obit Jul 70

Johnson, Eddie Bernice Jul 2001

Johnson, Edward Mar 43 obit Jun 59

Johnson, Elizabeth A. Nov 2002

Johnson, F. Ross May 89

Johnson, Frank M. Aug 78

obit Oct 99

Johnson, Hall Jan 45 obit Jun 70

Johnson, Harold K. May 66 obit Nov 83

Johnson, Harold Ogden Sep 40 [Olsen, John Sigvard; and Johnson, Harold Ogden] obit Apr 62

Johnson, Herschel V. Jul 46

Johnson, Hewlett May 43 obit Dec 66

Johnson, Hiram Feb 41 obit Sep 45

Johnson, Holgar J. Mar 50

Johnson, Howard A. Apr 64 obit Sep 74

Johnson, Howard B. Sep 66

Johnson, Howard E. obit Jun 41

Johnson, Hugh S. Sep 40 obit Jun 42

Johnson, J. Monroe Feb 45 obit Sep 64

Johnson, Jack obit Jul 46

Johnson, Jimmy Jul 94

Johnson, John H. Oct 68 obit Yrbk 2005

Johnson, Joseph B. Jul 56

Johnson, Joseph E. Nov 50 obit Jan 91

Johnson, Joseph T. Feb 52

Johnson, Kathie Lee *see* Gifford, Kathie Lee

Johnson, Keyshawn Oct 99

Johnson, Lady Bird *see* Johnson, Claudia Alta

Johnson, Leroy Sep 49 obit Jun 61

Johnson, Loren obit Feb 42

Johnson, Louis A. Jun 42 Apr 49 obit May 66

Johnson, Lyndon B. Jan 51 Mar 64 obit Mar 73

Johnson, Magic *see* Johnson, Earvin

Johnson, Malcolm Jun 49 obit Aug 76

Johnson, Marguerite Annie

see Angelou, Maya

Johnson, Michael Jul 96

Johnson, Mordecai Wyatt Apr 41

Johnson, Nelson T. Jan-Feb 40 obit Feb 55

Johnson, Nicholas Mar 68

Johnson, Nunnally Aug 41 obit May 77

Johnson, Osa Apr 40 obit Feb 53

Johnson, Pamela Hansford (WLB) Yrbk 48 obit Aug 81

Johnson, Paul B. obit Feb 44

Johnson, Paul Sep 94

Johnson, Philip G. obit Nov 44

Johnson, Philip Oct 57 Nov 91 obit Sep 2005

Johnson, Rafer Jun 61

Johnson, Randy Sep 2000

Johnson, Robert L. [publisher] Mar 48 obit Feb 66

Johnson, Robert L. [television executive] Apr 94

Johnson, Robert Wood Nov 43 obit Mar 68

Johnson, Roy W. May 58 obit Oct 65

Johnson, Sonia Feb 85

Johnson, Thomasina Walker Mar 47

Johnson, Thor Oct 49 obit Mar 75

Johnson, U. Alexis Oct 55 obit Jun 97

Johnson, Van Jul 45

Johnson, Virginia E. Apr 76

Johnson, Virginia May 85

Johnson, Walter Apr 57 obit Sep 85

Johnson, Wendell Apr 59 obit Nov 65

Johnson, William E. obit Mar 45

Johnston, Alvanley Jun 46 obit Nov 51

Johnston, Clem D. May 55 obit Jan 80

Johnston, Eric A. Apr 43 Oct

55 obit Oct 63

Johnston, Lynn Feb 98

Johnston, Olin D. Nov 51 obit Jun 65

Johnston, Victor Jul 49 obit May 67

Johnston, Wayne A. May 51 obit Feb 68

Johnstone, Margaret Blair, Rev. Jan 55

Johnstone-Wilson, Angus Frank see Wilson, Angus

Jolie, Angelina Oct 2000

Joliot-Curie, Frederic Oct 46 obit Oct 58

Joliot-Curie, Irène Apr 40 obit May 56

Jolson, Al Nov 40 obit Dec 50

Jónasson, Hermann Aug 41

Jones, Arthur Creech Jan 48 obit Jan 65

Jones, Barry Mar 58

Jones, Bill T. Jul 93

Jones, Billy obit Jan 41

Jones, Bobby Jun 2002

Jones, Buck obit Jan 43

Jones, Candy Oct 61 obit Mar 90

Jones, Carolyn Mar 67 obit Sep 83

Jones, Cherry May 98

Jones, Chester Lloyd obit Mar 41

Jones, Chipper May 2001

Jones, Chuck May 96 obit May 2002

Jones, Clara Stanton Jul 76

Jones, David C. Jul 82

Jones, David Robert see Bowie, David

Jones, E. Stanley May 40 obit Mar 73

Jones, Edward P. Mar 2004

Jones, Elaine Jun 2004

Jones, George Feb 95

Jones, Grace Sep 87

Jones, Grover obit Nov 40

Jones, Harold Spencer Mar 55 obit Jan 61

Jones, Howard P. Jul 63 obit

Nov 73

Jones, Idwal (WLB) Yrbk 48 obit Jan 65

Jones, Jack see Jones, John Joseph May 76

Jones, James Earl Sep 69 Nov 94

Jones, James Larkin see Jones, Jack

Jones, James R. Oct 81

Jones, Jennifer May 44

Jones, Jerry May 96

Jones, Jesse H. Oct 40 obit Sep 56

Jones, Joe Oct 40 obit Jun 63

Jones, John Daniel obit Jun 42

Jones, John Joseph Nov 40 obit Jan 42

Jones, K. C. Feb 87

Jones, Kimberly Denise see Lil' Kim

Jones, Larry Wayne Jr. see Jones, Chipper

Jones, Leroi May 70

Jones, Lewis Webster Oct 58

Jones, Marion Oct 98

Jones, Marvin Aug 43 obit Jan 84

Jones, Norah May 2003

Jones, Norman L. obit Jan 41

Jones, Preston Feb 77 obit Nov 79

Jones, Quincy Feb 77

Jones, Rickie Lee May 90

Jones, Robert Edmond Nov 46 obit Jan 55

Jones, Roger W. Nov 59 obit Aug 93

Jones, Roy Jr. Feb 99

Jones, Rufus Matthew Oct 41 obit Sep 48

Jones, Russell Oct 57 obit Aug 79

Jones, Sam Houston Mar 40 obit Yrbk 91 (died Feb 78)

Jones, Sarah Jul 2005

Jones, Shirley Oct 61

Jones, Tom Apr 70

Jones, Tommy Lee Oct 95

Jong, Erica Jul 75 Apr 97

Jonsson, John Erik Jan 61 obit

Nov 95

Jonze, Spike Apr 2003

Jooss, Kurt Jul 76 obit Jul 79

Jooste, G. P. Apr 51

Joplin, Janis Mar 70 obit Mar 70

Jordan, B. Everett Nov 59 obit May 74

Jordan, Barbara C. Sep 74 Apr 93 obit Apr 96

Jordan, Frank C. obit Apr 41

Jordan, Hamilton Aug 77

Jordan, I. King Jan 91

Jordan, James Edward see Jordan, Jim

Jordan, Jim Nov 41 obit May 88

Jordan, Marian Nov 41 obit Jun 61

Jordan, Michael H. Feb 98

Jordan, Michael Sep 87 Feb 97

Jordan, Mildred (WLB) Yrbk 51

Jordan, Neil Aug 93

Jordan, Sara M. Mar 54 obit Jan 60

Jordan, Vernon E., Jr. Feb 72 Aug 93

Jordan, Virgil Oct 47 obit Jun 65

Jordan, W. K. Mar 55 obit Jul 80

Jordana, Francisco Gomez Mar 44

Jorgensen, Anker Sep 78

Joseph, Keith Feb 75 obit Feb 95

Joseph, Mrs. Robert H. see de Jong, Dola

Joseph, Sister Mary Dec 42

Joseph, Stephen C. Jan 89

Josephs, Devereux C. Jul 53 obit Mar 77

Josephson, Walter S. obit Mar 40

Jospin, Lionel Robert Jun 2000

Jouhaux, Léon Jan 48 obit Jul

54

Jourdan, Louis Jan 67

Jouvet, Louis Oct 49 obit Oct 51

Jowitt, William Allen Jowitt, 1st Earl Aug 41 obit Nov 57

Joxe, Louis Apr 61 obit Jun 91

Joy, C. Turner Jun 51 obit Sep 56

Joyce, J. Avery Mar 59

Joyce, James obit Mar 41

Joyner, Florence Griffith see Griffith Joyner, Florence

Joyner, Tom Sep 2002

Joyner-Kersee, Jackie Jul 87

Juan Carlos I, King of Spain see Carlos, Prince Juan

Juan Carlos, Count of Barcelona see Carlos, Juan

Juan Carlos, Prince of Spain see Carlos, Prince Juan

Judd, Ashley Feb 2000

Judd, Charles Hubbard obit Sep 46

Judd, Jackie Sep 2002

Judd, Jacqueline Dee see Judd, Jackie

Judd, Nadine see Nerina, Nadia

Judd, Walter H. Sep 49 obit Apr 94

Judd, Wynonna see Wynonna

Judds see Wynonna

Judge, Mike May 97

Judson, Arthur Aug 45 obit Mar 75

Judson, Clara Ingram (WLB) Yrbk 48

Judson, Mrs. James McIntosh see Judson, Clara Ingram

Judson, Olivia Jan 2004

Juin, Alphonse Aug 43 obit Mar 67

Jules-Bois, H. A. obit Aug 43

Julia y Araelay, Raul Rafael Carlos see Julia, Raul

Julia, Raul Sep 82 obit Jan 95

Julian, Percy Lavon Sep 47 obit Jan 75

Juliana Queen of the Netherlands Sep 44 Jan 55 obit

Yrbk 2004

Jumblatt, Kamal Jan 77 obit Jan 77

Jung, Andrea May 2000

Jung, Carl Gustav Apr 43 Oct 53 obit Sep 61

Jurgensen, Sonny Jun 77

Just, Ward May 89

Justo, Agustin P. obit Mar 43

Kabakov, Ilya Apr 98

Kabila, Joseph Sep 2001

Kádár, János May 57 obit Aug 89

Kadare, Ismail Feb 92

Kael, Pauline Mar 74 obit Nov 2001

Kaempffert, Waldemar B. Sep 43 obit Feb 57

Kagan, Henry Enoch Sep 65 obit Oct 69

Kaganovich, Lazar M. Apr 42 Oct 55 obit Sep 91

Kagawa, Toyohiko Sep 41 obit Jun 60

Kagey, Rudolf obit Jun 46

Kahal, Irving obit Apr 42

Kahane, Meir Oct 72 obit Jan 91

Kahane, Melanie Jul 59 obit Feb 89

Kahmann, Chesley (WLB) Yrbk 52

Kahn, Albert obit Sep 42

Kahn, Alfred E. Mar 79

Kahn, Ely Jacques Aug 45 obit Nov 72

Kahn, Gus obit Dec 41

Kahn, Herman Oct 62 obit Aug 83

Kahn, Louis I. Oct 64 obit May 74

Kahn, Madeline May 77 obit Mar 2000

Kahn, Roger Jun 2000

Kaifu, Toshiki Jun 90

Kain, Karen May 80

Kainen, Jacob Feb 87 obit Aug 2001

Kaiser Wilhelm II see Hohenzollern, Friedrich Wilhelm

Victor Albert

Kaiser, Edgar F. Sep 64 obit Feb 82

Kaiser, Henry J. Oct 42 Mar 61 obit Nov 67

Kaiser, Jakob Feb 56 obit Jul 61

Kaiser, John B. May 43

Kaiser, Philip M. Oct 49

Kai-shek, Chiang *see* Chiang Kai-Shek

Kalb, Marvin Jul 87

Kalich, Mrs. Jacob *see* Picon, Molly

Kalikow, Peter S. Sep 88

Kaline, Al Dec 70

Kalinin, Mikhail Ivanovich Jun 42 obit Jul 46

Kallay de Nagy Kallo, Miklos *see* Kallay, Nicholas De

Kallay, Nicholas De Jun 42 obit May 67

Kallen, Horace M. Oct 53 obit Apr 74

Kallio, Kyosti obit Feb 41

Kalmus, Herbert T. Feb 49 obit Sep 63

Kaltenborn, Hans Von Aug 40 obit Sep 65

Kaltenbrunner, Ernst Apr 43 obit Nov 46

Kamali, Norma Nov 98

Kamau, Johnstone *see* Kenyatta, Jomo

Kamen, Dean Nov 2002

Kaminska, Ida Nov 69 obit Jul 80

Kaminski, Janusz Mar 2000

Kaminsky, Mel *see* Brooks, Mel

Kampelman, Max M. Jul 86

Kampmann, Viggo Jan 61 obit Jul 76

Kamprad, Ingvar Jun 98

Kanawa, Kiri Te *see* Te Kanawa, Kiri

Kander, Lizzie Black obit Sep 40

Kandinsky, Wassily obit Feb 45

Kane, Harnett T. (WLB) Yrbk 47 obit Yrbk 84

Kane, Joseph Nathan Nov 85 obit Nov 2002

Kani, John Jun 2001

Kania, Stanislaw Jun 81

Kanin, Garson Jan 41 Oct 52 obit Jun 99

Kan-In, Prince Kotohito obit Jun 45

Kann, Peter R. Mar 2003

Kanter, Albert L. Jul 53

Kanter, Rosabeth Moss Jun 96

Kantor, Michael *see* Kantor, Mickey

Kantor, Mickey Mar 94

Kantrowitz, Adrian Oct 67

Kantrowitz, Arthur Oct 66

Kanzler, Ernest C. Apr 42 obit Feb 68

Kapar, Karl obit Jun 41

Kapell, William May 48 obit Jan 54

Kapitza, P. L. Oct 55 obit May 84

Kaplan, Joseph Oct 56 obit Nov 91

Kaplan, Justin Jul 93

Kapp, Joe Sep 75

Kappel, Frederick R. Mar 57 obit Jan 95

Kaptur, Marcy Jan 2003

Kapuscinski, Ryszard Sep 92

Karadic, Radovan Oct 95

Karajan, Herbert von Oct 56 Sep 86 obit Sep 89

Karamanlis, Constantine *see* Caramanlis, Constantine

Karami, Rashid Nov 59 obit Jul 87

Karan, Donna Aug 90

Karbo, Karen May 2001

Kardelj, Edvard Dec 49 obit Apr 79

Karelitz, George B. obit Mar 43

Karfiol, Bernard Nov 47 obit Oct 52

Karinska, Barbara Jan 71

Karle, Isabella Jan 2003

Karloff, Boris Mar 41 obit

Mar 69

Karmal, Babrak Mar 81 obit Feb 97

Karman, Theodore von *see* Von Kármán, Theodore

Karmazin, Mel May 2000

Karno, Fred obit Nov 41

Karolyi, Bela Oct 96

Karon, Jan Mar 2003

Karp, David (WLB) Yrbk 57 obit Feb 2000

Karpov, Anatoly Nov 78

Karsh, Yousuf Dec 52 Feb 80 obit Nov 2002

Karsner, David obit Apr 41

Kartawidjaja, Djuanda *see* Djuanda

Karzai, Hamid May 2002

Kasavubu, Joseph Mar 61 obit May 69

Kasdan, Lawrence May 92

Kase, Toshikazu Apr 57 obit Yrbk 2004

Kasem, Casey Nov 97

Kasich, John R. Aug 98

Kasner, Edward Nov 43 obit Mar 55

Kasparov, Gary Apr 86

Kass, Leon R. Aug 2002

Kassebaum, Nancy Landon Feb 82

Kassem, Abdul Karim Nov 59 obit Mar 63

Kast, Ludwig W. obit Oct 41

Kasten, Bob *see* Kasten, Robert W.

Kasten, Robert W. Jun 89

Kastenmeier, Robert W. Jul 66

Kastler, Alfred Dec 67 obit Mar 84

Kästner, Erich Jul 64 obit Oct 74

Kaszon, Hans Heinrich Thyssen-Bornemisza De *see* Thyssen-Bornemisza De Kaszon, Hans Heinrich

Katayama, Tetsu Jan 48

Katchalski, Ephraim *see*

Katzir, Ephraim
Katchor, Ben May 2000
Katsav, Moshe Feb 2001
Katsh, Abraham I. Mar 62 obit Oct 98
Katz, Alex Jul 75
Katz, Jackson Jul 2004
Katz, Joel *see* Grey, Joel
Katz, Label A. Apr 60 obit Jun 75
Katz, Lillian Vernon *see* Vernon, Lillian
Katz, Milton Oct 50 obit Oct 95
Katzen, Mollie Oct 96
Katzenbach, Nicholas Deb Jul 65
Katzenberg, Jeffrey May 95
Katzir, Ephraim Jan 75
Katz-Suchy, Juliusz Jun 51 obit Dec 71
Kauffmann, Henrik Apr 56 obit Jul 63
Kaufman, Charlie Jul 2005
Kaufman, Cy *see* Coleman, Cy
Kaufman, George S. Aug 41 obit Sep 61
Kaufman, Henry Aug 81
Kaufman, Irving R. Apr 53 obit Apr 92
Kaunda, Kenneth Jul 66
Kaup, Felix F., Father obit Apr 40
Kaur, Rajkumari Amrit Oct 55 obit Mar 64
Kavanagh, Dan *see* Barnes, Julian
Kavner, Julie Oct 92
Kawabata, Yasunari Mar 69 obit Jun 72
Kawakami, Jotaro Mar 63 obit Jan 66
Kawakubo, Rei Aug 99
Kay, Beatrice Dec 42
Kay, Hershy Mar 62 obit Feb 82
Kaye, Danny Dec 41 Nov 52 obit Apr 87
Kaye, Nora Jan 53 obit Apr 87
Kay-Scott, Cyril *see* Well-

man, Frederick Creighton
Kazan, Elia Jan 48 Oct 72 obit Yrbk 2004
Kazanjian, Arlene Francis *see* Francis, Arlene
Kazantzakis, Nikos Jul 55 obit Jan 58
Kazin, Alfred May 66 obit Aug 98
Kcho Aug 2001
Keach, Stacy Nov 71
Kean, Thomas H. Jul 85
Keane, Doris obit Jan 46
Keane, Seán *see* Chieftains
Kearns, Carroll D. Sep 56
Kearns, Doris *see* Goodwin, Doris Kearns
Kearns, Mrs. Carroll D *see* Kearns, Nora Lynch
Kearns, Nora Lynch Sep 56
Keating, Kenneth B. Oct 50 obit Jun 75
Keating, Paul May 92
Keaton, Diane Jun 78 May 96
Keaton, Michael Jun 92
Keck, George Fred Sep 45
Keck, Lucile L. Mar 54
Keck, Mrs. George Fred *see* Keck, Lucile L.
Kee, Elizabeth Jan 54
Kee, John Jun 50 obit Jun 51
Kee, Mrs. John *see* Kee, Elizabeth
Keech, Richmond B. Mar 50
Keegan, John Oct 89
Keegan, Robert Jan 2004
Keeler, Ruby Dec 71 obit Apr 93
Keen, Sam Feb 95
Keenan, Joseph B. Sep 46 obit Feb 55
Keenan, Mike Mar 96
Keenan, Walter Francis Jr. obit Apr 40
Keene, Christopher Mar 90 obit Jan 96
Keene, Donald Jan 88
Keener, Catherine Oct 2002
Keeney, Barnaby C. Mar 56 obit Aug 80
Keeny, Spurgeon M. Jan 58

obit Jan 89
Keeshan, Bob May 65 obit Yrbk 2004
Keeton, Kathy Sep 93 obit Jan 98
Kefauver, Estes Jan 49 obit Oct 63
Keighley, William Nov 48 obit Aug 84
Keillor, Garrison Aug 85
Keino, Kipchoge Jun 67
Keita, Mobida Apr 60 obit Jul 77
Keitel, Harvey Mar 94
Keitel, Wilhelm Sep 40 obit Nov 46
Keith, Dora Wheeler obit Feb 41
Keith, Harold (WLB) Yrbk 58
Keith, Toby Oct 2004
Kekkonen, Urho K. Sep 50 obit Oct 86
Kelberine, Alexander obit Mar 40
Keldysh, Mstislav Feb 62 obit Aug 78
Kell, Joseph *see* Burgess, Anthony
Kellas, Eliza obit May 43
Kelleher, Herb Jan 2001
Kellems, Vivien Sep 48 obit Mar 75
Keller, Bill Oct 2003
Keller, Helen Dec 42 obit Jul 68
Keller, James Oct 51 obit Apr 77
Keller, K. T. May 47 obit Feb 66
Keller, Kasey Nov 98
Keller, Marthe Jul 2004
Keller, Thomas Jun 2004
Kelley, Augustine B. Apr 51 obit Feb 58
Kelley, Clarence M. May 74 obit Nov 97
Kelley, David E. May 98
Kelley, Edgar Stillman obit Jan 45
Kelley, Kitty Apr 92
Kellner, Erica *see* Anderson,

Erica

Kellogg, John Harvey obit Feb 44

Kellogg, Remington Nov 49

Kellogg, Winthrop N. Apr 63

Kelly, E. Lowell Mar 55 obit Apr 86

Kelly, Edna F. Mar 50 obit Feb 98

Kelly, Ellsworth May 70

Kelly, Emmett Jul 54 obit May 79

Kelly, Eugene Curran *see* Kelly, Gene

Kelly, Florence Finch obit Jan 40

Kelly, Gene Dec 45 Feb 77 obit Apr 96

Kelly, Grace *see* Grace, Princess of Monaco

Kelly, Howard A. obit Mar 43

Kelly, Jim Nov 92

Kelly, Joe Jun 45 obit Jul 59

Kelly, John B., Jr. Jun 71 obit Apr 85

Kelly, Joseph William *see* Kelly, Joe

Kelly, Judith Oct 41 obit Jul 57

Kelly, Mervin J. Oct 56 obit May 71

Kelly, Mrs. Norman H. *see* Kelly, Regina Z.

Kelly, Nancy Jun 55 obit Mar 95

Kelly, Patrick Sep 89 obit Mar 90

Kelly, Petra Mar 84 obit Jan 93

Kelly, R. Jun 99

Kelly, Regina Z. (WLB) Yrbk 56

Kelly, Robert *see* Kelly, R.

Kelly, Sharon Pratt Nov 92

Kelly, Walt Oct 56 obit Dec 73

Kelman, Charles Jun 84 obit Yrbk 2004

Kelsen, Hans Sep 57 obit Jun 73

Kelsey, Frances O. Apr 65

Kem, James P. Oct 50 obit Apr 65

Kemeny, John G. Feb 71 obit Feb 93

Kemmerer, E. W. Oct 41 obit Feb 46

Kemmis, Daniel Oct 96

Kemp, Hal obit Feb 41

Kemp, Jack Mar 80

Kemper, James S. Apr 41 obit Nov 81

Kempner, Robert M. W. May 43 obit Oct 93

Kempton, Murray Jun 73 obit Jul 97

Kemsley, James Gomer Berry, 1st Viscount *see* Berry, James Gomer

Kendall, Edward C. Dec 50 obit Jun 72

Kendall, William Mitchell obit Oct 41

Kendrew, John C. Oct 63 obit Nov 97

Kendrick, Baynard Feb 46 obit May 77

Keneally, Thomas Jun 87

Kennan, George F. Oct 47 Jan 59 obit Yrbk 2005

Kennedy, Anthony M. Jul 88

Kennedy, Arthur Nov 61

Kennedy, Claudia J. Jan 2000

Kennedy, David M. Jun 69 obit Jul 96

Kennedy, Donald Jul 84

Kennedy, Edward Moore Sep 63 Oct 78

Kennedy, Jacqueline *see* Onassis, Jacqueline Kennedy

Kennedy, John B. Feb 44 obit Oct 61

Kennedy, John F. Jun 50 Jul 61 obit Jan 64

Kennedy, John F., Jr. Jan 96 obit Sep 99

Kennedy, Joseph P. Nov 40

obit Jan 70

Kennedy, Joseph P., 2d Jun 88

Kennedy, Nigel Jul 92

Kennedy, Paul Oct 93

Kennedy, Randall Aug 2002

Kennedy, Robert F. Feb 58 obit Jul 68

Kennedy, Robert F. Jr. May 2004

Kennedy, Rose Nov 70 obit Mar 95

Kennedy, Stephen P. Jun 56 obit Jan 79

Kennedy, Thomas Jun 60 obit Feb 63

Kennedy, William May 85

Kennedy, William P. Jan 50 obit Jul 68

Kennelly, Ardyth (WLB) Yrbk 53

Kennelly, Martin H. Dec 49 obit Jan 62

Kenney, George C. Jan 43 obit Oct 77

Kennon, Robert F. Oct 54 obit Apr 88

Kenny G Nov 95

Kenny, Elizabeth Oct 42 obit Jan 53

Kent, Allegra Mar 70

Kent, Corita Feb 69 obit Nov 86

Kent, George Edward Alexander Edmund, Duke of obit Oct 42

Kent, Jeff May 2003

Kent, Raymond A. obit Apr 43

Kent, Rockwell Nov 42 obit Apr 71

Kenton, Stan Jun 79

Kentridge, William Oct 2001

Kenyatta, Jomo Oct 53 Apr 74 obit Oct 78

Kenyon, Cynthia Jan 2005

Kenyon, Dorothy Apr 47 obit Apr 72

Kenyon, Helen Oct 48

Kepes, György Mar 73 obit Mar 2002

Kepler, Asher Raymond, Rev.

obit Oct 42

Keppel, Francis May 63 obit Apr 90

Kerensky, Alexander Dec 66 obit Sep 70

Kerkorian, Kirk May 75 Mar 96

Kern, Jerome Jun 42 obit Dec 45

Kernan, W. F. Apr 42

Kerner, Otto Oct 61 obit Jul 76

Kerouac, Jack Nov 59 obit Dec 69

Kerr, Archibald Clark Dec 42 obit Sep 51 [Inverchapel of Loch Eck, Archibald John Kerr Clark Kerr, 1st Baron]

Kerr, Clark Apr 61 obit May 2004

Kerr, Deborah Sep 47

Kerr, James W. Oct 59

Kerr, Jean Jul 58 obit May 2003

Kerr, Mrs. Walter F see Kerr, Jean

Kerr, Mrs. Walter F see Kerr, Jean

Kerr, Robert Samuel May 50 obit Feb 63

Kerr, Steve Oct 98

Kerr, Walter Oct 53 obit Jan 97

Kerrey, Bob Feb 91

Kerrl, Hanns obit Feb 42

Kerry, John Jun 88 Sep 2004

Kerst, Donald William Apr 50 obit Oct 93

Kersten, Charles J. Sep 52

Kertész, André Aug 79 obit Nov 85

Kesey, Ken May 76 obit Feb 2002

Kesselring, Albert Nov 42 obit Oct 60

Kessing, O. O. Jun 49 obit Mar 63

Kessler, David A. Sep 91

Kessler, Henry H. Oct 57

Kestnbaum, Meyer May 53

obit Feb 61

Ketcham, Hank Jan 56 obit Sep 2001

Kettering, Charles Franklin May 40 Dec 51 obit Feb 59

Kevorkian, Jack Sep 94

Key, Ben Witt obit Jul 40

Key, William S. Jul 43 obit Mar 59

Keyhoe, Donald Edward Jun 56 obit Feb 89

Keynes, John Maynard Jun 41 obit May 46

Keys, Ancel Jan 66 obit Yrbk 2005

Keys, Charlene see Tweet

Keys, David A. Oct 58

Keyserling, Hermann, Count obit Jun 46

Keyserling, Leon H. Jan 47 obit Sep 87

Keyworth, George A., 2d Mar 86

Khachaturian, Aram Mar 48 obit Jun 78

Khalid, ibn Abul Aziz, King of Saudi Arabia see Khalid, King of Saudi Arabia

Khalid, King of Saudi Arabia Jan 76 obit Aug 82

Khama, Seretse May 67 obit Sep 80

Khamenei, Hojatoleslam Ali Nov 87

Khan, Aga see Aga Khan, The

Khan, Begum Liaquat Ali Jul 50

Khan, Chaka Jul 99

Khan, Liaquat Ali Jun 48 obit Dec 51

Khan, Michelle see Yeoh, Michelle

Khan, Mohammad Ayub see Ayub Khan, Mohammad

Khan, Taidje see Brynner, Yul

Khashoggi, Adnan Mar 86

Khatami, Mohammad Apr 98

Kheel, Theodore W. Sep 64

Khoman, Thanat Mar 58

Khomeini, Ayatollah Ruholla

Nov 79 obit Jul 89

Khorana, Har Gobind Dec 70

Khouri, Faris El- Sep 48 obit Feb 62

Khoury, Bechara El- Dec 51 obit Feb 64

Khrushchev, Nikita S. Jul 54 obit Oct 71

Kiam, Omar Dec 45 obit May 54

Kiarostami, Abbas Jul 98

Kid Rock Oct 2001

Kidd, Chip Jul 2005

Kidd, Isaac Campbell obit Feb 42

Kidd, Jason May 2002

Kidd, Michael Mar 60

Kidder, George W. Jul 49

Kidman, Nicole Mar 97

Kiefer, Anselm Jun 88

Kienholz, Edward Aug 89 obit Aug 94

Kiepura, Jan Nov 43 obit Nov 66

Kieran, John Apr 40 obit Feb 82

Kiesinger, Kurt Georg Apr 67 obit Apr 88

Kiesler, Frederick Jan 44 obit Feb 66

Kiéslowski, Krzysztof May 95 obit May 96

Kiessling, Laura Aug 2003

Kiewiet, Cornelis de see De Kiewiet, Cornelis W.

Kilbourne, Jean May 2004

Kilday, Paul J. Oct 58 obit Dec 68

Kiley, Richard Apr 73 obit May 99

Kilgallen, Dorothy Feb 52 [Kilgallen, Dorothy; and Kollmar, Richard] obit Jan 66

Kilgore, Harley M. Jun 43 obit May 56

Killanin, Michael Morris Apr 73 obit Jul 99

Killebrew, Harmon Feb 66

Killian, James R. Feb 49 May

59 obit Mar 88

Killion, George Nov 52

Killy, Jean-Claude Jun 68

Kilmer, Aline obit Dec 41

Kilmer, Mrs. Joyce *see* Kilmer, Aline

Kilmer, Val Jan 96

Kilmuir, David Patrick Maxwell Fyfe, 1st Earl of *see* Maxwell, David

Kilpatrick, James J. Jul 80

Kilpatrick, John Reed Jul 48 obit Jul 60

Kilpatrick, Kwame M. Apr 2004

Kim Dae Jung Sep 85

Kim Il Sung Sep 51 Yrbk 94 obit Yrbk 94

Kim Jong Il Oct 99

Kim Sung Ju *see* Kim Il Sung

Kim Young Sam Jun 95

Kimball, Abbott May 49 obit Nov 68

Kimball, Dan A. Sep 51 obit Oct 70

Kimball, James Henry obit Feb 44

Kimball, Lindsley F. Jul 51 obit Oct 92

Kimball, Spencer W. Feb 79 obit Jan 86

Kimball, Wilbur R. obit Sep 40

Kimble, George H. T. Oct 52

Kimbrel, M. Monroe Jun 63

Kimbrough, Emily Mar 44 obit Apr 89

Kimmel, Husband E. Jan 42 obit Jul 68

Kimpton, Lawrence A. Jun 51 obit Jan 78

Kincaid, Jamaica Mar 91

Kindelberger, J. H. Mar 51 obit Oct 62

Kinder, Katharine L. May 57

Kindler, Hans Sep 46 obit Oct 49

Kiner, Ralph May 54

King Hussein *see* Hussein, King of Jordan

King, Alan Jun 70 obit Yrbk

2004

King, Annette *see* Reid, Charlotte T.

King, B. B. Jun 70

King, Billie Jean Dec 67

King, Carole Jan 74

King, Cecil R. Feb 52 obit May 74

King, Charles Glen Dec 67 obit Mar 88

King, Coretta Scott May 69

King, Don Jun 84

King, Ernest Joseph Feb 42 obit Sep 56

King, John W. May 64 obit Nov 96

King, Larry May 85

King, Leslie Lynch, Jr. *see* Ford, Gerald R.

King, Martin Luther, Jr. May 57 May 65 obit May 68

King, Mary-Claire Feb 95

King, Mrs. Martin Luther, Jr. *see* King, Coretta

King, Muriel Apr 43 obit May 77

King, Riley B. *see* King, B. B.

King, Samuel Wilder Oct 53 obit Jun 59

King, Stephen Oct 81

King, William Lyon Mackenzie Aug 40 obit Sep 50

Kingdon, Frank Jul 44 obit Apr 72

Kingman, Dave Mar 82

Kingman, Dong Oct 62 obit Yrbk 2000

Kingsland, Lawrence C. Jan 49

Kingsley, Ben Nov 83

Kingsley, J. Donald Feb 50

Kingsley, Myra Apr 43

Kingsley, Sidney Jun 43 obit May 95

Kingsolver, Barbara Jul 94

Kingston, Maxine Hong Mar 90

Kinkade, Thomas Jun 2000

Kinkaid, Thomas C. Dec 44

obit Jan 73

Kinnear, Helen Apr 57

Kinnell, Galway Aug 86

Kinnock, Neil Apr 84

Kinsey, Alfred C. Jan 54 obit Oct 56

Kinski, Nastassja Jun 84

Kinsley, Michael May 95

Kintner, Earl W. Apr 60 obit Mar 92

Kintner, Robert E. Oct 50 obit Feb 81

Kiphuth, Robert J. H. Jun 57 obit Mar 67

Kipling, Caroline Starr Balestier obit Jan 40

Kiplinger, Willard Monroe Mar 43 Jan 62 obit Oct 67

Kipnis, Alexander Dec 43 obit Jul 78

Kipping, Norman Dec 49

Kirbo, Charles H. Sep 77 obit Nov 96

Kirby, George May 77 obit Jan 96

Kirby, Robert E. Sep 79 obit Mar 99

Kirby, Rollin Dec 44 obit Jun 52

Kirchner, Leon Dec 67

Kirchwey, Freda Dec 42 obit Feb 76

Kirchwey, George W. obit Apr 42

Kiriyenko, Sergei Aug 98

Kirk, Alan Goodrich Jul 44 obit Dec 63

Kirk, Alexander C. Feb 45

Kirk, Claude R., Jr. Oct 67

Kirk, Grayson L. May 51 obit Jan 98

Kirk, Norman T. Feb 44 obit Nov 60

Kirk, Paul G., Jr. Aug 87

Kirk, Russell Sep 62 obit Jun 94

Kirk, William T. Feb 60 obit Mar 74

Kirkland, Gelsey Oct 75

Kirkland, Lane May 80 obit

Oct 99

Kirkland, Winifred Margaretta obit Jul 43

Kirkpatrick, Chris *see* 'N Sync

Kirkpatrick, Helen May 41

Kirkpatrick, Ivone Jun 50 obit Jul 64

Kirkpatrick, Jeane Jul 81

Kirkpatrick, Miles W. Feb 72 obit Jul 98

Kirkpatrick, Ralph Sep 71 obit Aug 84

Kirkus, Virginia May 41 Jun 54 obit Nov 80

Kirshner, Sidney *see* Kingsley, Sidney

Kirstein, Lincoln Dec 52 Aug 90 obit Mar 96

Kirsten, Dorothy Feb 48 obit Jan 93

Kisevalter, George obit May 41

Kishi, Nobusuke Jun 57 obit Sep 87

Kiss Apr 99

Kissin, Evgeny Nov 97

Kissin, Yevgeny *see* Kissin, Evgeny

Kissinger, Henry Jun 58 Jun 72

Kistiakowsky, George B. Nov 60 obit Feb 83

Kistler, Darci Oct 91

Kitaj, R. B. Apr 82

Kitano, Takeshi Jul 98

Kitchell, Iva Dec 51 obit Jan 84

Kitson, Harry Dexter Apr 51 obit Nov 59

Kitt, Eartha Apr 55

Kittikachorn, Thanom Dec 69 obit Yrbk 2004

Kittredge, George Lyman obit Sep 41

Klahre, Ethel S. May 62

Klass, Perri May 99

Klassen, Elmer T. May 73 obit Jun 90

Klaus, Josef Jan 65 obit Oct

2001

Klaus, Václav Nov 97

Klee, Paul obit Aug 40

Kleffens, Eelco Van Oct 47

Kleiber, Carlos Jul 91 obit Yrbk 2004

Klein, Calvin Jul 78

Klein, Edward E. Sep 66 obit Sep 85

Klein, Herbert G. Feb 71

Klein, Julius Jul 48 obit May 84

Klein, Naomi Aug 2003

Klein, Robert Mar 77

Klein, William Mar 2004

Kleindienst, Richard G. Oct 72 obit Jun 2000

Kleinsmid, Rufus B. Von Jun 58 obit Sep 64

Kleist, Paul Ludwig Von Jul 43 obit Jan 55

Kleitman, Nathaniel Oct 57 obit Jan 2000

Klemperer, Otto Mar 65 obit Sep 73

Klenze, Camillo Von obit Apr 43

Kleppe, Thomas S. Aug 76

Klimecki, Tadeusz A. obit Aug 43

Kline, Allan B. Mar 48 obit Sep 68

Kline, Clarice May 61

Kline, Kevin Jul 86

Kline, Nathan S. Oct 65 obit May 83

Klopsteg, Paul E. May 59 obit Jul 91

Kluckhohn, Clyde Nov 51 obit Oct 60

Kluge, John Sep 93

Klumpp, Theodore G. Oct 58

Knabenshue, Paul obit Mar 42

Knappstein, Karl Heinrich Feb 65

Knatchbull-Hugessen, Hughe Mar 43 obit May 71

Knaths, Karl Jul 53 obit Apr 71

Knauer, Virginia H. Apr 70

Knickerbocker, Hubert Ren-

fro Sep 40 obit Sep 49

Knievel, Evel Feb 72

Knievel, Robbie Mar 2005

Knievel, Robert Craig *see* Knievel, Evel

Knight, Bobby May 87

Knight, Douglas M. May 64

Knight, Eric Mowbray Jul 42 obit Mar 43

Knight, Frances G. Oct 55 obit Nov 99

Knight, Gladys Feb 87

Knight, Goodwin Jan 55 obit Jul 70

Knight, John S. Apr 45 obit Aug 81

Knight, O. A. Jun 52

Knight, Philip H. Aug 97

Knight, Ruth Adams Aug 43 (WLB) Yrbk 55

Knipfel, Jim Mar 2005

Knipling, E. F. May 75 obit Yrbk 2000

Knoblock, Edward obit Aug 45

Knoll, Hans G. May 55

Knopf, Alfred A. Jun 43 Nov 66 obit Oct 84

Knopf, Blanche Jul 57 [Knopf, Mrs. Alfred A.] obit Jul 66

Knopf, Mrs. Alfred A. *see* Knopf, Blanche

Knopf, Mrs. Hans *see* Vanderbilt, Amy

Knopf, Sigard Adolphus obit Sep 40

Knopfler, Mark Apr 95

Knorr, Nathan H. Feb 57 obit Aug 77

Knott, Sarah Gertrude Jul 47

Knowland, William Fife Apr 47 obit Apr 74

Knowles, Beyoncé *see* Destiny's Child

Knowles, John H. Dec 70 obit May 79

Knowlson, James S. Nov 42

Knox, Frank Aug 40 obit Jun

44

Knox, Jean Sep 42

Knox, Louise Chambers obit Mar 42

Knox, Mrs. Charles Briggs *see* Knox, Rose Markward

Knox, Ronald Arbuthnott Jul 50 obit Nov 57

Knox, Rose Markward May 49 obit Nov 50

Knudsen, Semon E. Jan 74 obit Sep 98

Knudsen, William S. Jul 40 obit Jun 48

Knussen, Oliver Feb 94

Knuth-Winterfeldt, Kield Gustav, Count Sep 59

Knutson, Coya Mar 56 obit Jan 97

Knutson, Harold Jan 47 obit Oct 53

Kobak, Edgar Apr 47 obit Jul 62

Koch, Bill Mar 99

Koch, Ed Sep 78

Koch, Fred Jr. Oct 53 obit Yrbk 2000

Koch, Frederick H. obit Oct 44

Koch, John May 65 obit Jun 78

Koch, Kenneth Feb 78 obit Yrbk 2002

Koch, Theodore Wesley obit May 41

Koch, William I. *see* Koch, Bill

Kock, Karin Nov 48

Koenig, Joseph-Pierre *see* Koenig, Marie Pierre

Koenig, Marie Pierre Sep 44 obit Nov 70

Koestler, Arthur Apr 43 Jan 62 obit Apr 83

Koff, Clea Nov 2004

Koffka, Kurt obit Jan 42

Koga, Mineichi obit Oct 43

Kohl, Helmut Aug 77

Kohler, Foy D. Jan 50 obit Mar 91

Kohler, Walter J., Jr. Jan 53

obit May 76

Kohler, Walter Jodok obit May 40

Kohout, Pavel Feb 88

Kohoutek, Lubos Jun 74

Koivisto, Mauno Sep 82

Koizumi, Junichiro Jan 2002

Kokoschka, Oskar Oct 56 obit Apr 80

Kolár, Jirí Apr 86 obit Yrbk 2002

Kolarov, Vassil Dec 49 obit Mar 50

Kolb-Danvin, Mrs. Charles Louis *see* Radziwill, Catherine, Princess

Kolbe, Parke Rexford obit Apr 42

Kolff, Willem Johan May 83

Kollek, Teddy Oct 74 Mar 93

Kollmar, Richard Feb 52 [Kilgallen, Dorothy; and Kollmar, Richard] obit Feb 71

Kollontay, Alexandra Oct 43 obit Apr 52

Kolodin, Irving Jul 47 obit Jun 88

Kolvenbach, Peter-Hans May 84

Koma *see* Eiko and Koma

Komando, Kim Sep 2000

Komar, Vitali Oct 84 [Komar, Vitaly; and Melamid, Aleskandr]

Komarovsky, Mirra Oct 53 obit Apr 99

Kominski, David Daniel *see* Kaye, Danny

Konaré, Alpha Oumar Oct 2001

Koner, Pauline Oct 64 obit Apr 2001

Konev, Ivan S. Oct 43 Jan 56 obit Jul 73

Konijnenburg, Willem Adriaan Van obit Apr 43

Konoye, Fumimaro, Prince Sep 40 obit Feb 46

Konstantinu, Mrs. Ilias *see* Clark, Eugenie

Konstanty, Casimer James *see*

Konstanty, Jim

Konstanty, Jim Apr 51 obit Aug 76

Koo, V. K. Wellington Jul 41 obit Jan 86

Koogle, Tim Apr 2000

Koolhaas, Rem Nov 2000

Kooning, Elaine de *see* De Kooning, Elaine

Kooning, Willem de *see* De Kooning, Willem

Koons, Jeff May 90

Koontz, Elizabeth Duncan Jan 69 obit Apr 89

Koop, C. Everett Sep 83

Kopal, Zdenek Mar 69 obit Aug 93

Kopit, Arthur L. Dec 72

Kopp, Wendy Mar 2003

Koppel, Ted Jul 84

Kopple, Barbara Jul 98

Koprowski, Hilary Mar 68

Köprülü, Fuat Jan 53 obit Sep 66

Korbut, Olga Jul 73

Korda, Alexander Sep 46 obit Mar 56

Korda, Michael Aug 85

Koreff, Nora *see* Kaye, Nora

Korizis, Alexander Mar 41 obit Mar 41

Korman, Harvey Oct 79

Kornberg, Arthur Sep 68

Körner, Theodor Jul 51 obit Mar 57

Korngold, Erich Wolfgang Mar 43 obit Feb 58

Korngold, Julius obit Oct 45

Kors, Michael Jan 2000

Korth, Fred Jul 62 obit Jan 99

Kosaka, Zentaro Sep 61

Koscow, Sophia *see* Sidney, Sylvia

Kosinski, Jerzy Mar 74 obit Jul 91

Koslowski, Leon obit Jul 44

Kossak, Zofia Jun 44 obit Jun 68

Kostelanetz, André Jul 42 obit

Mar 80

Kostunica, Vojislav Jan 2001

Kosygin, Aleksei N. Sep 65 obit Feb 81

Kotelawala, John Oct 55

Kotschnig, Walter M. Oct 52 obit Sep 85

Kott, Jan Apr 69 obit Mar 2002

Kotto, Yaphet Mar 95

Kouchner, Bernard Aug 93

Koufax, Sandy Jan 64

Kournikova, Anna Jan 2002

Koussevitzky, Mrs. Serge see Koussevitzky, Natalya

Koussevitzky, Natalya obit Mar 42

Koussevitzky, Serge Nov 40 obit Jul 51

Kovacs, Ernie Feb 58 obit Mar 62

Kovic, Ron Aug 90

Kowalski, Frank Jr. Jul 60 obit Dec 74

Kozlenko, William Oct 41

Kozlov, Frol R. Nov 59 obit Mar 65

Kozol, Jonathan Jan 86

Kozyrev, Andrei V. Sep 92

Kozyrev, Nikolai A. Feb 70

Kraft, Christopher C., Jr. Feb 66

Kraft, Ole Björn Feb 53

Krag, Jens Otto Oct 62 obit Aug 78

Krainik, Ardis Nov 91 obit Mar 97

Kramer, Edward Adam obit Feb 42

Kramer, Jack see Kramer, Jake

Kramer, Jake May 47

Kramer, Joey see Aerosmith

Kramer, John Albert see Kramer, Jake

Kramer, Larry Mar 94

Kramer, Stanley May 51 obit May 2001

Kramm, Joseph Jul 52

Krampe, Hugh J. see O'Brian,

Hugh

Krantz, Judith May 82

Krasna, Norman May 52 obit Feb 85

Krasner, Lee Mar 74 obit Aug 84

Kratz, Althea Hallowell see Hottel, Althea Kratz

Kraus, Alfredo Jun 87 obit Nov 99

Kraus, Hans Peter Jul 60 obit Jan 89

Kraus, Lili Oct 75 obit Jan 87

Kraus, Rene Jul 41 obit Sep 47

Krause, Allen K. obit Jul 41

Krause, David W. Feb 2002

Kraushaar, Otto F. Nov 49 obit Nov 89

Krauss, Alison May 97

Krautter, Elisa Bialk see Bialk, Elisa

Kravchenko, Victor A. Jul 46 obit Mar 66

Kravchuk, Leonid M. Jan 93

Kravis, Henry R. Mar 89

Kravitz, Lenny Apr 96

Krebs, Hans Adolf Mar 54 obit Feb 82

Krebs, Richard Julius Herman see Valtin, Jan

Kreisky, Bruno Sep 60 obit Sep 90

Kreisler, Fritz Jul 44 obit Mar 62

Krekeler, Heinz L. Dec 51

Kremer, Gidon Mar 85

Krenek, Ernst Jul 42 obit Feb 92

Krens, Thomas Apr 89

Krenz, Egon Mar 90

Kreps, Juanita M. Jun 77

Kress, Samuel H. Oct 55

Kreutzberger, Mario see Francisco, Don

Krick, Irving P. Jul 50 obit Sep 96

Kriebel, Hermann obit Apr 41

Krim, Mathilde Aug 87

Kripke, Saul A. Oct 2004

Krips, Josef Jun 65 obit Dec

74

Krishna Menon, V. K. Mar 53 obit Nov 74

Krishnamurti, Jiddu Oct 74 obit Apr 86

Kristiansen, Mrs. Erling see Selinko, Annemarie

Kristofferson, Kris Nov 74

Kristol, Irving Sep 74

Kristol, William May 97

Krivitsky, Walter G. obit Mar 41

Kroc, Ray Mar 73 obit Mar 84

Krock, Arthur Feb 43 obit Jun 74

Kroeber, A. L. Oct 58 obit Dec 60

Kroft, Steve Nov 96

Krohg, Per Nov 54

Krol, John Jan 69 obit May 96

Kroll, Jack Sep 46 obit Jul 71

Kroll, John Jacob see Kroll, Jack

Kroll, Jules B. Feb 99

Kroll, Leon Mar 43 obit Dec 74

Krone, Julie Oct 89

Kronenberger, Louis Aug 44 obit Jul 80

Kross, Anna M. Nov 45 obit Oct 79

Krueger, Maynard C. May 40

Krueger, Walter Apr 43 obit Oct 67

Krueger, Wilhelm obit Jun 43

Krug, J. A. Oct 44 obit May 70

Kruger, Barbara Jul 95

Kruger-Gray, George obit Jun 43

Krugman, Paul Aug 2001

Kruif, Paul De see De Kruif, Paul

Krupa, Gene Sep 47 obit Dec 73

Krupp, Alfred May 55 obit Oct 67

Krupsak, Mary Anne Jul 75

Krutch, Joseph Wood Nov 59

obit Jul 70

Krzyzewski, Mike Jan 97

Kubelik, Jan obit Jan 41

Kubelik, Rafael Feb 51 obit Oct 96

Kubelsky, Benjamin *see* Benny, Jack

Kubitschek, Juscelino Apr 56 obit Nov 76

Kübler-Ross, Elisabeth Jun 80 obit Yrbk 2004

Kubly, Herbert Feb 59 obit Oct 96

Kubrick, Stanley Feb 63 obit May 99

Kuchel, Thomas H. Feb 54 obit Feb 95

Küchler, Georg Von Sep 43

Kuchma, Leonid Oct 97

Kucinich, Dennis J. Mar 79

Kucuk, Fazil *see* Kutchuk, Fazil

Kudelka, James Mar 95

Kuekes, Edward D. Mar 54 obit Mar 87

Kuhlman, Kathryn Jul 74 obit Apr 76

Kuhlmann, Frederick obit Jun 41

Kuhn, Bowie Jan 70

Kuhn, Edward W. Jun 66

Kuhn, Irene Feb 46 obit Mar 96

Kuhn, Maggie Jul 78 obit Jul 95

Kuhn, Margaret E. *see* Kuhn, Maggie

Kuiper, Gerard P. Feb 59 obit Feb 74

Kukoc, Toni Jul 97

Kulik, Grigory Jul 42

Kullmer, Ann Feb 49

Kumaratunga, Chandrika Bandaranaike Jan 96

Kumm, Henry W. Jun 55 obit Mar 91

Kundera, Milan Mar 83

Kung, H. H. Mar 43 obit Oct

67

Küng, Hans Jul 63

Kunin, Madeleine Jul 87

Kunitz, Stanley Mar 43 Nov 59

Kuniyoshi, Yasuo Jun 41 obit Jun 53

Kunstler, William M. Apr 71 obit Nov 95

Kunz, Alfred A. Dec 41

Kunz, Stanley H. obit Jun 46

Kuo T'ai-ch'i *see* Quo Tai-Chi

Kuok, Robert Jun 98

Kuralt, Charles Jul 81 obit Sep 97

Kurchatov, Igor V. Nov 57 obit Apr 60

Kureishi, Hanif Feb 92

Kurenko, Maria Sep 44

Kurosawa, Akira Apr 65 Jul 91 obit Nov 98

Kurtz, Efrem Feb 46 obit Sep 95

Kurtz, Swoosie Oct 87

Kurusu, Sabro Jan 42 obit May 54

Kusch, Polykarp Mar 56 obit May 93

Kushner, Harold S. Apr 97

Kushner, Tony Jul 2002

Kusner, Kathy Apr 73

Kusturica, Emir Nov 2005

Kutchuk, Fazil Feb 61 obit Mar 84

Kuter, Laurence S. Jul 48

Kutznetov, Vassili V. Jan 56 obit Aug 90

Kuusinen, Hertta May 49 obit May 74

Kuwatly, Shukri Al May 56 obit Oct 67

Kuzmin, Iosif I. Feb 59

Kuznets, Simon May 72 obit Sep 85

Kuznetsov, Nikolai G. Nov 42 obit Jan 75

Ky, Nguyen Cao Dec 66

Kyles, Cedric *see* Cedric the Entertainer

Kylian, Jiri Sep 82

Kyprianou, Spyros May 79

obit May 2002

Kyser, Kay Apr 41 obit Sep 85

L. Herndon, J. Marvin Nov 2003

L. L. Cool J Nov 97

L'amour, Louis Feb 80 obit Jul 88

L'engle, Madeleine Jan 97

L'esperance, Elise Nov 50 obit Apr 59

La Cava, Gregory Dec 41 obit Apr 52

La Farge, Oliver Jan 53 obit Oct 63

La Follette, Robert M. May 44 obit Apr 53

La Fontaine, Henri obit Jul 43

La Gorce, John Oliver Nov 54 obit Feb 60

La Guardia, Ernesto de, Jr. *see* Guardia, Ernesto De La, Jr.

La Guardia, Fiorello H. Oct 40 obit Nov 47

La Guardia, Ricardo Adolfo de *see* De La Guardia, Ricardo Adolfo

La India May 2002

La Montagne, Margaret *see* Spellings, Margaret

La Rocque, François

La Roe, Wilbur, Jr. Mar 48 obit Jul 57

La Russa, Tony Jul 2003

Labelle, Patti Jul 86

Labouisse, Henry R. Oct 61 obit May 87

Lack, Pearl *see* Lang, Pearl

Lacoste, Robert Nov 57

Lacroix, Christian Apr 88

Lacy, Dan Nov 54 obit Nov 2001

Ladd, Alan Sep 43 obit Mar 64

LaDuke, Winona Jan 2003

Ladurie, Emmanuel Le Roy *see* Le Roy Ladurie, Emmanuel

Laeri, J. Howard Sep 68 obit Aug 86

Lafarge, John Nov 42 obit Jan

64

Laffer, Arthur Feb 82

Laffoon, Ruby obit Apr 41

Lafleur, Guy Mar 80

Lafollette, Charles M. Feb 50

LaFontaine, Don Sep 2004

Lafontaine, Oskar Sep 90

Lagardère, Jean-Luc Aug 93 obit Aug 2003

Lagasse, Emeril May 99

Lagerfeld, Karl Jan 82

Lagerkvist, Pär Jan 52 obit Sep 74

Lagerlöf, Selma Apr 40

LaHaye, Tim and Jenkins, Jerry B. Jun 2003

LaHaye, Tim see LaHaye, Tim and Jenkins, Jerry B.

Lahey, Frank H. Mar 41 obit Sep 53

Lahr, Bert Jan 52 obit Feb 68

Laich, Katherine Jun 72

Laidlaw, Patrick Playfair obit Apr 40

Laidler, Harry W. Feb 45 obit Oct 70

Laine, Cleo Feb 86

Laine, Frankie Nov 56

Laing, Hugh Nov 46 obit Jun 88

Laing, R. D. Mar 73 obit Mar 89

Laird, Donald A. Sep 46

Laird, Melvin R. Nov 64

Lake, Anthony Oct 94

Lake, Harriette see Sothern, Ann

Lake, Simon obit Jul 45

Laker, Frederick A. Jun 78

Lalanne, Jack Oct 94

Lall, Anand see Lall, Arthur S.

Lall, Arthur S. Nov 56 obit Jan 99

Lally, Joe see Fugazi

Lamarsh, Judy Apr 68 obit Jan 81

LaMarsh, Julia Verlyn see

Lamarsh, Judy

Lamb, Brian Feb 95

Lamb, Willis E., Jr. Mar 56

Lambert, Janet (WLB) Yrbk 54

Lambert, Sylvester M. Oct 41 obit Feb 47

Lambert, W. V. Nov 55

Lamberton, Robert Eneas obit Oct 41

Lambsdorff, Otto May 80

Lamm, Norman Sep 78

Lamm, Richard D. May 85

Lamond, Felix obit Apr 40

Lamont, Corliss Jun 46 obit Jul 95

Lamont, Norman Aug 92

Lamont, Thomas William Oct 40 obit Feb 48

Lamorisse, Albert Jun 63 obit Jul 70

Lampert, Edward S. Sep 2005

Lancaster, Burt Jul 53 Apr 86 obit Jan 95

Lancaster, Osbert Oct 64 obit Sep 86

Lance, Bert Aug 77

Lanchester, Elsa May 50 obit Feb 87

Land, Edwin H. Nov 53 Mar 81 obit May 91

Land, Emory S. Sep 41 obit Jan 72

Landau, Jacob Dec 65

Landau, Lev Jul 63 obit May 68

Landers, Ann Nov 57 obit Nov 2002

Landes, Bertha K. obit Jan 44

Landis, James M. Mar 42 obit Oct 64

Landis, Kenesaw Mountain May 44 obit Jan 45

Landon, Alf Feb 44 obit Nov 87

Landon, Louise see Hauck, Louise Platt

Landon, Margaret Feb 45 obit Feb 94

Landon, Michael Jul 77 obit

Sep 91

Landowska, Wanda Nov 45 obit Nov 59

Landrieu, Maurice Edwin see Landrieu, Moon

Landrieu, Moon Jan 80

Landrum, Phil M. May 60 obit Jan 91

Landry, Tom Jun 72 obit Apr 2000

Landsbergis, Vytautas Jul 90

Landsteiner, Karl obit Aug 43

Lane, Allen May 54 obit Sep 70

Lane, Arbuthnot obit Mar 43

Lane, Arthur Bliss Apr 48 obit Oct 56

Lane, Burton Mar 67 obit Mar 97

Lane, Carl D. (WLB) Yrbk 51

Lane, Gertrude B. obit Nov 41

Lane, Keith Westmacott see West, Keith

Lane, Nathan Aug 96

Lane, William Arbuthnot see Lane, Arbuthnot

Lane, William Preston, Jr. Jun 49 obit Apr 67

Lang of Lambeth, Cosmo Gordon Lang, 1st Baron see Lang, Cosmo Gordon

Lang, Cosmo Gordon Aug 41 obit Jan 46

Lang, David Feb 2000

Lang, Fritz Jun 43 obit Sep 76

Lang, Helmut Apr 97

Lang, Jack Aug 83

Lang, K. D. Sep 92

Lang, Pearl Jan 70

Langan, Dory see Previn, Dory

Langdon, Harry obit Feb 45

Lange, David Sep 85 obit Yrbk 2005

Lange, Halvard M. Nov 47 obit Jul 70

Lange, Jessica May 83

Lange, John see Crichton, Michael

Lange, Oscar Apr 46 obit Dec

Yrbk 52

Lausche, Frank J. Apr 46 Nov 58 obit Jun 90

Lautenberg, Frank Jan 91

Lauterbach, Jacob Zallel obit Jun 42

Laval, Pierre Sep 40 obit Nov 45

Laver, Rod Feb 63

Laverty, Maura (WLB) Yrbk 47

Lavery, Emmet Jul 47

Lavery, John obit Mar 41

Lavigne, Avril Apr 2003

Lavin, Linda Nov 87

Law, Richard K. Feb 44

Law, Ty Oct 2002

Law, Vernon S. Apr 61

Lawe, John Jan 84 obit Apr 89

Lawes, Lewis Edward Oct 41 obit Mar 47

Lawford, Ernest obit Feb 41

Lawrence, Carol Nov 61

Lawrence, Charles Edward obit Apr 40

Lawrence, David Dec 43 obit Apr 73

Lawrence, David L. Jun 59 obit Jan 67

Lawrence, Ernest O. Feb 40 Jan 52 obit Nov 58

Lawrence, Geoffrey Jan 46 obit Yrbk 91 (died Aug 71)

Lawrence, Gertrude Aug 40 Sep 52

Lawrence, Hilda (WLB) Yrbk 47

Lawrence, Jacob Jul 65 Sep 88 obit Aug 2000

Lawrence, Marjorie Apr 40 obit Mar 79

Lawrence, Martin Oct 99

Lawrence, Mildred (WLB) Yrbk 53

Lawrence, Mrs. Clarence A. see Lawrence, Mildred

Lawrence, Steve Nov 64

Lawrence, William, Bishop

obit Jan 42

Lawson, Edward B. Jan 56

Lawson, Mary obit Jul 41

Lawson, Nigel Mar 87

Lawson, Robert Oct 41 obit Oct 57

Lawson, Ted Dec 43

Lawther, William Dec 49

Lawton, Frederick J. Mar 51

Lax, Peter D. Oct 2005

Laxalt, Paul Jan 79

Laxness, Halldór Oct 46 obit Apr 98

Lay, James S., Jr. Mar 50 obit Aug 87

Laybourne, Geraldine Apr 99

Laycock, Craven obit May 40

Laycock, R. E. May 44 obit May 68

Layton, Geoffrey Feb 42 (died Sep 64)

Layton, Joe Sep 70 obit Jul 94

Layton, Olivia Jan 52 obit Jan 76

Lazareff, Pierre May 42 obit Jun 72

Lazarsfeld, Paul F. Nov 64 obit Oct 76

Lazarus, Rochelle see Lazarus, Shelly

Lazarus, Shelly May 97

Lazzeri, Tony obit Sep 46

Le Carré, John Dec 74

Le Clercq, Tanaquil Jul 53 obit Mar 2001

Le Corbusier Apr 47 obit Nov 65

Le Duc Tho Mar 75 obit Jan 91

Le Gallienne, Eva Oct 42 Mar 55 obit Aug 91

Le Guin, Ursula K. Jan 83

Le Pen, Jean-Marie Jan 88

Le Roy Ladurie, Emmanuel Jul 84

Lea, Clarence F. Nov 46 obit Sep 64

Lea, Luke obit Jan 46

Leach, Alexander Archibald

see Grant, Cary

Leach, Penelope Aug 94

Leach, Robin Sep 90

Leach, Ruth M. Mar 48

Leachman, Cloris Oct 75

Leacock, Stephen obit May 44

Leader, George M. Jan 56

Leahy, Frank Dec 41 obit Sep 73

Leahy, Patrick J. Sep 90

Leahy, William D. Jan 41 obit Oct 59

Leake, Chauncey D. Apr 60 obit Mar 78

Leakey, Louis S. B. Mar 66 obit Dec 72

Leakey, Mary Apr 85 obit Feb 97

Leakey, Meave Jun 2002

Leakey, Richard Nov 76 Oct 95

Lean, David May 53 Jun 89 obit Jun 91

Leao Velloso, P. Sep 46 obit Mar 47

Lear, Ben Jul 42 obit Jan 67

Lear, Evelyn Apr 73

Lear, Frances Apr 91 obit Jan 97

Lear, Norman Feb 74

Lear, William P. Jul 66 obit Jul 78

Leary, Herbert F. Aug 42 obit Feb 58

Leary, John Joseph, Jr. obit Feb 44

Leary, Timothy Dec 70 obit Aug 96

Leathers, Frederick James Leathers, 1st Viscount Jun 41 obit May 65

Leavey, Edmond H. May 51 obit Apr 80

Leblanc, Georgette obit Dec 41

Leblanc, Maurice obit Jan 42

Lebowitz, Fran Mar 82

Leboyer, Frédérick Jul 82

Lebrun, Rico Sep 52 obit Jul

Johnson, Crockett

Leiter, Al Aug 2002

Leith-Ross, Frederick Oct 42

Lejeune, John A. obit Jan 43

Lelong, Lucien Nov 55 obit Sep 58

Lelouch, Claude Nov 82

Lelyveld, Joseph Nov 2005

Lem, Stanislaw Oct 86

Lemass, Sean F. Mar 60 obit Jun 71

Lemay, Curtis E. Dec 44 Nov 54 obit Nov 90

Lemieux, Mario Aug 88

Lemkin, Raphael May 50 obit Nov 59

Lemmon, Jack Feb 61 Aug 88 obit Oct 2001

Lemnitzer, Lyman L. Nov 55 obit Jan 89

Lemon, Ralph Feb 97

Lemond, Greg Oct 89

Lemonnier, André Nov 52 obit Jul 63

Lendl, Ivan Sep 84

Lengyel, Emil Feb 42 obit Apr 85

Lenhart, Jason Gregory see Gregory, Paul

Lennon, John Dec 65 obit Feb 81

Lennox, Annie May 88

Lennox-Boyd, Alan Tindal Jun 56 obit May 83

Leno, Jay Jun 88

Lenroot, Katharine F. May 40 Nov 50 obit Yrbk 91 (died Feb 82)

Lentaigne, Walter D. A. Jul 44 obit Oct 55

Lenya, Lotte Jun 59 obit Jan 82

Leon, Kenny Nov 2005

Leonard see Hackett, Buddy

Leonard see Hackett, Buddy

Leonard, Bill Nov 60 obit Feb 95

Leonard, Eddie obit Sep 41

Leonard, Edward F. obit Jan 41

Leonard, Elmore Sep 85

Leonard, Hugh Apr 83

Leonard, Lucille Putnam Feb 53 [Leonard, Mrs. Newton P.]

Leonard, Mrs. Newton P see Leonard, Lucille Putnam

Leonard, Sugar Ray Feb 81

Leonard, William A. see Leonard, Bill

Leone, Giovanni May 72 obit Feb 2002

Leone, Lucile Petry see Petry, Lucile

Leoni, Raúl Oct 64 obit Sep 72

Leonid Danilovich Kuchma see Kuchma, Leonid

Leonidoff, Leon Jul 41 obit Oct 89

Leonov, Aleksei Jul 65

Leontief, Wassily Jan 67 obit Apr 99

Leopold III, King of The Belgians Dec 44 obit Nov 83

Leopold, Alice K. Jan 55

Lepage, Robert Apr 95

Lepofsky, Manford see Lee, Manfred B.

Leppard, Raymond Mar 80

Lequerica Y Erquiza, José Félix De Jun 51 obit Jul 63

Lercaro, Giacomo Cardinal Sep 65 obit Jan 77

Lerch, Archer L. Nov 45 obit Oct 47

Lerman, Liz Nov 2000

Lerner, Alan Jay Jul 58 [Lerner, Alan Jay; and Loewe, Frederick] obit Aug 86

Lerner, Dorothy see Gordon, Dorothy

Lerner, Gerda Feb 98

Lerner, Max Oct 42 obit Aug 92

Lesage, Jean Nov 61 obit Feb 81

Lescaze, William Apr 42 obit

Apr 69

Lescot, Élie Jun 41 obit Dec 74

Leser, Tina Jun 57 obit Mar 86

Lesinski, John Jr. Jun 57

Lesinski, John Sr. Jul 49 obit Jul 50

Leslie, Chris see Fairport Convention

Leslie, Lisa Jan 98

LeSourd, Catherine Marshall see Marshall, Catherine

Lessing, Bruno obit Jan 40

Lessing, Doris Jan 76 Jan 95

Lester, Richard Apr 69

LeSueur, Larry Jun 43 obit Jun 2003

Letourneau, Jean Oct 52

Letourneau, R. G. Apr 58 obit Jul 69

Letterman, David Nov 80 Oct 2002

Lev, Ray Jan 49 obit Jul 68

Levant, Oscar Jan-Feb 40 Oct 52 obit Oct 72

Levay, Simon Oct 96

Levene, Phoebus Aaron Theodore obit Oct 40

Levenson, Sam Jul 59 obit Nov 80

Leverone, Nathaniel Nov 56 obit Jul 69

Levert, Gerald Oct 2003

Levertov, Denise Aug 91 obit Mar 98

Leveson-Gower, William Spencer Sep 50 obit Sep 53

Lévesque, René Jan 75 obit Jan 88

Levi, Carlo Dec 52 obit Feb 75

Levi, Edward H. Jan 69 obit Jul 2000

Levi, Julian Apr 43 obit Apr 82

Levi, Primo Mar 87 obit Mar 87

Leviero, Anthony Sep 52 obit

Nov 56

Levi-Montalcini, Rita Nov 89

Levin, Carl May 2004

Levin, Ira Aug 91

Levin, Meyer Apr 40 obit Sep 81

Levin, Yehuda Leib Sep 69 obit Jan 72

Levine, David Feb 73

Levine, Irving R. Jul 59

Levine, Jack Jun 56

Levine, James Apr 75

Levine, Joseph E. Oct 79 obit Sep 87

Levine, Mel Nov 2005

Levine, Philip May 47 obit Nov 87

Levinson, Barry Jul 90

Levinson, Salmon Oliver obit Mar 41

Lévi-Strauss, Claude Mar 72

Levi-Tanai, Sara May 58

Levitt, William J. Nov 56 obit Mar 94

Levitzki, Mischa obit Feb 41

LeVox, Gary *see* Rascal Flatts

Lévy, Bernard-Henri Nov 93

Levy, David H. Jan 95

Levy, David Mar 98

Levy, Eugene Jan 2002

Levy, Marv Feb 98

Levy, William Auerbach- *see* Auerbach-Levy, William

Lewi, Mrs. Jack *see* Armstrong, Charlotte

Lewin, Murray obit Sep 43

Lewing, Adele obit Apr 43

Lewis, Albert Buell obit Yrbk 40

Lewis, Ananda Jun 2005

Lewis, C. S. Jan 44 obit Jan 64

Lewis, Carl Nov 84 Yrbk 96

Lewis, Cecil Day- *see* Day-Lewis, C.

Lewis, Chester M. May 56 obit Jun 90

Lewis, Claudius *see* Lewis, Lennox

Lewis, Clyde A. Feb 50

Lewis, Daniel Day- *see* Day-

Lewis, Daniel

Lewis, David Levering May 2001

Lewis, David S. Jr. Aug 75 obit Yrbk 2004

Lewis, Dean obit Dec 41

Lewis, Drew Feb 82

Lewis, Ethelreda obit Sep 46

Lewis, Flora Jan 89 obit Yrbk 2002

Lewis, Francis Park obit Oct 40

Lewis, Fulton, Jr. Nov 42 obit Nov 66

Lewis, Henry Feb 73 obit Apr 96

Lewis, Jerry Nov 62

Lewis, John [civil rights activist] Sep 80

Lewis, John [musician] Jan 62 obit Jun 2001

Lewis, John L. Mar 42 obit Jul 69

Lewis, Joseph Anthony Nov 55

Lewis, Juliette Feb 96

Lewis, Kenneth Apr 2004

Lewis, Lawrence obit Jan 44

Lewis, Lennox Jan 99

Lewis, Loida Nicolas Apr 97

Lewis, Marvin Nov 2004

Lewis, Mary [executive] Sep 40

Lewis, Mary [opera singer] obit Feb 42

Lewis, Oscar Apr 68 obit Feb 71

Lewis, Ramsey Oct 96

Lewis, Richard Jul 93

Lewis, Roger Dec 73 obit Jan 88

Lewis, Shari Mar 58 obit Oct 98

Lewis, Willmott May 41 obit Feb 50

Lewis, Wilmarth Sheldon Jul 73 obit Jan 80

Lewitt, Sol Jul 86

Ley, Robert Sep 40 obit Dec 45

Ley, Willy Jun 41 Feb 53 obit

Sep 69

Leyburn, James G. Apr 43

Leyland, Jim Nov 98

Lhevinne, Josef obit Jan 45

Lhevinne, Rosina Nov 61 obit Jan 77

Li Lian Jie *see* Li, Jet

Li Lieh-Chun obit Apr 46

Li Lieh-hsun *see* Li Lieh-Chun

Li Peng Nov 88

Li Tsung-Jen Nov 42 [Li Tsung-Jen; and Pai Tsung-Hsi] obit Mar 69

Li, Choh-hao Apr 63 obit Jan 88

Li, Gong *see* Gong Li

Li, Jet Jun 2001

Liaquat Ali Khan *see* Khan, Liaquat Ali

Liaquat Ali Khan, Begum *see* Khan, Begum Liaquat Ali

Libby, Frederick J. Apr 49 obit Sep 70

Libby, Willard F. Nov 54 obit Nov 80

Liberace Nov 54 Mar 86 obit Mar 87

Liberman, Alexander May 87 obit Mar 2000

Liberman, Evsei Jun 68 obit May 83

Libeskind, Daniel Jun 2003

Lichtenberg, Bernard obit Nov 44

Lichtenberger, Andre obit Apr 40

Lichtenberger, Arthur Apr 61 obit Nov 68

Lichtenstein, Harvey May 87

Lichtenstein, Roy Feb 69 obit Jan 98

Lichtman, Joseph *see* Layton, Joe

Liddel, Urner May 51

Liddell Hart, Basil Henry Jan-Feb 40 obit Mar 70

Liddy, G. Gordon Oct 80

Lie, Jonas Jan 40

Lie, Trygve Mar 46 obit Feb

69

Liebenow, Robert C. May 56

Lieberman, Joseph I. Jul 94

Liebermann, Rolf Sep 73 obit Mar 99

Lieberson, Goddard Mar 76 obit Jul 77

Liebes, Dorothy Apr 48 obit Dec 72

Liebler, Theodore A. obit Jun 41

Liebling, Leonard obit Dec 45

Liebman, Joshua Loth Oct 46 obit Jul 48

Liebman, Max Apr 53 obit Sep 81

Lifeson, Alex see Rush Lilly, John C. obit Feb 2002

Lifshitz, Ralph see Lauren, Ralph

Lifton, Robert Jay Nov 73

Ligachev, Yegor K. Aug 90

Liggett, Louis Kroh obit Jul 46

Lightfoot, Gordon Aug 78

Lightner, Milton C. Nov 58 obit May 68

Lil' Kim Oct 2000

Lilienthal, David E. Jun 44 obit Mar 81

Lillard, George W. obit Yrbk 40

Lillehei, C. Walton May 69 obit Nov 99

Lillie, Beatrice Feb 45 Sep 64 obit Mar 89

Lilly, John C. Nov 62 obit Feb 2002

Lilly, Kristine Apr 2004

Lima do Amor, Sisleide see Sissi Lincoln, Abbey Sep 2002

Lima, Sigrid de see De Lima, Sigrid

Liman, Arthur L. Jan 88 obit Oct 97

Limann, Hilla Jun 81 obit Apr 98

Limb, Ben C. Jan 51

Limbaugh, Rush Mar 93

Limón, José Jun 53 Apr 68

obit Jan 73

Lin Ch'ang-jen see Lin Sen

Lin Piao May 67 obit Oct 72

Lin Sen obit Sep 43

Lin, Maya Apr 93

Lin, Yutang May 40 obit May 76

Lincoln, Blanche Lambert Mar 2002

Lincoln, Joseph C. obit Apr 44

Lincoln, Leroy A. Jun 46 obit Jun 57

Lincoln, Murray D. Mar 53 obit Jan 67

Lind, Joseph Conrad see Hayes, Peter Lind

Lindbergh, Anne Morrow Nov 40 Jun 76

Lindbergh, Anne Morrow Jun 76 obit Apr 2001

Lindbergh, Charles A. Jul 41 Jan 54 obit Oct 74

Lindemann, Frederick Alexander Mar 52 obit Sep 57

Linden, Hal Jan 87

Lindenberg, Hedda see Sterne, Hedda

Lindfors, Viveca Apr 55 obit Jan 96

Lindgren, Astrid Oct 96 obit Apr 2002

Lindley, Ernest Hiram obit Oct 40

Lindley, Ernest K. Jun 43 obit Yrbk 91 (died Jun 79)

Lindo, Delroy Mar 2001

Lindros, Eric Apr 98

Lindsay, Howard Apr 42 [Lindsay, Howard; and Stickney, Dorothy] obit Apr 68

Lindsay, John V. Nov 62 obit Mar 2001

Lindsay, Ronald obit Sep 45

Lindsey, Ben B. obit May 43

Lindsley, Thayer Jan 57 obit Jul 76

Lindt, Auguste R. Nov 59 obit Yrbk 2000

Ling, James J. Apr 70 obit

Yrbk 2005

Lingle, Linda Jun 2003

Link, Edwin Jan 74 obit Yrbk 83 (died Sep 81)

Link, O. Winston Jun 95 obit Apr 2001

Linkin Park Mar 2002

Linkletter, Art Nov 53

Linlithgow, Victor Alexander John Hope, 2d Marquess of see Hope, Victor Alexander John

Linnell, John see They Might Be Giants

Linowitz, Sol M. Mar 67 obit Yrbk 2005

Linton, Frank B. A. obit Jan 44

Lion of Kashmir see Abdullah, Mohammad

Lionni, Leo Sep 97 obit Feb 2000

Liotta, Ray May 94

Li-pai see Tsung-Jen Li and Tsung-Hsi Pai

Lipchitz, Chaim Jacob see Lipchitz, Jacques

Lipchitz, Jacques Nov 48 Apr 62 obit Jul 73

Lipinski, Ann Marie Jul 2004

Lipinski, Tara Apr 98

Lipmann, Fritz Mar 54 obit Sep 86

Lippincott, Joseph Wharton May 55 obit Jan 77

Lippincott, Joshua Bertram obit Jan 40

Lippmann, Walter Sep 40 Nov 62 obit Jan 75

Lippold, Richard Nov 56 obit Yrbk 2002

Lipschitz, Chaim U. Dec 66

Lipsky, Eleazar (WLB) Yrbk 59 obit Apr 93

Lipton, Seymour Nov 64 obit Feb 87

Litchfield, Edward H. Nov 53 obit May 68

Litchfield, P. W. Dec 50 obit

72 obit Feb 85

Long, Andrew Theodore obit Jul 46

Long, Breckinridge Nov 43 obit Dec 58

Long, Earl K. Dec 50 obit Nov 60

Long, Edward V. Jul 64 obit Jan 73

Long, Oren E. Sep 51 obit Jun 65

Long, Richard Sep 95

Long, Russell B. Dec 51 Oct 65 obit Yrbk 2003

Long, Tania May 46 obit Jun 99

Long, Westray see Boyce, Westray Battle

Long, William Ivey Mar 2004

Longbaugh, Harry see Goldman, William

Longman, Hubert Harry obit Apr 40

Longo, Luigi Feb 66 obit Jan 81

Longo, Robert Oct 90

Longstreth, T. Morris (WLB) Yrbk 50

Longworth, Alice Roosevelt Jun 43 Aug 75 obit Apr 80

Loomis, Daniel P. Jan 60

Loomis, Orland S. obit Jan 43

Loos, Anita Feb 74 obit Oct 81

Loosli, E. Fritz Jan 42

Lopes, Francisco Higino Craveiro see Craveiro Lopes, Francisco Higino

López Bravo, Gregorio Jul 71 obit Apr 85

López Mateos, Adolfo Mar 59 obit Nov 69

López Michelsen, Alfonso Apr 75

López Portillo, José Jun 77 obit Yrbk 2004

López Rodó, Laureano Feb 72

Lopez, Al Feb 60

López, Alfonso Sep 42 obit

Jan 60

Lopez, Barry Jul 95

Lopez, Encarnacion see Argentinita

Lopez, Nancy Sep 78

Lopez, Trini Mar 68

Lopez, Vincent Nov 60 Nov 75

Loquasto, Santo Jun 81

Loram, Charles Templeman obit Sep 40

Lord Caradon see Foot, Hugh

Lord Irwin see Halifax, Edward Frederick Lindley Wood, 1st Earl of

Lord, F. T. obit Jan 42

Lord, John Wesley May 71 obit Jan 90

Lord, Mary Stimson Pillsbury see Lord, Mrs. Oswald B.

Lord, Milton E. Feb 50

Lord, Mrs. Oswald B. Oct 52 [Lord, Mary Stimson Pillsbury]

Lord, Walter Oct 72 obit Yrbk 2002

Loren, Sophia Mar 59

Lorentz, Pare Apr 40 obit May 92

Lorenz, John G. Sep 66

Lorenz, Konrad Jul 55 Oct 77 obit Apr 89

Lorenzo, Frank Feb 87

Lorge, Irving Jul 59 obit Apr 61

Loring, Eugene Mar 72 obit Oct 82

Loring, Jules see Mackaye, Julia Gunther

Loring, Peter see Shellabarger, Samuel

Lortel, Lucille Feb 85 obit Jul 99

Los Angeles, Victoria de see Angeles, Victoria de los

Los Lobos Oct 2005

Losch, Tilly Jul 44 obit Feb 76

Losey, Joseph Dec 69 obit Aug 84

Lothar, Ernst (WLB) Yrbk 47

Lothian, Philip Henry Kerr,

11th Marquis of obit Yrbk 40

Lott, Ronnie Feb 94

Lott, Trent Sep 96

Lou, Liza Jan 2000

Louchheim, Aline B. see Saarinen, Aline B.

Louchheim, Katie Jun 56 obit Apr 91

Louchheim, Mrs. Walter C., Jr. see Louchheim, Katie

Loud, Pat Jul 74

Loudon, Alexander Jul 42 obit Mar 53

Loudon, Dorothy Jun 84 obit Yrbk 2004

Louganis, Greg Oct 84

Lougheed, Peter Aug 79

Loughlin, Anne Feb 50

Louis, Joe Oct 40 obit Jun 81

Louis, Murray Oct 68

Louis-Dreyfus, Julia Oct 95

Louise Caroline Alberta, Duchess of Argyll, Princess obit Jan 40

Loutfi, Omar Jan 57 obit Jul 63

Louw, Eric H. Mar 62 obit Sep 68

Lovano, Joe Mar 98

Love, Courtney Jun 96

Love, George H. Mar 50 obit Sep 91

Love, Iris Aug 82

Love, J. Spencer Nov 57 obit Mar 62

Love, John A. Nov 63 obit Apr 2002

Love, Susan M. Oct 94

LoVecchio, Frank Paul see Laine, Frankie

Loveless, Herschel C. Jul 58 obit Jul 89

Lovell, Bernard Oct 59

Lovell, James A., Jr. Mar 69

Lovelock, James Nov 92

Loveman, Amy Jun 43 obit Feb 56

Lovett, Lyle Sep 97

Lovett, Robert A. Aug 42 Nov

51 obit Jun 86

Lovett, Robert Morss Aug 43 obit Apr 56

Lovins, Amory B. Jun 97

Low, David Jan-Feb 40 obit Nov 63

Lowden, Frank O. obit May 43

Lowdermilk, W. C. Feb 49 obit Jul 74

Lowe, Jack Jan 54 [Whittemore, Arthur; and Lowe, Jack] obit Aug 96

Lowe, Rob Jul 2000

Lowell, A. Lawrence obit Feb 43

Lowell, Mike Sep 2003

Lowell, Robert Jul 47 Jan 72 obit Nov 77

Lowenstein, Allard K. Sep 71 obit May 80

Lowery, Joseph E. Nov 82

Lowey, Nita M. Sep 97

Lownsbery, Eloise (WLB) Yrbk 47

Lowrie, Jean E. Jun 73

Lowry, Edward G. obit Sep 43

Loy, Myrna Oct 50 obit Feb 94

Loynd, Harry, J. Feb 52

Lozano, Conrad see Los Lobos Lucas, George May 2002

Lozovsky, S. A. Nov 41

Lozowick, Louis Apr 42 obit Nov 73

Lubbers, Ruud May 88

Lubell, Samuel Nov 56 obit Oct 87

Lubic, Ruth Watson Sep 96

Lubin, Isador Oct 41 Jan 53 obit Sep 78

Lübke, Heinrich Jan 60 obit May 72

Lubovitch, Lar Mar 92

Luca, Giuseppe De see De Luca, Giuseppe

Lucas, Craig Sep 91

Lucas, George Apr 78 May

2002

Lucas, Jerry Jun 72

Lucas, John Oct 95

Lucas, Martha B. see Pate, Martha B.

Lucas, Scott W. Dec 47 obit Apr 68

Lucci, Susan Oct 89

Luccock, Halford E. Jun 60 obit Jan 61

Luce, Charles F. Dec 68

Luce, Clare Boothe Nov 42 Apr 53 obit Nov 87

Luce, Henry R. Jul 41 Jan 61 obit Apr 67

Luce, Robert obit May 46

Lucet, Charles Dec 67

Lucioni, Luigi Oct 43 obit Sep 88

Luckman, Charles Oct 47 obit Apr 99

Luckovich, Mike Jan 2005

Luckstone, Isidore obit May 41

Ludacris Jun 2004

Ludington, Flora B. Nov 53

Ludlam, Charles Aug 86 obit Jul 87

Ludlum, Robert Nov 82 obit Jul 2001

Ludwig, Christa Mar 71

Ludwig, Daniel Keith May 79 obit Oct 92

Ludwig, Ken May 2004

Lugar, Richard G. Oct 77

Luhan, Mabel Dodge Jan-Feb 40 obit Oct 62

Luhring, Oscar Raymond obit Oct 44

Lujack, Johnny Dec 47

Lujan, Manuel, Jr. Sep 89

Lukas, J. Anthony Jan 87 obit Aug 97

Lukas, Paul Feb 42 obit Oct 71

Luke, Delilah Rene see Delilah

Lumet, Sidney Sep 67 Jun 2005

Lumley, Roger Jan 58 obit

Sep 69

Lumpkin, Alva M. obit Sep 41

Lumumba, Patrice Nov 60 obit Apr 61

Lund, Wendell L. Sep 42

Lundeberg, Harry Nov 52 obit Mar 57

Lundeen, Ernest obit Oct 40

Lunden, Joan May 89

Lunn, Katharine Fowler see Fowler-Billings, Katharine

Luns, Joseph M. A. H. Feb 58 Apr 82 obit Yrbk 2002

Lunt, Alfred Jun 41 [Lunt, Alfred; and Fontanne, Lynn] obit Sep 77

Lunt, Storer B. Nov 58

Lunts, The see Alfred Lunt and Lynn Fontanne

Lupescu, Magda Oct 40 obit Aug 77

Lupica, Mike Mar 2001

Lupino, Ida Sep 43 obit Oct 95

Lupino, Stanley obit Aug 42

Lupone, Patti Apr 89

Luquiens, Frederick Bliss obit May 40

Lurçat, Jean Sep 48 obit Feb 66

Luria, S. E. Feb 70 obit Apr 91

Lurie, Alison Feb 86

Lusk, Georgia L. Oct 47 obit Feb 71

Lustiger, Cardinal see Lustiger, Jean Marie

Lustiger, Jean Marie Feb 84

Lutes, Della Thompson obit Sep 42

Luthuli, Albert John Feb 62 obit Oct 67

Lutoslawski, Witold Aug 91 obit Apr 94

Lutyens, Edwin L. Jun 42 obit Feb 44

Lutz, Frank E. obit Jan 44

Lutz, Robert A. Jan 94

Luzhkov, Yuri Nov 99

Lydenberg, Harry Miller Sep

41 obit Jun 60

Lydon, John Nov 96

Lyle, Sparky Jul 78

Lynch, Daniel F. Jul 55

Lynch, David May 87

Lynch, J. Joseph Oct 46 obit Aug 87

Lynch, John May 67 obit Feb 2000

Lynch, Peg Feb 56

Lynch, Peter Nov 94

Lynch, William J. obit Aug 41

Lynd, Staughton May 83

Lynde, Paul Nov 72 obit Feb 82

Lyndon, Edward obit Yrbk 40

Lyne, Adrian Jan 94

Lynen, Feodor Jun 67 obit Oct 79

Lynes, Russell Nov 57 obit Nov 91

Lyng, Richard E. Sep 86 obit Jun 2003

Lynn, Diana Nov 53 obit Feb 72

Lynn, James T. Dec 73

Lynn, Loretta Oct 73

Lynne, Shelby Jul 2001

Lyons, Eugene Jan 44 obit Mar 85

Lyons, Harry Oct 57

Lysenko, T. D. Oct 52 obit Feb 77

Lyttelton, Oliver Sep 41 Jan 53 obit Mar 72

Lyubimov, Yuri Nov 88

M. C. Hammer *see* Hammer

M'bow, Amadou-Mahtar May 87

Ma Chi-Chuang Jul 53

Ma, G. John *see* Ma Chi-Chuang

Ma, Yo-Yo Jul 82

Maas, Melvin J. Nov 57 obit Jun 64

Maathai, Wangari Sep 93

Maazel, Lorin Dec 65

Mabley, Jackie *see* Mabley, Moms

Mabley, Moms Jan 75 obit Aug 75

Mabovitz, Goldie *see* Meir, Golda

Mac, Bernie Jun 2002

Macalarney, Robert E. obit Jan 46

Macapagal, Diosdado Nov 62 obit Jul 97

Macarthur, Douglas Oct 41 May 48 obit May 64

Macarthur, Douglas, 2d Nov 54 obit Jan 98

Macartney, William Napier obit Aug 40

Macauley, Jane Hamilton Sep 49

Macauley, Mrs. Robert W. *see* Macauley, Jane Hamilton

Macbride, Ernest William obit Jan 41

Macbride, Sean Jun 49 obit Mar 88

Maccallum, William George obit Mar 44

Maccormick, Austin H. May 40 Jul 51 obit Jan 80

Maccracken, Henry Noble Sep 40 obit Jun 70

Macdermot, Galt Jul 84

Macdonald, Betty Feb 46 obit Apr 58

Macdonald, Brian Jul 68

Macdonald, Cordelia Howard obit Oct 41

Macdonald, Duncan Black, Rev. obit Oct 43

Macdonald, Dwight Nov 69 obit Mar 83

Macdonald, George obit Sep 40

Macdonald, John D. Oct 86 obit Feb 87

Macdonald, John Ross *see* Macdonald, Ross

Macdonald, Malcolm Nov 54 obit Mar 81

Macdonald, Pirie obit Jun 42

Macdonald, Ross (WLB) Yrbk 53 [Millar, Kenneth] Aug 79 obit Sep 83

Macdonald, William J. obit May 46

MacDowell, Andie Nov 99

MacEachen, Allan J. Apr 83

MacEwen, Walter obit May 43

MacFarlane, F. N. Mason Feb 43

MacGowan, Gault Jan 45

MacGregor, Ellen (WLB) Yrbk 54

Machado, Alexis Leyva *see* Kcho

Machado, Alfredo obit Sep 46

Machado, Bernardino obit Jun 44

Machel, Graça Simbine Oct 97

Machel, Samora Mar 84 obit Jan 87

Machito Feb 83 obit Jun 84

Machold, Earle J. Nov 58

Macinnes, Helen Nov 67 obit Nov 85

Maciver, Loren Nov 53 Nov 87 obit Aug 98

Mack, Connie Jun 44 obit Apr 56

Mack, Julian W. obit Oct 43

Mack, Lawrence L. Apr 57

Mack, Nila Dec 52 obit Mar 53

Mack, Pauline Beery Dec 50

Mack, Ted Apr 51 obit Sep 76

Mack, Walter S. Feb 46 obit May 90

Mackay, Iven Giffard Apr 41 obit Jan 67

Mackay, John A. Feb 52 obit Aug 83

Mackaye, David L. (WLB) Yrbk 49 [MacKaye, David L.; and MacKaye, Julia Gunther]

MacKaye, Ian *see* Fugazi

Mackaye, Julia Gunther (WLB) Yrbk 49 [MacKaye, David L.; and MacKaye, Julia Gunther]

MacKaye, Loring *see* Mackaye, David L.; Mackaye,

Julia Gunther

Mackenzie, C. J. Jun 52

Mackenzie, Clinton obit Mar 40

MacKenzie, Gisele Nov 55 obit Jul 2004

MacKenzie, Gisele obit Jul 2004

MacKenzie, Marie Marguerite Louise Gisele La Fleche *see* Mackenzie, Gisele

Mackenzie, Warren Sep 94

Mackenzie, William Warrender, 1st Baron *see* Amulree, William Warrender Mackenzie, 1st Baron of Strathbraan

Mackie, Bob Oct 88

Mackinnon, Catharine A. Jun 94

Mackintosh, Cameron Mar 91

Maclachlan, Kyle Aug 93

Maclaine, Shirley Dec 59 Jul 78

Maclean, Basil C. May 57 obit Apr 63

Maclean, Malcolm Shaw Jul 40

Macleish, Archibald Oct 40 Nov 59 obit Jun 82

Maclennan, Hugh (WLB) Yrbk 46 obit Jan 91

MacLeod, Dorothy Shaw Apr 49

Macleod, Iain Apr 56 obit Oct 70

Macleod, Mrs. W. Murdoch *see* MacLeod, Dorothy Shaw

Macmahon, Arthur W. Apr 58 obit Apr 80

Macmillan, Donald Baxter Sep 48 obit Nov 70

Macmillan, Ernest Mar 55 obit Jun 73

Macmillan, Harold Mar 43 Jan 55 obit Feb 87

MacMitchell, Leslie Apr 46

Macmurray, Fred Feb 67 obit

Feb 92

Macneil, Cornell Jan 76

Macneil, Neil May 40

Macneil, Robert Feb 80

Macphail, Larry Mar 45 obit Nov 75

Macrae, John obit Apr 44

Macrossie, Allan, Rev. obit Mar 40

Macveagh, Lincoln Nov 41 Jun 52 obit Mar 72

Macy, Edith Dewing Dec 52 obit Oct 67

Macy, George Nov 54 obit Sep 56

Macy, John W., Jr. Jan 62 obit Apr 87

Macy, Mrs. Edward W. *see* Macy, Edith Dewing

Madariaga, Salvador De Jan 64 obit Feb 79

Madden, John Aug 85

Madden, Ray J. Apr 53 obit Nov 87

Maddox, Lester Dec 67 obit Yrbk 2003

Maddox, William P. Nov 47 obit Dec 72

Maddux, Greg Feb 96

Maddy, Joseph E. Apr 46 obit May 66

Madeira, Jean Oct 63 obit Sep 72

Madeleva, Sister Mary Feb 42 obit Oct 64

Madigan, Edward R. Nov 92 obit Feb 95

Madonna May 86

Madrid, Miguel de la *see* De La Madrid, Miguel

Madsen, Michael Apr 2004

Maenner, T. H. Nov 49 obit Mar 58

Magallanes, Nicholas May 55 obit Jul 77

Magaziner, Ira C. Apr 95

Magee, Elizabeth S. Oct 50

Magee, James C. May 43

Maggiolo, Walter A. Jul 52 obit Yrbk 2000

Magill, Roswell Mar 48 obit

Feb 64

Maglie, Sal Jun 53 obit Feb 93

Maglione, Luigi, Cardinal obit Oct 44

Magloire, Paul E. Feb 52 obit Nov 2001

Magnani, Anna Apr 56 obit Nov 73

Magner, Thomas F. obit Feb 46

Magnuson, Paul B. Jun 48 obit Jan 69

Magnuson, Warren G. Oct 45 obit Jul 89

Magoffin, Ralph Van Deman obit Jul 42

Magritte, René Sep 66 obit Oct 67

Magruder, William M. Mar 72 obit Nov 77

Magsaysay, Ramón Dec 52 obit May 57

Maguiness, William Edward *see* Mack, Ted

Maguire, Tobey Sep 2002

Mahady, Henry J. Jul 54

Mahal, Taj Nov 2001

Mahan, John W. Jul 59

Maharaj Ji, Guru Dec 74

Mahathir Bin Mohamad Aug 88

Mahendra, King of Nepal Jul 56 obit Mar 72

Maher, Ahmed, Pasha obit Apr 45

Maher, Aly Mar 52 obit Nov 60

Maher, Bill Jul 97

Mahesh Yogi, Maharishi Dec 72

Mahfouz, Naguib May 89

Mahmoud Hassan *see* Hassan, Mahmoud

Mahon, George H. Mar 58 obit Jan 86

Mahoney, John Aug 99

Maier, Walter A. May 47 obit Feb 50

Maile, Boniface R. Feb 51

Mailer, Norman Oct 48 Feb

70

Mailhouse, Max obit Dec 41

Maillol, Aristide May 42 obit Nov 44

Main, Charles Thomas obit Apr 43

Main, Marjorie Oct 51 obit Jun 75

Mainbocher Feb 42 obit Mar 77

Maines, Natalie *see* Dixie Chicks

Maisky, Ivan Sep 41 obit Oct 75

Major, John Oct 90 Apr 97

Makarios III May 56 obit Sep 77

Makarova, Natalia Feb 72

Makeba, Miriam Jun 65

Makemson, Maud W. Jun 41

Maki, Fumihiko Jul 2001

Makin, Norman J. O. Mar 46

Makins, Roger Jan 53 obit Jan 97

Makonnen, Tafari *see* Haile Selassie I

Malamud, Bernard (WLB) Yrbk 58 Jul 78 obit May 86

Malan, Daniel François

Malbin, Elaine Feb 59

Malcolm, George A. Nov 54

Malden, Karl Apr 57

Malenkov, Georgi M. Jun 52 obit Mar 88

Malick, Terrence Jun 99

Malik, Adam Nov 70 obit Nov 84

Malik, Charles H. Apr 48 obit Feb 88

Malik, Jacob Apr 49 obit Apr 80

Malin, Patrick Murphy Mar 50 obit Feb 65

Malina, Joshua Apr 2004

Malinovsky, Rodion Y. Mar 44 Nov 60 obit May 67

Malinowski, Bronislaw Jun 41 obit Jul 42

Malkovich, John May 88

Mallakh, Kamal, El *see* El

Mallakh, Kamal

Malle, Louis Feb 76 obit Feb 96

Mallette, Gertrude E. (WLB) Yrbk 50

Malley, Matt *see* Counting Crows

Mallory, C. C. Feb 56 obit Mar 59

Mallory, F. B. obit Nov 41

Mallory, L. D. Sep 60 obit Sep 94

Malone, George W. Dec 50 obit Jul 61

Malone, John C. Aug 95

Malone, Karl Jan 93

Malone, Moses Jun 86

Malone, Ross L. Mar 59 obit Oct 74

Maloney, Carolyn B. Apr 2001

Maloney, Francis T. obit Mar 45

Maloney, Walter E. Oct 52

Malott, Deane W. Mar 51 obit Nov 96

Malraux, André Mar 59 obit Feb 77

Maltz, Albert Jan-Feb 40 obit Jul 85

Malvern, Godfrey Huggins, 1st Viscount *see* Huggins, Godfrey

Mamet, David Aug 78 Mar 98

Mamlok, Hans J. obit Yrbk 40

Mamoulian, Rouben Mar 49 obit Jan 88

Manchester, William Nov 67 obit Yrbk 2004

Mancini, Henry Jul 64 obit Aug 94

Mandel, Georges Yrbk 40

Mandela, Nelson Jan 84 Nov 95

Mandela, Winnie Jan 86

Mandelbrot, Benoit Jun 87

Mandlikova, Hana Jan 86

Mandrell, Barbara Aug 82

Manessier, Alfred May 57 obit Oct 93

Maney, Richard Jul 64 obit

Sep 68

Mangione, Chuck May 80

Mangione, Jerre Mar 43 obit Nov 98

Mangrum, Lloyd Sep 51 obit Jan 74

Manilow, Barry Jul 78

Mankiewicz, Joseph L. Sep 49 obit Apr 93

Mankiller, Wilma P. Nov 88

Mankin, Helen Douglas Apr 46

Mankind *see* Foley, Mick

Mankoff, Robert May 2005

Mankowitz, Wolf (WLB) Yrbk 56 obit Aug 98

Manley, Michael Jan 76 obit May 97

Manley, Norman W. Nov 59 obit Nov 69

Manly, John Matthews obit May 40

Mann, Emily Jun 2002

Mann, Erica *see* Jong, Erica

Mann, Erika Yrbk 40 obit Nov 69

Mann, Klaus Yrbk 40 obit Jul 49

Mann, Marty Jun 49 obit Sep 80

Mann, Michael Jan 93

Mann, Thomas C. Apr 64 obit Apr 99

Mann, Thomas May 42 obit Oct 55

Mann, Tom obit May 41

Manna, Charlie Jan 65 obit Dec 71

Mannerheim, Carl Gustaf Emil von Apr 40 obit Feb 51

Mannes, Marya Apr 59

Manning, Ernest Dec 59 obit May 96

Manning, Harry May 52 obit Oct 74

Manning, Marie *see* Fairfax, Beatrice

Manning, Peyton Sep 98

Manning, Reg Jun 51

Manning, William Thomas,

Bishop Apr 40 obit Jan 50

Mansbridge, Albert Jun 42

Mansfield, Michael J. *see* Mansfield, Mike

Mansfield, Mike Apr 52 Jan 78 obit Jan 2002

Manship, Paul May 40 obit Mar 66

Mansholt, Sicco L. May 66

Manson, John T. obit Apr 44

Manson, Marilyn May 99

Mansouri, Lotfi Apr 90

Manstein, Fritz Erich Von Oct 42 obit Sep 73

Mantle, Burns Nov 44 obit Mar 48

Mantle, Mickey Jul 53 obit Oct 95

Manuilsky, Dmitri Z. Dec 48 obit May 59

Manzù, Giacomo Mar 61 obit Mar 91

Mao Tse-Tung *see* Mao Zedong

Mao Zedong Feb 43 May 62 obit Oct 76

Mapes, Victor obit Jan 44

Mapplethorpe, Robert May 89 obit May 89

Maradona, Diego Nov 90

Marais, Jean Apr 62 obit Jan 99

Marble, Alice Nov 40 obit Mar 91

Marburg, Theodore obit Apr 46

Marcantonio, Vito Feb 49 obit Oct 54

Marca-Relli, Conrad Sep 70 obit Nov 2000

Marceau, Marcel Feb 57

March, Charles Hoyt obit Sep 45

March, Fredric Mar 43 [March, Fredric; and Eldridge, Florence] obit Jun 75

Marchais, Georges Jun 76 obit Jan 98

Marchal, Léon Sep 43 obit Dec 56 Yrbk 57

Marcial-Dorado, Carolina

obit Sep 41

Marciano, Rocky Sep 52 obit Nov 69

Marcinko, Richard Mar 2001

Marcos, Ferdinand E. Feb 67 obit Nov 89

Marcus, Greil Oct 99

Marcus, Jacob R. May 60 obit Jan 96

Marcus, Stanley Jun 49 obit Apr 2002

Marcuse, Herbert Mar 69 obit Sep 79

Marcy, Geoffrey W. *see* Marcy, Geoffrey W., and Butler, R. Paul

Marcy, Geoffrey W., and Butler, R. Paul Nov 2002

Marden, Brice Aug 90

Marden, Orison S. Jul 67 obit Oct 75

Mardikian, George M. Nov 47

Marek, Kurt W. Jan 57 obit Jun 72

Marella, Paolo, Cardinal Oct 64

Marett, Robert R. obit Apr 43

Margai, Milton Feb 62 obit Jun 64

Margaret, Princess of Great Britain Nov 53 obit May 2002

Marge *see* Damerel, Donna

Margesson, Henry David Reginald Margesson, 1st Viscount Feb 41 obit Feb 66

Margoliouth, David Samuel obit Apr 40

Margret, Ann *see* Ann-Margret

Margrethe II, Queen of Denmark Nov 72

Margueritte, Victor obit May 42

Margulis, Lynn Jul 92

Maria Theresa, Archduchess of Austria obit Apr 44

Marías, Julián Feb 72

Marie, Andre Sep 48 obit Sep 74

Marin, John Jul 49 obit Dec

53

Marín, Luis Muñoz *see* Munoz Marin, Luis

Marini, Marino Jan 54 obit Oct 80

Marino, Dan Jan 89

Marion, George obit Jan 46

Maris, Roger Nov 61 obit Feb 86

Marisol Apr 68

Maritain, Jacques May 42 obit Jun 73

Marius, Emilie Alexander obit Apr 40

Marjolin, Robert Dec 48 obit Jun 86

Mark, Herman F. May 61 obit Jun 92

Mark, Louis obit May 42

Mark, Mary Ellen Sep 99

Mark, Rebecca May 99

Markel, Lester Dec 52 obit Jan 78

Marker, Laurie Feb 2000

Marker-Kraus, Laurie *see* Marker, Laurie

Markey, Edward J. Nov 97

Markham, Beryl Nov 42 obit Oct 86

Markham, Edwin Mar 40

Markova, Alicia Sep 43 obit Yrbk 2005

Markovic, Ante Nov 91

Marks, Leonard H. Jun 66

Marks, Simon Marks, 1st Baron Nov 62 obit Feb 65

Marland, Sidney P., Jr. Apr 72 obit Jul 92

Marland, William C. Apr 56 obit Jan 66

Marlette, Doug Jul 2002

Marples, Ernest May 60

Marquand, Hilary A. Apr 51

Marquand, John Apr 42 obit Oct 60

Marquardt, Alexandria obit Jun 43

Marquis, Albert Nelson obit Feb 44

Marquis, Frederick James Marquis, 1st Baron Woolton *see* Woolton, Frederick James Marquis, 1st Earl

Marriner, Neville Aug 78

Marriott, Alice Lee (WLB) Yrbk 50 obit May 92

Marriott, J. Willard Jun 72 obit Oct 85

Marriott, John obit Jul 45

Marrow, Tracy *see* Ice-T

Marsalis, Branford Sep 91

Marsalis, Ellis Aug 2000

Marsh, Ernest Sterling Feb 60

Marsh, Jean Nov 77

Marsh, John, Rev. Dr. Mar 60

Marsh, Reginald Sep 41 obit Sep 54

Marshak, Robert E. Jul 73 obit Feb 93

Marshall, Barry J. Sep 96

Marshall, Burke Feb 65 obit Yrbk 2003

Marshall, C. Herbert, Jr. Oct 49

Marshall, Catherine Jan 55 obit May 83

Marshall, David Jul 56 obit Feb 96

Marshall, E. G. Jun 86 obit Nov 98

Marshall, Garry Nov 92

Marshall, George C. Oct 40 Mar 47 obit Dec 59

Marshall, Grant *see* Massive Attack

Marshall, Lois Jun 60 obit May 97

Marshall, M. Lee Sep 48 obit Oct 50

Marshall, Penny Mar 80 May 92

Marshall, Peter, Rev. Apr 48 obit Feb 49

Marshall, Ray Nov 77

Marshall, Rob Jun 2003

Marshall, Rosamond Aug 42 obit Feb 58

Marshall, S. L. A. Nov 53 obit Mar 78

Marshall, Susan Jul 99

Marshall, Thurgood Nov 54 Sep 89 obit Mar 93

Marshall, Tully obit Apr 43

Marshall, Verne Feb 41 obit May 65

Marshall, Walter P. Apr 50 obit Jun 69

Marsten, Richard *see* Hunter, Evan

Martel, Giffard Le Quesne Jul 43 obit Nov 58

Martell, Edward Nov 64

Martens, Wilfried Feb 87

Martin Artajo, Alberto Nov 49

Martin, A. J. P. *see* Martin, Archer

Martin, Agnes Sep 89 obit Apr 2005

Martin, Alfred Manuel *see* Martin, Billy

Martin, Allie Beth Jun 75 obit Jun 76

Martin, Archer John Porter Nov 53 obit Yrbk 2002

Martin, Billy Oct 76 obit Feb 90

Martin, Charles H. obit Nov 46

Martin, Chris *see* Coldplay

Martin, Christy Oct 97

Martin, Collier Ford obit May 41

Martin, Dean Nov 64 obit Mar 96

Martin, Dick Sep 69

Martin, Edgar Stanley Jr. obit Sep 40

Martin, Edmund F. Jan 62 obit Mar 93

Martin, Edward Oct 45 obit May 67

Martin, Fletcher Feb 58 obit Jul 79

Martin, Frank L. obit Sep 41

Martin, George Brown obit Dec 45

Martin, George R. R. Jan 2004

Martin, Glenn L. Feb 43 obit Feb 56

Martin, Harry Jun 48 obit Mar 59

Martin, Helen *see* Rood, Helen Martin

Martin, Jackie Apr 43

Martin, James S. Jr. Mar 77 obit Yrbk 2002

Martin, John Bartlow (WLB) Yrbk 56 obit Mar 87

Martin, Joseph W., Jr. Oct 40 May 48 obit Apr 68

Martin, Judith Jun 86

Martin, Kenyon Jan 2005

Martin, Kevin J. Aug 2005

Martin, Lillien J. Apr 42 obit May 43

Martin, Lynn Oct 89

Martin, Mark Mar 2001

Martin, Mary Jan 44 obit Jan 91

Martin, Paul Dec 51 obit Nov 92

Martin, Percy Alvin obit Apr 42

Martin, Ricky Sep 99

Martin, Steve Aug 78 Nov 2000

Martin, Thomas E. Mar 56 obit Sep 71

Martin, Walter B. Nov 54 obit May 66

Martin, William C., Bishop Apr 53

Martin, William McChesney, Jr. May 51 obit Oct 98

Martinelli, Giovanni Jan 45 obit Mar 69

Martínez Trueba, Andrés Nov 54 obit Feb 60

Martinez, Alicia *see* Alonso, Alicia

Martínez, Maximiliano Hernández *see* Hernández Martínez, Maximiliano

Martinez, Pedro Jun 2001

Martinez, Rueben Jun 2005

Martinez, Vilma Jul 2004

Martini, Helen Jul 55

Martini, Mrs. Fred *see* Martini, Helen

Martino, Gaetano May 56 obit

Oct 67

Martins, Peter Jun 78

Martinu, Bohuslav Nov 44 obit Nov 59

Martland, Harrison Stanford Nov 40 obit Jun 54

Marton, Eva Apr 85

Martos, Rafael *see* Raphael

Marty, Martin E. Jun 68

Martz, Judy Mar 2005

Marvel, Elizabeth Newell Apr 62 [Marval, Mrs. Archie D.]

Marvin, Charles F. obit Jul 43

Marvin, Cloyd H. Dec 49 obit Jun 69

Marvin, Dwight Edwards, Rev. obit Mar 40

Marvin, Harry obit Jan 40

Marvin, Lee Sep 66 obit Oct 87

Marx, Chico May 48 [Marx, Chico; Marx, Groucho; and Marx, Harpo] obit Dec 61

Marx, Elizabeth Lisl Weil *see* Weil, Lisl

Marx, Groucho Mar 48 [Marx, Chico; Marx, Groucho; and Marx, Harpo] Feb 73 obit Oct 77

Marx, Harpo Mar 48 [Marx, Chico; Marx, Groucho; and Marx, Harpo] obit Nov 64

Mary Alice Nov 95

Mary Joseph Butler, Mother obit Jan 40

Mary Kay *see* Ash, Mary Kay

Marzotto, Gaetano, Count Jul 53

Masaryk, Jan May 44 obit Apr 48

Mascagni, Pietro obit Sep 45

Masekela, Hugh Mar 93

Masina, Giulietta Apr 58 obit Jun 94

Masina, Guilia Anna *see* Masina, Giulietta

Masliansky, Zvei Hirsch,

Rev. obit Mar 43

Mason, Bobbie Ann Sep 89

Mason, Jackie Jul 87

Mason, James May 47 obit Sep 84

Mason, Joseph Warren Teets obit Jul 41

Mason, Lowell B. Jun 49

Mason, Marsha Apr 81

Mason, Noah M. Nov 57 obit May 65

Mason, Norman P. Jun 59

Massee, W. Wellington obit Oct 42

Masserman, Jules H. Jul 80 obit Jan 95

Massevitch, Alla G. Jan 64

Massey, Raymond Feb 46 obit Sep 83

Massey, Vincent Oct 51 obit Feb 68

Massey, Walter E. Jun 97

Massigli, René May 56

Massine, Leonide Apr 40 obit May 79

Massive Attack Jun 2004

Masson, André Nov 74 obit Jan 88

Masters, Kelly Ray *see* Ball, Zachary

Masters, William H. Nov 68 obit May 2001

Mastroianni, Marcello Jun 63 obit Feb 97

Mastroianni, Umberto Sep 60

Masursky, Harold Aug 86 obit Oct 90

Matalin, Mary Sep 96

Mateos, Adolfo López *see* López Mateos, Adolfo

Mates, Leo Nov 56

Mather, Kirtley F. Jan 51

Mathers, Marshall *see* Eminem

Matheson, Samuel Pritchard, Archbishop obit Jul 42

Mathews, David Jan 76

Mathews, Shailer, Rev. obit Dec 41

Mathewson, Lemuel Dec 52

obit Apr 70

Mathias, Charles McC., Jr. Dec 72

Mathias, Robert Bruce Sep 52

Mathis, Johnny Jul 65 Feb 93

Matisse, Henri May 43 Jun 53 obit Jan 55

Matlin, Marlee May 92

Matola, Sharon Jun 93

Matskevich, Vladimir V. Nov 55

Matson, Randy Sep 68

Matsudaira, Koto Nov 58

Matsui, Connie L. Aug 2002

Matsui, Keishiro, Baron obit Jul 46

Matsui, Robert T. Oct 94 obit Apr 2005

Matsuoka, Yosuke Mar 41 obit Jul 46

Matta Echauren, Roberto Antonio Sebastian *see* Matta

Matta Nov 57 obit Yrbk 2003

Mattei, Enrico Apr 59 obit Jan 63

Matthau, Walter Jun 66 obit Sep 2000

Matthews, Burnita Shelton Apr 50 obit Jun 88

Matthews, Francis P. Sep 49 obit Dec 52

Matthews, H. Freeman Mar 45 obit Jan 87

Matthews, Herbert L. Nov 43 obit Sep 77

Matthews, J. B. May 43

Matthews, T. S. Apr 50 obit Mar 91

Matthews, W. Donald Sep 52

Matthiessen, Peter Oct 75

Mattingly, Don Oct 88

Mattingly, Garrett Nov 60 obit Feb 63

Mattson, Henry Jan 56 obit Nov 71

Mature, Victor Dec 51 obit Oct 99

Matzinger, Polly Oct 98

Mauch, Gene Dec 74 obit Yrbk 2005

Maudling, Reginald May 60

obit Apr 79

Maugham, W. Somerset Jan 63 obit Jan 66

Mauldin, Bill Yrbk 45 Nov 64 obit July 2003

Mauldin, William Henry *see* Mauldin, Bill

Maunoury, Maurice Bourgès *see* Bourgès-Maunoury, Maurice

Maura, Carmen Apr 92

Maurer, Ion Gheorghe Sep 71 obit Jul 2000

Mauriac, Claude Sep 93 obit Jun 99

Maurier, Daphne du *see* Du Maurier, Daphne

Mauroy, Pierre Jun 82

Maverick, Maury, Sr. Mar 44 obit Sep 54

Maw, Herbert B. Oct 48 obit Jan 91

Max, Adolphe obit Jan 40

Max, Peter May 71

Maximos, Demetrios Mar 48 obit Dec 55

Maxon, Lou R. Aug 43 obit Jul 71

Maxton, James obit Sep 46

Maxtone Graham, Joyce *see* Struther, Jan

Maxwell Davies, Peter *see* Davies, Peter Maxwell

Maxwell, David Dec 51 obit Mar 67 [Kilmuir, David Patrick Maxwell Fyfe, 1st Earl of]

Maxwell, David F. Jun 57

Maxwell, Elsa Mar 43 obit Jan 64

Maxwell, Robert Sep 88 obit Feb 92

Maxwell, Russell L. Nov 42 obit Jan 69

Maxwell, Vera Jul 77 obit Mar 95

Maxwell, William (WLB) Yrbk 49 obit Oct 2000

May, Andrew Jackson Apr 41

obit Nov 59

May, Catherine Jan 60

May, Charles H. obit Jan 44

May, Elaine Mar 61

May, Geraldine P. Feb 49

May, Henry John obit Jan 40

May, John L. Jan 91 obit Jun 94

May, Rollo Jun 73 obit Jan 95

Maybank, Burnet R. Apr 49 obit Nov 54

Mayer, Daniel Nov 49

Mayer, Jane *see* Jaynes, Clare

Mayer, Jean Sep 70 obit Feb 93

Mayer, Louis B. Jun 43 obit Jan 58

Mayer, Maria Goeppert Jun 64 obit Apr 72

Mayer, René May 48 obit Feb 73

Mayes, Mrs. Gilford *see* Mayes, Rose Gorr

Mayes, Rose Gorr May 50

Mayle, Peter Oct 92

Maynard, John A. F., Rev. Oct 43

Maynard, Joyce Jan 99

Maynard, Robert C. Jun 86 obit Oct 93

Mayne, Ethel C. obit Jun 41

Mayne, Thom Oct 2005

Maynor, Dorothy Jan-Feb 40 Dec 51 obit May 96

Mayo, Charles W. Nov 41 Nov 54 obit Oct 68

Mayo, Katherine obit Yrbk 40

Mayo, Robert P. Feb 70

Mayr, Ernst Nov 84 obit May 2005

Mays, Benjamin E. May 45 obit May 84

Mays, Ewing W. Jan 52

Mays, L. Lowry Aug 2003

Mays, Willie May 55 Dec 66

Mayweather, Floyd Oct 2004

Maza, José Nov 55 obit Jul 64

Mazen, Abu *see* Abbas, Mahmoud

Mazey, Emil Jan 48 obit Nov

83

Mazowiecki, Tadeusz Feb 90

Mazursky, Paul May 80

Mazzo, Kay Jul 71

Mbeki, Thabo Aug 98

Mboya, Tom Jun 59 obit Sep 69

McAdie, Alexander George obit Dec 43

McAdoo, William Gibbs obit Mar 41

McAfee, Mildred H. Sep 42 obit Jan 95

McAlary, Michael obit Mar 99

McAuliffe, Anthony C. Feb 50 obit Oct 75

McBain, Ed *see* Hunter, Evan

McBride, Christian Jan 2000

McBride, Katharine E. Feb 42 obit Jul 76

McBride, Lloyd Feb 78 obit Jan 84

McBride, Martina Mar 2004

McBride, Mary Margaret Apr 41 Mar 54 obit Jun 76

McBride, Patricia Jul 66

McCabe, Gibson Feb 63 obit Yrbk 2000

McCabe, Thomas B. Sep 48 obit Jul 82

McCaffrey, Barry R. Jul 97

McCaffrey, John L. Nov 50

McCain, John S. 3d. Feb 89

McCain, John S. Sr. Oct 43 obit Oct 45

McCain, John S., Jr. Jun 70 obit Jun 81

McCall, Duke K. Nov 59

McCall, Tom Jun 74 obit Mar 83

McCambridge, Mercedes Jun 64 obit Yrbk 2004

McCann, Renetta May 2005

McCardell, Claire Nov 54 obit Jun 58

McCarey, Leo Jul 46 obit Sep 69

McCarl, John Raymond obit Sep 40

McCarran, Patrick A. Jul 47

obit Dec 54

McCarrens, John S. obit Sep 43

McCarthy, Carolyn Mar 98

McCarthy, Clem Oct 41 obit Jul 62

McCarthy, Eugene J. Nov 55

McCarthy, Frank Sep 45 obit Feb 87

McCarthy, Joe May 48 obit Mar 78

McCarthy, Joseph R. Jan 50 obit Jul 57

McCarthy, Joseph Vincent see McCarthy, Joe

McCarthy, Kenneth C. Nov 53

McCarthy, Leighton Oct 42 obit Nov 52

McCarthy, Mary (WLB) Yrbk 55 Feb 69 obit Jan 90

McCartney, Paul Nov 66 Jan 86

McCarty, Dan Jul 53

McCarver, Tim May 2000

McCaw, Craig Sep 2001

McClanahan, Rue May 89

McCleery, Albert Feb 55 obit Jul 72

McClellan, Harold C. Oct 54 obit Sep 79

McClellan, John L. Apr 50 obit Feb 78

McClintic, Guthrie May 43 obit Jan 62

McClintock, Barbara Mar 84 obit Nov 92

McClintock, Robert Mills Apr 55

McClinton, Katharine Morrison Mar 58 obit Mar 93

McClinton, Mrs. Harold L. see McClinton, Katharine Morrison

McCloskey, John Robert see McCloskey, Robert

McCloskey, Mark A. Nov 55 obit Jan 78

McCloskey, Paul N., Jr. Nov 71

McCloskey, Robert Sep 42

obit Yrbk 2003

McCloy, John J. Apr 47 Nov 61 obit May 89

McCobb, Paul Nov 58 obit Apr 69

McColough, C. Peter Jan 81

McComas, O. Parker Nov 55 obit Feb 58

McConachie, G. W. Grant Nov 58 obit Sep 65

McCone, John A. Jan 59 obit Apr 91

McConnell, F. B. Jul 52 obit Feb 62

McConnell, Joseph H. Nov 50 obit May 97

McConnell, Page see Phish

McConnell, Samuel K., Jr. Nov 56

McCormack, Arthur Thomas obit Sep 43

McCormack, Emmet J. Jul 53 obit Apr 65

McCormack, John obit Oct 45

McCormack, John W. Jun 43 Apr 62 obit Jan 81

McCormick, Anne O'Hare Mar 40 obit Jul 54

McCormick, Edward J. Nov 53 obit Feb 75

McCormick, Edward T. May 51 obit Oct 91

McCormick, Fowler Jun 47 obit Feb 73

McCormick, Jay Apr 43

McCormick, Lynde D. Feb 52 obit Oct 56

McCormick, Myron Jan 54 obit Oct 62

McCormick, Robert R. Aug 42 obit May 55

McCormick, William Patrick Glyn, Rev. obit Yrbk 40

McCourt, Frank Feb 98

McCovey, Willie Nov 70

McCowen, Alec Oct 69

McCoy, Charles B. Jul 70 obit Mar 95

McCoy, Frank R. Nov 45 obit

Sep 54

McCracken, Craig Feb 2004

McCracken, Harold (WLB) Yrbk 49

McCracken, James Nov 63 obit Jun 88

McCracken, Joan Jun 45 obit Jan 62

McCracken, Paul W. Dec 69

McCracken, Robert James Jul 49 obit Apr 73

McCrady, Edward Jan 57

McCrary, Jinx Jul 53 [McCrary, Tex; and McCrary, Jinx]

McCrary, Tex Jul 53 obit Yrbk 2003 [McCrary, Tex; and McCrary, Jink]

McCreery, Richard L. May 45 obit Dec 67

McCullers, Carson Sep 40 obit Dec 67

McCullough, Colleen Apr 82

McCullough, David Jan 93

McCune, Charles Andrew obit Yrbk 40

McCune, Francis K. Mar 61

McCune, George S. obit Feb 42

McCurdy, William Albert, Rev. obit Feb 42

McCurry, Michael D. Nov 96

McCurry, Steve Nov 2005

McDaniel, Glen May 52

McDaniel, Hattie Sep 40 obit Dec 52

McDaniel, James Feb 2000

McDermott, Alice Sep 92

McDermott, Michael J. Feb 51 obit Oct 55

McDevitt, James L. Mar 59 obit May 63

McDiarmid, E. W. Dec 48

McDivitt, James A. Nov 65

McDonagh, Martin Aug 98

McDonald, Audra Apr 99

McDonald, David J. Jun 53 obit Oct 79

McDonald, David L. Nov 63

obit Mar 98

McDonald, Erroll Oct 99

McDonald, Eugene F., Jr. Oct 49 obit Oct 58

McDonald, Gabrielle Kirk Oct 2001

McDonald, James G. Apr 49 obit Dec 64

McDonnell, Mary May 97

McDonnell, William A. Feb 59

McDonough, Roger H. Jun 68

McDormand, Frances Sep 97

McDowall, Roddy Apr 61 obit Jan 99

McDowell, Malcolm Dec 73

McElroy, Neil H. Apr 51 obit Jan 73

McEnroe, John Feb 80

McEntee, Gerald W. Oct 2000

McEntire, Reba Oct 94

McEwan, Ian Jul 93

McEwen, Terence A. Jul 85 obit Jan 99

McFadden, Mary Apr 83

McFarland, Ernest W. Jan 51 obit Aug 84

McFarlane, Robert C. May 84

McFarlane, Todd Feb 99

McGannon, Donald H. Feb 71 obit Jul 84

McGarry, William J. obit Nov 41

McGeachy, Mary Craig Apr 44

McGee, Fibber *see* Jordan, Jim

McGee, Frank Jun 64 obit Jun 74

McGee, Gale Nov 61 obit Jun 92

McGee, Molly *see* Jordan, Marian

McGhee, George Crews Sep 50 obit Yrbk 2005

McGill, Ralph Jun 47 obit Mar 69

McGill, William J. Jun 71 obit Jan 98

McGillicuddy, Cornelius *see*

Mack, Connie

McGinley, Laurence J. Jun 49 obit Oct 92

McGinley, Phyllis Feb 41 Nov 61 obit Apr 78

McGinnis, Patrick B. Nov 55 obit Apr 73

McGinniss, Joe Jan 84

McGovern, Francis Edward obit Jun 46

McGovern, George S. Mar 67

McGovern, John W. Nov 61 obit Jun 75

McGovern, Maureen Feb 90

McGrady, Tracy Feb 2003

McGranery, James P. May 52 obit Feb 63

McGrath, Earl James Apr 49 obit Apr 93

McGrath, J. Howard Jan 48 obit Nov 66

McGrath, Judy Feb 2005

McGraw, Curtis W. Jun 50 obit Nov 53

McGraw, Eloise Jarvis (WLB) Yrbk 55 obit Mar 2001

McGraw, Phillip Jun 2002

McGraw, Tim Sep 2002

McGreal, Elizabeth *see* Yates, Elizabeth

McGreal, Mrs. William *see* Yates, Elizabeth

McGregor, G. R. Mar 54 obit Apr 71

McGregor, J. Harry Oct 58

McGroarty, John Steven obit Sep 44

McGruder, Aaron Sep 2001

McGuane, Thomas Nov 87

McGuigan, James Sep 50 obit Jun 74

McGuire, Dorothy Sep 41 obit Nov 2001

McGuire, William Anthony obit Nov 40

McGurn, Barrett Apr 65

McGwire, Mark Jul 98

McHale, Kathryn Jan 47 obit

Dec 56 Yrbk 57

McHenry, Donald F. Sep 80

McInerney, Jay Nov 87

McIntire, Carl Oct 71 obit Jun 2002

McIntire, Ross T. Oct 45 obit Feb 60

McIntosh, Millicent Carey Jul 47 obit Mar 2001

McIntyre, James Francis Feb 53 obit Sep 79

McIntyre, James T., Jr. Jan 79

McIntyre, Marvin H. obit Feb 44

McIntyre, Natalie *see* Gray, Macy

McIntyre, Thomas J. Nov 63 obit Oct 92

McIver, Pearl Mar 49

McKay, David O. Jun 51 obit Mar 70

McKay, Douglas May 49 obit Oct 59

McKay, Jim Oct 73

McKayle, Donald Jun 71

McKeen, John E. Jun 61 obit Apr 78

McKeever, Ed Nov 45

McKeldin, Theodore R. Oct 52 obit Oct 74

McKellar, K. D. Jan 46 obit Jan 58

McKellen, Ian Jan 84

McKelway, B. M. Jan 58 obit Oct 76

McKenna, F. E. May 66 obit Feb 79

McKenna, Reginald obit Oct 43

McKenna, Siobhan Nov 56 obit Jan 87

McKenney, Eileen *see* West, Nathanael

McKenney, Ruth Aug 42 obit Oct 72

McKenzie, Kevin Jan 2000

McKenzie, Roderick Duncan obit Jan 40

McKenzie, Vashti Murphy Nov 2000

McKenzie, William P. obit

Oct 42

McKeon, Jack Apr 2004

McKinley, Chuck Nov 63 obit Sep 86

McKinney, Cynthia A. Aug 96

McKinney, Frank E. Jan 52 obit Mar 74

McKinney, Robert Jan 57 obit Yrbk 2001

McKissick, Floyd B. Jan 68 obit Jun 91

McKittrick, Thomas H. Jul 44 obit Mar 70

McKneally, Martin B. Mar 60 obit Aug 92

McKuen, Rod Feb 70

McLain, Dennis Jan 69

McLaren, Malcolm Aug 97

McLaughlin, Ann Dore Nov 88

McLaughlin, Audrey Jul 90

McLaughlin, John [guitarist] Feb 2004

McLaughlin, John [commentator] Jul 87

McLaughlin, Leo May 70 obit Nov 96

McLean, A. J. see Backstreet Boys

McLean, Alice T. Jul 45 obit Dec 68

McLean, Don May 73

McLean, Evalyn Walsh May 43 obit May 47

McLean, Jackie Mar 2001

McLean, John Lenwood see McLean, Jackie

McLean, Robert Nov 51 obit Feb 81

McLennan, Isabel Stewart see McMeekin, Isabel McLennan

McLintock, Gordon Nov 53 obit Jun 90

McLuhan, Marshall Jun 67 obit Feb 81

McLurkin, James Sep 2005

McMahon, Brien Dec 45 obit

Sep 52

McMahon, Ed Apr 77

McMahon, Vince Feb 99

McMahon, William Sep 71 obit May 88

McManamy, Frank obit Nov 44

McManus, James Kenneth see McKay, Jim

McMath, Sid Mar 49 obit Jan 2004

McMeekin, Clark see Clark, Dorothy Park; McMeekin, Isabel McLennan

McMeekin, Isabel McLennan Sep 42 (WLB) Yrbk 57 [McMeekin, Isabel McLennan; and Clark, Dorothy Park]

McMein, Neysa Feb 41 obit Jun 49

McMillan, Edwin M. Feb 52 obit Nov 91

McMillan, John L. Nov 56

McMillan, Terry Feb 93

McMillen, Tom Jan 93

McMinnies, Mary (WLB) Yrbk 59

McMurrin, Sterling M. Jun 61 obit Jun 96

McMurtrie, Douglas C. Jul 44

McMurtry, Larry Jun 84

McNabb, Donovan Jan 2004

McNair, Arnold D. Feb 55

McNair, Barbara Nov 71

McNair, Lesley J. Nov 42 obit Sep 44

McNair, Steve Jan 2005

McNair, Sylvia Nov 97

McNally, Andrew 3d Nov 56 obit Feb 2002

McNally, Terrence Mar 88

McNamara, James Barnabas obit Apr 41

McNamara, Patrick V. Nov 55 obit Jun 66

McNamara, Robert S. Sep 61 Mar 87

McNamee, Graham obit Jul 42

McNarney, Joseph T. Nov 44

obit Mar 72

McNary, Charles L. Aug 40 obit Apr 44

McNaughton, Andrew Nov 42 obit Nov 66

McNealy, Scott Apr 96

McNeely, Eugene J. Nov 62 obit Feb 74

McNeil, Hector Dec 46 obit Dec 55

McNeil, Wilfred J. Feb 58 obit Oct 79

McNeill, Don Jul 49 obit Aug 96

McNellis, Maggi Jan 55 obit Aug 89

McNicholas, John T. May 49 obit Jun 50

McNichols, Stephen L. R. Oct 58 obit Feb 98

McNutt, Paul V. Feb 40 obit May 55

McPartland, Marian Jun 76

McPharlin, Paul Nov 45 obit Nov 48

McPhee, John Oct 82

McPherson, Aimee Semple obit Nov 44

McPherson, James Alan Sep 96

McQueen, Alexander Feb 2002

McQueen, Steve Oct 66 obit Jan 81

McRae, Carmen Apr 83 obit Jan 95

McReynolds, James Clark obit Oct 46

McSwigan, Marie (WLB) Yrbk 53 obit Sep 62

McWhinney, Madeline H. Jul 76

McWhirter, Norris D. Nov 79 obit Yrbk 2004

McWhorter, John H. Feb 2003

McWilliams, Carey Oct 43 obit Aug 80

Mead, Charles Larew, Bishop obit Jul 41

Mead, George H. Oct 46 obit

Feb 63

Mead, James M. Jul 44 obit Apr 64

Mead, Kate Campbell obit Feb 41

Mead, Margaret Nov 40 May 51 obit Jan 79

Mead, Sylvia Earle May 72

Meader, George Jul 56

Meadowcroft, Enid (WLB) Yrbk 49

Meadows, A. H. Apr 60

Meadows, Audrey May 58 obit Apr 96

Meadows, Jayne May 58

Means, Helen Hotchkin Jan 46

Means, Mrs. Alan Hay *see* Means, Helen Hotchkin

Means, Russell Jan 78

Meany, George Jan 42 Mar 54 obit Mar 80

Mearns, David C. Jul 61 obit Jul 81

Mearns, Hughes Jan-Feb 40 obit Apr 65

Mears, Helen Mar 43

Mechau, Frank, Jr. obit Apr 46

Mechem, Edwin L. Jul 54 obit Yrbk 2003

Mechem, Merritt Cramer obit Jun 46

Meciar, Vladimír Jul 94

Medaris, John B. Feb 58

Medawar, Peter B. Apr 61 obit Nov 87

Medawar, Peter Brian *see* Medawar, Peter B.

Medeiros, Cardinal *see* Medeiros, Humberto

Medeiros, Humberto Nov 71 obit Nov 83

Médici, Emílio Garrastazú Oct 71 obit Jan 86

Medina Angarita, Isaías Mar 42 obit Nov 53

Medina, Harold R. Apr 49 obit May 90

Medina-Sidonia, Duchess of

Apr 72

Medvedev, Roy Sep 84

Medvedev, Zhores A. Nov 73

Meehan, Thomas F. obit Sep 42

Meeker, Mary Aug 99

Meerloo, Joost A. M. Jan 62 obit Feb 77

Meese, Edwin, 3d Sep 81

Mehaffey, Joseph C. Jan 48 obit Apr 63

Mehta, G. L. Nov 52 obit Jun 74

Mehta, Hansa Jul 47

Mehta, Ved Sep 75

Mehta, Zubin Mar 69

Mei Lanfang obit Sep 43

Meier, Richard Jan 85

Meiling, Richard L. May 50

Meir, Golda May 50 [Meyerson, Mrs. Golda] Dec 70 obit Feb 79

Meiselas, Susan Feb 2005

Meisner, Sanford Apr 91 obit Apr 97

Meitner, Lise Sep 45 obit Sep 68

Melamid, Aleksandr Oct 84 [Komar, Vitaly; and Melamid, Aleksandr]

Melas, George V. Jul 56

Melcher, Frederic G. Jul 45 obit Apr 63

Melchior, Lauritz Jan 41 obit May 73

Mellencamp, John Mar 88

Mellers, Wilfred Howard Feb 62

Mellett, Lowell May 42 obit May 60

Mello Franco, Afranio De obit Feb 43

Mellon, Paul Apr 66 obit Apr 99

Mellon, Richard K. May 65 obit Jul 70

Mellon, William Larimer, Jr. Jun 65 obit Oct 89

Mellor, Walter obit Jan 40

Meloney, Franken *see* Fran-

ken, Rose

Meloney, Mrs. William Brown obit Aug 43

Melton, James Sep 45 obit Jun 61

Melzer, Roman F. obit Jun 43

Menchú, Rigoberta Oct 93

Mende, Erich Jul 66

Mendelsohn, Erich Nov 53

Mendenhall, Harlan George, Rev. obit Jul 40

Mendenhall, Thomas Corwin 2nd May 60 obit Sep 98

Menderes, Adnan Nov 54 obit Nov 61

Mendes, Sam Oct 2002

Mendès-France, Pierre Oct 54 obit Jan 83

Menem, Carlos Saúl Nov 89

Meng, John J. Nov 61 obit Apr 88

Mengistu Haile Mariam Jul 81

Menjou, Adolphe Jun 48 obit Jan 64

Menken, Alan Jan 2001

Mennin, Peter Nov 64 obit Aug 83

Menninger, Karl Oct 48 obit Sep 90

Menninger, William Claire Sep 45 obit Nov 66

Menocal, Mario Garcia obit Oct 41

Menon, K. P. S. Mar 57 obit Yrbk 83 (died Nov 82)

Menon, V. K. Krishna *see* Krishna Menon, V. K.

Menotti, Gian Carlo Dec 47 Jan 79

Menshikov, Mikhail A. May 58 obit Sep 76

Menthon, Francois De Mar 44

Menuhin, Yehudi Feb 41 May 73 obit Jun 99

Menzel, Donald H. Apr 56 obit Mar 77

Menzies, Robert G. Feb 41 Jan 50 obit Jul 78

Mercer, Johnny Jun 48 obit

Aug 76

Mercer, Mabel Feb 73 obit Jun 84

Mercer, Samuel A. B. Feb 53

Merchant, Ismail Mar 93 obit Yrbk 2005

Merchant, Livingston T. Nov 56 obit Jul 76

Merchant, Natalie Jan 2003

Merck, George W. Dec 46 obit Jan 58

Mercouri, Melina Jul 65 Mar 88 obit May 94

Meredith, Burgess Jul 40 obit Nov 97

Mérida, Carlos Jan 60

Merivale, Philip obit Apr 46

Meriwether, John Mar 99

Meriwether, W. Delano Jan 78

Merle-Smith, Van Santvoord obit Dec 43

Merman, Ethel Oct 41 May 55 obit Apr 84

Meron, Theodor Mar 2005

Merriam, C. Hart obit May 42

Merriam, Charles Edward Feb 47 obit Feb 53

Merriam, George Ernest, Rev. obit May 41

Merriam, John Campbell obit Dec 45

Merrick, David Jan 61 obit Jul 2000

Merrick, Elliott (WLB) Yrbk 50 obit Jul 97

Merrifield, R. Bruce Mar 85

Merrill, Charles E. Apr 56

Merrill, Frank Jul 44 obit Feb 56

Merrill, James Aug 81 obit Apr 95

Merrill, John Douglas obit Jan 40

Merrill, Linda see Ashley, Merrill

Merrill, Robert Mar 52 obit Feb 2005

Merritt, Matthew J. obit Nov 46

Merry Del Val, Alfonso, 2d

Marquis De Nov 65

Merton, Robert K. Sep 65 obit Yrbk 2003

Merwin, W. S. May 88

Merz, Charles Nov 54 obit Nov 77

Meservey, Robert Preston see Preston, Robert

Meskill, Thomas J. Mar 74

Messer, Thomas M. Nov 61

Messerschmitt, Willy Apr 40 obit Nov 78

Messersmith, George S. Oct 42 obit Apr 60

Messiaen, Olivier Feb 74 obit Jun 92

Messick, Dale Jul 61 obit Yrbk 2005

Messier, Jean-Marie May 2002

Messier, Mark Jul 95

Messing, Debra Aug 2002

Messmer, Pierre Nov 63

Messner, Reinhold Mar 80

Mesta, Perle Sep 49 obit May 75

Meta, Ilir Feb 2002

Metaxas, John Yrbk 40 obit Mar 41

Metcalf, Jesse H. obit Dec 42

Metcalf, Lee Feb 70 obit Mar 78

Metheny, Pat May 96

Metrovic, Ivan Oct 40 obit Mar 62

Metzelthin, Pearl V. Nov 42 obit Jan 48

Metzenbaum, Howard M. Jul 80

Metzman, G. Jul 46 obit Jun 60

Meyer, Agnes E. Jan 49 obit Nov 70

Meyer, Albert Jan 60 obit May 65

Meyer, Cord Jr. Mar 48 obit Aug 2001

Meyer, Debbie May 69

Meyer, Edgar Jun 2002

Meyer, Eugene Sep 41 obit

Oct 59

Meyer, Jean Nov 55

Meyer, K. F. Mar 52 obit Jun 74

Meyer, Mrs. Eugene see Meyer, Agnes E.

Meyer, Ron Mar 97

Meyerowitz, William May 42

Meyers, George Julian obit Jan 40

Meyers, Nancy Feb 2002

Meyerson, Golda see Meir, Golda

Meyner, Robert B. Apr 55 obit Jul 90

Mfume, Kweisi Jan 96

Michael V, King of Rumania Oct 44

Michael, George Nov 88

Michael, Moina obit Jun 44

Michaels, Lorne Aug 99

Michals, Duane Apr 81

Michel, Robert H. Sep 81

Michel, Sia Sep 2003

Michelin, Edouard obit Oct 40

Michelman, Kate Nov 2000

Michelson, Charles Aug 40 obit Jan 48

Michener, Daniel Roland Jan 68 obit Nov 91

Michener, James A. Jun 48 Aug 75 obit Jan 98

Michie, Allan A. Nov 42 obit Jan 74

Michnik, Adam Jul 90

Mickelson, Phil Mar 2002

Middelhoff, Thomas Feb 2001

Middlecoff, Cary Jul 52 obit Nov 98

Middleton, Arthur see O'Brien, Edward J.

Middleton, Drew Sep 43 obit Mar 90

Midgley, Thomas, Jr. obit Dec 44

Midler, Bette Jun 73 Nov 97

Midori Jun 90

Mielziner, Jo Mar 46 obit May 76

Miers, Earl Schenck (WLB)

Yrbk 49 Sep 67 obit Jan 73

Mies Van Der Rohe, Ludwig Oct 51 obit Oct 69

Mifune, Toshiro Jun 81 obit Mar 98

Mignone, Francisco Jun 42

Mihajlov, Mihajlo Jan 79

Mihajlovic, Dragoliub *see* Mikhailovitch, Draja

Mikell, Henry Judah, Bishop obit Apr 42

Mikhailov, Nikolai A. Nov 58

Mikhailovitch, Draja Mar 42 obit Sep 46

Mikhalkov, Nikita Oct 95

Miki, Takeo Apr 75 obit Jan 89

Mikita, Stan Oct 70

Mikolajczyk, Stanislaw Mar 44 obit Feb 67

Mikoyan, Anastas I. May 55 obit Jan 79

Mikulski, Barbara A. Nov 85

Mikva, Abner J. Jul 80

Milam, Carl H. Jun 45 obit Oct 63

Milanov, Zinka Jul 44 obit Jul 89

Milchan, Arnon Oct 2000

Miles, Mary Nov 42

Milgram, Stanley Aug 79 obit Mar 85

Milhaud, Darius Jun 41 May 61 obit Sep 74

Milland, Ray Feb 46 obit Apr 86

Millar, Alexander Copeland, Rev. obit Yrbk 40

Millar, George (WLB) Yrbk 49

Millar, Kenneth *see* Macdonald, Ross

Millar, Margaret (WLB) Yrbk 46 obit Jun 94

Millar, Mrs. Kenneth *see* De Mille, Agnes; Millar, Margaret

Millard, Bailey obit May 41

Mille, Cecil B. de *see* De Mille, Cecil B.

Miller, Alice Duer Sep 41 obit

Oct 42

Miller, Ann Apr 80 obit Yrbk 2004

Miller, Arjay Jan 67

Miller, Arnold Nov 74 obit Sep 85

Miller, Arthur Oct 47 Feb 73 obit Jul 2005

Miller, Bebe Apr 99

Miller, Benjamin Meek obit Mar 44

Miller, Dayton C. obit Apr 41

Miller, Douglas Nov 41

Miller, Edward G., Jr. Jun 51 obit Jun 68

Miller, Frieda S. Feb 45 obit Oct 73

Miller, G. William Jun 78

Miller, George P. Feb 64

Miller, Gilbert Apr 58 obit Feb 69

Miller, Glenn Feb 42 obit Yrbk 91 (died Dec 44)

Miller, Harry W. Mar 62 obit Mar 77

Miller, Henry Nov 70 obit Jul 80

Miller, Irving Nov 52 obit Feb 81

Miller, J. Cloyd Dec 51

Miller, J. Irwin Nov 61 obit Yrbk 2004

Miller, James C., 3d May 86

Miller, Jason Jan 74 obit Yrbk 2001

Miller, John Aug 2003

Miller, John *see* Miller, Jason

Miller, Johnny Sep 74

Miller, Jonathan Oct 70 Nov 86

Miller, Justin Jan 47 obit Mar 73

Miller, Lee P. Jul 59

Miller, Marshall E. Oct 53

Miller, Marvin May 73

Miller, Max May 40 obit Feb 68

Miller, Merle (WLB) Yrbk 50

obit Jul 86

Miller, Mildred Jun 57

Miller, Mitch Jul 56

Miller, Neal Jul 74 obit Jun 2002

Miller, Nicole Mar 95

Miller, Reggie Mar 96

Miller, Roger Sep 86 obit Jan 93

Miller, Shannon Jul 96

Miller, Watson B. Sep 47 obit Apr 61

Miller, Webb obit Jan 40

Miller, William E. Feb 62 obit Aug 83

Miller, William Lash obit Oct 40

Miller, Zell Jul 96

Millerand, Alexander obit May 43

Milles, Carl Yrbk 40 Dec 52 obit Nov 55

Millett, John D. Feb 53 obit Jan 94

Millett, Kate Jan 71 Jun 95

Milligan, Mary Louise May 57

Millikan, Robert A. Jun 40 Jun 52 obit Feb 54

Millikin, Eugene D. Apr 48 obit Oct 58

Million, J. W. obit Nov 41

Millionaire, Tony Jul 2005

Millis, Harry Alvin Nov 40 obit Sep 48

Millman, Dan Aug 2002

Millo, Aprile Apr 88

Mills, Frederick C. Nov 48 obit Apr 64

Mills, Hayley Apr 63

Mills, John May 63 obit Yrbk 2005

Mills, Wilbur D. Nov 56 obit Jul 92

Milnes, Sherrill Nov 70

Milosevic, Slobodan Apr 90

Milosz, Czeslaw Oct 81 obit Yrbk 2004

Milstein, Nathan Mar 50 obit Feb 93

Minard, George Cann obit

Aug 40

Mindszenty, József Jan 57 obit Jun 75

Miner, Tony see Miner, Worthington C.

Miner, Worthington C. Feb 53 obit Mar 83

Mingus, Charles Feb 71 obit Mar 79

Mink, Patsy Takemoto Sep 68 obit Jan 2003

Minnelli, Liza Oct 70 Jul 88

Minnelli, Vincente May 75 obit Sep 86

Minner, Ruth Ann Aug 2001

Minor, Halsey Oct 98

Minor, Robert Apr 41 obit Jan 53

Minow, Newton N. Oct 61

Minsky, Marvin Sep 88

Mintoff, Dom Mar 84

Minton, Sherman Mar 41 Dec 49 obit May 65

Mirabal, Robert Aug 2002

Mirabella, Grace Oct 91

Miranda, Carmen Jun 41 obit Oct 55

Miró Cardona, José Nov 61 obit Oct 74

Miró, Joan May 40 Nov 73 obit Feb 84

Mirren, Helen Jul 95

Mirvish, Edwin Apr 89

Mirvish, Robert F. (WLB) Yrbk 57

Mirza, Iskander May 56 obit Jan 70

Mistral, Gabriela Feb 46 obit Mar 57

Mitchell, Arthur Oct 66

Mitchell, Dean Aug 2002

Mitchell, George J. Apr 89

Mitchell, H. L. Jan 47

Mitchell, Howard May 52 obit Aug 88

Mitchell, James P. Sep 55 obit Dec 64

Mitchell, Joan Mar 86 obit Jan 93

Mitchell, John Newton Jun 69

obit Jan 89

Mitchell, Joni Oct 76

Mitchell, Pat Aug 2005

Mitchell, Stephen A. Oct 52 obit Jun 74

Mitchell, William D. Jan 46 obit Nov 55

Mitchell, William L. Nov 59

Mitchum, Robert Sep 70 obit Sep 97

Mitford, Jessica Sep 74 obit Oct 96

Mitha, Tehreema May 2004

Mitropoulos, Dimitri Mar 41 Mar 52 obit Jan 61

Mitscher, Marc A. Aug 44 obit Mar 47

Mitsotakis, Constantine Nov 90

Mittell, Philip obit Mar 43

Mittermeier, Russell A. Oct 92

Mitterrand, François Dec 68 Oct 82 obit Mar 96

Mix, Tom obit Yrbk 40

Miyake, Issey Nov 97

Miyazaki, Hayao Apr 2001

Miyazawa, Kiichi Feb 92

Mizner, Elizabeth Howard see Howard, Elizabeth

Mizrahi, Isaac Jan 91

Mnouchkine, Ariane Mar 93

Moats, Alice-Leone May 43 obit Jul 89

Mobutu Sese Seko Sep 66 [Mobutu, Joseph D.] May 97

Mobutu, Joseph Désiré see Mobutu Sese Seko

Moby Apr 2001

Moch, Jules Oct 50 obit Nov 85

Modjeski, Ralph obit Aug 40

Moën, Lars May 41

Moffat, J. Pierrepont obit Mar 43

Moffatt, James obit Aug 44

Moffo, Anna May 61

Mohammad, Bakshi Ghulam see Bakshi, Ghulam Mo-

hammad

Mohammed Riza Shah Pahlevi Jan 50 Sep 77 obit Sep 80

Mohammed V, King of Morocco Oct 51 [Sidi Mohammed, Sultan of Morocco] obit Apr 61

Mohammed Zahir Shah Mar 56

Mohammed, Ghulam Jul 54 obit Nov 56

Mohammed, W. Deen Jan 2004

Mohrhardt, Foster E. Jun 67

Moi, Daniel Arap May 79

Moir, Phyllis Apr 42

Moiseev, Igor see Moiseyev, Igor

Moiseiwitsch, Tanya Nov 55 obit Jul 2003

Moiseyev, Igor Nov 58

Moisseiff, Leon S. obit Oct 43

Moley, Raymond Jul 45 obit Apr 75

Molina, Alfred Feb 2004

Molina, Rafael L. Trujillo see Trujillo Molina, Rafael Leónidas

Molinari, Susan Mar 96

Mollenhoff, Clark R. Nov 58 obit May 91

Mollet, Guy Sep 50 obit Nov 75

Mollison, Amy see Johnson, Amy

Molloy, Daniel M. obit Mar 44

Molloy, Matt see Chieftains

Molloy, Robert (WLB) Yrbk 48 obit Mar 77

Moloney, Paddy see Chieftains

Molotov, Viacheslav M. Jan-Feb 40 Jun 54 obit Jan 87

Molyneux, Edward H. Jun 42 obit May 74

Momaday, N. Scott Apr 75

Momsen, C. B. Jul 46 obit Jul 67

Monaco, Mario del see Del

Monaco, Mario

Monaghan, Francis Joseph obit Jan 43

Monaghan, Frank Nov 43 obit Sep 69

Monaghan, Thomas Jun 90

Monckton of Brenchley, Walter Turner Monckton, 1st Viscount Dec 51 obit Feb 65

Monckton, Walter Turner see Monckton of Brenchley, Walter Turner Monckton, 1st Viscount

Mondale, Joan Jan 80

Mondale, Walter F. Jan 69 May 78

Mondavi, Robert Apr 99

Mondriaan, Piet obit Mar 44

Monk, Art Apr 95

Monk, Meredith Feb 85

Monk, T. S. Feb 2002

Monk, Thelonious Oct 64 obit Apr 82

Monnet, Jean Sep 47 obit May 79

Monod, Jacques Jul 71 obit Jul 76

Monroe, Anne S. obit Dec 42

Monroe, Earl May 78

Monroe, Lucy Aug 42 obit Nov 87

Monroe, Marilyn Jul 59 obit Oct 62

Monroe, Vaughn Jul 42 obit Jul 73

Monroney, A. S. Mike Nov 51 obit Apr 80

Monsarrat, Nicholas (WLB) Yrbk 50 obit Oct 79

Monseu, Stephanie see Nelson, Keith and Monseu, Stephanie

Monsky, Henry Nov 41 obit Jun 47

Montagnier, Luc Aug 88

Montagu, Ashley Feb 67 obit Mar 2000

Montagu, Ewen Jun 56 obit Sep 85

Montague, James J. obit Feb 42

Montale, Eugenio Apr 76 obit Nov 81

Montana, Claude Jan 92

Montana, Joe Sep 83

Montanari, A. J. Feb 68

Montand, Yves Jul 60 Sep 88 obit Jan 92

Montebello, Philippe de see De Montebello, Philippe

Montenegro, Fernanda Oct 99

Montessori, Maria Nov 40 obit Jun 52

Monteux, Pierre Apr 46 obit Sep 64

Montgomery of Alamein, Bernard Law Montgomery, 1st Viscount see Montgomery, Bernard Law

Montgomery, Bernard Law Dec 42 obit May 76 [Montgomery of Alamein, Bernard Law Montgomery, 1st Viscount]

Montgomery, Deane Nov 57 obit May 92

Montgomery, Elizabeth Rider (WLB) Yrbk 52

Montgomery, James Shera Apr 48 obit Sep 52

Montgomery, L. M. obit Jun 42

Montgomery, Robert Bruce see Crispin, Edmund

Montgomery, Robert Jan 48 obit Nov 81

Montgomery, Ruth Feb 57

Montini, Giovanni Battista see Paul VI, Pope

Montoya, Carlos Mar 68 obit May 93

Montoya, Joseph M. Mar 75 obit Jul 78

Montresor, Beni Dec 67 obit Feb 2002

Moody, Blair Sep 51 obit Oct 54

Moody, Joseph E. Dec 48 obit Jul 84

Moody, Ralph (WLB) Yrbk 55

Moon, Bucklin (WLB) Yrbk 50

Moon, Sun Myung Mar 83

Moon, Warren Nov 91

Mooney, Edward Apr 46 obit Jan 59

Mooney, Thomas J. obit Apr 42

Mooney, Tom see Mooney, Thomas J.

Moore, Ann Aug 2003

Moore, Archie Nov 60 obit Feb 99

Moore, Brian Jan 86 obit Mar 99

Moore, Bryant E. Feb 49 obit Mar 51

Moore, Charlotte Emma see Sitterly, Charlotte Moore

Moore, Demi Sep 93

Moore, Douglas Nov 47 obit Oct 69

Moore, Dudley Jun 82 obit Yrbk 2002

Moore, Edward Caldwell obit May 43

Moore, Elisabeth Luce Oct 60 obit Yrbk 2002

Moore, Garry Nov 54 obit Jan 94

Moore, George E. Jan 68

Moore, George S. May 70 obit Yrbk 2000

Moore, Gerald Oct 67 obit May 87

Moore, Gordon E. Apr 2002

Moore, Grace Apr 44 obit Mar 47

Moore, Henry Feb 54 Feb 78 obit Oct 86

Moore, Henry R. Sep 43 obit May 78

Moore, Julianne Oct 98

Moore, Marianne Dec 52 Apr 68 obit Mar 72

Moore, Mary Tyler Feb 71

Moore, Melba Jan 73

Moore, Michael C. Aug 97

Moore, Michael May 97

Moore, Mike see Moore,

Michael C.

Moore, Mrs. Maurice T. *see* Moore, Elisabeth Luce

Moore, Paul Jr. Jan 67 obit Yrbk 2003

Moore, Preston J. Apr 59

Moore, R. Walton obit Apr 41

Moore, Raymond obit Mar 40

Moore, Robert Webber obit Jan 43

Moore, Roger Feb 75

Moore, Ruth (WLB) Yrbk 54

Moore, T. Albert obit Apr 40

Moore, Thomas W. Sep 67

Moore-Brabazon, J. C. T. May 41

Moorehead, Agnes Jun 52 obit Jun 74

Moorer, Thomas H. Apr 71 obit Yrbk 2004

Moorland, Jesse Edward obit Jan 40

Moos, Malcolm C. Nov 68

Mora, Francis Luis obit Jul 40

Mora, José A. Nov 56 obit Mar 75

Moraes, Frank Nov 57 obit Jul 74

Moran Cho *see* Cho, Margaret

Moran, Léon obit Oct 41

Morano, Albert P. Mar 52 obit Feb 88

Morath, Max Nov 63

Moravia, Alberto Apr 70 obit Nov 90

Mordkin, Mikhail obit Sep 44

More, Adelyne *see* Ogden, C. K.

Moreau, Jeanne Dec 66

Moreell, Ben Jun 46 obit Sep 78

Morehead, Albert H. Mar 55 obit Dec 66

Morehead, John H. obit Jul 42

Morehouse, Daniel Walter obit Mar 41

Morehouse, Ward Jan-Feb 40 obit Feb 67

Morell, Parker obit Apr 43

Morella, Constance A. Feb

2001

Moreno, Mario *see* Cantinflas

Moreno, Rita Sep 85

Morfit, Thomas Garrison *see* Moore, Garry

Morgan, Anne Jan 46 obit Mar 52

Morgan, Arthur E. Jul 56 obit Jan 76

Morgan, Edward P. [government official] May 51

Morgan, Edward P. [journalist] Apr 64 obit Mar 93

Morgan, Frederick Feb 46 obit May 67

Morgan, Henry Mar 47 obit Jul 94

Morgan, J. Pierpont obit Apr 43

Morgan, Joe Sep 84

Morgan, Joy Elmer Jan 46

Morgan, Lorrie Apr 99

Morgan, Lucy Mar 59

Morgan, Thomas A. Mar 50 obit Jan 68

Morgan, Thomas E. Jun 59 obit Oct 95

Morgan, Thomas Hunt obit Feb 46

Morganfield, McKinley *see* Waters, Muddy

Morgenstierne, Wilhelm Munthe De May 49 obit Sep 63

Morgenthau, Hans J. Mar 63 obit Sep 80

Morgenthau, Henry, Jr. Sep 40 obit Apr 67

Morgenthau, Robert M. Jan 86

Morial, Marc Jan 2002

Moriarty, Michael Jul 76

Morin, Relman Nov 58 obit Oct 73

Morini, Erica Apr 46 obit Jan 96

Moríñigo, Higinio Jun 42

Morison, Samuel Eliot Oct 51 Sep 62 obit Jul 76

Morissette, Alanis May 97

Morita, Akio Feb 72 obit Feb

2000

Morley, Malcolm Jun 84

Morley, Robert Nov 63 obit Aug 92

Moro, Aldo Jun 64 obit Jun 78

Morón, Alonzo G. Oct 49 obit Dec 71

Morricone, Ennio Oct 2000

Morrill, J. L. Feb 51

Morris, Butch Jul 2005

Morris, Dave Hennen obit Jun 44

Morris, Desmond Nov 74

Morris, Earl Jun 68 obit Jul 92

Morris, Edmund Jul 89

Morris, Errol Feb 2001

Morris, James [Journalist] *see* Morris, Jan

Morris, James [opera singer] Jul 86

Morris, James T. [organization official] Mar 2005

Morris, Jan Jan 64 Jun 86

Morris, Lawrence *see* Morris, Butch

Morris, Mark Aug 88

Morris, Newbold Mar 52 obit Apr 66

Morris, Robert Apr 71

Morris, Roland Sletor obit Jan 46

Morris, Steveland Judkins *see* Wonder, Stevie

Morris, William Richard Apr 41 [Nuffield, William Richard Morris, 1st Viscount] obit Oct 63

Morris, Willie Jan 76 obit Oct 99

Morris, Wright May 82 obit Jul 98

Morrison of Lambeth, 1st Baron *see* Morrison, Herbert

Morrison, Adrienne obit Jan 41

Morrison, Delesseps S. Nov 49 obit Jul 64

Morrison, Frank B. May 64

Morrison, Frank *see* Spillane,

Mickey

Morrison, Henry Clinton obit May 45

Morrison, Herbert Jul 40 Feb 51 obit Apr 65 [Morrison of Lambeth, 1st Baron]

Morrison, Margaret Mackie *see* Cost, March

Morrison, Marion Michael *see* Wayne, John

Morrison, Peggy *see* Cost, March

Morrison, Philip Jul 81 obit Aug 2005

Morrison, Toni May 79

Morrison, Van Sep 96

Morrison, William Shepherd Jan 52 obit Apr 61 [Dunrossil, William Shepherd Morrison, 1st Viscount]

Morrow, Elizabeth Cutter Apr 43 obit Mar 55

Morrow, Honore Willsie obit May 40

Morrow, Mrs. Dwight Whitney *see* Morrow, Elizabeth Cutter

Morsch, Lucile M. Jun 57 obit Nov 72

Morse, Carol *see* Hall, Marjory

Morse, Clarence G. Nov 57

Morse, David A. Mar 49 obit Mar 91

Morse, John Lovett obit May 40

Morse, Marston Mar 57 obit Aug 77

Morse, Philip M. Jun 48 obit Nov 85

Morse, Robert Nov 62

Morse, True D. Nov 59 obit Sep 98

Morse, Wayne Apr 42 Nov 54 obit Sep 74

Mortensen, Viggo Jun 2004

Mortenson, Norma Jean *see* Monroe, Marilyn

Mortier, Gérard Jul 91

Mortimer, Charles G. Nov 55

obit Feb 79

Mortimer, John Apr 83

Morton, Craig Jun 78

Morton, Elizabeth Homer Jul 61

Morton, Florrinell F. Jul 61

Morton, Henry Holdich obit Jul 40

Morton, James F. obit Dec 41

Morton, James Madison Jr. obit Aug 40

Morton, James obit Oct 43

Morton, Joe Feb 99

Morton, John Jamieson, Jr. Mar 55

Morton, Rogers C. B. Nov 71 obit Jun 79

Morton, Thruston B. Nov 57 obit Oct 82

Mos Def Apr 2005

Mosbacher, Emil, Jr. Mar 63 obit Nov 97

Mosbacher, Robert Jun 89

Mosca, Gaetano obit Jan 42

Moschen, Michael Jul 2000

Moscicki, Ignace obit Nov 46

Mosconi, Willie Jun 63 obit Nov 93

Moscoso, Teodoro Oct 63 obit Aug 92

Moscovitch, Maurice obit Aug 40

Moseka, Aminata *see* Lincoln, Abbey

Mosel, Tad Nov 61

Moseley-Braun, Carol Jun 94

Moser, Annemarie *see* Proell, Annemarie

Moser, Fritz Jun 55

Moses, Bob *see* Moses, Robert P.

Moses, Edwin Nov 86

Moses, George Higgins obit Feb 45

Moses, Grandma Jan 49 obit Feb 62

Moses, Harry M. Oct 49 obit Jun 56

Moses, John obit Apr 45

Moses, Robert Nov 40 Feb 54

obit Sep 81

Moses, Robert P. Apr 2002

Mosher, A. R. Dec 50 obit Dec 59

Mosher, Gouverneur Frank obit Sep 41

Mosher, Ira Feb 45 obit May 68

Mosley, J. Brooke Sep 70 obit Apr 88

Mosley, Oswald Jul 40 obit Feb 81

Mosley, Sugar Shane Jan 2001

Mosley, Timothy *see* Timbaland

Mosley, Walter Sep 94

Moss, Adam Mar 2004

Moss, Cynthia May 93

Moss, Frank E. Dec 71 obit Jun 2003

Moss, John E., Jr. Nov 56 obit Feb 98

Mossadegh, Mohammed May 51 obit May 67

Mössbauer, Rudolf L. May 62

Mostel, Zero Apr 43 Nov 63 obit Nov 77

Moten, Etta *see* Barnett, Etta Moten

Motherwell, Hiram obit Jan 46

Motherwell, Robert Nov 62 obit Sep 91

Motley, Arthur H. Jan 61 obit Jul 84

Motley, Constance Baker May 64

Moton, Robert Russa obit Jul 40

Motrico, José María de Areilza, Count of *see* Areilza, José Maria de, Count of Motrico

Mott, C. S. Sep 69 obit Apr 73

Mott, Frank Luther Oct 41 obit Dec 64

Mott, James W. obit Dec 45

Mott, John R. Jan 47 obit Mar

55

Mott, Lewis F. obit Jan 42

Mott, Stewart R. Apr 75

Motta, Giuseppe obit Jan 40

Moulton, F. R. Jan 46 obit Jan 53

Moulton, Harold G. Nov 44 obit Feb 66

Mountbatten of Burma, 1st Earl *see* Mountbatten, Louis

Mountbatten, Louis Jun 42 obit Oct 79 [Mountbatten of Burma, 1st Earl]

Mountbatten, Philip Oct 47 [Edinburgh, Philip, 3d Duke of]

Mountevans, Edward R. G. R. Evans, 1st Baron *see* Evans, Edward R. G. R.

Mouskos, Michael Christedoulos *see* Makarios III

Moutet, Marius Jul 47 obit Dec 68

Mowat, Farley Feb 86

Mowat, Robert B. obit Nov 41

Mowery, Edward J. Nov 53 obit Feb 71

Mowinckel, Johan Ludwig obit Nov 43

Mowrer, Edgar Ansel Oct 41 Jul 62 obit May 77

Mowrer, Lilian Thomson May 40 obit Jan 91

Mowrey, Corma Nov 50

Moya, Manuel A. De Nov 57

Moyers, Bill Jan 66 Feb 76

Moylan, Mary Ellen Feb 57

Moyne, Walter Edward Guinness, 1st Baron *see* Guinness, Walter Edward

Moynihan, Daniel Patrick Feb 68 Feb 86 obit Yrbk 2003

Mr. John Oct 56 obit Sep 93

Mubarak Hosni Apr 82

Muccio, John J. Jan 51 obit Jul 89

Muck, Karl Mar 40

Mudd, Emily Nov 56 obit Jul 98

Mudd, Roger Jan 81

Mueller, Frederick H. Dec 59

obit Oct 76

Mueller, George E. Nov 64

Mueller, Mildred *see* Miller, Mildred

Mueller, R. H. Apr 64 obit Sep 82

Muench, Aloisius Apr 60 obit Apr 62

Mugabe, Robert Apr 79

Muggeridge, Malcolm Apr 55 Jul 75 obit Jan 91

Muhammad, Elijah Jan 71 obit Apr 75

Muhammed, Warith Deen *see* Mohammed, W. Deen

Muir, James May 50 obit Jan 60

Muir, Malcolm Apr 53 obit Mar 79

Muir, P. H. Apr 63

Muir, Percy *see* Muir, P. H.

Muir, Ramsay obit Jun 41

Mujibur Rahman Jan 73 obit Oct 75

Mukherjee, Bharati Apr 92

Mulcahy, Anne M. Nov 2002

Muldoon, Robert D. Feb 78 obit Sep 92

Muldowney, Shirley Oct 97

Muller, H. J. Feb 47 obit Jun 67

Müller, Paul Oct 45 [Läuger, Paul; and Müller, Paul] obit Dec 65

Mulligan, Gerry Dec 60 obit Mar 96

Mulliken, Robert S. Sep 67 obit Jan 87

Mullis, Kary B. Feb 96

Mulloy, Gardnar Nov 57

Mulroney, Brian Apr 84

Mumford, Ethel Watts obit Jan 40

Mumford, L. Quincy Jun 54 obit Jan 83

Mumford, Lewis Nov 40 Mar 63 obit Mar 90

Münch, Charles Dec 47 obit Dec 68

Munch, Edvard Yrbk 40 obit

Mar 44

Mundt, Karl E. Jul 48 obit Oct 74

Mundy, Talbot Chetwynd obit Sep 40

Muni, Paul Jan 44 obit Nov 67

Muniz, João Carlos Sep 52 obit Sep 60

Munk, Kaj obit Feb 44

Munn, Biggie *see* Munn, Clarence L.

Munn, Clarence L. Nov 53

Munn, Frank May 44 obit Dec 53

Münnich, Ferenc May 59 obit Jan 68

Munoz Marin, Luis Oct 42 Nov 53 obit Jun 80

Munro, Alice Sep 90

Munro, Leslie Knox Nov 53 obit Apr 74

Munsel, Patrice Mar 45

Munson, Thurman Nov 77 obit Sep 79

Murakami Harakui Sep 97

Murayama, Makio Oct 74

Murch, Walter Apr 2000

Murdoch, Iris (WLB) Yrbk 58 Aug 80 obit Apr 99

Murdoch, Rupert May 77

Murdock, George J. obit Sep 42

Murdock, George Peter Mar 57

Murdock, Victor obit Aug 45

Muren, Dennis Mar 97

Murkowski, Frank H. Jul 2003

Murphree, Eger V. Sep 56 obit Jan 63

Murphy, Charles S. Apr 50 obit Oct 83

Murphy, Eddie Nov 83

Murphy, Frank Jul 40 obit Sep 49

Murphy, Franklin D. Mar 71 obit Aug 94

Murphy, Franklin W. obit Jan 41

Murphy, Frederick E. obit

Mar 40

Murphy, Gardner May 60 obit May 79

Murphy, George Dec 65 obit Jul 92

Murphy, Mark Sep 2004

Murphy, Patricia Apr 62

Murphy, Patrick V. Nov 72

Murphy, Robert D. Feb 43 Nov 58 obit Mar 78

Murphy, Thomas A. Oct 79

Murphy, Thomas F. Mar 51 obit Jan 96

Murphy, W. B. Nov 55 obit Aug 94

Murray, Albert May 94

Murray, Anne Jan 82

Murray, Arthur Apr 43 obit May 91

Murray, Augustus Taber obit Mar 40

Murray, Bill Jan 85 Sep 2004

Murray, Charles A. Jul 86

Murray, Charlie obit Sep 41

Murray, Don Sep 59

Murray, Dwight H. May 57 obit Nov 74

Murray, Elizabeth Apr 95

Murray, J. Harold obit Feb 41

Murray, James E. Aug 45 obit May 61

Murray, John Courtney May 61 obit Oct 67

Murray, Jonathan *see* Bunim, Mary-Ellis, and Murray, Jonathan

Murray, Patty Aug 94

Murray, Philip Jan 41 Feb 49 obit Dec 52

Murray, Thomas E. Sep 50 obit Sep 61

Murray, Tom Nov 56 obit Jan 72·

Murray, Ty May 2002

Murray, William S. obit Mar 42

Murrell, Ethel Ernest Oct 51

Murrell, Mrs. John Moore *see* Murrell, Ethel Ernest

Murrow, Edward R. Feb 42

Nov 53 obit Jun 65

Murtaugh, Daniel Feb 61 obit Feb 77

Murville, Maurice Couve de *see* Couve de Murville, Maurice

Museveni, Yoweri Aug 90

Musgrave, Thea May 78

Musharraf, Pervaiz *see* Musharraf, Pervez

Musharraf, Pervez Mar 2001

Musial, Stan Dec 48

Muskie, Edmund S. Feb 55 Dec 68 obit Jun 96

Musmanno, Michael A. Jun 67 obit Dec 68

Mussert, Anton Nov 42

Mussolini, Benito Mar 42 obit May 45

Mussolini, Bruno obit Oct 41

Muste, Abraham Johannes Oct 65 obit Apr 67

Muster, Thomas May 97

Muti, Ettore obit Oct 43

Muti, Riccardo Jul 80

Mutombo, Dikembe Feb 2000

Mutter, Anne-Sophie Jan 90

Muzorewa, Abel T. Mar 79

Mwinyi, Ali Hassan Jun 95

Mydans, Carl M. May 45 [Mydans, Carl M.; and Mydans, Shelley Smith] obit Yrbk 2004

Mydans, Shelley Smith May 45 [Mydans, Carl M.; and Mydans, Shelley Smith] obit Aug 2002

Myer, Dillon S. Jul 47 obit Jan 83

Myers, C. Kilmer Feb 60

Myers, Dee Dee Aug 94

Myers, Francis J. Apr 49 obit Sep 56

Myers, Gustavus obit Jan 43

Myers, Jerome obit Aug 40

Myers, Joel N. Apr 2005

Myers, Margaret Jane *see* My-

ers, Dee Dee

Myers, Mike Aug 97

Myers, Norman May 93

Myers, Richard B. Apr 2002

Myhrvold, Nathan Sep 97

Myrdal, Alva Dec 50 obit Mar 86

Myrdal, Gunnar Sep 46 Mar 75 obit Jul 87

Mysore, Maharaja of *see* Wadiyar, Sri Krishnaraja, Bahadur Maharaja of Mysore

'N Sync Nov 2000

N'dour, Youssou Jan 96

Nabarro, Gerald Nov 63 obit Jan 74

Nabokov, Vladimir May 66 obit Aug 77

Nabors, Jim Nov 69

Nabrit, James M., Jr. Jan 61 obit Mar 98

Nabrit, S. M. Jan 63 obit Yrbk 2004

Nabulsi, Suleiman Mar 57

Nader, Ralph Nov 68 Apr 86

Nadler, Marcus May 55 obit Jun 65

Nagano, Osami Jul 42 obit Feb 47

Naguib, Mohammed Oct 52

Nagy, Ivan May 77

Nahas, Mustafa Jul 51 obit Nov 65

Naidu, Sarojini May 43 obit Mar 49

Naifeh, Steven Mar 98 [Naifeh, Steven; and Smith, Gregory White]

Naipaul, V. S. Jul 77

Nair, Mira Nov 93

Naisbitt, John Nov 84

Naish, J. Carrol Jan 57 obit Mar 73

Nájera, Francisco Castillo *see* Castillo Nájera, Francisco

Najib Ahmadzi *see* Najibullah, Mohammed

Najibullah, Mohammed Jun

88 obit Jan 97

Najimy, Kathy Oct 2002

Nakasone, Yasuhiro Jun 83

Nakian, Reuben Feb 85 obit Feb 87

Nam Il Sep 51 obit Apr 76

Namath, Joe Dec 66

Namboodiripad, E. M. S. Nov 76

Namphy, Henri Sep 88

Napolitano, Janet Oct 2004

Narasimha Rao, P. V. *see* Rao, P. V. Narasimha

Narayan, Jaya Prakash May 58 obit Nov 79

Narayan, R. K. Sep 87 obit Jul 2001

Narelle, Marie obit Mar 41

Narendra Shiromani, Maharajah of Bikaner *see* Shiromani, Narendra

Nares, Owen obit Sep 43

Nash, Ogden Apr 41 obit Jul 71

Nash, Paul obit Sep 46

Nash, Philleo Nov 62 obit Jan 88

Nash, Steve Mar 2003

Nash, Walter Oct 42 Mar 58 obit Jul 68

Nason, John W. Jul 53 obit Feb 2002

Nasser, Gamal Abdel Nov 54 obit Nov 70

Nasser, Jacques Apr 2001

Nast, Condé obit Nov 42

Nastase, Ilie Oct 74

Nathan, Daniel *see* Dannay, Frederic

Nathan, George Jean Apr 45 obit Jun 58

Nathan, Robert R. Sep 41 obit Nov 2001

Natta, Giulio Nov 64

Nauman, Bruce Nov 90

Navarre, Henri Nov 53

Navarro, Mary De obit Jul 40

Navasky, Victor S. May 86

Navon, Yitzhak May 82

Navratilova, Martina Sep 77

Feb 2004

Naylor, Gloria Apr 93

Nazarbayev, Nursultan Oct 2000

Nazimova, Alla obit Aug 45

Nazimuddin, Khwaja Mar 49 obit Dec 64

Ne Win Apr 71 obit Yrbk 2003

Neagle, Anna Nov 45 [Neagle, Anna; and Wilcox, Herbert] obit Jul 86

Neal, Herbert Vincent obit Mar 40

Neal, Patricia Sep 64

Neals, Otto Feb 2003

Nearing, Scott Oct 71 obit Oct 83

Nederlander, James Morton Apr 91

Neel, Alice Aug 76 obit Jan 85

Neeleman, David Sep 2003

Neely, Matthew M. Jan 50 obit Mar 58

Neeson, Liam Nov 94

Neghelli, Marchese di *see* Graziani, Rodolfo

Negrín, Juan Sep 45 obit Jan 57

Negroponte, John Apr 2003

Nehru, B. K. Feb 63 obit Feb 2002

Nehru, Jawaharlal Jan 41 Apr 48 obit Jul 64

Neier, Aryeh Nov 78

Neill, A. S. Apr 61 obit Nov 73

Neill, Charles Patrick obit Nov 42

Neill, Stephen Charles Mar 60

Neilson, Frances Fullerton (WLB) Yrbk 55

Neilson, Mrs. Winthrop *see* Neilson, Frances Fullerton

Neilson, William Allan obit

Mar 46

Neiman, Leroy Jul 96

Nelles, Percy Walker Feb 44

Nelligan, Kate Jul 83

Nelly Oct 2002

Nelson, Byron Mar 45

Nelson, Donald M. Mar 41 obit Dec 59

Nelson, Gaylord May 60 obit Yrbk 2005

Nelson, Harriet May 49 [Nelson, Ozzie; and Nelson, Harriet] obit Jan 95

Nelson, Keith and Monseu, Stephanie Jun 2005

Nelson, Keith *see* Nelson, Keith and Monseu, Stephanie

Nelson, Marilyn Carlson Oct 2004

Nelson, Ozzie May 49 [Nelson, Ozzie; and Nelson, Harriet] obit Aug 75

Nelson, Stanley May 2005

Nelson, Willie Feb 79

Nemerov, Howard Oct 64 obit Sep 91

Nemirovich-Dantchenko, Vladimir obit Jun 43

Nenni, Pietro Mar 47 obit Feb 80

Neptunes May 2004

Nerina, Nadia Nov 57

Nernst, Walter H. obit Jan 42

Neruda, Pablo Dec 70 obit Nov 73

Nervi, Pier Luigi Jan 58 obit Mar 79

Nervo, Luis Padilla *see* Padilla Nervo, Luis

Nesbitt, Cathleen Nov 56 obit Sep 82

Nesmeianov, Aleksandr N. Nov 58

Nessen, Ron Jan 76

Nestingen, Ivan A. Mar 62 obit Jun 78

Netanyahu, Benjamin Jun 96

Netherwood, Douglas B. obit

Oct 43

Nettles, Graig Jul 84

Neuberger, Maurine B. Oct 61 obit Jul 2000

Neuberger, Richard L. Feb 55 obit May 60

Neuharth, Allen H. Apr 86

Neuhaus, Richard John Jun 88

Neuman, Leo Handel obit May 41

Neumann, Emanuel Mar 67 obit Jan 81

Neumann, Heinrich obit Jan 40

Neumann, John Von *see* Von Neumann, John

Neumeier, John Jul 91

Neurath, Otto obit Feb 46

Neustadt, Richard E. Nov 68 obit Yrbk 2004

Neutra, Richard J. May 47 Jul 61 obit Jun 70

Neuwirth, Bebe Nov 97

Nevelson, Louise Oct 67 obit May 88

Neville, John Jan 59

Neville, Robert A. R. Nov 53

Nevins, Allan Oct 68 obit Apr 71

Nevinson, Christopher R. W. obit Nov 46

Newall, Cyril Louis Norton Aug 40

Newberry, Truman H. obit Nov 45

Newbolt, Francis George obit Jan 41

Newby, P. H. (WLB) Yrbk 53

Newcombe, Don Feb 57

Newcombe, John Oct 77

Newcomer, Francis K. Mar 50 obit Oct 67

Newcomer, Mabel Sep 44

Newell, Edward Theodore obit Apr 41

Newell, Homer E., Jr. Nov 54 obit Sep 83

Newell, Horatio B. obit Oct

Newhall, Arthur B. Oct 42

Newhart, Bob Mar 62

Newhouse, Maggi *see* Mc-Nellis, Maggi

Newhouse, Samuel I. Mar 61 obit Oct 79

Newley, Anthony Oct 66 obit Jul 99

Newlon, Jesse H. obit Oct 41

Newman, Alfred Jul 43 obit Apr 70

Newman, Arnold Oct 80

Newman, Barnett Sep 69 obit Sep 70

Newman, Bernard Apr 59 obit Apr 68

Newman, Edwin Sep 67

Newman, J. Wilson Apr 55 obit Yrbk 2003

Newman, Paul Nov 59 May 85

Newman, Randy Oct 82

Newmark, Craig Jun 2005

Newsom, Carroll Vincent Apr 57 obit Apr 90

Newsom, Herschel D. Apr 51 obit Sep 70

Newsom, Lee Ann Oct 2004

Newton, Alfred Edward obit Nov 40

Newton, Christopher Feb 95

Newton, Cleveland Alexander obit Oct 45

Newton, Eric Feb 56 obit Apr 65

Newton, Helmut Nov 91 obit Yrbk 2004

Newton, Huey P. Feb 73 obit Oct 89

Newton, Wayne Feb 90

Newton-John, Olivia Nov 78

Ney, Hubert Nov 56

Ngawang Lobsang Yishey Tenzing Gyatso *see* Dalai Lama

Ngo Dinh Diem Mar 55 obit Jan 64

Nguyen Cao Ky *see* Ky, Nguyen Cao

Nguyen Tat Thanh *see* Ho Chi

Minh

Nguyen Thi Binh Jul 76

Nguyen Van Thieu *see* Thieu, Nguyen Van

Nguyen Van Thieu *see* Thieu, Nguyen Van

Niall, Michael *see* Breslin, Howard

Niarchos, Stavros May 58 obit Jun 96

Nice, Harry obit Apr 41

Nichols, Dudley Sep 41 obit Mar 60

Nichols, Herbert B. Sep 47

Nichols, Kenneth D. Nov 48 obit Sep 2000

Nichols, Mike Mar 61 Jan 92

Nichols, Roy Franklin Jul 49 obit Mar 73

Nichols, William I. Jun 58

Nichols, William T. Oct 53

Nicholson, Ben Jan 58 obit Apr 82

Nicholson, Jack *see* Steen, Marguerite Oct 74 Apr 95

Nicholson, Margaret Nov 57

Nickerson, Albert L. Nov 59 obit Nov 94

Nicklaus, Jack Nov 62

Nicol, Simon *see* Fairport Convention

Nicolet, Marcel Nov 58

Nicolson, Harold George May 67 obit Jun 68

Nicolson, Marjorie Hope Apr 40 obit Jun 81

Nidetch, Jean Dec 73

Niebuhr, Reinhold Mar 41 Nov 51 obit Jul 71

Niederland, William G. Oct 80 obit Oct 93

Nielsen, A. C. Dec 51 obit Jul 80

Nielsen, Alice obit Apr 43

Niemeyer, Oscar Feb 60

Niemöller, Martin Mar 43 Mar 65 obit May 84

Niggli, Josephina (WLB) Yrbk 49

Nijinsky, Waslaw Oct 40 obit

May 50

Nikolais, Alwin Feb 68 obit Jul 93

Nikolayev, Andrian Nov 64 obit Yrbk 2004

Nikolayevna-Tereshkova, Valentina see Tereshkova, Valentina

Niles, John Jacob Nov 59 obit Apr 80

Nilsson, Birgit May 60

Nimeiry, Gaafar Muhammad Al- Nov 77

Nimitz, Chester W. Feb 42 obit Mar 66

Nimoy, Leonard Feb 77

Nin, Anaïs Feb 44 Sep 75 obit Mar 77

Nipkow, Paul Gottlieb obit Oct 40

Nirenberg, Marshall W. Apr 65

Nitze, Paul H. Feb 62 obit Mar 2005

Niven, David Mar 57 obit Sep 83

Nixon, Agnes Apr 2001

Nixon, Lewis obit Nov 40

Nixon, Patricia Jan 70 obit Aug 93

Nixon, Richard M. Jul 48 Jun 58 Dec 69 Yrbk 94 obit Jun 94

Nizer, Louis Nov 55 obit Jan 95

Nkomo, Joshua Apr 76 obit Sep 99

Nkrumah, Kwame Jul 53 obit Jun 72

No Name see Senarens, Luis Philip

Noah, Yannick Aug 87

Noble, Adrian Aug 99

Noble, Allan May 57

Noble, Edward J. Jan 44 obit Mar 59

Noble, Gladwyn Kingsley obit Jan 41

Nobs, Ernst Sep 49 obit Jun 57

Nock, Albert Jay May 44 obit

Sep 45

Noel-Baker, Philip John Feb 46 obit Mar 83

Nofziger, Lyn Jan 83

Noguchi, Isamu Sep 43 obit Feb 89

Noguès, Auguste Feb 43 obit Jun 71

Noguès, Charles see Noguès, Auguste

Nolan, Christopher Sep 88

Nolan, Lloyd Nov 56 obit Nov 85

Nolan, W. I. obit Sep 43

Noland, Kenneth Sep 72

Nolde, O. Frederick Feb 47 obit Sep 72

Nolte, Nick Nov 80

Nomura, Kichisaburo Apr 41 obit Jul 64

Noon, Malik Firoz Khan Jun 57

Noonan, Peggy Jul 90

Noor al-Hussein Apr 91

Norden, Carl L. Jan 45 obit Sep 65

Nordhoff, Heinz Nov 56 obit Jun 68

Nordmann, Charles obit Yrbk 40

Norell, Norman Nov 64 obit Dec 72

Norford, Thomasina Johnson see Johnson, Thomasina Walker

Norgay, Tenzing see Tenzing Norgay

Noriega, Manuel Antonio Mar 88

Norkey, Tenzing see Tenzing Norkey

Norman, Greg Aug 89

Norman, Jessye Feb 76

Norman, Marsha May 84

Norman, Montagu Yrbk 40 obit Mar 50

Norodom Sihanouk Mar 54 Aug 93

Norrington, Roger Jan 90

Norris, Charles G. obit Aug

45

Norris, Chuck Jan 89

Norris, George W. obit Oct 44

Norris, Henry Hutchinson obit May 40

Norris, James Flack obit Sep 40

Norstad, Lauris May 48 Feb 59 obit Oct 88

North, Andrew see Norton, Andre

North, John Ringling Jun 51 obit Jul 85

North, Oliver L. Mar 92

North, Sterling Nov 43 obit Feb 75

Northrop, John H. Jun 47 obit Sep 87

Northrop, John K. Mar 49 obit Apr 81

Northrup, Edwin Fitch obit Jan 40

Norton, Alice Mary see Norton, Andre

Norton, Andre Jan 57 obit Yrbk 2005

Norton, Edward Jun 2000

Norton, Eleanor Holmes Nov 76

Norton, Gale A. Jun 2001

Norton, Howard M. Jun 47

Norton, John Richard Brinsley, 5th Baron of Grantley see Grantley, John Richard Brinsley Norton, 5th Baron

Norton, Mary T. Nov 44 obit Nov 59

Norton, Thomas obit Jan 42

Norton, W. W. obit Dec 45

Norville, Deborah Apr 90

Norway, Nevil Shute see Shute, Nevil

Norwich, Alfred Duff Cooper, 1st Viscount see Cooper, Alfred Duff

Notman, J. Geoffrey Jan 58

Nottage, Lynn Nov 2004

Noue, Jehan De, Comte Jan 47

Nourse, Edwin G. Oct 46 obit

Jun 74

Novacek, Michael J. Sep 2002

Novaës, Guiomar Jun 53 obit May 79

Novak, Joseph see Kosinski, Jerzy

Novak, Kim Apr 57

Novak, Marilyn Pauline see Novak, Kim

Novak, Michael Feb 85

Novello, Antonia May 92

Novikov, Nikolai V. Feb 47

Novotn, Antonín May 58 obit Mar 75

Novotna, Jarmila Mar 40 obit Apr 94

Nowitzki, Dirk Jun 2002

Noyes, W. Albert, Jr. Oct 47

Noyes, William A. obit Dec 41

Nozick, Robert Jun 82 obit Apr 2002

Nu, Thakin Dec 51 obit Apr 95

Nuckols, William P. May 52

Nufer, Albert F. Mar 55 obit Jan 57

Nuffield, William Richard Morris, 1st Viscount see Morris, William Richard

Nugent, Elliott Jul 44 obit Oct 80

Nugent, Ted Apr 2005

Nujoma, Sam Feb 90

Nuñez Portuondo, Emilio Apr 57

Nunn, Sam Jan 80

Nunn, Trevor Nov 80

Nur el Hussein see Noor al-Hussein

Nureyev, Rudolf Jul 63 obit Feb 93

Nuri As-Said Jun 55 obit Oct 58

Nuridsany, Claude Jun 97 [Nuridsany, Claude; and Pérennou, Marie]

Nutting, Anthony Feb 55 obit

May 99

Nutting, Wallace obit Sep 41

Nyad, Diana Aug 79

Nyborg, Victor H. Feb 54

Nye, Archibald E. Feb 42 obit Jan 68

Nye, Bill Jul 98

Nye, Gerald Prentice Nov 41 obit Sep 71

Nye, Russell Blaine Jul 45 obit Nov 93

Nyerere, Julius K. Apr 63 obit Jan 2000

Nykvist, Sven Jun 89

Nylander, Olof O. obit Sep 43

Nyrop, Donald W. Jun 52

Nystrom, Paul H. Mar 51 obit Oct 69

Oakes, Grant W. Jan 50

Oaksey, Geoffrey Lawrence see Lawrence, Geoffrey

Oates, Joyce Carol Sep 70 Jun 94

Obama, Barack Jul 2005

Obando Y Bravo, Miguel Mar 88

Obasanjo, Olusegun Jul 99

Oberlin, Russell Jul 60

Oberon, Merle Nov 41 obit Jan 80

Oberteuffer, George obit Jan 40

Oberth, Hermann Apr 57 obit Mar 90

Obolensky, Serge Oct 59 obit Nov 78

Oboler, Arch Mar 40 obit May 87

Obote, Milton Apr 81

O'Boyle, Patrick Jul 73 obit Sep 87

Obraztsov, Sergei Nov 64

Obraztsova, Elena Feb 83

O'Brian, Hugh Jul 58

O'Brian, Patrick Jun 95 obit

Mar 2000

O'Brien, Conan May 96

O'Brien, Conor Cruise Apr 67

O'Brien, Dan Jul 96

O'Brien, Ed see Radiohead

O'Brien, Edna Sep 80

O'Brien, Edward J. obit Apr 41

O'Brien, Lawrence F. Nov 61 Apr 77 obit Nov 90

O'Brien, Leo W. Jun 59 obit Jul 82

O'Brien, Pat Mar 66 obit Jan 84

O'Brien, Tim Aug 95

Obst, Lynda Oct 2000

Obuchi, Keizo May 99 obit Aug 2000

O'Byrne, Mrs. Roscoe C. Nov 48

O'Casey, Sean Nov 62 obit Nov 64

Ochoa, Severo Jun 62 obit Jan 94

Ochsner, Alton Oct 66 obit Nov 81

Ocker, William C. obit Nov 42

O'Connell, Hugh obit Mar 43

O'Connell, William Jun 41 obit Jun 44

O'Connor, Andrew obit Aug 41

O'Connor, Basil Sep 44 obit May 72

O'Connor, Carroll Jul 72 obit Sep 2001

O'Connor, Donald May 55 obit Apr 2004

O'Connor, Edwin Nov 63 obit May 68

O'Connor, Flannery (WLB) Yrbk 58 obit Sep 65

O'Connor, James Francis obit Mar 45

O'Connor, John J. Jun 84 obit Jul 2000

O'Connor, Sandra Day Jan 82

O'Connor, Sinéad Jun 91

O'Conor, Herbert R. Feb 50

obit May 60

O'Daniel, W. Lee Oct 47 obit Jun 69

O'Day, Anita Jun 90

O'Day, Caroline Goodwin obit Feb 43

Odell, George C. D. Dec 44 obit Dec 49

Odets, Clifford Nov 41 obit Nov 63

Odetta Dec 60

Odishaw, Hugh Feb 71 obit Jun 84

Odlin, Reno Jul 65

Odlum, Floyd B. Nov 41 obit Aug 76

Odlum, Mrs. Floyd B. *see* Cochran, Jacqueline

O'Donnell, Donat *see* O'Brien, Conor Cruise

O'Donnell, Edwin P. obit Jun 43

O'Donnell, Emmett, Jr. Jul 48 obit Feb 72

O'Donnell, Rosie Aug 95

O'Dowd, George A. *see* Boy George

Odria, Manuel A. Nov 54 obit Apr 74

Oduber, Daniel Jul 77

O'Dwyer, Paul Sep 69 obit Sep 98

O'Dwyer, William Sep 41 May 47 obit Jan 65

Oe, Hikari May 99

Oe, Kenzaburo May 96

Oechsner, Frederick Cable Mar 43 obit Jun 92

Oenslager, Donald Sep 46 obit Aug 75

Oettinger, Katherine Brownell Nov 57 obit Jan 98

O'Faoláin, Séan Apr 90 obit Jun 91

O'Flanagan, Michael obit Sep 42

Ogata, Sadako Oct 97

Ogburn, Charlton Feb 55 obit Apr 62

Ogburn, William F. Feb 55

obit Jul 59

Ogden, C. K. Jan 44 obit Jun 57

Ogilvie, Elisabeth (WLB) Yrbk 51

Ogilvy, David M. Jul 61 obit Oct 99

O'Gorman, James A. obit Jul 43

O'Gorman, Juan Nov 56

O'Gorman, Patrick F. obit Apr 40

O'Hair, Madalyn Murray Jan 77 obit Jun 2001

O'Hara, John Feb 41 obit Jun 70

O'Hara, Mary Jan 44 obit Jan 81

O'Hara, Maureen Feb 53

Ohga, Norio Jun 98

Ohira, Masayoshi Mar 64 obit Aug 80

Ohlin, Lloyd E. Apr 63

Ohlsson, Garrick Jun 75

O'Horgan, Tom Apr 70

Oistrakh, David Mar 56 obit Dec 74

Ojike, Mbonu Jul 47

Ojukwu, Chukuemeka Odumegwu Feb 69

O'Keefe, Sean Jan 2003

O'Keeffe, Georgia Jun 41 Feb 64 obit Apr 86

O'Kelly, Sean T. Jul 48 obit Jan 67

O'Konski, Alvin E. Nov 55 obit Aug 87

Okrent, Daniel Nov 2004

Okun, Arthur M. Feb 70 obit May 80

Olaf V, King of Norway *see* Olav V, King of Norway

Olajuwon, Hakeem Nov 93

Olav V, King of Norway Jan 62 obit Mar 91

Oldenbroek, Jacobus H. Mar 50

Oldenburg, Claes Feb 70

Oldfield, Barney obit Nov 46

Oldman, Gary Jan 96

Olds, Irving S. Oct 48 obit

Apr 63

O'Leary, Hazel R. Jan 94

O'Leary, James A. obit May 44

Oleson, Lloyd F. Jun 47

Olin, Lena Jun 2003

Oliphant, Marcus L. Dec 51 obit Oct 2000

Oliphant, Pat Jul 91

Olitski, Jules Oct 69

Oliveira Salazar, Antonio de *see* Salazar, Antonio De Oliveira

Oliver, Edna May obit Jan 43

Oliver, James A. Jan 66 obit May 82

Oliver, Lunsford E. Sep 47

Olivero, Magda Apr 80

Olivetti, Adriano Jan 59 obit Apr 60

Olivier, Lady *see* Plowright, Joan

Olivier, Laurence Jun 46 Jan 79 obit Sep 89

Ollenhauer, Erich Jan 53 obit Feb 64

Ollila, Jorma Aug 2002

Olmedo, Alex Dec 59

Olmedo y Rodriguez Alejandro *see* Olmedo, Alex

Olmos, Edward James Aug 92

Olmstead, Albert Ten Eyck obit May 45

Olmsted, Frederick Law Jun 49 obit Mar 58

Olsen, John Sep 40 [Olsen, John Sigvard; and Johnson, Harold Ogden] obit Mar 63

Olsen, Kenneth H. Mar 87

Olson, Harry F. Nov 55 obit Jun 82

Olsson, Ann-Margret *see* Ann-Margret

Oltman, Florine May 70

O'Mahoney, Joseph C. Oct 45 obit Jan 63

O'Malley, Sean Patrick Jan 2004

O'Malley, Walter F. Mar 54 obit Oct 79

O'Meara, Walter (WLB) Yrbk

58 obit Nov 89

O'Melveny, Henry W. obit Jun 41

Onassis, Aristotle Socrates Mar 63 obit May 75

Onassis, Christina Feb 76 obit Jan 89

Onassis, Jacqueline Kennedy Oct 61 [Kennedy, Jacqueline] obit Jul 94

Ondaatje, Michael Oct 93

O'Neal, A. Daniel Jun 79

O'Neal, Edward A. Sep 46 obit May 58

O'Neal, Frederick Nov 46 obit Oct 92

O'Neal, Jermaine Jun 2004

O'Neal, Ryan Feb 73

O'Neal, Shaquille Jul 96

O'Neal, Stanley May 2003

O'Neil, George obit Jul 40

O'Neil, James F. Nov 47 obit Sep 81

O'Neil, Thomas F. Nov 55 obit Jun 98

O'Neill, C. William Jul 58

O'Neill, Eugene F. Apr 63

O'Neill, Francis A., Jr. Dec 60 obit Mar 92

O'Neill, Gerard K. Feb 79 obit Jun 92

O'Neill, J. E. Jun 52

O'Neill, Paul H. Jul 2001

O'Neill, Terence Sep 68 obit Sep 90

O'Neill, Thomas P., Jr. Apr 74 obit Mar 94

O'Neill, Tip see O'Neill, Thomas P., Jr.

O'Neill, William A. Feb 85

Ongania, Juan Carlos Oct 68 obit Aug 95

Onís, Harriet De see De Onís, Harriet

Ono, Yoko Nov 72

Onsager, Lars Apr 58 obit Jan 77

Oort, Jan Hendrik Jun 69 obit

Jan 93

Oosterbaan, Benjamin Gaylord see Oosterbaan, Bennie

Oosterbaan, Bennie Dec 49 obit Jan 91

Opel, John R. Mar 86

Ophuls, Marcel Jun 77

Oppenheim, E. Phillips obit Mar 46

Oppenheimer, Eric see Newton, Eric

Oppenheimer, Franz obit Nov 43

Oppenheimer, Harry Frederick Feb 61 obit Nov 2000

Oppenheimer, J. Robert Nov 45 Apr 64 obit Apr 67

Orbach, Jerry May 70 obit Apr 2005

O'Reilly, Bill Oct 2003

Orff, Carl Aug 76 obit May 82

Orlando, Vittorio Emanuele Feb 44 obit Jan 53

Orlean, Susan Jun 2003

Orlebar, Augustus H. obit Sep 43

Orlemanski, Stanislaus, Rev. Jun 44

Orman, Suze May 2003

Ormandy, Eugene Jan 41 obit May 85

Ormond, Julia Mar 99

Ormsby-Gore, David Mar 61 obit Mar 85

Ornish, Dean Apr 94

Orowitz, Eugene Maurice see Landon, Michael

Orozco, Jose Clemente Sep 40 obit Oct 49

Orr, Bobby Nov 69

Orr, H. Winnett Oct 41

Orr, John Boyd see Boyd-Orr, John Boyd Orr

Orr, Louis M. Apr 60 obit Jul 61

Orsborn, Albert Nov 46 obit Apr 67

Ortega, Daniel Oct 84

Ortega Saavedra, Daniel see

Ortega, Daniel

Ortiz, David Aug 2005

Ortiz, Roberto M. obit Sep 42

Ortner, Sherry B. Nov 2002

Orton, Helen Fuller Jan 41 obit Apr 55

Orville, Howard T. May 56 obit Jul 60

Osato, Sono Oct 45

Osawa, Sandra Sunrising Jan 2001

Osborn, Fairfield Sep 49 obit Nov 69

Osborn, Frederick Nov 41 obit Mar 81

Osborn, Robert C. Jun 59 obit Feb 95

Osborne, Barrie M. Feb 2005

Osborne, John Jun 59 obit Feb 95

Osborne, Oliver Thomas obit Yrbk 40

Osborne, Tom Mar 98

Osborne, William Hamilton obit Feb 43

Osbourne, Ozzy Nov 98

Osbourne, Sharon Jan 2001

Oscar of the Waldorf see Tschirky, Oscar

Osgood, Charles E. Apr 62

O'Shea, Milo Jun 82

O'Shea, William F. obit Apr 45

Osmeña, Sergio Sep 44 obit Dec 61

Osmond, Donny Feb 98

Ospina Perez, Mariano Feb 50 obit Jun 76

Osterberg, James Newell see Pop, Iggy

Osumi, Mineo Osumi, Baron obit Apr 41

Otake, Koma see Eiko and Koma

Otero, Miguel Antonio obit Sep 44

O'Toole, Peter Sep 68

Ott, Mel Jul 41 obit Jan 59

Ottaviani, Alfredo Dec 66 obit

Sep 79

Otter, Anne Sofie von Sep 95

Ottinger, Nathan obit Jan 41

Ottley, Roi Oct 43 obit Dec 60

Otto, Frei Oct 71

Otto of Austria, Archduke Jun 41

Ötüken, Adnan Jun 54

Oudolf, Piet Apr 2003

Ouédraogo, Idrissa May 93

Oumansky, Constantine Feb 41 obit Mar 45

Oursler, Fulton Oct 42 obit Jul 52

Ousmane, Sembène see Sembène, Ousmane

OutKast Apr 2004

Ovanda Candia, Alfredo Mar 70 obit Mar 82

Overholser, Winfred Nov 53 obit Dec 64

Overman, Lynne obit Apr 43

Overstreet, Harry A. Sep 50 obit Oct 70

Ovitz, Michael S. Oct 95

Owen, A. David K. May 46 obit Sep 70

Owen, David Sep 77

Owen, Ruth Bryan see Rohde, Ruth Bryan Owen

Owen, Steve Dec 46 obit Jul 64

Owens, Clarence Julian obit Apr 41

Owens, Dana see Queen Latifah

Owens, James Cleveland see Owens, Jesse

Owens, Jesse Nov 56 obit May 80

Owens, Robert Bowie obit Yrbk 40

Owings, Nathaniel A. May 71 obit Aug 84

Oxenham, John obit Mar 41

Oxford And Asquith, Margot Asquith, Countess of see Asquith, Margot

Oxnam, G. Bromley Nov 44

obit Apr 63

Oz, Amos Jul 83

Oz, Frank Oct 99

Oz, Mehmet C. Apr 2003

Özal, Turgut Jun 85 obit Jun 93

Ozawa, Seiji Feb 68 Jul 98

Ozbirn, Catharine Freeman Jan 62 [Ozbirn, Mrs. E. Lee] obit Mar 74

Ozick, Cynthia Aug 83

Oznowicz, Frank see Oz, Frank

P'ing, Lan see Jiang Qing

Paar, Jack Apr 59 obit Yrbk 2004

Paasikivi, Juho Kusti May 44 obit Feb 57

Pacciardi, Randolfo Mar 44 obit Jul 91

Pace, Charles Ashford obit Feb 41

Pace, Frank, Jr. Feb 50 obit Feb 88

Pacelli, Eugenio Maria Giuseppe Giovanni see Pius XII, Pope

Pacheco E Chaves, João Nov 54

Pacino, Al Jul 74

Packard, David Jun 69 obit Jun 96

Packard, Eleanor Apr 41 obit Jun 72

Packard, Frank L. obit Apr 42

Packard, Vance Apr 58 obit Feb 97

Packard, Winthrop obit May 43

Packer, Fred L. obit Feb 57

Packwood, Bob Jan 81

Padover, Saul K. Oct 52 obit Apr 81

Paepcke, Walter P. Apr 60

Page, Clarence Jan 2003

Page, Geraldine Nov 53 obit Aug 87

Page, Irvine H. Jun 66 obit Aug 91

Page, Joe Apr 50 obit Jun 80

Page, Larry see Brin, Sergey,

and Page, Larry

Page, Patti Sep 65

Page, Robert Morris Nov 64 obit Jul 92

Page, Ruth Jun 62 obit Jul 91

Pagels, Elaine Hiesey Feb 96

Paglia, Camille Aug 92

Pagnanelli, George see Carlson, John Roy

Pagnol, Marcel Mar 56 obit Jun 74

Pahlevi, Farah Diba see Farah Diba Pahlevi

Pahlevi, Mohammed Riza see Mohammed Zahir Shah

Pahlmann, William C. Oct 64 obit Jan 88

Pai Tsung-Hsi Nov 42 [Li Tsung-Jen; and Pai Tsung-Hsi] obit Feb 67

Paicovitch, Yigal see Allon, Yigal

Paige, Janis Jan 59

Paige, Leroy Sep 52 obit Aug 82

Paige, Roderick R. Jul 2001

Paige, Satchel see Paige, Leroy

Paik, Nam June Mar 83

Paine, Thomas Otten Mar 70 obit Jul 92

Pais, Abraham Jan 94 obit Oct 2000

Paisley, Ian Jan 71 Jun 86

Pak, Chong-Hui see Park, Chung Hee

Pak, Jung Hi see Park, Chung Hee

Pak, Se Ri Jan 99

Pakenham, Antonia see Fraser, Antonia

Pakula, Alan J. Jun 80 obit Feb 99

Palade, George E. Jul 67

Palance, Jack Aug 92

Palethorpe-Todd, Richard Andrew see Todd, Richard

Paley, Grace Mar 86

Paley, William S. Oct 40 Dec

51 obit Jan 91

Palin, Michael Feb 2000

Palinurus see Connolly, Cyril

Palme, Olof May 70 obit Apr 86

Palmeiro, Rafael Aug 2001

Palmer, Arnold Sep 60

Palmer, Jim May 80

Palmer, John Leslie obit Sep 44

Palmer, Lilli May 51 obit Mar 86

Palmieri, Eddie Jun 92

Paltrow, Gwyneth Jan 2005

Pandit, Mrs. Ranjit see Pandit, Vijaya Lakshmi

Pandit, Vijaya Lakshmi Jan 46 obit Feb 91

Panetta, Leon E. Jun 93

Panic, Milan Jun 93

Panofsky, Wolfgang K. H. Jun 70

Panov, Valery Oct 74

Pant, Govind Ballabh Jan 59 obit May 61

Pantaleoni, Helenka A. Nov 56 obit Mar 87

Pantaleoni, Mrs. Guido see Pantaleoni, Helenka A.

Pantani, Marco Feb 99

Papaleo, Anthony see Franciosa, Anthony

Papandreou, Andreas May 70 Apr 83 obit Sep 96

Papandreou, George Dec 44 obit Dec 68

Papashvily, George Mar 45 [Papashvily, George; and Papashvily, Helen] obit May 78

Papashvily, Helen Mar 45 [Papashvily, George; and Papashvily, Helen]

Papen, Franz Von Jun 41 obit Jun 69

Papp, Joseph May 65 obit Jan 92

Parcells, Bill Apr 91

Paretsky, Sara May 92

Parizeau, Jacques Jul 93

Park, Chung Hee Jan 69 obit

Jan 80

Park, Dorothy Dowden see Clark, Dorothy Park

Park, Linda Sue Jun 2002

Park, Rosemary Jan 64 obit Yrbk 2004

Park, Thomas Jan 63 obit Jun 92

Parkening, Christopher Apr 87

Parker, Alan Mar 94

Parker, John J. Dec 55 obit May 58

Parker, Mrs. James C. see Parker, Karla V.

Parker, Raymond K. see Parker, Buddy

Parker, Robert B. Nov 93

Parker, Robert M. May 2005

Parker, Sarah Jessica Sep 98

Parker, Trey May 98 [Parker, Trey; and Stone, Matt]

Parkes, Henry Bamford Mar 54

Parkinson, C. Northcote Dec 60 obit May 93

Parks, Bert Feb 73 obit Apr 92

Parks, Gordon Oct 68 Oct 92

Parks, Rosa May 89

Parks, Suzan-Lori Apr 99

Parmoor, Charles Alfred Cripps, 1st Baron see Cripps, Charles Alfred

Parnis, Mollie May 56 obit Sep 92

Parodi, Alexandre Jun 46

Parr, Albert Eide Jul 42 obit Sep 91

Parran, Thomas Aug 40 obit Apr 68

Parrish, Maxfield Nov 65 obit Apr 66

Parrish, Mrs. Wayne William see Knight, Frances G.

Parry, Albert Apr 61 obit Jul 92

Parseghian, Ara Feb 68

Parsons, Estelle Oct 75

Parsons, Harriet Jan 53 obit Mar 83

Parsons, Louella Oct 40 obit

Oct 73

Parsons, Mrs. William Barclay see Parsons, Rose Peabody

Parsons, Richard D. Apr 2003

Parsons, Rose Peabody Dec 59 obit Jun 85

Parsons, Talcott Jan 61 obit Jul 79

Pärt, Arvo Feb 95

Partch, Harry Sep 65 obit Oct 74

Partch, Virgil Franklin Jul 46 obit Oct 84

Parton, Dolly Aug 77

Partridge, Deborah see Wolfe, Deborah Partridge

Partridge, Eric Jan 63 obit Jul 79

Pascal, Amy Mar 2002

Pasionaria, La see Ibárruri, Dolores

Pasolini, Pier Paolo Jul 70 obit Jan 76

Passman, Otto, E. Oct 60 obit Sep 88

Passos, John Dos see Dos Passos, John

Pasternak, Boris Leonidovich Feb 59 obit Jul 60

Pastora Gómez, Edén Jul 86

Pastore, John O. Apr 53 obit Yrbk 2000

Pastrana Borrero, Misael Jul 71 obit Nov 97

Pataki, George E. Apr 96

Patch, Alexander M. May 43 obit Jan 46

Patchett, Ann Apr 2003

Pate, Martha B. May 47 obit Jul 83

Patel, Vallabhbhai Mar 48 obit Jan 51

Paterno, Joe Feb 84

Paterson, Chat Mar 48 obit May 92

Paterson, Katherine Nov 97

Patinkin, Mandy Jan 99

Patino, Simon I. Oct 42 obit May 47

Patman, Wright Feb 46 obit

William George

Penney, William George Feb 53 obit May 91

Penniman, Richard Wayne *see* Little Richard

Penzias, Arno A. Sep 85

Pepitone, Joe Jan 73

Peppard, George Dec 65 obit Jul 94

Pepper, Claude Feb 41 Jan 83 obit Jul 89

Pepys, Mark Everard obit Sep 43

Per Krohg *see* Krohg, Per

Perahia, Murray Mar 82

Percy, Charles H. Dec 59 Aug 77

Percy, Walker Sep 76 obit Jul 90

Perdue, Frank Jun 79 obit Oct 2005

Pereira, I. Rice Nov 53 obit Feb 71

Pereira, William L. Jan 79 obit Jan 86

Perelman, Ronald Owen Jan 91

Perelman, S. J. Mar 71 obit Jan 80

Pérennou, Marie Jun 97 [Nuridsany, Claude; and Pérennou, Marie]

Peres, Shimon Jan 76 Mar 95

Péret, Raoul obit Sep 42

Pérez De Cuéllar, Javier Aug 82

Pérez Esquivel, Adolfo Mar 81

Pérez Jiménez, Marcos Nov 54 obit Feb 2002

Pérez, Carlos Andrés Feb 76

Pérez, Louie *see* Los Lobos

Perez, Manuel Benitez *see* El Cordobés

Perez, Mariano Ospina *see* Ospina Perez, Mariano

Perez, Rosie Sep 95

Perfect, Josephine Holt *see* Bay, Mrs. Charles Ulrick

Perkins, Anthony Sep 60 obit

Nov 92

Perkins, Carl D. Feb 68 obit Sep 84

Perkins, Charles Jan 69 obit Feb 2001

Perkins, Dan *see* Tomorrow, Tom

Perkins, Dexter Jan 58 obit Jul 84

Perkins, Frances Yrbk 40 obit Jul 65

Perkins, James A. Apr 64 obit Nov 98

Perkins, Marlin Oct 51 obit Aug 86

Perle, Richard Jul 2003

Perlman, Alfred E. Apr 55 obit Jul 83

Perlman, Itzhak May 75

Perón, Eva De Mar 49 obit Sep 52

Perón, Isabel Jan 75

Perón, Juan Jun 44 Feb 74 obit Feb 74

Perón, María Estele Martínez de *see* Perón, Isabel

Perot, Ross Jul 71 Yrbk 96

Perrin, Francis Jul 51

Perrine, Valerie Oct 75

Perry, Anne Aug 96

Perry, Frank Oct 72 obit Nov 95

Perry, Gaylord Nov 82

Perry, Harold R. Oct 66 obit Sep 91

Perry, Joe *see* Aerosmith

Perry, Tyler Jun 2005

Perry, William J. Jan 95

Perse, St.-John *see* Léger, Alexis Saint-Léger

Person, Houston Jun 2003

Pertinax *see* Geraud, André

Pertschuk, Michael Sep 86

Perutz, Max Nov 63 obit Apr 2002

Pesci, Joe Mar 94

Pétain, Henri Philippe Aug 40 obit Sep 51

Peter II of Yugosavia Nov 43

obit Dec 70

Peters, Bernadette Sep 84

Peters, Charles Aug 90

Peters, Roberta Apr 54

Peters, Tom Oct 94

Petersen, Donald E. Mar 88

Petersen, Wolfgang Jul 2001

Peterson, David Feb 88

Peterson, Esther Dec 61 obit Mar 98

Peterson, Oscar Oct 83

Peterson, Peter G. Jun 72

Peterson, Roger Tory Apr 59 obit Oct 96

Petherbridge, Margaret *see* Farrar, Margaret

Pethick-Lawrence, Frederick William Jun 46 obit Nov 61

Petiot, Henry Jules Charles *see* Daniel-Rops, Henry

Petit, Philippe Sep 88

Petit, Roland Apr 52

Petitpierre, Max Dec 53 obit Jun 94

Petri, Egon Nov 42 obit Jul 62

Petrillo, James C. Yrbk 40 obit Jan 85

Petronio, Stephen Mar 98

Petry, Ann Mar 46 obit Jul 97

Pettibon, Raymond Apr 2005

Pettit, Robert Oct 61

Petty, Richard Aug 80

Petty, Tom Nov 91

Peurifoy, John E. Jan 49 obit Oct 55

Pevsner, Antoine Mar 59 obit Jun 62

Peyroux, Madeleine Nov 2005

Pfeiffer, Eckhard Jun 98

Pfeiffer, Michelle Mar 90

Pflimlin, Pierre Nov 55 obit Oct 2000

Pfost, Gracie May 55 obit Oct 65

Pham Van Dong Feb 75 obit Sep 2000

Phan Dinh Khai *see* Le Duc

Tho

Phelps, Michael Aug 2004

Phelps, William Lyon Jan 43

Philbin, Regis Oct 94

Philbrick, Herbert A. Mar 53 obit Oct 93

Philip, André Aug 43 obit Sep 70

Phillips, Caryl Jul 94

Phillips, H. I. Sep 43 obit Apr 65

Phillips, Irna Apr 43 obit Feb 74

Phillips, Kevin Sep 94

Phillips, Morgan Sep 49 obit Feb 63

Phillips, Pauline Esther Friedman *see* Van Buren, Abigail

Phillips, Sam Apr 2001

Phillips, Scott *see* Creed

Phillips, Thomas Hal (WLB) Yrbk 56

Phillips, William [diplomat] Jul 40 obit Apr 68

Phillips, William [editor] Oct 84 obit Yrbk 2002

Phipps, Joyce Irene *see* Grenfell, Joyce

Phish Jul 2003

Phoenix *see* Linkin Park

Phoui Sananikone *see* Sananikone, Phoui

Phouma, Souvanna *see* Souvanna Phouma

Phumiphon Aduldet *see* Rama IX, King of Thailand

Piaf, Edith Dec 50 obit Nov 63

Piaget, Jean Dec 58 obit Nov 80

Piano, Renzo Apr 2001

Piatigorsky, Gregor Oct 45 obit Sep 76

Piazza, Mike Jul 99

Picasso, Pablo Jan 43 Nov 62 obit May 73

Picasso, Paloma Apr 86

Piccard, Auguste Sep 47 [Piccard, Auguste; and Piccard,

Jean Felix] obit May 62

Piccard, Jacques Dec 65

Piccard, Jean Felix Sept 47 [Piccard, Auguste; and Piccard, Jean Felix] obit Mar 63

Picciotto, Guy *see* Fugazi

Pickens, Jane Dec 49 obit Apr 92

Pickens, T. Boone Jul 85

Pickering, William H. Nov 58 obit Yrbk 2004

Pickersgill, J. W. Mar 68

Pickford, Mary Apr 45 obit Jul 79

Picon, Molly Jun 51 obit Jun 92

Pidgeon, Walter Sep 42 obit Nov 84

Piëch, Ferdinand Sep 99

Piel, Gerard Jun 59 obit Feb 2005

Pierce, Bob Dec 61

Pierce, David Hyde Apr 2001

Pierce, J. R. *see* Pierce, John Robinson

Pierce, John Robinson Feb 61 obit Jun 2002

Pierce, Lorne Nov 56

Pierce, Paul Nov 2002

Pierce, Samuel R. Jr. Nov 82 obit Feb 2001

Piercy, Marge Nov 94

Pierlot, Hubert, Count May 43 obit Feb 64

Pifer, Alan Apr 69

Pike, James A. May 57 obit Nov 69

Pile, Frederick Alfred Feb 42 obit Yrbk 91 (died Nov 76)

Pileggi, Nicholas Jan 99

Pilgrim, David *see* Saunders, Hilary Aidan St. George

Pinay, Antoine Apr 52 obit Feb 95

Pincay, Laffit Sep 2001

Pincherle, Alberto *see* Moravia, Alberto

Pincus, Gregory May 66 obit Oct 67

Pindling, Lynden Oscar May

68 obit Yrbk 2000

Pineau, Christian Jul 56 obit Jun 95

Piñero Jesús T. Oct 46 obit Jan 53

Piñero, Miguel Nov 83 obit Aug 88

Pingree, Chellie Jan 2005

Piniella, Lou Aug 86

Pinilla, Gustavo Rojas *see* Rojas Pinilla, Gustavo

Pinker, Steven A. Sep 98

Pinnock, Trevor Sep 89

Pinochet Ugarte, Augusto Dec 74

Pinsky, Robert Feb 99

Pinter, Harold Nov 63

Pinza, Ezio Feb 41 Dec 53 obit Jul 57

Piper, John Apr 64 obit Aug 92

Pipher, Mary Aug 99

Pippen, Scottie Mar 94

Pippin, Horace Aug 45 obit Yrbk 47

Pire, Georges May 59 obit Mar 69

Piscator, Erwin Oct 42 obit Apr 66

Piston, Walter Jun 48 Dec 61 obit Jan 77

Pitino, Rick Jan 98

Pitt, Brad Mar 96

Pitt, Harvey Nov 2002

Pittman, Robert Jul 2000

Pitts, Leonard Jr. Oct 2004

Pius XII, Pope Apr 41 Mar 50 obit Dec 58

Pivot, Bernard Oct 90

Plain, Belva Feb 99

Plant, Robert Oct 98

Plavsic, Biljana Feb 98

Player, Gary Nov 61

Plaza Lasso, Galo Oct 51 Apr 69 obit Mar 87

Pleasence, Donald Jun 69 obit Apr 95

Pleven, René Jun 50 obit Mar 93

Plimpton, George Feb 69 obit

Jan 2004

Plimpton, Martha Apr 2002

Plisetskaya, Maya Jun 63

Plotkin, Mark J. Jun 97

Plowden, David Feb 96

Plowden, Edwin Noel Jul 47

Plowright, Joan Feb 64

Plummer, Christopher Jul 56 Aug 88

Plunkett, Jim Sep 71 Feb 82

Poage, W. R. Dec 69 obit Mar 87

Podgorny, Nikolai V. May 66 obit Mar 83

Podhoretz, Norman Oct 68

Pogorelich, Ivo Sep 88

Pogrebin, Letty Cottin Nov 97

Poindexter, John M. Nov 87

Poinso-Chapuis, Germaine Jun 48

Poitier, Sidney May 59 Sep 2000

Pol Pot Apr 80 obit Jun 98

Polanski, Roman Jun 69

Polese, Kim Jul 97

Poletti, Charles Sep 43 obit Yrbk 2002

Poling, Daniel Nov 43 obit Mar 68

Pollack, Jack H. Dec 57 obit Feb 85

Pollack, Sydney Sep 86

Pollini, Maurizio Nov 80

Pollitt, Harry May 48 obit Sep 60

Pollitt, Katha Oct 2002

Pollock, Jackson Apr 56

Pomeroy, Wardell B. Jul 74 obit Yrbk 2001

Pompidou, Georges Nov 62 obit May 74

Poncins, Gontran, Vicomte De Jun 41

Ponnamperuma, Cyril Apr 84 obit Mar 95

Ponnelle, Jean-Pierre Mar 83 obit Sep 88

Pons, Lily Jan 44 obit Apr 76

Poole, Elijah *see* Muhammad, Elijah

Poor, Henry Varnum Apr 42

obit Jan 71

Poorten, Hein Ter *see* Ter Poorten, Hein

Pop, Iggy Jan 95

Popcorn, Faith Feb 93

Pope John Paul I *see* John Paul I, Pope

Pope John Paul II *see* John Paul II, Pope

Pope John XXIII *see* John XXIII, Pope

Pope Paul VI *see* Paul VI, Pope

Pope Pius XII *see* Pius XII, Pope

Pope, Liston Apr 56 obit Jun 74

Popeil, Ron Mar 2001

Popenoe, Paul Dec 46

Popham, Robert Brooke- *see* Brooke-Popham, Robert

Popkin, Zelda (WLB) Yrbk 51 obit Jul 83

Popov, Oleg Mar 64

Popovic, Koca Jan 57 obit Jan 93

Popper, Karl Raimund Jan 63 obit Nov 94

Portal of Hungerford, Charles Frederick Algernon Portal, 1st Viscount *see* Portal, Charles

Portal, Charles Mar 41 obit Jun 71 [Portal of Hungerford, Charles Frederick Algernon Portal, 1st Viscount]

Porter, Cole Jul 40 obit Dec 64

Porter, Eliot Nov 76 obit Jan 91

Porter, Katherine Anne May 40 Mar 63 obit Nov 80

Porter, Mrs. Eugene Vandergrift *see* Porter, Elizabeth K.

Porter, Richard William Nov 58 obit Jan 97

Porter, Sylvia Oct 41 Apr 80 obit Aug 91

Porter, William J. Mar 74 obit May 88

Portinari, Candido Yrbk 40

obit Mar 62

Posey, Parker Mar 2003

Posner, Richard A. Jan 93

Post, Emily Mar 41 obit Nov 60

Poston, Tom Apr 61

Pot, Pol *see* Pol Pot

Potok, Chaim May 83 obit Yrbk 2002

Potter, Beatrix obit Mar 44

Potter, Dan M. Feb 64

Potter, Dennis Jul 94 obit Jul 94

Potter, Myrtle S. Aug 2004

Potter, William E. Dec 57 obit Feb 89

Potvin, Denis Oct 86

Poujade, Pierre Apr 56 obit Yrbk 2004

Pound, Ezra Nov 42 May 63 obit Dec 72

Pound, Roscoe May 47 obit Sep 64

Pousette-Dart, Richard Mar 76 obit Jan 93

Poussaint, Alvin F. Jul 73

Powdermaker, Hortense Feb 61 obit Sep 70

Powell, Adam Clayton Apr 42 obit May 72

Powell, Anthony Sep 77 obit Aug 2000

Powell, Benjamin E. Jun 59

Powell, Colin L. Jun 88 Nov 2001

Powell, Dick Feb 48 obit Feb 63

Powell, J. Enoch Nov 64 obit Jun 99

Powell, Jane Dec 74

Powell, Jody Jul 77

Powell, Kevin Jan 2004

Powell, Lawrence Clark Jun 60

Powell, Lewis F., Jr. Feb 65 obit Nov 98

Powell, Michael Aug 87 obit Apr 90

Powell, Michael K. May 2003

Powell, Mike Oct 93

Powell, Richard Stillman *see*

obit May 55

Pumarejo, Alfonso López *see* López, Alfonso

Purcell, Edward M. Sep 54 obit May 97

Puryear, Martin Aug 99

Pusey, Merlo J. Jul 52 obit Jan 86

Pusey, Nathan M. Dec 53 obit Feb 2002

Putin, Vladimir Apr 2000

Putnam, Roger L. Jan 52

Puttnam, David Feb 89

Puzo, Mario Mar 75 obit Sep 99

Pyle, Ernest Taylor *see* Pyle, Ernie

Pyle, Ernie Apr 41 obit May 45

Pym, Francis Sep 82

Pynchon, Thomas Oct 87

Qabus Bin Said Aug 78

Qaddafi, Muammar Al- Sep 73 Mar 92

Qing, Jiang *see* Jiang Qing

Quadros, Jânio da Silva Jun 61 obit Apr 92

Quaison-Sackey, Alex Mar 66 obit Feb 93

Quant, Mary Jan 68

Quasimodo, Salvatore Mar 60 obit Sep 68

Quay, Jan Eduard de May 63 obit Aug 85

Quayle, Anthony Dec 71 obit Jan 90

Quayle, Dan Jun 89

Queen Latifah Feb 97

Queen Noor *see* Noor al-Hussein

Queen, Ellery *see* Dannay, Frederic; Lee, Manfred B.

Queloz, Didier Feb 2002

Quennell, Peter May 84 obit Jan 94

Quesada, Elwood Richard Apr 50 Jan 60 obit Apr 93

Queuille, Henri Oct 48 obit Sep 70

Quezon, Manuel L. Aug 41

obit Sep 44

Quigley, Jane *see* Alexander, Jane

Quill, Michael J. Aug 41 Mar 53 obit Mar 66

Quimby, Edith H. Jul 49 obit Mar 83

Quimby, Mrs. Shirley L. *see* Quimby, Edith H.

Quindlen, Anna Apr 93

Quine, W. V. Nov 99 obit Mar 2001

Quine, Willard van Orman *see* Quine, W. V.

Quinn, Aidan Apr 2005

Quinn, Anthony Dec 57 obit Sep 2001

Quinn, Sally Oct 88

Quintanilla, Luis Nov 40

Quintero, Joaquin Alvarez *see* Alvarez Quintero, Joaquin

Quintero, José Apr 54 obit May 99

Quirino, Elpidio Sep 48 obit May 56

Quisling, Vidkun Nov 40 obit Yrbk 46

Quo Tai-Chi May 46 obit Apr 52

Quoirez, Françoise *see* Sagan, Françoise

Raab, Julius Apr 54 obit Feb 64

Rabassa, Gregory Jan 2005

Rabe, David Jul 73

Rabi, I. I. Apr 48 obit Mar 88

Rabi, Isidor Isaac *see* Rabi, I. I.

Rabin, Yitzhak Sep 74 Jan 95 obit Jan 96

Raborn, William Francis Jul 58 obit Jun 90

Racette, Patricia Feb 2003

Rackmil, Milton R. Nov 52 obit Jan 92

Radcliffe, Cyril John Jun 63 obit May 77

Raddall, Thomas (WLB) Yrbk 51

Radhakrishnan, Sarvepalli

Jun 52 obit Jun 75

Radiohead Jun 2001

Radner, Gilda Feb 80 obit Jul 89

Radvanyi, Netty *see* Seghers, Anna

Radziwill, Catherine, Princess obit Jul 41

Radziwill, Lee Apr 77

Rae, Bob Feb 91

Rae, Edna *see* Burstyn, Ellen

Raeder, Erich Apr 41 obit Jan 61

Raedler, Dorothy Dec 54 obit Feb 94

Rafferty, Max Jan 69 obit Aug 82

Rafsanjani, Hashemi Nov 89

Rafshoon, Gerald Jul 79

Ragland, Rags obit Oct 46

Ragon, Heartsill obit Nov 40

Rahman, Abdul Dec 57 obit Mar 91

Rahman, Abdul, Paramount Ruler of Malaya Dec 57 obit May 60

Rahman, Sheik Mujibur *see* Mujibur Rahman

Rahman, Ziaur Jun 81

Rahner, Karl Jul 70 obit May 84

Raimi, Sam Jul 2002

Raimu, Jules obit Nov 46

Raines, Franklin D. Oct 2000

Rainey, Froelich G. Feb 67 obit Jan 93

Rainey, Homer P. Nov 46 obit Feb 86

Rainier III, Prince of Monaco Nov 55 obit Yrbk 2005

Rains, Albert McKinley Sep 59 obit May 91

Rains, Claude Nov 49 obit Jul 67

Rainwater, Richard Apr 99

Rajagopalachari, Chakravarti Jul 42 obit Feb 73

Rakic, Patricia Goldman *see* Goldman-Rakic, Patricia

Rakosi, Matyas Mar 49 obit

Mar 71

Rakowski, Mieczyslaw Apr 89

Rall, Ted May 2002

Ralls, Charles C. Jan 51

Ralston, Dennis Oct 65

Ralston, Joseph W. Jan 2001

Ram, Jagjivan Oct 78 obit Aug 86

Rama IX, King of Thailand Jul 50

Rama Rau, Benegal see Rau, Benegal Rama

Rama Rau, Dhanvanthi Apr 54 obit Sep 87

Rama Rau, Santha Aug 45 (WLB) Yrbk 59

Ramadier, Paul Jun 47 obit Dec 61

Raman, Chandrasekhara Venkata Nov 48 obit Jan 71

Ramaphosa, Cyril Sep 95

Rambam, Cyvia see Rambert, Marie

Rambert, Marie Feb 81 obit Aug 82

Rameau, Jean obit Apr 42

Ramey, Howard K. obit May 43

Ramey, Samuel Jul 81

Ramirez, Manny Jun 2002

Ramírez, Pedro P. Aug 43 obit Sep 62

Ramirez, Tina Nov 2004

Ramm, Fredrik obit Jan 44

Ramo, Simon Apr 58 [Ramo, Simon; and Wooldridge, Dean E.]

Ramos, Fidel Mar 94

Ramos, Jorge Mar 2004

Rampal, Jean-Pierre Mar 70 obit Aug 2000

Rampersad, Arnold Sep 98

Ramphele, Mamphela Jul 97

Rampling, Anne see Rice, Anne

Rampling, Charlotte Jun 2002

Rampone, Christie Oct 2004

Ramsay, Bertram Mar 44 obit Feb 45

Ramsey, Arthur Michael Apr

60 obit Jun 88

Ramsey, Dewitt C. Jan 53 obit Nov 61

Ramsey, Norman F. Dec 63

Ramspeck, Robert Jun 51 obit Dec 72

Rance, Hubert Elvin Dec 53 obit Mar 74

Rand, Ayn May 82

Rand, Ellen obit Feb 42

Rand, James Henry, Sr. obit Nov 44

Rand, William M. May 53

Randall, Clarence B. Jun 52 obit Oct 67

Randall, Jean see Hauck, Louise Platt

Randall, John D. May 60

Randall, Mrs. J. G. see Randall, Ruth Painter

Randall, Ruth Painter (WLB) Yrbk 57

Randall, Tony Jan 61 obit Yrbk 2004

Randers, Gunnar Jan 57

Randi, James May 87

Randi, The Amazing see Randi, James

Randolph, Asa Philip May 40 Oct 51 obit Jul 79

Randolph, Jennings Jan 62 obit Jul 98

Randolph, Willie Sep 2005

Randolph, Woodruff May 48 obit Jan 67

Ranganathan, S. R. Sep 65 obit Dec 72

Rangel, Charles B. Mar 84

Rania Feb 2001

Rank, J. Arthur Nov 45 obit May 72 [Rank, Joseph, Arthur Rank, 1st Baron]

Rank, Joseph obit Jan 44

Rankin, J. Lee Feb 59 obit Sep 96

Rankin, John E. Feb 44 obit Jan 61

Rankin, Karl Lott Apr 55 obit Apr 91

Ransom, John Crowe Jul 64

obit Sep 74

Ranson, S. Walter obit Oct 42

Rao, P. V. Narasimha Jan 92 obit Yrbk 2005

Rao, Shanta Dec 57

Rapacki, Adam Jul 58 obit Dec 70

Raphael Aug 91

Raphael, Chaim Dec 63 obit Jan 95

Raphaël, Sally Jessy Feb 90

Rapp, William J. obit Oct 42

Rappard, William E. Oct 51 obit Jul 58

Rascal Flatts Aug 2003

Raskin, A. H. May 78 obit Feb 94

Raskin, Abraham Henry see Raskin, A. H.

Raskin, Judith Apr 64 obit Feb 85

Rasminsky, Louis Dec 61

Rasmussen, Gustav Dec 47 obit Nov 53

Rassweiler, Clifford F. Oct 58

Rathbone, Basil Mar 51 obit Oct 67

Rathbone, Eleanor Jun 43 obit Feb 46

Rathbone, Josephine Adams obit Jul 41

Rathbone, Monroe J. Mar 57 obit Sep 76

Rather, Dan May 75

Ratoff, Gregory Aug 43 obit Feb 61

Rattigan, Terence Dec 56 obit Feb 78

Rattle, Simon Feb 88

Rattner, Abraham Mar 48 obit Apr 78

Ratushinskaya, Irina Jul 88

Ratzinger, Cardinal see Ratzinger, Joseph

Ratzinger, Joseph Apr 86

Ratzinger, Joseph see Benedict XVI

Rau, Benegal Narsing Dec 51 obit Feb 54

Rau, Benegal Rama Feb 49

obit Feb 70

Rau, Dhanvanthi Rama *see* Rama Rau, Dhanvanthi

Rau, Johannes Mar 87

Rau, Santha Rama *see* Rama Rau, Santha

Rauh, Joseph L., Jr. Apr 65 obit Nov 92

Rauschenberg, Robert Oct 65 Oct 87

Rauschning, Hermann May 41 obit Apr 83

Rautenberg, Robert Mar 40

Ravdin, I. S. Apr 68 obit Oct 72

Raven, Peter H. Feb 94

Raver, Paul J. Sep 41

Rawalt, Marguerite Mar 56

Rawl, Lawrence G. Feb 92 obit Yrbk 2005

Rawlings, Bernard Aug 45 obit Dec 62

Rawlings, Jerry Jun 82

Rawlings, Marjorie Kinnan Jul 42 obit Feb 54

Rawls, Lou Mar 84

Ray, Amy *see* Indigo Girls

Ray, Charles obit Jan 44

Ray, Dixy Lee Jun 73 obit Mar 94

Ray, Gordon Norton Mar 68 obit Feb 87

Ray, Man Dec 65 obit Jan 77

Ray, Rachael Aug 2005

Ray, Randolph Apr 45 obit Jul 63

Ray, Robert D. Jan 77

Ray, Satyajit Mar 61 obit Jun 92

Ray, Ted obit Oct 43

Rayburn, Sam Oct 40 Mar 49 obit Jan 62

Raye, Martha Jul 63 obit Jan 95

Raymond, Lee Nov 99

Razmara, Ali Oct 50 obit Mar 51

Rea, Gardner May 46 obit Feb 67

Read, Herbert Mar 62 obit

Sep 68

Reading, Stella, Marchioness of Apr 48 obit Jul 71

Reagan, Nancy May 82

Reagan, Patricia Ann *see* Davis, Patti

Reagan, Ron Feb 92

Reagan, Ronald Dec 49 Feb 67 Nov 82 obit Sep 2004

Reagon, Bernice Johnson Aug 99

Reardon, John Nov 74 obit Jun 88

Reasoner, Harry Feb 66 obit Oct 91

Reavey, Mrs. George *see* Pereira, I. Rice

Reavis, Smith Freeman obit Mar 40

Reba *see* McEntire, Reba

Reber, Samuel Sep 49 obit Feb 72

Reckord, Milton A. Mar 45

Redd, Michael Mar 2005

Redding, J. Saunders Apr 69 obit Apr 88

Reddy, Helen Apr 75

Reddy, N. Sanjiva Mar 81 obit Aug 96

Redfield, Robert Dec 53 obit Jan 59

Redford, Robert Apr 71 Mar 82

Redgrave, Lynn Sep 69

Redgrave, Michael Feb 50 obit May 85

Redgrave, Steven Jan 2000

Redgrave, Vanessa Dec 66 Sep 2003

Redman, Joshua Jan 97

Redpath, Anne Jan 57 obit Mar 65

Redpath, Jean Feb 84

Redstone, Sumner Jan 96

Redway, Jacques Wardlaw obit Jan 43

Reece, B. Carroll May 46 obit May 61

Reed, Carol Mar 50 obit Jun

76

Reed, Daniel A. May 53 obit Apr 59

Reed, Edward Bliss obit Mar 40

Reed, Herbert Calhoun obit Sep 40

Reed, Ishmael Oct 86

Reed, James A. obit Oct 44

Reed, James, Sr. obit Sep 41

Reed, John Howard obit Mar 40

Reed, John S. Jan 85

Reed, Lou Jul 89

Reed, Margie Yvonne *see* Raye, Martha

Reed, Philip D. Jan 49 obit May 89

Reed, Ralph Mar 96

Reed, Ralph T. Apr 51 obit Mar 68

Reed, Rex Jan 72

Reed, Stanley F. Feb 42 obit May 80

Reed, Willis Jan 73

Rees, Edward H. Jan 58 obit Dec 69

Rees, Mina S. Nov 57 obit Jan 98

Reese, Della Sep 71

Reese, Everett D. Mar 54

Reese, Harold Jun 50 obit Oct 99

Reese, Pee Wee *see* Reese, Harold

Reeve, Christopher May 82 obit Jan 2005

Reeve, Sidney A. obit Aug 41

Reeves, Dan Oct 2001

Reeves, Jesse S. obit Aug 42

Reeves, Keanu May 95

Regan, Donald T. Nov 81 obit Yrbk 2003

Regan, Judith Sep 2000

Reggio, Godfrey Jul 95

Régine Apr 80

Rehnquist, William H. Apr 72 Nov 2003 obit Yrbk 2005

Reich, Charles A. Jun 72

Reich, Nathaniel Julius obit

Nov 43

Reich, Robert B. Apr 93

Reich, Steve Apr 86

Reich, Walter Aug 2005

Reichelderfer, F. W. May 49 obit Mar 83

Reichenau, Walter Von obit Mar 42

Reichmann, Paul Jan 91

Reichstein, Tadeus Feb 51 obit Oct 96

Reid, Antonio *see* Reid, L. A.

Reid, Charlotte T. Jan 75

Reid, Frank R., Sr. obit Mar 45

Reid, Harry Mar 2003

Reid, Helen Rogers Feb 41 May 52 obit Oct 70

Reid, Ira De A. Jul 46 obit Oct 68

Reid, Kate Mar 85 obit May 93

Reid, L. A. Aug 2001

Reid, Mont R. obit Jun 43

Reid, Mrs. Ogden Mills *see* Reid, Helen Rogers

Reid, Ogden R. Feb 56

Reid, Patricia *see* Stanley, Kim

Reid, Whitelaw Dec 54

Reilly, John C. Oct 2004

Reilly, Rick Feb 2005

Reilly, William K. Jul 89

Reinartz, F. Eppling Jul 53

Reiner, Carl Apr 61

Reiner, Fritz Apr 41 Dec 53 obit Jan 64

Reiner, Rob May 88

Reinhard, Johan Aug 99

Reinhardt, Aurelia Henry May 41 obit Feb 48

Reinhardt, Max obit Dec 43

Reinhardt, Uwe E. Mar 2004

Reinking, Ann Jun 2004

Reischauer, Edwin O. May 62 obit Nov 90

Reiser, Paul Apr 96

Reisner, Christian Fichthorne obit Sep 40

Reisner, George Andrew obit

Jul 42

Reith, John Charles Walsham Nov 40 obit Jul 71

Reitman, Ivan Mar 2001

Reizenstein, Elmer Leopold *see* Rice, Elmer

Relander, Lauri Kristian obit Apr 42

Rell, M. Jodi Sep 2005

Remick, Lee Oct 66 obit Sep 91

Remington, John W. Feb 60

Remnick, David Oct 98

Remorino, Jerónimo Sep 51

Renaud, Madeleine Mar 53 [Barrault, Jean-Louis; and Renaud, Madeleine] obit Nov 94

Renault, Louis obit Dec 44

Renault, Mary Jan 59 obit Feb 84

Rendell, Ed Apr 98

Rendell, Ruth Apr 94

Renne, Roland R. Jun 63

Rennebohm, Oscar Jul 50 obit Dec 68

Renner, Karl Sep 45 obit Jan 51

Rennert, Gunther Jun 76 obit Sep 78

Reno, Janet Sep 93

Renoir, Jean Dec 59 obit Apr 79

Rentzel, Delos Wilson Oct 48 obit Jan 92

Reshevsky, Samuel Feb 55 obit Jul 92

Resnais, Alain Feb 65

Resnick, Louis obit May 41

Resnik, Regina Jan 56

Resor, Stanley B. Jul 49 obit Dec 62

Resor, Stanley R. Sep 69

Ressler, Robert K. Feb 2002

Reston, James Mar 43 Nov 80 obit Feb 96

Retton, Mary Lou Feb 86

Reubens, Paul Jan 88 [Herman, Pee Wee]

Reuss, Henry S. Oct 59 obit

Mar 2002

Reuter, Ernst Oct 49 obit Dec 53

Reuter, Gabriele obit Jan 42

Reuther, Victor Dec 53 obit Yrbk 2004

Reuther, Walter Apr 41 Nov 49 obit Jun 70

Reutz, Janice *see* DeGaetani, Jan

Revel, Jean-François

Revelle, Roger Mar 57 obit Sep 91

Reventlow, Ernst, Graf Zu obit Jan 44

Revercomb, Chapman Jun 58

Reves, Emery Jul 46

Revueltas, Silvestro obit Yrbk 40

Rexroth, Kenneth Apr 81 obit Aug 82

Rey, Fernando Mar 79 obit May 94

Reybold, Eugene Jun 45 obit Jan 62

Reynaud, Paul Apr 40 May 50 obit Nov 66

Reynolds, Albert Pierce *see* Reynolds, Allie

Reynolds, Albert Sep 94

Reynolds, Allie Jun 52 obit Mar 95

Reynolds, Burt Oct 73

Reynolds, Debbie Dec 64

Reynolds, Helen Wilkinson obit Feb 43

Reynolds, James A. obit May 40

Reynolds, John W. Jr. Apr 64 obit Mar 2002

Reynolds, Quentin Mar 41 obit Apr 65

Reynolds, R. S., Sr. Feb 53 obit Oct 55

Reynolds, Richard S., Jr. May 67 obit Nov 80

Reynolds, Robert Rice Oct 40 obit Mar 63

Reynolds, William Bradford

Jul 88

Reynoso, Cruz Mar 2002

Reza, Yasmina Sep 98

Rhee, Syngman Sep 47 obit Sep 65

Rhine, J. B. Jan 49 obit Apr 80

Rhoades, Cornelia Harsen obit Jan 41

Rhoades, Nina *see* Rhoades, Cornelia Harsen

Rhoads, C. P. Mar 53 obit Nov 59

Rhodes, Edgar Nelson obit May 42

Rhodes, James A. Mar 49 Apr 76 obit Jul 2001

Rhodes, John J. Sep 76 obit Yrbk 2004

Rhodes, Randi Feb 2005

Rhone, Sylvia Jun 98

Rhyne, Charles S. May 58 obit Yrbk 2003

Rhys, Ernest obit Jan 46

Rhys, Jean Dec 72 obit Jul 79

Riad, Mahmoud Nov 71 obit Mar 92

Riasanovsky, Antonina *see* Fedorova, Nina

Ribbentrop, Joachim Von May 41 obit Nov 46

Ribbs, Willy T. Nov 2000

Ribicoff, Abraham A. Jun 55 obit May 98

Ricard, Jean-François *see* Revel, Jean-François

Rice, Alice Caldwell Hegan obit Apr 42

Rice, Anne Jul 91

Rice, Condoleezza Apr 2001

Rice, Elmer Apr 43 obit Jul 67

Rice, Grantland Sep 41 obit Sep 54

Rice, Greg Dec 41 obit Aug 91

Rice, Jerry Apr 90

Rice, Jim Sep 79

Rice, Paul North Nov 47 obit Jun 67

Rich, Adrienne Cecile Feb 76

Rich, Buddy Jun 73 obit May

87

Rich, Daniel Catton Dec 55 obit Feb 77

Rich, Frank Apr 99

Rich, Louise Dickinson May 43 obit Jul 91

Richard, Louis obit Sep 40

Richard, Maurice Dec 58 obit Yrbk 2000

Richards, A. N. Sep 50 obit Apr 66

Richards, Ann W. Feb 91

Richards, C. R. obit Jan 41

Richards, Dickinson W. Mar 57 obit Apr 73

Richards, I. A. Dec 72 obit Oct 79

Richards, James P. Sep 51 obit Apr 79

Richards, John G. obit Dec 41

Richards, John S. Jun 55

Richards, Keith Feb 89

Richards, Laura E. obit May 43

Richards, Lloyd Oct 87

Richards, Michael Nov 97

Richards, Robert E. Jun 57

Richards, Vincent Jul 47 obit Dec 59

Richards, Wayne E. Jul 54

Richardson, Bill Apr 96

Richardson, Bobby May 66

Richardson, Elliot L. Mar 71 obit Mar 2000

Richardson, Henrietta *see* Richardson, Henry Handel

Richardson, Henry Handel obit May 46

Richardson, Kevin *see* Backstreet Boys

Richardson, Miranda Feb 94

Richardson, Norval obit Yrbk 40

Richardson, Ralph Nov 50 obit Nov 83

Richardson, Robert Clinton, Jr. *see* Richardson, Bobby

Richardson, Seth Feb 48 obit May 53

Richardson, Tony Dec 63 obit

Feb 92

Richberg, Donald R. Dec 49 obit Jan 61

Richie, Lionel Jul 84

Richler, Mordecai May 75 obit Oct 2001

Richman, Charles J. obit Jan 41

Richmond, Charles Alexander obit Sep 40

Richmond, Mitch Jun 99

Richter, Burton Sep 77

Richter, Charles Francis May 75 obit Nov 85

Richter, Conrad Jun 51 obit Dec 68

Richter, George Martin obit Jul 42

Richter, Gerhard Jun 2002

Richter, Sviatoslav Feb 61 obit Oct 97

Rickenbacker, Eddie *see* Rickenbacker, Edward Vernon

Rickenbacker, Edward Vernon Nov 40 Feb 52 obit Oct 73

Ricketts, Louis Davidson obit Mar 40

Rickey, Branch Oct 45 obit Jan 66

Rickey, George W. Feb 80 obit Yrbk 2002

Rickey, James W. obit Jun 43

Rickover, Hyman G. May 53 obit Aug 86

Riddell, R. Gerald Sep 50 obit Apr 51

Riddleberger, James W. May 57 obit Jan 83

Ride, Sally K. Oct 83

Ridenour, Nina Apr 51

Ridge, Lola obit Jul 41

Ridge, Tom Feb 2001

Ridgway, Matthew B. Jul 47 obit Sep 93

Riebel, John P. Jan 57

Riecken, Henry W. Dec 61

Riefenstahl, Berta Helene Amalia *see* Riefenstahl,

Leni

Riefenstahl, Leni May 75 obit Yrbk 2004

Riefler, Winfield W. May 48 obit Jun 74

Riegle, Donald W., Jr. Oct 86

Riesenberg, Felix, Jr. (WLB) Yrbk 57

Riesman, David [educator] obit Jul 40

Riesman, David [social scientist] Jan 55 obit Yrbk 2002

Rieve, Emil Jul 46 obit Mar 75

Rifkin, Jeremy Feb 86

Rifkind, Simon H. May 46 obit Jan 96

Rigg, Diana Oct 74

Rigg, Edgar T. Jun 61

Riggio, Leonard Jun 98

Riggio, Vincent Jul 49 obit Nov 60

Riggs, Austen Fox obit Mar 40

Riggs, Bobby see Riggs, Robert Larimore

Riggs, Robert Larimore Sep 49 obit Jan 96

Riggs, T. L. obit Jun 43

Righter, Carroll Oct 72 obit Jun 88

Rigling, Alfred obit Jan 41

Riiser-Larsen, Hjalmar Nov 51 obit Jul 65

Riklis, Meshulam Dec 71

Riles, Wilson Dec 71

Riley, Bridget Sep 81

Riley, Pat Aug 88

Riley, Richard W. Oct 93

Riley, Susan B. Feb 53

Riley, Terry Apr 2002

Riley, William E. Nov 51

Rimes, Leann May 98

Rimm, Sylvia B. Feb 2002

Rimsza, Skip Jul 2002

Rincón de Gautier, Felisa see Gautier, Felisa Rincón De

Rinehart, Stanley M., Jr. Dec

54 obit Jun 69

Rines, Robert H. Jan 2003

Rinfret, Pierre A. Jul 72

Ring, Barbara T. obit Nov 41

Ringgold, Faith Feb 96

Ringling, Robert E. May 45 obit Feb 50

Ringwald, Molly May 87

Rio, Carlos Alberto Arroyo del see Arroyo Del Río, Carlos Alberto

Riopelle, Jean-Paul Oct 89 obit Yrbk 2002

Riordan, Richard May 2000

Ríos Montt, José Efraín May 83

Rios, Juan Antonio Apr 42 obit Jul 46

Ripken, Cal, Jr. Jun 92

Ripley, Alexandra Mar 92 obit Yrbk 2004

Ripley, Elizabeth (WLB) Yrbk 58

Ripley, Joseph obit Nov 40

Ripley, Robert L. Jul 45 obit Jul 49

Ripley, S. Dillon Oct 66 obit Aug 2001

Ripley, William Z. obit Oct 41

Ritchard, Cyril Jan 57 obit Feb 78

Ritchie, Dennis Mar 99

Ritchie, Jean Oct 59

Ritchie, Robert James see Kid Rock

Riter, Henry G., 3d Oct 55 obit Sep 58

Ritner, Ann (WLB) Yrbk 53

Ritt, Martin Nov 79 obit Feb 91

Rittenhouse, Constance Mar 48 [Rittenhouse, Mrs. Paul]

Rittenhouse, Mrs. Paul see Rittenhouse, Constance

Ritter, Bruce Jun 83 obit Feb 2000

Ritter, John Jun 80 obit Yrbk 2004

Ritter, Joseph Elmer Dec 64 obit Oct 67

Ritter, Thelma Dec 57 obit

Feb 74 (died Feb 69)

Rivera, Chita Oct 84

Rivera, Diego Jul 48 obit Feb 58

Rivera, Geraldo May 75

Rivero, Jose Ignacio obit May 44

Rivers, Joan Jan 70 Mar 87

Rivers, L. Mendel Oct 60 obit Feb 71

Rivers, Larry Apr 69 obit Nov 2002

Rivers, Thomas M. Jul 60 obit Jul 62

Rives, Amelie see Troubetzkoy, Amelie

Rives, Hallie Erminie (WLB) Yrbk 56

Rivkin, Dorothy Carnegie see Carnegie, Dorothy

Rivlin, Alice M. Oct 82

Riza Shah Pahlavi obit Sep 44

Rizzo, Frank L. Mar 73 obit Sep 91

Rizzuto, Phil Jul 50

Roa, Raúl Nov 73 obit Sep 82

Robards, Jason Jr. Oct 59 obit Mar 2001

Robarts, John P. Dec 62 obit Jan 83

Robb, Charles S. Apr 89

Robb, Hunter obit Jan 40

Robb, Inez Dec 58 obit Jun 79

Robb, J. D. see Roberts, Nora

Robbe-Grillet, Alain Dec 74

Robbins, Anthony see Robbins, Tony

Robbins, Frederick C. Jun 55 [Enders, John F; Robbins, Frederick C; and Weller, Thomas H.] obit Yrbk 2003

Robbins, Harold May 70 obit Jan 98

Robbins, Jerome May 47 May 69 obit Oct 98

Robbins, Tim Jul 94

Robbins, Tom Jun 93

Robbins, Tony Jul 2001

Robbins, William J. Feb 56

Robens, Alfred Jun 56

Robert Stephenson Smyth

Baden-Powell obit Mar 41

Robert, Georges Jun 43

Roberts, Albert H. obit Jul 46

Roberts, C. Wesley Apr 53 obit Jun 75

Roberts, Charles G. D. obit Jan 44

Roberts, Cokie May 94

Roberts, Dennis J. Dec 56 obit Sep 94

Roberts, Dorothy James (WLB) Yrbk 56 obit Jun 90

Roberts, Elizabeth Madox obit May 41

Roberts, Florence obit Jul 40

Roberts, George Lucas obit Apr 41

Roberts, Goodridge May 55

Roberts, Julia May 91

Roberts, Kate L. obit Oct 41

Roberts, Marcus Mar 94

Roberts, Nora Sep 2001

Roberts, Oral Nov 60

Roberts, Owen J. Oct 41 obit Jul 55

Roberts, Robin Dec 53

Roberts, Walter Orr Dec 60 obit May 90

Robertson, A. Willis Dec 49 obit Dec 71

Robertson, Anna Mary see Moses, Grandma

Robertson, Ben, Jr. Nov 42

Robertson, Brian Sep 48 obit Jun 74

Robertson, Cliff Dec 69

Robertson, Constance (WLB) Yrbk 46

Robertson, D. B. May 50 obit Dec 61

Robertson, Ethel Florence Lindesay see Richardson, Henry Handel

Robertson, Marion Gordon see Robertson, Pat

Robertson, Mrs. Miles E. see Robertson, Constance

Robertson, Norman A. Dec 57

obit Sep 68

Robertson, Oscar Jan 66

Robertson, Pat Sep 87

Robertson, R. B. May 57

Robertson, Reuben B., Jr. Dec 55 obit May 60

Robertson, Walter S. Dec 53 obit May 70

Robeson, Eslanda Goode Sep 45 obit Yrbk 91 (died Dec 65)

Robeson, Mrs. Paul see Robeson, Eslanda Goode

Robeson, Paul Mar 41 Mar 76

Robey, Ralph W. May 41 obit Sep 72

Robichaud, Louis J. May 68

Robins, Edward obit Jul 43

Robins, Margaret Dreier obit Apr 45

Robins, Mrs. Raymond see Robins, Margaret Dreier

Robinson, Arthur H. Mar 96 obit Yrbk 2005

Robinson, Bill Feb 41 obit Jan 50

Robinson, Boardman Dec 41 obit Oct 52

Robinson, Brooks Sep 73

Robinson, David Jul 93

Robinson, Eddie Jun 88

Robinson, Edward G. Jan 50 obit Mar 73

Robinson, Elmer E. Nov 55

Robinson, Frank Jun 71

Robinson, Frederick B. obit Dec 41

Robinson, Henry Morton Jul 50 obit Mar 61

Robinson, Holton D. obit Jun 45

Robinson, Jack Roosevelt see Robinson, Jackie

Robinson, Jackie Feb 47 obit Dec 72

Robinson, Janet L. Mar 2003

Robinson, John Feb 65 obit Feb 84

Robinson, Kim Stanley Nov 98

Robinson, M. R. Dec 56 obit

May 82

Robinson, Marilynne Oct 2005

Robinson, Mary Apr 91

Robinson, Randall Sep 98

Robinson, Ray see Robinson, Sugar Ray

Robinson, Samuel M. Feb 42

Robinson, Smokey Jul 80

Robinson, Spottswood W. Mar 62 obit Jan 99

Robinson, Sugar Ray Mar 51 obit Jun 89

Robinson, William E. Feb 58 obit Jul 69

Robinson, William Heath obit Nov 44

Robinson, William, Jr. see Robinson, Smokey

Robison, Emily see Dixie Chicks

Robison, Paula May 82

Robitzek, Edward H. Dec 53 obit May 84

Robles, Marco A. Jun 68 obit Jun 90

Robsjohn-Gibbings, T. H. Sep 65 obit Feb 77

Robson, Flora Jan 51 obit Sep 84

Robson, May obit Dec 42

Robus, Hugo Dec 62 obit Feb 64

Roca, Julio A. obit Nov 42

Rocard, Michel Oct 88

Rochberg, George Sep 85 obit Yrbk 2005

Roche, James M. Feb 67 obit Yrbk 2004

Roche, Josephine Aug 41 obit Sep 76

Roche, Kevin Nov 70

Roche, Margaret Eleanor see McNellis, Maggi

Rock, John Dec 64 obit Jan 85

Rockefeller, David Mar 59

Rockefeller, John D. 4th Mar 78

Rockefeller, John D., 3d Jun 53 obit Sep 78

Rockefeller, John D., Jr. Jul

41 obit Jul 60

Rockefeller, Laurance S. Jun 59 obit Yrbk 2004

Rockefeller, Nelson A. Mar 41 Mar 51 obit Mar 79

Rockefeller, Winthrop Sep 59 obit Apr 73

Rockley, Alicia-Margaret Amherst, Baroness *see* Amherst, Alicia-Margaret

Rockwell, Norman Jun 45 obit Jan 79

Rodahl, Kaare Feb 56

Roddick, Andy Jan 2004

Roddick, Anita Sep 92

Roderick, David M. Apr 87

Rodgers and Hart *see* Rodgers, Richard; Hart, Lorenz

Rodgers, Bill Aug 82

Rodgers, Richard May 40 [Rodgers, Richard; and Hart, Lorenz] Apr 51 obit Feb 80

Rodin, Judith Jun 99

Rodino, Peter W., Jr. Oct 54 obit Yrbk 2005

Rodman, Dennis Sep 96

Rodriguez, Alex Apr 2003

Rodriguez, Andrés Sep 91 obit Jun 97

Rodriguez, Arturo Mar 2001

Rodriguez, Cecilia May 99

Rodriguez, Chi Chi Oct 69

Rodriguez, Eloy May 2000

Rodriguez, Jorge Alessandri *see* Alessandri, Jorge

Rodriguez, Juan *see* Rodriguez, Chi Chi

Rodriguez, Nicolas obit Sep 40

Rodriguez, Robert Aug 96

Rodzinski, Artur Aug 40 obit Feb 59

Roebling, Mary G. Oct 60 obit Jan 95

Roeg, Nicolas Jan 96

Roehm, Carolyne Feb 92

Roelofs, Henrietta obit Mar 42

Roemer, Buddy Nov 90

Roemer, Charles Elson, 3d

see Roemer, Buddy

Rogers, Bernard W. Oct 84

Rogers, Bruce Dec 46 obit Jul 57

Rogers, Carl R. Dec 62 obit Mar 87

Rogers, Dale Evans Sep 56 obit Apr 2001

Rogers, Edith Nourse Apr 42 obit Nov 60

Rogers, Frank B. Jun 62

Rogers, Fred Jul 71 obit Jul 2003

Rogers, Ginger Apr 41 Dec 67 obit Jul 95

Rogers, Kenny Jan 81

Rogers, Lynn L. Oct 94

Rogers, Mark Homer obit Nov 41

Rogers, Norman McLeod obit Jul 40

Rogers, Paul Mar 60

Rogers, Robert Emmons obit Jul 41

Rogers, Roy Mar 48 Oct 83 obit Sep 98

Rogers, Rutherford David Jun 62

Rogers, Will, Jr. Dec 53 obit Sep 93

Rogers, William P. Feb 58 Sep 69 obit Mar 2001

Rogge, O. John Feb 48 obit Jun 81

Roh Tae Woo Feb 88

Rohatyn, Felix G. May 78

Rohde, Ruth Bryan Owen Dec 44 obit Oct 54

Rohe, Vera-Ellen *see* Vera-Ellen

Rohmer, Eric Apr 77

Rojas Pinilla, Gustavo Jun 56 obit Mar 75

Rokossovsky, Konstantin Jan 44 obit Oct 68

Rolland, Romain obit Feb 45

Rollin, Betty Aug 94

Rollins, Carl Purington Sep

48 obit Jan 61

Rollins, Edward J. Mar 2001

Rollins, Henry Sep 2001

Rollins, Sonny Apr 76

Rolvaag, Karl F. Feb 64 obit Mar 91

Roman, Nancy G. Dec 60

Romano, Emanuel Mar 40 obit Feb 85

Romano, Umberto Mar 54 obit Nov 82

Romanoff, Alexis L. Dec 53

Rombauer, Irma S. Dec 53 obit Dec 62

Romberg, Sigmund Mar 45 obit Dec 51

Rome, Harold Apr 42 obit Jan 94

Romenesko, Jim Feb 2004

Romer, John Jul 2003

Romero Barceló, Carlos Oct 77

Romero, Anthony Jul 2002

Rommel, Erwin Aug 42 obit Dec 44

Romnes, H. I. Feb 68 obit Jan 74

Romney, George Jun 58 obit Oct 95

Romulo, Carlos P. Mar 43 Apr 57 obit Feb 86

Ronaldo Aug 98

Ronan, William J. Oct 69

Roncalli, Angelo Giuseppe *see* John XXIII, Pope

Roney, Marianne May 57 [Cohen, Barbara; and Roney, Marianne]

Ronne, Finn Feb 48 obit Mar 80

Ronstadt, Linda Jan 78

Rood, Helen Martin obit Mar 43

Rooks, Lowell W. Apr 47

Roome, Mrs. Charles O. *see* Goertz, Arthémise

Rooney, Andy Jul 82

Rooney, Joe Don *see* Rascal

Rooney, John J. Dec 64 obit Jan 76

Rooney, Mickey Feb 42 Sep

65

Roosa, Robert V. Dec 62 obit Mar 94

Roosevelt, Alice Lee *see* Longworth, Alice Roosevelt

Roosevelt, Anna C. Jun 97

Roosevelt, Eleanor Nov 40 Jan 49 obit Jan 63

Roosevelt, Elliott Dec 46 obit Jan 91

Roosevelt, Franklin D. Mar 42 obit Apr 45

Roosevelt, Franklin D., Jr. Jan 50 obit Sep 88

Roosevelt, James Apr 50 obit Nov 91

Roosevelt, Kermit obit Jul 43

Roosevelt, Mrs. Franklin Delano *see* Roosevelt, Eleanor

Roosevelt, Sara Delano obit Oct 41

Roosevelt, Theodore, Jr. obit Sep 44

Root, Oren Aug 40 Jul 52 obit Mar 95

Root, Waverley Lewis May 43 obit Jan 83

Rootes, William Edward Rootes, 1st Baron Nov 51 obit Feb 65

Rooth, Ivar Dec 52 obit Apr 72

Roper, Daniel C. obit May 43

Roper, Elmo Jan 45 obit Jun 71

Roquelaure, A. N. *see* Rice, Anne

Rorem, Ned Jul 67

Rorimer, James J. Dec 55 obit Jun 66

Rosanoff, Aaron J. obit Feb 43

Rose, Alex Dec 59 obit Feb 77

Rose, Arnold Josef obit Oct 46

Rose, Billy Aug 40 obit Mar 66

Rose, Charlie Jan 95

Rose, George Sep 84 obit Jun

Rose, Jalen Mar 2004

Rose, Jim Mar 2003

Rose, Leonard Jan 77 obit Jan 85

Rose, Mary D. Swartz obit Mar 41

Rose, Maurice obit May 45

Rose, Murray Jun 62

Rose, Pete Aug 75

Rose, William C. Mar 53 obit Jan 86

Roseanne *see* Barr, Roseanne

Rosellini, Albert D. Dec 58

Rosen, Al Jul 54

Rosen, Benjamin M. Jun 97 [Rosen, Benjamin; and Rosen, Harold A.]

Rosen, Harold A. Jun 97 [Rosen, Benjamin; and Rosen, Harold A.]

Rosen, Robert *see* Rossen, Robert

Rosen, Samuel Feb 74 obit Jan 82

Rosenbach, A. S. W. May 46 obit Sep 52

Rosenberg, Alfred Oct 41 obit Nov 46

Rosenberg, Anna M. *see* Hoffman, Anna Rosenberg

Rosenberg, Arthur obit Mar 43

Rosenberg, John Paul *see* Erhard, Werner

Rosenberg, Steven A. Feb 91

Rosenberg, William Samuel *see* Rose, Billy

Rosenfeld, Henry Nov 48

Rosenfeld, Kurt obit Nov 43

Rosenfeld, Paul obit Sep 46

Rosenfield, Harry N. Apr 52 obit Aug 95

Rosenman, Dorothy Apr 47 obit Mar 91

Rosenman, Dorothy Reuben *see* Rosenman, Samuel I.

Rosenman, Samuel I. Aug 42 obit Sep 73

Rosenquist, James Sep 70

Rosenstock, Joseph Jan 54

obit Jan 86

Rosenthal, A. M. Dec 60

Rosenthal, Joe Jun 45

Rosenthal, Moriz obit Oct 46

Rosenwald, Lessing J. Feb 47 obit Aug 79

Rosett, Joshua obit May 40

Rosewall, Ken Dec 56

Ros-Lehtinen, Ileana Aug 2000

Ross, C. Ben obit May 46

Ross, Charles Jun 45 obit Jan 51

Ross, Diana Mar 73

Ross, Edward Denison obit Nov 40

Ross, Gary May 2004

Ross, Harold W. May 43 obit Jan 52

Ross, Herbert Aug 80 obit Feb 2002

Ross, Leonard Q. *see* Rosten, Leo

Ross, Malcolm Feb 44 obit Jul 65

Ross, Nancy Wilson (WLB) Yrbk 52 obit May 86

Ross, Nellie Tayloe May 40 obit Feb 78

Ross, Robert Oct 2002

Rossellini, Isabella Aug 88

Rossellini, Roberto Jul 49 obit Aug 77

Rossen, Robert Oct 50 obit Mar 66

Rosset, Barnet Apr 72

Rossiter, Clinton Apr 67 obit Dec 70

Rostand, Jean Dec 54 obit Jan 78

Rosten, Leo Oct 42 obit Apr 97

Rosten, Norman Apr 44 obit May 95

Rostenkowski, Dan Jan 82

Rostow, Eugene V. Apr 61 obit Yrbk 2003

Rostow, Walt W. May 61 obit Jul 2003

Rostropovich, Mstislav May

66 Nov 88

Roszak, Theodore [artist] Jun 66 obit Oct 81

Roszak, Theodore [historian] Apr 82

Rotblat, Joseph Jul 97

Rote, Kyle May 65 obit Yrbk 2002

Roth, Almon E. Oct 46

Roth, Ann Mar 97

Roth, Henry Jan 89 obit Jan 96

Roth, Philip Mar 70 May 91

Roth, William V., Jr. Apr 83 obit Yrbk 2004

Rotha, Paul Apr 57 obit May 84

Rothenberg, Susan Mar 85

Rothenstein, John Apr 57

Rothenstein, William obit Apr 45

Rothermere, Esmond Cecil Harmsworth, Viscount see Harmsworth, Esmond Cecil

Rothermere, Harold Sidney Harmsworth, 1st Viscount see Harmsworth, Harold Sidney

Rothery, Agnes (WLB) Yrbk 46 obit Oct 54

Rothko, Mark May 61 obit Apr 70

Rothschild, Guy, Baron De Mar 73

Rothschild, Louis S. Dec 57 obit Oct 84

Rothschild, Miriam Oct 92 obit Yrbk 2005

Rothwell, Joan Dorothy see Benesh, Joan

Rotten, Johnny see Lydon, John

Rouault, Georges May 45 obit Apr 58

Roudebush, Richard L. Jun 76 obit Apr 95

Roueché, Berton (WLB) Yrbk 59 obit Jul 94

Rountree, Martha Feb 57 obit Nov 99

Rountree, William M. Jun 59

obit Jan 96

Rourke, Constance Mayfield obit May 41

Rourke, Mickey Oct 91

Rous, Peyton Mar 67 obit Apr 70

Rouse, James W. Feb 82 obit Jun 96

Rouse, Milford O. Jun 68

Roussy de Sales, Raoul de see De Roussy De Sales, Raoul

Routley, T. Clarence Jan 56 obit Jun 63

Rove, Karl Oct 2000

Rovere, Richard H. Apr 77 obit Jan 80

Rowan, Andrew S. obit Mar 43

Rowan, Carl T. Jan 58 obit Jan 2001

Rowan, Chad see Akebono

Rowan, Dan Sep 69 obit Nov 87

Rowans, Virginia see Tanner, Edward Everett, 3d

Rowe, L. S. Aug 45 obit Jan 47

Rowell, Chester H. Yrbk 40 obit May 48

Rowland, John G. Oct 97

Rowland, Kelly see Destiny's Child

Rowlands, Gena Nov 75

Rowlands, Virginia Cathryn see Rowlands, Gena

Rowley, James J. Jan 63 obit Jan 93

Rowley, Janet D. Mar 2001

Rowntree, Cecil obit Dec 43

Rowntree, David see Blur

Rowse, A. L. Jul 79 obit Jan 98

Roxas, Manuel May 46 obit May 48

Roy Jan 98 [Siegfried and Roy]

Roy, Maurice Feb 58 obit Jan 86

Roy, Patrick Nov 99

Royal, Forrest B. obit Jul 45

Royall, Kenneth C. Jan 47

obit Sep 71

Royden, Maude Apr 42 obit Oct 56

Royen, Jan Herman Van Dec 53

Royko, Mike Jun 94 obit Jul 97

Royle, Edwin Milton obit Apr 42

Royster, Vermont C. Dec 53 obit Oct 96

Rozelle, Pete Jun 64 obit Feb 97

Rózsa, Miklós Feb 92 obit Oct 95

Rubattel, Rodolphe Dec 54 obit Dec 61

Rubbia, Carlo Jun 85

Rubenstein, Atoosa Oct 2004

Rubicam, Raymond Dec 43 obit Jul 78

Rubik, Erno Feb 87

Rubín De La Borbolla, Daniel F. Feb 60

Rubin, Barbara Jo Dec 69

Rubin, Reuven Apr 43 obit Jan 75

Rubin, Robert E. Jul 97

Rubin, Theodore Isaac Feb 80

Rubin, William Nov 86

Rubinstein, Artur Dec 45 Feb 66 obit Mar 83

Rubinstein, Atoosa Oct 2004

Rubinstein, Helena Jun 43 obit May 65

Rubottom, R. R., Jr. May 59

Ruckelshaus, William D. Jul 71

Ruckstull, F. Wellington obit Jul 42

Rudd, Paul Sep 77

Rudd, Phil see AC/DC

Rudel, Julius Jul 65

Ruder, David S. Nov 88

Rudkin, Margaret Sep 59 obit Oct 67

Rudkin, Mrs. Henry Albert see Rudkin, Margaret

Rudman, Warren B. Nov 89

Rudolph, Paul Feb 72 obit

Nov 97

Rudolph, Wilma Sep 61 obit Jan 95

Rueff, Jacques Feb 69 obit Jun 78

Ruffin, William H. Feb 51

Ruffing, Charles Nov 41 obit Apr 86

Ruffing, Red see Ruffing, Charles

Rugambwa, Laurean Cardinal Sep 60 obit Feb 98

Rugg, Harold Ordway May 41 obit Jul 60

Ruiz Cortines, Adolfo Sep 52 obit Jan 74

Ruiz Guiñazú, Enrique Apr 42 obit Jan 68

Ruiz Soler, Antonio Jun 68

Rukeyser, Louis Feb 83

Rukeyser, Muriel Mar 43 obit Apr 80

Rule, Ann Sep 2000

Rule, Ja see Ja Rule

Ruml, Beardsley May 43 obit Jun 60

Rummel, Joseph F. Jun 59 obit Jan 65

Rumor, Mariano Jul 69 obit Mar 90

Rumpler, Edmund obit Oct 40

Rumsfeld, Donald H. Apr 70 Mar 2002

Runbeck, Margaret Lee (WLB) Yrbk 52 obit Dec 56

Runcie, Robert Nov 80 obit Oct 2000

Rundstedt, Gerd von see Rundstedt, Karl Von

Rundstedt, Karl Von Nov 41 obit Apr 53

Runkle, Erwin W. obit Apr 41

Runyon, Damon Nov 42 obit Jan 47

Runyon, Mefford R. May 49

Rupertus, William H. obit

May 45

Rus, Daniela Feb 2004

Rusby, Henry H. obit Jan 41

Ruscha, Edward Oct 89

Rusesabagina, Paul May 2005

Rush Feb 2001

Rush, Kenneth May 75 obit Feb 95

Rushdi, Tevfik Bey see Aras, Tevfik Rüstü

Rushdie, Salman Nov 86

Rushing, Matthew Jul 2000

Rushmore, David Barker obit Jul 40

Rusk, Dean Jun 49 Jul 61 obit Feb 95

Rusk, Howard A. Mar 46 May 67 obit Jan 90

Ruslander, Mark see Russell, Mark

Russell, Anna Apr 54

Russell, Bertrand Apr 40 Jan 51 obit Mar 70

Russell, Bill see Russell, William F. Jul 75 [Russell, William F.]

Russell, Charles Ellsworth see Russell, Pee Wee

Russell, Charles H. Dec 55 obit Nov 89

Russell, Charles obit Jun 41

Russell, Donald J. May 62 obit Feb 86

Russell, Harold Jan 50 Jan 66 obit Apr 2002

Russell, Herbrand Arthur, 11th Duke of Bedford see Herbrand Arthur Russell

Russell, James Earl obit Dec 45

Russell, James S. Jan 62

Russell, Ken Oct 75

Russell, Kurt Nov 2004

Russell, Mark Mar 81

Russell, Mary Annette Russell obit Mar 41

Russell, Pee Wee Aug 44 obit Apr 69

Russell, Richard B. Nov 49 obit Mar 71

Russell, Rosalind Jan 43 obit

Feb 77

Russell, William F. Apr 47 obit Jun 56

Russell, William Felton see Russell, Bill

Russert, Tim Oct 97

Russo, Rene Jul 97

Rust, Bernhard Jul 42

Rustin, Bayard Jun 67 obit Oct 87

Rutan, Burt Jun 2005

Rutenberg, Pinhas obit Mar 42

Rutenborn, Günter, Rev. Oct 60

Ruth, Babe Aug 44 obit Oct 48

Ruth, George Herman see Ruth, Babe

Rutherford, Joseph Franklin Nov 40 obit Mar 42

Rutherford, Margaret Jan 64 obit Jul 72

Rutledge, Brett see Paul, Elliot

Rutledge, Wiley May 43 obit Oct 49

Ryan, George H. Sep 2001

Ryan, John obit Oct 45

Ryan, Joseph P. Jan 49 obit Sep 63

Ryan, Meg May 99

Ryan, Nolan Oct 70

Ryan, Patrick J. May 55

Ryan, Robert Dec 63 obit Sep 73

Ryan, T. Claude Jan 43 obit Nov 82

Ryan, Thelma Catherine see Nixon, Patricia

Ryan, William F. May 67 obit Dec 72

Ryder, Jonathan see Ludlum, Robert

Ryder, Winona Jun 94

Ryer, Jonathan see Ludlum, Robert

Rykiel, Sonia May 90

Ryle, Martin Sep 73 obit Jan 85

Rysanek, Leonie Mar 66 obit

May 98

Ryti, Risto Feb 41 obit Jan 57

Ryun, Jim May 68

Saab, Elie Aug 2004

Saarinen, Aline B. Dec 56 obit Sep 72

Saarinen, Eero Oct 49 obit Nov 61

Saarinen, Eliel Oct 42 obit Sep 50

Saatchi, Maurice Jan 89

Sabah, Jaber Al-Ahmad Al-Jaber Al-, Sheik Aug 88

Sabath, Adolph J. Jul 46 obit Dec 52

Sabatier, Paul obit Oct 41

Sabatini, Gabriela Jun 92

Sabato, Ernesto Oct 85

Sabin, Albert B. Feb 58 obit Apr 93

Sabin, Florence R. Apr 45 obit Dec 53

Sabry, Hassan, Pasha obit Yrbk 40

Sachar, Abram Leon Nov 49 obit Sep 93

Sachs, Bernard obit Mar 44

Sachs, Curt Aug 44 obit Apr 59

Sachs, Jeffrey D. Nov 93

Sachs, Nelly Mar 67 obit Jul 70

Sackett, Frederic M., Jr. obit Jul 41

Sacks, Oliver Feb 85

Sadak, Necmeddin Jan 50 obit Dec 53

Sadat, Anwar Mar 71 obit Nov 81

Sadat, Jihan Aug 86

Saddler, Donald Jan 63

Sade Sep 86

Sadik, Nafis Feb 96

Sadler, Michael obit Dec 43

Saerchinger, Cesar Apr 40

Safdie, Moshe Sep 68

Safer, Morley Jul 80

Safina, Carl Apr 2005

Safire, William Dec 73

Sagan, Carl Apr 70 obit Feb

97

Sagan, Françoise Sep 60 obit Feb 2005

Sage, Dean obit Aug 43

Sagendorph, Robb Dec 56 obit Sep 70

Sager, Ruth Jul 67 obit Jun 97

Sahl, Mort Dec 60

Said Bin Taimur Oct 57 obit Aug 78 (died Oct 72)

Said, Edward W. Nov 89 obit Feb 2004

Said, Nuri as- see Nuri As-Said

Saillant, Louis Jul 48 obit Jan 75

Saint Exupery, Antoine De Jan-Feb 40 obit May 45

Saint, Eva Marie Jun 55

Sainte-Marie, Buffy Jul 69

Saint-Gaudens, Homer Oct 41 obit Feb 59

Saionji, Kimmochi, Prince obit Jan 41

Sajak, Pat Jul 89

Sakel, Manfred Jan 41 obit Feb 58

Sakharov, Andrei Dmitrievich Jul 71 obit Feb 90

Salam, Abdus Apr 88 obit Jan 97

Salant, Richard S. Nov 61 obit Apr 93

Salazar, Alberto May 83

Salazar, Antonio De Oliveira May 41 May 52 obit Oct 70

Sale, Rhys M. Dec 57

Saleh, Allah-Yar Feb 53

Salerno-Sonnenberg, Nadja Nov 87

Sales, Nykesha Jun 99

Sales, Soupy Jan 67

Saliers, Emily see Indigo Girls

Salinas De Gortari, Carlos Mar 89

Salinger, Pierre Jul 61 Mar 87 obit Feb 2005

Salisbury, Harrison E. Jul 55 Jan 82 obit Sep 93

Salit, Norman, Rabbi Mar 55

obit Oct 60

Salk, Jonas May 54 obit Aug 95

Salk, Lee Sep 79 obit Jul 92

Salle, David Sep 86

Salomon, Henry, Jr. Dec 56 obit Apr 58

Salote Tupou, Queen of Tonga Dec 53 obit Feb 66

Salten, Felix obit Nov 45

Salter, Alfred obit Sep 45

Salter, Andrew May 44 obit Jan 97

Salter, Arthur Mar 44

Saltonstall, Leverett Jun 44 Apr 56 obit Sep 79

Saltzman, Charles E. Oct 47 obit Aug 94

Salvemini, Gaetano Dec 43 obit Nov 57

Salverson, Laura Goodman (WLB) Yrbk 57

Salzmann, Siegfried see Salten, Felix

Samaranch, Juan Antonio Feb 94

Samaras, Lucas Nov 72

Samaroff, Olga Mar 46 obit Jun 48

Sammartino, Peter Dec 58 obit May 92

Sampras, Pete May 94

Sampson, Edith S. Dec 50 obit Jan 80

Samuel, Bernard Sep 49 obit Mar 54

Samuel, Herbert 1st Viscount Apr 55 obit Mar 63

Samuel, Sealhenry see Seal

Samuelson, Joan Aug 96

Samuelson, Paul Anthony May 65

San Martin, Ramon Grau see Grau San Martin, Ramón

Sananikone, Phoui Sep 59 obit Feb 84

Sanborn, David Aug 92

Sanborn, Pitts obit Apr 41

Sánchez Vicario, Arantxa

Aug 98

Sánchez, David Nov 2001

Sandage, Allan Jan 99

Sandberg, Ryne Nov 94

Sandburg, Carl Jun 40 Dec 63 obit Oct 67

Sandefer, Jefferson Davis obit Apr 40

Sander, Jil Oct 97

Sanders, Barry Sep 93

Sanders, Bernard Jun 91

Sanders, Carl E. Dec 64

Sanders, Colonel *see* Sanders, Harland

Sanders, Deion Jan 95

Sanders, George Jun 43 obit Jun 72

Sanders, Harland Apr 73 obit Feb 81

Sanders, Jared Young obit May 44

Sanders, Lawrence Apr 89 obit May 98

Sanders, Marlene Feb 81

Sanders, Ric *see* Fairport Convention

Sanderson, Derek Apr 75

Sandford, John Mar 2002

Sandler, Adam May 98

Sandor, Gyorgy Jul 47

Sandström, Emil Jan 51 obit Sep 62

Sandys, Duncan May 52

Sanford, John Elroy *see* Foxx, Redd

Sanford, Terry Nov 61 obit Jul 98

Sanger, Frederick Jul 81

Sanger, Margaret Aug 44 obit Nov 66

Sanger, Stephen W. Mar 2004

Santa Cruz, Hernan Dec 49

Santana, Manuel Sep 67

Santayana, George Apr 44 obit Nov 52

Santelmann, William F. Apr 53

Santmyer, Helen Hooven Feb 85 obit Apr 86

Santolalla, Irene Silva De Dec

56 obit Sep 92

Santos, José Edwardo Dos May 94

Santos, José Nov 2003

Santos, Rufino J. Dec 60 obit Nov 73

Sapieha, Princess *see* Peterson, Virgilia

Sapolsky, Robert Jan 2004

Saposs, David Nov 40 obit Jan 69

Sapp, Warren Sep 2003

Sar, Saloth *see* Pol Pot

Saracoglu, Sükrü Jun 42 obit Mar 54

Saragat, Giuseppe Dec 56 Jul 65 obit Jul 88

Sarah, Duchess of York Mar 87

Sarajoglu Shukri, Bey *see* Saracoglu, Sükrü

Saralegui, Cristina Jan 99

Saramago, José Jun 2002

Sarandon, Susan Sep 89

Sarasin, Pote Dec 55

Sarbanes, Paul S. Jan 97

Sardauna of Sokoto *see* Ahmadu, Alhaji, Sardauna of Sokoto

Sardi, Melchiorre Pio Vincenzo *see* Sardi, Vincent, Sr.

Sardi, Vincent, Jr. May 57 [Sardi, Vincent, Sr.; and Sardi, Vincent, Jr.]

Sardi, Vincent, Sr. May 57 [Sardi, Vincent, Sr.; and Sardi, Vincent, Jr.] obit Jan 70

Sardina, Adolfo *see* Adolfo

Sarg, Tony obit Apr 42

Sargeant, Howland H. Dec 52 obit Apr 84

Sargent, Francis W. Jun 71 obit Jan 99

Sargent, Malcolm Watts Dec 45 obit Jan 68

Sargent, Porter Jul 41 obit May 51

Sarkis, Elias Mar 79 obit Aug

85

Sarney, José Mar 86

Sarnoff, David Nov 40 Oct 51 obit Feb 72

Sarnoff, Robert W. Dec 56 obit May 97

Sarojini Nayadu *see* Naidu, Sarojini

Saroyan, William Jul 40 Nov 72 obit Jul 81

Sarraute, Nathalie Jun 66 obit Jan 2000

Sarton, George Jul 42 obit May 56

Sarton, May May 82 obit Sep 95

Sartre, Jean Paul Mar 47 May 71 obit Jun 80

Sassa, Scott Jan 2000

Sasser, James R. Jul 93

Sassoon, Vidal Apr 99

Sastroamidjojo, Ali Jun 50 obit May 75

Satcher, David Feb 97

Sato, Eisaku Dec 65 obit Aug 75

Satterfield, John C. Jul 62

Sauckel, Fritz obit Nov 46

Saud, King of Saudi Arabia Apr 54 obit Apr 69

Sauer, Emil Von obit Jun 42

Sauer, George Nov 48 obit Apr 94

Saul, Ralph S. Feb 71

Saulnier, Raymond J. Dec 57

Saund, Dalip S. Jun 60 obit Jun 73

Saunders, Carl M. Jun 50 obit Nov 74

Saunders, Hilary Aidan St. George Jun 43 obit Feb 52

Saunders, John Monk obit Apr 40

Saunders, Robert Dec 51 obit Mar 55

Saunders, Stuart T. Apr 66 obit Mar 87

Saura, Carlos Sep 78

Sauvé, Jeanne Aug 84 obit Mar 93

Savage, Augusta Jan 41 obit

May 62

Savage, John Lucian Apr 43 obit Feb 68

Savage, Michael Joseph obit Apr 40

Savage, Rick *see* Def Leppard

Savalas, Aristoteles *see* Savalas, Telly

Savalas, Telly Feb 76 obit Mar 94

Savery, Constance (WLB) Yrbk 48

Saville, Curtis Jan 86 [Saville, Curtis; and Saville, Kathleen]

Saville, Kathleen Jan 86 [Saville, Curtis; and Saville, Kathleen]

Savimbi, Jonas Aug 86 obit Jun 2002

Savitch, Jessica Jan 83 obit Mar 84

Savitt, Dick *see* Savitt, Richard

Savitt, Richard Jun 52

Sawhill, John C. Apr 79 obit Yrbk 2000

Sawyer, Charles Jul 48 obit Jun 79

Sawyer, Diane Oct 85

Sawyer, Eddie Nov 50 obit Jan 98

Sawyer, Edwin Milby *see* Sawyer, Eddie

Sawyer, Helen Oct 54

Sawyer, John E. Jul 61 obit Apr 95

Saxbe, William B. Jul 74

Saxon, James J. Dec 63 obit Apr 80

Saxon, Lyle obit May 46

Saxton, Alexander Nov 43

Sayão, Bidú Feb 42 obit Jun 99

Sayegh, Fayez A. Jul 57

Sayles Belton, Sharon Jan 2001

Sayles, John Feb 84

Sayles, R. W. obit Dec 42

Saylor, Michael Sep 2000

Sayre, Francis B. Jan-Feb 40

obit May 72

Sayre, Francis B., Jr. Dec 56

Sayre, Morris Jan 48 obit Apr 53

Sayre, Mrs. Raymond May 49 [Sayre, Ruth Buxton]

Sayre, Ruth Buxton *see* Sayre, Mrs. Raymond

Scali, John Sep 73 obit Jan 96

Scalia, Antonin Nov 86

Scammon, Richard M. Mar 71 obit Sep 2001

Scarbrough, Roger Lumley, 11th Earl of *see* Lumley, Roger

Scardino, Marjorie Apr 2000

Scargill, Arthur Jan 85

Scaturro, Pasquale V. Oct 2005

Scavullo, Francesco May 85 obit Yrbk 2004

Scdoris, Rachael Jul 2005

Scelba, Mario May 53 obit Feb 92

Schaap, Phil Sep 2001

Schacht, Al May 46 obit Sep 84

Schacht, Hjalmar Oct 44 obit Sep 70

Schachter, Mrs. Jules *see* Edwards, Joan

Schaefer, George Feb 70 obit Jan 98

Schaefer, Vincent J. Jan 48 obit Sep 93

Schaefer, William Donald Jul 88

Schäffer, Fritz Mar 53 obit May 67

Schain, Josephine Jul 45

Schakowsky, Jan Jul 2004

Schaller, George B. Aug 85

Schama, Simon Nov 91

Schanberg, Sydney H. Aug 90

Schapiro, Meyer Jul 84 obit May 96

Schapiro, Miriam Aug 2000

Schärf, Adolf Oct 57 obit Apr 65

Schary, Dore May 48 obit Sep

80

Schaufuss, Peter May 82

Schechter, A. A. May 41 obit Aug 89

Scheck, Barry Mar 98

Scheel, Walter Feb 71

Scheele, Leonard A. May 48 obit Mar 93

Scheer, Alan Austin Jan 64

Scheffer, Victor B. Apr 94

Scheiberling, Edward N. Dec 44 obit Jan 68

Schell, Jonathan Jul 92

Schell, Maria Jun 61 obit Yrbk 2005

Schell, Maximilian Dec 62

Schelling, Ernest Jan-Feb 40

Schemm, Mrs. Ferdinard Ripley *see* Walker, Mildred

Scherbo, Vitaly *see* Shcherbo, Vitaly

Scherer, Jean-Marie Maurice *see* Rohmer, Eric

Scherer, Paul May 41 obit May 69

Scherer, Roy Jr. *see* Hudson, Rock

Schereschewsky, Joseph Williams obit Sep 40

Scherman, Harry Sep 43 Jul 63 obit Jan 70

Scherman, Thomas Dec 54 obit Jul 79

Schertz, Ruth Louise *see* Phillips, Ruth

Schertzinger, Victor obit Dec 41

Scheuer, James Apr 68

Schiaparelli, Elsa Jan-Feb 40 Nov 51 obit Jan 74

Schick, Bela Jul 44 obit Feb 68

Schickele, Peter May 79

Schiff, Dorothy Jul 45 Jan 65 obit Oct 89

Schiffrin, André Jan 2000

Schilder, Paul Ferdinand obit Jan 41

Schildkraut, Joseph Apr 56

obit Mar 64

Schillebeeckx, Edward Jun 83

Schiller, Karl Dec 71 obit Mar 95

Schilling, Curt Oct 2001

Schillinger, Joseph obit May 43

Schindler, Alexander M. Sep 87 obit Feb 2001

Schindler, John A. Mar 56 obit Jan 58

Schiotz, Aksel Mar 49 obit Jun 75

Schiotz, Fredrik Axel Apr 72 obit May 89

Schippers, Thomas Apr 70 obit Feb 78

Schirra, Walter M., Jr. Jun 66

Schisgal, Murray Jan 68

Schjeldahl, Peter Oct 2005

Schlafly, Phyllis Jun 78

Schlamme, Martha Feb 64 obit Jan 86

Schlauch, Margaret Dec 42 obit Sep 86

Schlee, Mrs. George Matthias see Valentina

Schleich, Michel obit Jun 45

Schlein, Miriam (WLB) Yrbk 59 obit Yrbk 2005

Schlesinger, Arthur M. Oct 46 Jan 79

Schlesinger, Bruno see Walter, Bruno

Schlesinger, Frank obit Aug 43

Schlesinger, James R. Oct 73

Schlesinger, John Nov 70 obit Yrbk 2003

Schlessinger, Laura Sep 97

Schlink, Frederick John Mar 41 obit Mar 95

Schlöndorff, Volker Aug 83

Schlosser, Alex L. obit Mar 43

Schmelkes, Franz C. obit Feb 43

Schmid, Carlo Feb 65 obit

Apr 80

Schmidt, Benno C., Jr. Aug 86

Schmidt, Fritz obit Aug 43

Schmidt, Helmut Oct 74

Schmidt, Maarten Sep 66

Schmitt, Bernadotte E. Dec 42 obit May 69

Schmitt, Gladys Mar 43 obit Dec 72

Schmitt, Harrison H. Jul 74

Schmoke, Kurt L. Feb 95

Schnabel, Artur Jul 42 obit Sep 51

Schnabel, Julian Nov 83

Schneerson, Menachem M. Sep 83 obit Aug 94

Schneider, Alan Dec 69 obit Jun 84

Schneider, Alexander Mar 76 obit Mar 93

Schneider, Alma K. Dec 54

Schneider, Eugene obit Jan 43

Schneider, Hannes Mar 41 obit Jun 55

Schneider, Mrs. Daniel Jacob see Schneider, Alma K.

Schneider, Romy Jan 65 obit Jul 82

Schneiderman, Rose Feb 46 obit Oct 72

Schneirla, T. C. Dec 55 obit Nov 68

Schnittke, Alfred Jul 92 obit Oct 98

Schnitzler, William F. Apr 65

Schnurer, Carolyn Mar 55

Schnurer, Mrs. Harold T. see Schnurer, Carolyn

Schoenberg, Arnold Apr 42 obit Sep 51

Schoenberg, Loren Feb 2005

Schoenbrun, David Jan 60 obit Jul 88

Schoendienst, Albert Fred see Schoendienst, Red

Schoendienst, Red Dec 64

Schoeneman, George J. Nov 47

Schoen-René, Anna Eugénie obit Jan 43

Schoeppel, Andrew F. Mar 52

obit Mar 62

Schoff, Hannah Kent obit Feb 41

Schofield, Frank H. obit Apr 42

Scholder, Fritz Apr 85 obit Yrbk 2005

Schollander, Don Sep 65

Schomburg, August Nov 60

Schoonmaker, Edwin Davies obit Jan 40

Schoonmaker, Thelma Mar 97

Schoonmaker-Powell, Thelma see Schoonmaker, Thelma

Schoonover, Lawrence (WLB) Yrbk 57 obit Mar 80

Schopf, J. William May 95

Schorr, Daniel Sep 59 Feb 78

Schorr, Friedrich Jul 42 obit Jun 54

Schott, Marge Aug 99 obit Yrbk 2004

Schottland, Charles I. Dec 56 obit Sep 95

Schrader, Paul Aug 81

Schram, Emil Oct 41 May 53 obit Nov 87

Schranz, Karl Jan 71

Schratt, Katharina obit May 40

Schreiber, Georges May 43

Schreiber, J.-J. Servan- see Servan-Schreiber, J.-J

Schreiber, Walther Feb 54 obit Sep 58

Schrembs, Joseph obit Dec 45

Schrempp, Juergen Oct 99

Schreyer, Edward Richard Feb 81

Schricker, Henry F. Sep 50 obit Feb 67

Schriever, Bernard A. Oct 57 obit Yrbk 2005

Schrift, Shirley see Winters, Shelley

Schröder, Gerhard Dec 62 Nov 98 obit Mar 90

Schroeder, Frederick R., Jr.

Oct 49

Schroeder, Patricia Oct 78

Schroeder, R. W. Jul 41

Schroeder, Ted *see* Schroeder, Frederick R., Jr.

Schuchert, Charles obit Jan 43

Schuck, Arthur A. Apr 50 obit Apr 63

Schulberg, Budd Jun 41 May 51

Schuller, Gunther Apr 64

Schuller, Mary Craig *see* McGeachy, Mary Craig

Schuller, Robert H. Jun 79

Schulte, Karl Joseph, Cardinal obit May 41

Schultes, Richard Evans Mar 95 obit Sep 2001

Schulthess, Edmund obit Jun 44

Schultz, Ed Aug 2005

Schultz, Howard M. May 97

Schultz, Richard D. Jul 96

Schultz, Sigrid Apr 44

Schultze, Charles L. Jan 70

Schulz, Charles M. Dec 60 obit Apr 2000

Schulz, Leo obit Oct 44

Schumacher, Kurt Feb 48 obit Oct 52

Schuman, Robert Jan 48 obit Nov 63

Schuman, William Jun 42 Dec 62 obit Apr 92

Schumann, Maurice Apr 70 obit Apr 98

Schumer, Charles E. Jul 95

Schurman, Jacob G. obit Oct 42

Schuster, M. Lincoln Jul 41 [Simon, Richard L; and Schuster, M. Lincoln] obit Feb 71

Schwartz, Arthur Nov 79 obit Oct 84

Schwartz, Bernard *see* Curtis, Tony

Schwartz, Delmore Jun 60 obit Nov 66

Schwartz, Felice N. May 93

obit Apr 96

Schwartz, Maurice Feb 56 obit Jul 60

Schwartz, Tony Jul 85

Schwarz, Gerard Apr 86

Schwarzenegger, Arnold Apr 79 Oct 91 Aug 2004

Schwarzhaupt, Elisabeth Jan 67 obit Jan 87

Schwarzkopf, Elisabeth Dec 55

Schwarzkopf, H. Norman May 91

Schwarzschild, Martin Feb 67 obit Jun 97

Schwebel, Stephen M. Jul 52

Schweiker, Richard S. Feb 77

Schweitzer, Albert Jan 48 Jul 65

Schweitzer, Pierre-Paul Dec 63 obit Mar 94

Schwellenbach, Lewis B. Jun 45 obit Jul 48

Schwidetzky, Oscar Dec 43 obit Nov 63

Schwinger, Julian Oct 67 obit Sep 94

Schygulla, Hanna Jul 84

Scicolone, Sophia *see* Loren, Sophia

Scobie, Ronald M. Feb 45

Scofield, Paul Mar 62

Scoggin, Margaret C. Jul 52 obit Sep 68

Scorsese, Martin Feb 79

Scott, Arthur Carroll obit Yrbk 40

Scott, Barbara Ann Jul 48

Scott, C. Kay- *see* Wellman, Frederick Creighton

Scott, David R. Oct 71

Scott, George C. Apr 71 obit Nov 99 obit Yrbk 2005

Scott, George [Blind Boys of Alabama] obit Yrbk 2005

Scott, Harold Dec 50

Scott, Hazel Aug 43 obit Nov 81

Scott, Henry L. Jun 49

Scott, Hugh Sep 48 obit Sep

94

Scott, James B. obit Aug 43

Scott, Jill Jan 2002

Scott, John R. K. obit Feb 46

Scott, K. Frances Nov 48

Scott, Michael Apr 53 obit Apr 85

Scott, Peter Markham May 68 obit Nov 89

Scott, Raymond Jul 41 obit May 94

Scott, Ridley Oct 91

Scott, Robert L., Jr. Oct 43

Scott, Sheila Nov 74 obit Jan 89

Scott, Tom Nov 46

Scott, Tony Nov 2004

Scott, W. Kerr Apr 56 obit Jul 58

Scott, Willard Jul 89

Scotto, Renata Sep 78

Scottoline, Lisa Jul 2001

Scourby, Alexander Jul 65 obit Apr 85

Scowcroft, Brent Jul 87

Scranton, William W. Jan 64

Scribner, Fred C., Jr. Dec 58 obit Apr 94

Scrugham, James Graves obit Jul 45

Scudder, Janet obit Jul 40

Scull, Robert C. Apr 74 obit Feb 86

Sculley, John Aug 88

Scully, Vin Oct 2001

Seaborg, Glenn T. Jul 48 Dec 61 obit May 99

Seabrook, William B. Nov 40 obit Oct 45

Seabury, David Sep 41 obit May 60

Seaga, Edward Apr 81

Seagrave, Gordon S. Nov 43 obit May 65

Seagren, Bob Jun 74

Seal Feb 97

Seamans, Robert C., Jr. Dec 66

Searing, Annie E. P. obit Jun 42

Sears, Martha *see* Sears, William and Martha

Sears, Paul B. Jul 60

Sears, Robert Richardson Jul 52 obit Aug 89

Sears, William and Martha Aug 2001

Sears, William Joseph, Sr. obit May 44

Seaton, Fred A. Nov 56 obit Mar 74

Seau, Junior Sep 2001

Seaver, George Thomas *see* Seaver, Tom

Seaver, Tom Mar 70

Sebald, William J. Oct 51

Sebelius, Kathleen Nov 2004

Seberg, Jean Apr 66 obit Oct 79

Sebrell, W. H., Jr. May 51 obit Nov 92

Sec *see* Mannes, Marya

Secondari, John H. Apr 67 obit Apr 75

Sedaka, Neil Oct 78

Sedaris, Amy Apr 2002

Sedaris, David Jul 97

Sedgman, Francis Arthur *see* Sedgman, Frank

Sedgman, Frank Nov 51

Seefried, Irmgard Feb 56 obit Jan 89

Seeger, Pete Dec 63

Seferis, George *see* Sepheriades, Georgios S.

Segal, Bernard G. Jun 70 obit Aug 97

Segal, Erich Apr 71

Segal, George [actor] Nov 75

Segal, George [artist] Jan 72 obit Sep 2000

Seger, George N. obit Oct 40

Seghers, Anna Dec 42 obit Jul 83

Segni, Antonio Dec 55 obit Jan 73

Segovia, Andrés May 48 Jun 64 obit Jul 87

Segré, Emilio Apr 60 obit Jul 89

Segura, Francisco Sep 51

Seibert, Florence B. Nov 42

obit Oct 91

Seibold, Louis obit Jun 45

Seid, Ruth *see* Sinclair, Jo

Seidel, Martie *see* Dixie Chicks

Seidelman, Susan May 90

Seidman, L. William Sep 76

Seifert, Elizabeth (WLB) Yrbk 51 obit Oct 83

Seifert, Shirley (WLB) Yrbk 51

Seif-Ul-Islam Abdullah, Prince Dec 47 obit Sep 55

Seinfeld, Jerry Aug 92

Seitz, Frederick Apr 56

Seitz, George B. obit Aug 44

Seixas, E. Victor, Jr. Jul 52

Sekulovich, Mladen *see* Malden, Karl

Selassie, Haile *see* Haile Selassie I

Selden, David Jul 74 obit Aug 98

Seldes, George Sep 41 obit Sep 95

Seles, Monica Nov 92

Self, Henry Oct 42

Selfridge, H. Gordon Mar 41 obit Jun 47

Selig, Allan H. *see* Selig, Bud

Selig, Bud Jan 99

Selincourt, Ernest de *see* De Selincourt, Ernest

Selinko, Annemarie Jan 55

Sell, Hildegarde Loretta *see* Hildegarde

Sellars, Peter Jan 86

Selleck, Tom Nov 83

Sellers, Peter Dec 60 obit Sep 80

Seltzer, Louis B. Dec 56 obit Jun 80

Selway, Phil *see* Radiohead

Selwyn, Edgar obit Apr 44

Selwyn-Lloyd, Baron Apr 52 obit Jul 78

Selye, Hans Jun 53 Jan 81 obit Jan 83

Selzer, Richard Apr 93

Selznick, David O. Jun 41 obit

Sep 65

Selznick, Myron obit May 44

Sembène, Ousmane Apr 94

Semenov, Nikolay Nikolaevich Mar 57

Semon, Waldo Lonsbury Yrbk 40 obit Aug 99

Sen, Binay Ranjan Dec 52 obit Aug 93

Sen, Hun *see* Hun Sen

Senanayake, Don Stephen Apr 50 obit May 52

Senanayake, Dudley Dec 52 obit Jun 73

Senarens, Luis Philip obit Jan 40

Sendak, Maurice Jun 68 Jun 89

Sender, Toni May 50

Senghor, Léopold Sédar Mar 62 Jul 94 obit Mar 2002

Sengstacke, John H. Nov 49 obit Aug 97

Senior, Clarence Dec 61 obit Nov 74

Senn, Milton J. E. Jun 50 obit Aug 90

Sensenich, Roscoe L. Jun 49 obit Feb 63

Sepheriades, Georgios S. May 64 obit Nov 71

Serban, Andrei Feb 78

Seredy, Kate May 40 obit May 75

Sereno, Paul C. Jun 97

Sergio, Lisa Jun 44 obit Aug 89

Sergius, Metropolitan obit Jul 44

Serkin, Peter Jun 86

Serkin, Rudolf Jul 40 Jun 90 obit Jul 91

Serlin, Oscar Mar 43 obit Apr 71

Serling, Rod Dec 59 obit Aug 75

Serov, Ivan A. Dec 56

Serra, Richard Jan 85

Serrano Súñer, Ramón Nov 40 obit Yrbk 2004

Serratosa Cibils, Joaquin Feb

54

Sert, José Luis Apr 74 obit May 83

Sert, Jose Maria obit Jan 46

Sert, Josep Lluis *see* Sert, José Luis

Servan-Schreiber, J.-J. Jan 55

Sessions, Roger Jan 75 obit May 85

Sessions, William S. Jul 88

Seton, Anya (WLB) Yrbk 53 obit Jan 91

Seton, Ernest Thompson May 43 obit Dec 46

Settle, Mary Lee (WLB) Yrbk 59

Setzer, Philip *see* Emerson String Quartet

Seuss, Dr. *see* Geisel, Theodor Seuss

Sevareid, Eric Jul 42 Oct 66 obit Aug 92

Severance, H. Craig obit Nov 41

Seversky, Alexander de *see* De Seversky, Alexander

Sevier, Henry Hulme obit Mar 40

Sevigny, Chloë Aug 2000

Sevitzky, Fabien Jul 46 obit Apr 67

Sewell, James Luther *see* Sewell, Luke

Sewell, Luke Nov 44

Sewell, Winifred Jun 60

Sexton, W. R. obit Oct 43

Seyferth, O. A. Jul 50

Seymour, Charles May 41 obit Nov 63

Seymour, Flora Warren Jun 42

Seymour, Harriet Ayer obit Sep 44

Seymour, Lesley Jane Nov 2001

Seymour, Lynn Nov 79

Seymour, Stephanie Oct 2002

Seymour, Whitney North May 61 obit Jul 83

Seyss-Inquart, Artur Von May 41 obit Nov 46

Sforza, Carlo, Count Jun 42 obit Oct 52

Shabandar, Moussa Feb 56

Shafer, Paul W. Jul 52 obit Oct 54

Shaffer, Peter May 67 Nov 88

Shafik, Doria May 55

Shagari, Alhaji Shehu Aug 80

Shah of Iran *see* Mohammed Riza Shah Pahlevi

Shah, Idries Jun 76 obit Feb 97

Shahade, Jennifer Sep 2005

Shaham, Gil Apr 97

Shaheen, Jeanne Jan 2001

Shahn, Ben Dec 54 obit May 69

Shakespeare, Frank Sep 70

Shalala, Donna Mar 91

Shalhoub, Tony Nov 2002

Shalikashvili, John Nov 95

Shambaugh, Benjamin Franklin obit May 40

Shamir, Yitzhak Feb 83 Yrbk 96

Shandling, Garry Apr 89

Shang Chen Jul 44

Shange, Ntozake Sep 78

Shankar, Ravi Apr 68

Shanker, Albert Apr 69 obit May 97

Shannon, James A. Jan 65 obit Jul 94

Shannon, Peggy obit Jul 41

Shannon, William V. Jan 79 obit Nov 88

Shantz, Bobby *see* Shantz, Robert Clayton

Shantz, Robert Clayton Apr 53

Shaoqi, Liu *see* Liu Shao-ch'i

Shapiro, Harry Lionel Dec 52 obit Mar 90

Shapiro, Irving S. Nov 76 obit Nov 2001

Shapiro, Karl Oct 44 obit Aug 2000

Shapiro, Neal May 2003

Shapley, Harlow Jan 41 Dec

52 Dec 72

Shaposhnikov, Boris Mar 42 obit May 45

Shapp, Milton J. Jul 73 obit Feb 95

Sharansky, Natan *see* Shcharansky, Anatoly

Sharett, Moshe *see* Shertok, Moshe

Sharif, Mohammad Nawaz Sep 98

Sharif, Omar May 70

Sharon, Ariel Apr 81

Sharp, Harry Clay obit Yrbk 40

Sharp, Mitchell Jul 66

Sharpton, Al, Jr. Nov 95

Shastri, Lal Bahadur Dec 64 obit Feb 66

Shatner, William Jul 87

Shaver, Dorothy Jan 46 obit Sep 59

Shaver, Erwin L., Rev. Mar 49

Shaver, Mary obit Mar 42

Shaw, Artie May 41 obit Apr 2005

Shaw, Bernard Feb 95

Shaw, George Bernard Jun 44 obit Dec 50

Shaw, Henry obit May 41

Shaw, Irwin Oct 42 obit Jul 84

Shaw, Lau Oct 45

Shaw, Lloyd Sep 43

Shaw, Louis Agassiz obit Oct 40

Shaw, Patricia Hearst *see* Hearst, Patricia

Shaw, Ralph R. Jun 56 obit Dec 72

Shaw, Robert [actor] May 68 obit Oct 78

Shaw, Robert [conductor] Sep 49 Jul 66 obit Jul 66

Shawcross, Hartley Dec 45 obit Yrbk 2003

Shawkey, Morris Purdy obit Apr 41

Shawn, Ted Oct 49 obit Feb

Mar 85

Shockley, William Dec 53 obit Oct 89

Shoemaker, Bill *see* Shoemaker, Willie

Shoemaker, Eugene M. Jun 67 obit Oct 97

Shoemaker, Samuel M. Apr 55 obit Dec 63

Shoemaker, Willie Jul 66 obit Apr 2004

Sholokhov, Mikhail Alecksandrovich Jan 42 Feb 60 obit Apr 84

Shone, Terence Allen Nov 46 obit Dec 65

Shope, Richard E. Dec 63 obit Dec 66

Shore, Dinah Jun 42 Dec 66 obit May 94

Shoriki, Matsutaro Feb 58

Short, Bobby Jul 72 obit Nov 2005

Short, Dewey Dec 51 obit Feb 80

Short, Hassard Nov 48 obit Dec 56

Short, Joseph Feb 51 obit Nov 52

Short, Martin Sep 92

Short, Walter C. Jan 46 obit Oct 49

Shorter, Wayne Apr 96

Shortz, Will Apr 96

Shostakovich, Dmitrii Dmitrievich May 41 obit Oct 75

Shotton, Burt Jun 49 obit Oct 62

Shotwell, James T. Oct 44 obit Sep 65

Shoulders, Harrison H. Nov 46 obit Jan 64

Shoup, Carl Feb 49 obit Sep 2000

Shoup, David M. Jan 60 obit Mar 83

Shoup, Oliver Henry obit Nov 40

Shreeve, Herbert Edward obit

Jun 42

Shreve, Earl Owen Oct 47

Shreve, R. H. Nov 45 obit Oct 46

Shridharani, Krishnalal Jan 42 obit Oct 60

Shriver, Eunice Kennedy Jul 96

Shriver, Lionel Sep 2005

Shriver, Maria Nov 91

Shriver, R. Sargent Dec 61

Shu, Ch'ing-ch'un *see* Shaw, Lau

Shula, Don Mar 74

Shull, Martha A. Apr 57

Shulman, Harry Apr 52 obit May 55

Shulman, Irving (WLB) Yrbk 56 obit Jun 95

Shulman, Max Oct 59 obit Oct 88

Shultz, George P. May 69 Apr 88

Shuman, Charles B. Feb 56

Shu-meng, Luan *see* Jiang Qing

Shumlin, Herman Mar 41 obit Aug 79

Shumway, Norman E. Apr 71

Shurlock, Geoffery M. Jan 62 obit Jun 76

Shuster, George Nauman Jan 41 Oct 60 obit Mar 77

Shute, Nevil Jul 42 obit Mar 60

Shvernik, Nikolai Oct 51 obit Feb 71

Shyamalan, M. Night Mar 2003

Sibley, Antoinette Dec 70

Sickert, Walter Richard obit Mar 42

Siddons, Anne Rivers Jan 2005

Sides, John H. Jan 61 obit Jun 78

Sidi Mohammed, Sultan of Morocco *see* Mohammed V, King of Morocco

Sidney, Sylvia Oct 81 obit

Sep 99

Siebert, Mickie *see* Siebert, Muriel

Siebert, Muriel Aug 97

Siegel, Bernie S. Jun 93

Siegfried Jan 98 [Siegfried and Roy]

Siemiller, P. L. Nov 66

Siepi, Cesare Dec 55

Sigerist, Henry Ernest Sep 40 obit Jun 57

Signoret, Simone Dec 60 obit Nov 85

Sihanouk, Norodom *see* Norodom Sihanouk

Sikorski, Wladyslaw Jan-Feb 40 obit Aug 43

Sikorsky, Igor I. Oct 40 Dec 56 obit Dec 72

Silber, John R. Feb 84

Silberman, Charles E. Jul 79

Siles Zuazo, Hernán Sep 58 Jun 85 obit Oct 96

Siles, Hernando obit Jan 43

Sillanpää, Frans Eemil Jan-Feb 40 obit Jul 64

Sillcox, Lewis Ketcham Dec 54 obit May 89

Sills, Beverly Nov 69 Feb 82

Silva de Santolalla, Irene *see* Santolalla, Irene Silva De

Silva, Maria Helena Vieira da *see* Vieira Da Silva, Maria Helena

Silver, Abba Hillel Dec 41 May 63 obit Jan 64

Silver, Joel Nov 2003

Silverman, Fred Nov 78

Silvers, Phil Dec 57 obit Jan 86

Silzer, George Sebastian obit Yrbk 40

Simenon, Georges Apr 70 obit Nov 89

Simionato, Giulietta Apr 60

Simkhovitch, Mary Melinda Kingsbury Mar 43 obit Dec 51

Simkin, William E. Jan 67 obit May 92

Simmons, Adele Smith May

91

Simmons, Earl *see* DMX

Simmons, Furnifold McLendell obit Jan 40

Simmons, Gene *see* Kiss

Simmons, Jean Feb 52

Simmons, Richard May 82

Simmons, Russell Jun 98

Simmons, Ruth J. Jan 96

Simms, Hilda Nov 44 obit May 94

Simms, John F. Sep 56 obit Jun 75

Simms, Phil Oct 94

Simms, Ruth Hanna McCormick obit Feb 45

Simon and Schuster *see* Simon, Richard L.; Schuster, Lincoln M.

Simon, Carly Aug 76

Simon, Charlie May (WLB) Yrbk 46

Simon, Claude May 92 obit Yrbk 2005

Simon, Edith (WLB) Yrbk 54

Simon, Herbert A. Jun 79 obit May 2001

Simon, John Allsebrook Simon, 1st Viscount Jul 40 obit Mar 54

Simon, Mrs. Howard *see* Simon, Charlie May

Simon, Neil Feb 68 Mar 89

Simon, Norton Mar 68 obit Aug 93

Simon, Paul [musician] Mar 75

Simon, Paul [senator] Jan 88 obit Yrbk 2004

Simon, Richard L. Jul 41 [Simon, Richard L; and Schuster, M. Lincoln] obit Oct 60

Simon, William E. Apr 74 obit Aug 2000

Simonds, Frederic W. obit May 41

Simonds, G. G. Oct 43 obit Jul 74

Simone, Nina Apr 68 obit

Yrbk 2003

Simonetta Dec 55

Simons, David G. Dec 57

Simons, Elwyn L. Jun 94

Simons, Hans Mar 57 obit May 72

Simonson, Lee Nov 47 obit Mar 67

Simpson, Adele Nov 70 obit Oct 95

Simpson, Alan Feb 64 obit Jul 98

Simpson, Alan K. Oct 90

Simpson, Carole Nov 99

Simpson, George Gaylord Dec 64 obit Jan 85

Simpson, Harriette Louisa *see* Arnow, Harriette Simpson

Simpson, Helen De Guerry obit Yrbk 40

Simpson, Howard E. May 58 obit Apr 85

Simpson, Kenneth F. obit Mar 41

Simpson, Lorna Nov 2004

Simpson, Louis Dec 64

Simpson, Milward L. Jan 57 obit Aug 93

Simpson, Mona Feb 93

Simpson, O. J. Apr 69

Simpson, Richard M. Dec 53 obit Mar 60

Simpson, Valerie Apr 97 [Ashford, Nickolas; and Simpson, Valerie]

Simpson, Wallis Warfield *see* Windsor, Wallis Warfield

Simpson, William H. Feb 45 obit Oct 80

Sims, Hugo S., Jr. Oct 49

Sims, William L., 2d Dec 56

Sin, Jaime L. Sep 95 obit Yrbk 2005

Sinatra, Frank Jun 43 Oct 60 obit Jul 98

Sinbad Feb 97

Sinclair, Adelaide Helen Grant Macdonald *see* Sinclair, D. B.

Sinclair, April Sep 99

Sinclair, Archibald Sep 40

obit Oct 70 [Thurso, Archibald Henry Sinclair Macdonald, 1st Viscount]

Sinclair, D. B. Apr 51 [Sinclair, Adelaide Helen Grant Macdonald]

Sinclair, D. B. obit Jan 83

Sinclair, Jo Mar 46 obit Jun 95

Sinclair, May obit Dec 46

Sinclair, Upton Dec 62 obit Jan 69

Sinclair-Cowan, Bertha Muzzy *see* Bower, Bertha Muzzy

Sinding, Christian obit Jan 42

Singer, Adam *see* Karp, David

Singer, Bryan Apr 2005

Singer, Isaac Bashevis Jan 69 Sep 91

Singer, Israel J. obit Mar 44

Singer, Kurt D. Dec 54

Singer, Peter Mar 91

Singer, Richard obit Mar 40

Singer, S. Fred Dec 55

Singh, Giani Zail Sep 87 obit Mar 95

Singh, Swaran Mar 71 obit Jan 95

Singh, Vishwanath Pratap May 90

Singher, Martial Feb 47 obit May 90

Singletary, Mike Mar 93

Singleton, John Feb 97

Sinise, Gary Apr 97

Sink, M. Virginia Mar 64

Sinnott, Edmund W. Oct 48 obit Mar 68

Sinopoli, Giuseppe Mar 91 obit Sep 2001

Sinsheimer, Robert L. Jun 68

Sinyavsky, Andrei D. Jul 75 obit May 97

Siple, Paul A. Feb 57 obit Jan 69

Siqueiros, David Alfaro Jun 59 obit Feb 74

Sirica, John J. May 74 obit Oct 92

Sirikit Kitiyakara, Consort of

Bhumibol Adulyadej, King of Thailand *see* Sirikit Kitiyakara, Consort of Rama IX, King of Thailand

Sirikit Kitiyakara, Consort of Rama IX, King of Thailand Dec 60

Sirin *see* Nabokov, Vladimir

Siroky, Viliam Apr 57 obit Nov 71

Sisavang Vong, King of Laos Apr 54 obit Jan 60

Sisco, Joseph J. Jan 72 obit Yrbk 2005

Sissi Jun 2001

Sister Wendy *see* Beckett, Wendy

Sitgreaves, Beverley obit Sep 43

Sitterly, Charlotte Moore Jan 62 obit Jun 90

Sitwell, Osbert Sep 65 obit Jun 69

Six, Robert F. Oct 70 obit Nov 86

Siza, Alvaro Feb 2000

Sizoo, Joseph R. Dec 64 obit Nov 66

Skelton, Red Nov 47 obit Nov 97

Skelton, Richard Bernard *see* Skelton, Red

Skidmore, Hubert Standish obit Mar 46

Skidmore, Louis Dec 51 obit Dec 62

Skillin, Edward S. May 49 obit Yrbk 2000

Skilton, Charles Sanford obit May 41

Skinner, B. F. Jan 64 Nov 79 obit Oct 90

Skinner, Cornelia Otis Jan 42 Dec 64 obit Sep 79

Skinner, Eleanor Oakes *see* Skinner, Mrs. James M., Jr.

Skinner, Mrs. James M., Jr. May 51 [Skinner, Eleanor Oakes]

Skinner, Otis obit Feb 42

Skinner, Samuel K. Aug 89

Skira, Albert Apr 67 obit Jun 90

Skocpol, Theda Aug 2000

Skolnick, Mark H. Jun 97

Skouras, Spyros P. Jun 43 obit Nov 71

Skrowaczewski, Stanislaw Dec 64

Skutt, V. J. Dec 59 obit Apr 93

Slade, Roy Jun 85

Slaney, Mary Decker *see* Decker, Mary

Slater, John E. Nov 51

Slater, Kelly Jul 2001

Slater, Rodney Jan 99

Slatkin, Leonard Feb 86

Slaughter, Frank G. Oct 42

Slaughter, Louise M. Apr 99

Slavenska, Mia Feb 54 obit Apr 2003

Slayton, Donald K. Feb 76 obit Aug 93

Sleeper, Ruth Oct 52 obit Feb 93

Slemon, C. Roy Dec 56

Slezak, Walter Mar 55 obit Jun 83

Slichter, Sumner H. Jun 47 obit Dec 59

Slick, Grace Apr 82

Sligh, Charles R., Jr. Apr 53

Slim, Mongi Mar 58 obit Dec 69

Slim, William Joseph Slim, Viscount Jun 45 obit Feb 71

Sliwa, Curtis Feb 83

Sloan, Alfred Pritchard, Jr. Nov 40 obit Mar 66

Sloan, George A. Jan 52 obit Jul 55

Sloan, Samuel obit May 45

Sloane, Eric Sep 72 obit May 85

Sloane, Everett Jan 57 obit Oct 65

Slobodkin, Louis Apr 57 obit Aug 75

Slocum, Harvey Feb 57 obit

Jan 62

Slonimsky, Nicolas Apr 55 Feb 91 obit Mar 96

Slye, Maud Yrbk 40 obit Nov 54

Smadel, Joseph E. May 63

Small, John D. Feb 46 obit Mar 63

Small, John Humphrey obit Sep 46

Smallens, Alexander May 47 obit Jan 73

Smallpeice, Basil Oct 69

Smallwood, Joseph R. Feb 53 obit Mar 92

Smallwood, Robert B. Mar 56 obit Sep 74

Smart, David A. Jun 44

Smathers, George A. Apr 54

Smeal, Eleanor Cutri Mar 80

Smedberg, William Renwick, 3d Dec 57

Smedley, Agnes Jan 44 obit Jun 50

Smedley, Constance obit Apr 41

Smetona, Antanas obit Feb 44

Smiley, Jane Apr 90

Smiley, Tavis Apr 2003

Smith, Albert W. obit Oct 42

Smith, Alfred E. Sep 44

Smith, Amy Jun 2005

Smith, Anna Deavere Sep 94

Smith, Austin E. Mar 50 obit Jan 94

Smith, Barbara Jul 98

Smith, Ben Oct 45 obit Jul 64

Smith, Betty Nov 43 obit Mar 72

Smith, Bruce [football player] Mar 95

Smith, Bruce [police administrator] Feb 53 obit Nov 55

Smith, C. Aubrey Sep 44 obit Jan 49

Smith, C. R. Sep 45 obit Jun 90

Smith, Carleton Apr 61 obit Jul 84

Smith, Carleton Sprague Dec

60 obit Nov 94

Smith, Cecil Woodham- *see* Woodham-Smith, Cecil Blanche Fitzgerald

Smith, Chesterfield H. Nov 74 obit Yrbk 2003

Smith, Clara E. obit Jul 43

Smith, Clyde Harold obit May 40

Smith, Courtney Dec 59 obit Mar 69

Smith, Cyril Stanley Jul 48 obit Oct 92

Smith, Dante Terrell *see* Mos Def

Smith, David T. Oct 50

Smith, Dean Apr 94

Smith, Dick Mar 59

Smith, E. Durant obit Jan 45

Smith, Elinor Mar 2001

Smith, Elizabeth Rudel Dec 61

Smith, Emmitt Nov 94

Smith, Ernest Bramah *see* Bramah, Ernest

Smith, Frances Octavia *see* Rogers, Dale Evans

Smith, Frederick W. Jun 2000

Smith, George Adam obit Apr 42

Smith, George Albert Nov 47 obit May 51

Smith, Gerald L. K. Aug 43 obit Jun 76

Smith, Gerard C. Oct 70 obit Sep 94

Smith, Gregory White Mar 98 [Naifeh, Steven; and Smith, Gregory White]

Smith, H. Alexander Apr 48 obit Jan 67

Smith, H. Allen May 42 obit May 76

Smith, Harold D. Jul 43 obit Mar 47

Smith, Harrison Dec 54 obit Feb 71

Smith, Hazel Brannon Sep 73 obit Jul 94

Smith, Hedrick Jun 91

Smith, Holland M. Apr 45

obit Mar 67

Smith, Howard K. Mar 43 Jul 76 obit Aug 2002

Smith, Howard W. Feb 41 obit Nov 76

Smith, Ian Douglas May 66

Smith, Ida B. Wise Feb 43 obit Apr 52

Smith, James H., Jr. Jan 58 obit Feb 83

Smith, James Todd *see* L. L. Cool J

Smith, Jeff Aug 91 obit Yrbk 2004

Smith, Jim *see* Dale, Jim

Smith, John L. Jun 52 obit Dec 58

Smith, Kate Yrbk 40 Nov 65 obit Aug 86

Smith, Kevin Feb 98

Smith, Kiki Mar 2005

Smith, Lady Eleanor obit Nov 45

Smith, Lillian May 44 obit Dec 66

Smith, Liz May 87

Smith, Logan Pearsall obit Apr 46

Smith, Maggie Jul 2002

Smith, Maggie Jun 70

Smith, Margaret Chase Feb 45 Mar 62 obit Aug 95

Smith, Margaret Nicholson *see* Nicholson, Margaret

Smith, Martin Cruz Nov 90

Smith, Mary Alice *see* Mary Alice

Smith, Mary Carter Feb 96

Smith, Mary Elizabeth *see* Smith, Liz

Smith, Mary Louise Oct 76 obit Nov 97

Smith, Merriman Dec 64 obit Nov 93 (died Apr 70)

Smith, Oliver Sep 61 obit Mar 94

Smith, Orin C. Nov 2003

Smith, Ozzie Feb 97

Smith, Page Sep 90 obit Nov

95

Smith, Patti Apr 89

Smith, Paul C. Apr 43 obit Sep 76

Smith, Red *see* Smith, Walter Wellesley

Smith, Rex Jan 42

Smith, Richard Emerson *see* Smith, Dick

Smith, Robert Paul Dec 58

Smith, Robert Sep 2000

Smith, Robyn Nov 76

Smith, Roger B. May 86

Smith, Rosamund *see* Oates, Joyce Carol

Smith, Roy Burnett obit Feb 41

Smith, Sidney Jan 55 obit May 59

Smith, Sylvester C., Jr. Jul 63

Smith, T. V. Feb 56 obit Jul 64

Smith, Thomas R. obit Jun 42

Smith, Virginia B. Jun 78

Smith, Walter Bedell Apr 44 Dec 53 obit Nov 61

Smith, Walter Wellesley Apr 59 obit Feb 82

Smith, Wilbur Fisk obit Sep 40

Smith, Will Sep 96

Smith, William French Jan 82 obit Jan 91

Smith, William Jay Mar 74

Smith, William Ward Feb 48 obit Jul 66

Smith, Zadie Aug 2000

Smithdas, Robert J. Dec 66

Smoot, George Apr 94

Smoot, Reed obit Mar 41

Smothers, Dick Dec 68

Smothers, Tom Dec 68

Smuin, Michael Oct 84

Smuts, Jan Christiaan Aug 41 obit Oct 50

Smylie, Robert E. Feb 56 obit Yrbk 2004

Smyslov, Vassily Jul 67

Smyth, Ethel Mary obit Jun 44

Smyth, H. D. *see* Smyth, Henry Dewolf

Smyth, Henry Dewolf Dec 48 obit Nov 86

Snavely, Guy E. Apr 51

Snead, Sam Jun 49 obit Yrbk 2002

Snead, Samuel Jackson *see* Snead, Sam

Sneider, Vern (WLB) Yrbk 56 obit Jun 81

Snell, Foster Dee Jan 43

Snell, George D. May 86 obit Aug 96

Snell, Henry Bayley obit Mar 43

Snell, Henry Snell, 1st Baron May 41

Snell, Peter Dec 62

Snider, Duke May 56

Snider, Edwin Donald *see* Snider, Duke

Snipes, Wesley Sep 93

Snodgrass, W. D. Nov 60

Snook, H. Clyde obit Nov 42

Snow of Leicester, Baron *see* Snow, C. P.

Snow, C. P. (WLB) Yrbk 54 Dec 61 obit Aug 80

Snow, Clyde Collins Apr 97

Snow, Edgar Jun 41 obit Apr 72

Snow, Edward Rowe (WLB) Yrbk 58

Snow, Glenn E. Nov 47

Snow, John Aug 2003

Snowdon, Lord *see* Armstrong-Jones, Antony

Snowe, Olympia J. May 95

Snyder, Alice D. obit Apr 43

Snyder, Gary Nov 78

Snyder, Howard McC Feb 55 obit Nov 70

Snyder, J. Buell obit Apr 46

Snyder, Janet *see* Lambert, Janet

Snyder, John W. Jul 45 obit Jan 86

Snyder, Peggy Lou *see* Nel-son, Harriet

Snyder, Solomon H. Apr 96

Snyder, Tom Jun 80

Soames, Christopher, Baron of Fletching Aug 81 obit Oct 87

Soares, Mário Oct 75

Sobchak, Anatoly A. Jul 92 obit Jul 2000

Sobeloff, Simon E. Mar 55 obit Sep 73

Sobhuza II, King of Swaziland Mar 82 obit Mar 82

Sobolev, Arkady A. Apr 55 obit Jan 65

Socarras, Carlos Prio *see* Prío Socarrás, Carlos

Sockman, Ralph W. Jun 46 obit Nov 70

Soderberg, C. Richard Feb 58 obit Jan 80

Soderbergh, Steven Oct 98

Sodero, Cesare Mar 43 obit Jan 48

Söderström, Elisabeth Nov 85

Soeharto Jun 67 Oct 92

Soekarno *see* Sukarno

Soffer, Olga Jul 2002

Soglow, Otto Sep 40 obit May 75

Soheily, Ali Sep 43 obit Jul 58

Sokolovsky, Vassily D. Dec 53 obit Jul 68

Sokolow, Anna Feb 69 obit Sep 2000

Sokolsky, George E. May 41 obit Jan 63

Solandt, Omond M. Mar 74

Solarz, Stephen J. Nov 86

Solberg, Thorvald A. Dec 48

Soldati, Mario Apr 58 obit Nov 99

Soler, Antonio Ruiz *see* Ruiz Soler, Antonio

Soleri, Paolo Feb 72

Solh, Sami Feb 58 obit Jan 69

Solomon, Susan Jul 2005

Solti, Georg Mar 64 obit Nov 97

Solzhenitsyn, Aleksandr Feb 69 Jul 88

Somers, Jane *see* Lessing, Doris

Somervell, Brehon Aug 42 obit Apr 55

Somerville, James Apr 43 obit Apr 49

Somes, Michael Dec 55 obit Feb 95

Sommerfeld, A. Apr 50 obit May 51

Somoza, Anastasio [1896-1956] Jun 42 obit Dec 56

Somoza, Anastasio [1925-1980] Mar 78 obit Nov 80

Sondheim, Stephen Nov 73

Songgram, Luang Pibul *see* Pibul Songgram, Luang

Sonnenfeld, Barry Nov 98

Sontag, Susan Jun 69 Feb 92 obit May 2005

Soong, Chingling *see* Sun Yat-Sen

Soong, T.V. Mar 41 obit Jun 71

Sophoulis, Themistocles Nov 47 obit Sep 49

Sordoni, Andrew J. Jul 56 obit Apr 63

Sorel, Edward Mar 94

Sorensen, Theodore Dec 61

Sorensen, Virginia (WLB) Yrbk 50

Sorkin, Aaron Jun 2000

Sorokin, Pitirim Alexandrovich Jul 42 obit Apr 68

Soros, George Apr 97

Sorvino, Mira Aug 98

Sosa, Sammy May 99

Soss, Wilma Porter Mar 65 obit Jan 87

Soth, Lauren K. Dec 56 obit Jun 98

Sothern, Ann Dec 56 obit Aug 2001

Souers, Sidney W. Feb 49 obit Mar 73

Soukup, Frantisek obit Yrbk 40

Soulages, Pierre Apr 58

Soule, George Henry Dec 45

obit Jun 70

Soustelle, Jacques Dec 58 obit Oct 90

Souter, David H. Jan 91

Southworth, Billy Nov 44 obit Jan 70

Southworth, James L. Jun 43 [Hingson, Robert A.; Edwards, Waldo B.; and Southworth, James L.]

Southworth, William H. *see* Southworth, Billy

Souvanna Phouma Nov 62 obit Mar 84

Souzay, Gérard Jan 66 obit Yrbk 2004

Sovern, Michael I. Feb 81

Sowell, Thomas Jul 81

Soyer, Isaac Mar 41 [Soyer, Isaac; Soyer, Moses; and Soyer, Raphael] obit Sep 81

Soyer, Moses Mar 41 [Soyer, Isaac; Soyer, Moses; and Soyer, Raphael] obit Oct 74

Soyer, Raphael Mar 41 [Soyer, Isaac; Soyer, Moses; and Soyer, Raphael] obit Jan 88

Soyinka Akinwande Oluwole *see* Soyinka, Wole

Soyinka, Wole Dec 74

Spaak, Paul-Henri May 45 Apr 58 obit Oct 72

Spaatz, Carl Sep 42 obit Sep 74

Spacek, Sissy Jan 78

Spacey, Kevin Apr 97

Spaeth, Sigmund Jul 42 obit Jan 66

Spahn, Warren May 62 obit Yrbk 2004

Spain, Frances Lander Jun 60

Spalding, Albert Jan 44 obit Jul 53

Spang, J. P., Jr. Jun 49 obit Feb 70

Spangler, Harrison E. Aug 43 obit Oct 65

Spark, Muriel Nov 75

Sparkman, John J. Mar 50 obit Jan 86

Sparks, Nicholas Feb 2001

Sparling, Edward J. Jul 48

Spassky, Boris Nov 72

Spaulding, Rolland H. obit May 42

Speakes, Larry Mar 85

Speaks, John Charles obit Dec 45

Speare, Elizabeth George (WLB) Yrbk 59 obit Jan 95

Spearman, Charles E. obit Oct 45

Spears, Britney Apr 2000

Specter, Arlen Aug 88

Spector, Phil Jul 89

Spectorsky, A. C. Jan 60 obit Mar 72

Speer, Albert Oct 76 obit Oct 81

Speicher, Eugene Oct 47 obit Jul 62

Speidel, Hans Apr 52 obit Feb 85

Spelling, Aaron May 86

Spellings, Margaret Jun 2005

Spellman, Francis Apr 40 Apr 47 obit Jan 68

Spence, Brent Sep 52 obit Jan 68

Spence, Hartzell Oct 42 obit Yrbk 2001

Spencer, John Jan 2001

Spencer, Lady Diana *see* Diana, Princess of Wales

Spencer, P. C. Jul 51 obit Jan 70

Spencer, Scott Jul 2003

Spencer-Churchill, Clementine Ogilvy Hozier Jul 53 [Churchill, Lady] obit Mar 78

Spender, J. Alfred obit Aug 42

Spender, Percy C. Mar 50

Spender, Stephen Jan 40 Mar 77 obit Sep 95

Spergel, David Jan 2005

Sperry, Armstrong Oct 41

Sperry, Roger W. Jan 86 obit Jun 94

Sperry, Willard L., Rev. Dr.

May 52 obit Sep 54

Sperti, George Speri Jan 40 obit Jul 91

Spiegel, Clara *see* Jaynes, Clare

Spiegelman, Sol Nov 80 obit Mar 83

Spielberg, Steven Jul 78 Feb 96

Spilhaus, Athelstan Jun 65 obit Jun 98

Spillane, Mickey Sep 81

Spiller, William Gibson obit Apr 40

Spingarn, Arthur B. Jan 65 obit Jan 72

Spinola, Antonio De Sep 74 obit Nov 96

Spiropulu, Maria May 2004

Spitalny, Phil Oct 40 obit Dec 70

Spitz, Mark Oct 72

Spitzer, Eliot Mar 2003

Spitzer, Lyman, Jr. Jan 60 obit Jun 97

Spivak, Lawrence E. May 56 obit May 94

Spivakov, Vladimir Feb 96

Spock, Benjamin Dec 56 Nov 69 obit Jun 98

Spofford, Charles M. Feb 51 obit May 91

Sporborg, Constance Nov 47 [Sporborg, Mrs. William Dick] obit Feb 61 [Sporborg, Mrs. William Dick]

Sporn, Philip Nov 66

Spottswood, James obit Yrbk 40

Spottswood, Stephen Gill Apr 62 obit Jan 75

Sprague, Embert Hiram obit Mar 40

Sprague, Robert Chapman Jan 51 obit Nov 91

Sprewell, Latrell Feb 2001

Spring, Howard Jan 41 obit

Jun 65

Springer, Adele I. Apr 47

Springer, Axel Dec 68 obit Nov 85

Springsteen, Bruce Apr 78 Aug 92

Sprinkel, Beryl Jul 87

Sproul, Allan Dec 50 obit Jun 78

Sproul, Robert Gordon Jul 45 obit Nov 75

Spruance, Raymond Ames Apr 44 obit Mar 70

Spry, Constance May 40 obit Mar 60

Spurgeon, Caroline F. E. obit Dec 42

Spyrou, Aristocles Matthew *see* Athenagoras I, Patriarch

Squires, Richard Anderson obit May 40

St. Clair Sinclair, Mary Amelia *see* Sinclair, May

St. Denis, Ruth Oct 49 obit Oct 68

St. George, Katharine Dec 47 obit Jul 83

St. George, Mrs. George B. *see* St. George, Katharine

St. George, Thomas R. Jan 44

St. John, Robert Jun 42 obit Yrbk 2003

St. Johns, Adela Rogers Aug 76 obit Sep 88

St. Laurent, Louis S. Mar 48 obit Oct 73

St. Laurent, Yves Dec 64

Staats, Elmer B. Jun 67

Stabler, Ken Oct 79

Stace, W. T. Apr 61 obit Oct 67

Stack, Andy *see* Rule, Ann

Stackhouse, Jerry Nov 2001

Stacy, Walter P. Jan 46 obit Oct 51

Stade, Frederica Von *see* Von Stade, Frederica

Stader, Maria Jul 58 obit Aug 99

Stafford, Jean (WLB) Yrbk 51

obit May 79

Stafford, Robert T. Sep 60

Stafford, Thomas P. Jan 77

Stagg, Alonzo Mar 44 obit Apr 65

Staggers, Harley O. Mar 71 obit Nov 91

Stahl, Lesley Jun 96

Stahle, Nils K. Apr 56

Stahr, Elvis J., Jr. Sep 61 obit Feb 99

Stainback, Ingram Macklin Dec 47 obit Jun 61

Stakman, E. C. Dec 49 obit Mar 79

Staley, Dawn Apr 2005

Staley, Oren Lee Sep 65 obit Nov 88

Stalin, Joseph Mar 42 obit Apr 53

Stalina, Svetlana Iosifovna *see* Alliluyeva, Svetlana

Stallone, Sylvester Oct 77 Feb 94

Stalnaker, John M. Jul 58 obit Oct 90

Stamm, John S. Feb 49 obit May 56

Stamos, Theodoros Jan 59 obit Apr 97

Stamp, Josiah Charles Stamp, 1st Baron obit Jun 41

Standish, Burt L. *see* Patten, Gilbert

Standley, W. H. May 42 obit Dec 63

Stanfield, Robert Lorne Dec 58 obit Yrbk 2004

Stanfield, Robert Nelson obit Jun 45

Stanford, Otis Binet *see* Whyte, William H. Jr.

Stankiewicz, Richard Jun 67 obit May 83

Stanky, Eddie Jun 51 obit Aug 99

Stanky, Edward Raymond *see* Stanky, Eddie

Stanley, Freelan O. obit Nov 40

Stanley, Kim May 55 obit Jan

2002

Stanley, Oliver Apr 43 obit Jan 51

Stanley, Paul *see* Kiss

Stanley, Thomas B. Dec 55 obit Oct 70

Stanley, Wendell Meredith Apr 47 obit Sep 71

Stanley, Winifred Jun 43

Stans, Maurice H. Dec 58 obit Jun 98

Stanton, Andrew Feb 2004

Stanton, Bill May 2001

Stanton, Frank Nov 45 Oct 65

Stanwyck, Barbara Jul 47 obit Mar 90

Staples, Brent May 2000

Stapleton, Jean Dec 72

Stapleton, Maureen May 59

Stapp, John Paul Dec 59 obit May 2000

Stapp, Scott *see* Creed

Starch, Daniel Jan 63

Stargell, Willie Jun 80 obit Sep 2001

Stark, Harold Raynsford May 40 obit Oct 72

Stark, Louis Jun 45 obit Sep 54

Starkenborgh Stachouwer, A. W. L., Tjarda Van Feb 42

Starker, Janos May 63

Starkie, Walter Fitzwilliam May 64 obit Feb 77

Starr, Bart Jan 68

Starr, Cecile Mar 55

Starr, Chauncey Apr 54

Starr, Kenneth W. May 98

Starr, Louis E. Jun 47

Starr, Mark Jul 46 obit Jul 85

Starr, Ringo Dec 65

Starzl, Thomas E. Mar 93

Stassen, Harold E. May 40 Mar 48 obit May 2001

Statz, Hermann Jan 58

Staubach, Roger Apr 72

Staudinger, Hermann Apr 54 obit Nov 65

Stauning, Thorvald obit Jun 42

Stauss, Emil Georg Von obit

Feb 43

Stavropoulos, George Mar 85 obit Feb 91

Steacie, E. W. R. Jan 53 obit Nov 62

Steadman, Ralph May 99

Steagall, Henry Bascom obit Jan 44

Stearns, Harold E. obit Oct 43

Stebbins, George Coles obit Nov 45

Steber, Eleanor Mar 43 obit Jan 91

Steel, Danielle Jul 89

Steel, David Jul 78

Steel, Johannes Jun 41 obit Feb 89

Steel, Kurt *see* Kagey, Rudolf

Steele, Claude M. Feb 2001

Steele, Frederic Dorr obit Aug 44

Steele, Michael S. Jul 2004

Steele, Shelby Feb 93

Steell, Willis obit Mar 41

Steelman, John R. May 41 Nov 52 obit Nov 99

Steen, Marguerite Oct 41 obit Sep 75

Stefan, Paul obit Jan 44

Stefánsson, Vilhjalmur Oct 42 obit Nov 62

Stegner, Wallace Apr 77 obit Jun 93

Steichen, Edward Oct 42 Dec 64 obit May 73

Steig, William Jul 44 obit Apr 2004

Steiger, Rod Jun 65 obit Yrbk 2002

Stein, Benjamin J. Sep 2001

Stein, Gertrude obit Sep 46

Stein, Herbert Mar 73 obit Feb 2000

Stein, Jules May 67 obit Jun 81

Steinbeck, John Feb 40 May 63 obit Feb 69

Steinberg, Hans Wilhelm *see* Steinberg, William Sep 40

Steinberg, Milton Mar 40 obit

Apr 50

Steinberg, Saul Mar 57 obit Jul 99

Steinberg, William Mar 58 obit Jul 78

Steinbrenner, George Michael 3d Feb 79

Steincrohn, Peter J. Mar 57

Steinem, Gloria Mar 72 Mar 88

Steiner, George Oct 83

Steiner, Max Sep 43 obit Feb 72

Steiner, Walter Ralph obit Jan 43

Steinfeld, Jesse L. Apr 74

Steingraber, Sandra Sep 2003

Steinhardt, Laurence A. Jul 41 obit Apr 50

Steinhaus, Edward A. Dec 55

Steinkraus, Herman W. Nov 49 obit Jul 74

Steinman, D. B. Dec 57 obit Nov 60

Steinman, Mrs. John F. *see* Watkins, Shirley

Stekel, Wilhelm obit Aug 40

Stella, Antonietta Dec 59

Stella, Frank Apr 71 Apr 88

Stella, Joseph obit Dec 46

Stelle, John Jan 46 obit Sep 62

Steloff, Frances Nov 65 obit Jun 89

Stengel, Casey Jun 49 obit Nov 75

Stengel, Charles Dillon *see* Stengel, Casey

Stenmark, Ingemar Apr 82

Stennis, John C. Jan 53 obit Jul 95

Stephanie, Princess of Monaco Aug 86

Stephanopoulos, George Jan 95

Stephanopoulos, Stephanos Jul 55

Stephens, Hubert D. obit Apr 46

Stephens, John A. Dec 56

Stephens, Ward obit Nov 40

Stephens, William D. obit Jun

44

Stephenson, James obit Sep 41

Stepinac, Alojzije Feb 53 obit Apr 60

Stepovich, Michael A. Nov 58

Steptoe, Patrick Mar 79 obit Jun 88

Sterling, J. E. Wallace Jan 51 obit Aug 85

Stern, Arthur Cecil Apr 56 obit Jul 92

Stern, Bill Jun 41 obit Jan 72

Stern, David Apr 91

Stern, Howard Jan 96

Stern, Isaac Apr 49 Feb 89 obit Jan 2002

Stern, Leonard Mar 91

Stern, Martha Dodd *see* Dodd, Martha

Stern, Richard Jun 94

Stern, Robert A. M. Jun 2000

Sterne, Hedda Mar 57

Sterne, Maurice Apr 43 obit Oct 57

Stettinius, Edward R., Jr. Jul 40 obit Dec 49

Steuer, Max David obit Oct 40

Stevens, Edmund Jul 50 obit Jul 92

Stevens, George Apr 52 obit May 75

Stevens, George, Jr. Dec 65

Stevens, John Paul May 76

Stevens, Risë Nov 41

Stevens, Robert T. Jul 53 obit Mar 83

Stevens, Roger L. Dec 55 obit Apr 98

Stevens, Ted Oct 2001

Stevenson, Adlai E. Jan 49 Sep 61 obit Sep 65

Stevenson, Adlai E., 3d Apr 74

Stevenson, Bryan Mar 96

Stevenson, E. Robert Jan 40

Stevenson, Elizabeth (WLB) Yrbk 56

Stevenson, George S. Dec 46

Stevenson, McLean Jun 80

obit Apr 96

Stevenson, William E. Nov 43 obit May 85

Stever, H. Guyford Jan 81

Steward, David L. Nov 2004

Stewart, Alice Jul 2000 obit Yrbk 2002

Stewart, Anna Bird (WLB) Yrbk 48

Stewart, Donald Ogden Jul 41 obit Sep 80

Stewart, Ellen Jun 73

Stewart, George Craig, Bishop obit Jan 40

Stewart, George R. Jan 42 obit Nov 80

Stewart, Harris B., Jr. Mar 68

Stewart, James "Bubba" Feb 2005

Stewart, James Apr 41 Dec 60 obit Sep 97

Stewart, Jon Jul 2004

Stewart, Kenneth Dec 43

Stewart, Martha Aug 93

Stewart, Michael Sep 65 obit Jun 90

Stewart, Mrs. Gordon Neil *see* Johnson, Pamela Hansford

Stewart, Patrick Aug 94

Stewart, Potter Dec 59 obit Feb 86

Stewart, Rod Aug 79

Stewart, Thomas May 74

Stewart, William G. obit Sep 41

Stewart, William H. Apr 66

Stewart-Murray, John George, 8th Duke of Atholl *see* John George Stewart-Murray

Stickney, Dorothy Apr 42 [Lindsay, Howard; and Stickney, Dorothy] obit Aug 98

Stiebeling, Hazel K. Apr 50

Stiefel, Ethan Apr 2004

Stieglitz, Alfred Jan 40 obit Sep 46

Stigler, George Joseph Jul 83 obit Feb 92

Stignani, Ebe Feb 49 obit

Yrbk 91 (died Oct 74)

Stigwood, Robert Oct 79

Stikker, Dirk U. Feb 50 Feb 62

Stiles, Charles Wardell obit Mar 41

Still, Clyfford Sep 71 obit Aug 80

Still, William Grant Jan 41 obit Feb 79

Stiller, Ben Nov 99

Stillwell, Lewis Buckley obit Mar 41

Stilwell, Joseph W. May 42 obit Nov 46

Stilwell, Richard Feb 86

Stimson, Frederic Jesup obit Jan 44

Stimson, Henry L. Aug 40 obit Dec 50

Stimson, Julia Catherine Nov 40 obit Nov 48

Stine, Charles Milton Altland Jan 40 obit Sep 54

Stipe, Michael Apr 97

Stirnweiss, George Mar 46 obit Dec 58

Stock, Frederick obit Dec 42

Stockberger, W. W. Aug 41

Stockbridge, Frank Parker obit Jan 41

Stockhausen, Karlheinz Dec 71

Stockman, David Aug 81

Stockton, John Jun 95

Stockwell, Dean Feb 91

Stoddard, Alexandra Jun 96

Stoddard, Brandon Feb 89

Stoddard, Frederick Lincoln obit Mar 40

Stoddard, George D. Jul 46 obit Feb 82

Stoessel, Albert obit Jul 43

Stoessel, Mrs. Henry Kurt *see* Chastain, Madye Lee

Stoessel, Walter J., Jr. Jun 70 obit Feb 87

Stoica, Chivu Jan 59 obit Apr 75

Stokes, Anson Phelps, Jr. Jul

62 obit Jan 87

Stokes, Carl B. Apr 68 obit Jun 96

Stokes, Edward C. obit Dec 42

Stokes, I. N. Phelps obit Feb 45

Stokes, Richard R. Sep 51 obit Oct 57

Stokes, Thomas L. May 47 obit Sep 58

Stokowski, Leopold Feb 41 Jul 53 obit Nov 77

Stokowski, Olga Samaroff *see* Samaroff, Olga

Stolk, William C. Mar 53

Stoltenberg, Gerhard Sep 89 obit Mar 2002

Stolz, Mary (WLB) Yrbk 53

Stolz, Robert Aug 43 obit Aug 75

Stone, Abraham Mar 52 obit Oct 59

Stone, Edward C. Feb 90

Stone, Edward D. Jun 58 obit Sep 78

Stone, Hannah obit Sep 41

Stone, Harlan Fiske Aug 41 obit Jun 46

Stone, I. F. Sep 72 obit Aug 89

Stone, Irving Dec 67 obit Oct 89

Stone, John Charles obit Jul 40

Stone, Matt May 98 [Parker, Trey; and Stone, Matt]

Stone, Oliver Jun 87

Stone, Robert Jan 87

Stone, Sharon Apr 96

Stone, W. Clement Feb 72 obit Yrbk 2002

Stone, William S. Jun 60 obit Feb 69

Stonehaven, John Lawrence Baird, 1st Viscount *see* Baird, John Lawrence

Stookey, Charley Jan 40

Stoopnagle, Colonel Oct 47 obit Jul 50

Stoph, Willi Oct 60 obit Aug

99

Stoppard, Tom Jul 74

Storey, David Sep 73

Storey, Robert G. Nov 53

Storke, Thomas M. Dec 63

Storms, Harrison A., Jr. Jan 63 obit Sep 92

Storr, Anthony Jun 94 obit Sep 2001

Storr, Vernon Faithfull, Rev. obit Yrbk 40

Stott, John May 2005

Stout, Rex Mar 46 obit Jan 76

Stout, Ruth A. Jan 59

Stout, Wesley Winans Jun 41 obit Jan 72

Stout, William Bushnell Mar 41 obit May 56

Stowe, Leland Jul 40 obit Mar 94

Stowell, Clarence Warner obit Jan 41

Strachan, Paul A. Jan 52

Strachey, John Jun 46 obit Sep 63

Straight, Michael Aug 44 obit Yrbk 2004

Strait, George Feb 2000

Strakakis, Anastasia see Stratas, Teresa

Stranahan, Frank Sep 51

Strand, Paul Jul 65 obit May 76

Strang, Ruth Dec 60 obit Feb 71

Strasberg, Lee Oct 60 obit Apr 82

Strasberg, Susan May 58 obit Apr 99

Strasser, Otto Sep 40 obit Oct 74

Stratas, Teresa Jan 80

Stratemeyer, George E. Feb 51 obit Oct 69

Strathmore And Kinghorne, Claud George Bowes-Lyon, 14th Earl of see Bowes-Lyon, Claud George

Stratton, Dorothy C. Jun 43

Stratton, Julius A. May 63 obit Aug 94

Stratton, Samuel S. Jan 66 obit Jan 91

Stratton, William G. Apr 53 obit Aug 2001

Straub, Peter Feb 89

Straus, Jack I. Mar 52 obit Nov 85

Straus, Michael W. Jun 52

Straus, Nathan May 44 obit Nov 61

Straus, Oskar Mar 44 obit Mar 54

Straus, Percy Selden obit May 44

Straus, Roger W. Jul 52 obit Oct 57

Straus, Roger W., Jr. Aug 80 obit Yrbk 2004

Strauss, Anna Lord Nov 45 obit Apr 79

Strauss, Franz Josef Feb 57 Feb 87 obit Nov 88

Strauss, J. G. N. Jan 51

Strauss, Lewis L. Feb 47 obit Mar 74

Strauss, Richard Jul 44 obit Oct 49

Strauss, Robert S. Mar 74 Jul 92

Stravinsky, Igor May 40 Apr 53 obit May 71

Strawberry, Darryl Jun 84

Strawbridge, Anne West obit Nov 41

Streb, Elizabeth Apr 2003

Streep, Meryl Aug 80 Mar 97

Street, James (WLB) Yrbk 46 obit Nov 54

Street, Jessie Sep 47

Street, Picabo Apr 98

Streeter, Ruth Cheney Jul 43 obit Jan 91

Strehler, Giorgio Mar 91 obit Mar 98

Streibert, Theodore C. Feb 55 obit Mar 87

Streicher, Julius obit Nov 46

Streisand, Barbra Jun 64

Streit, Clarence K. May 40 May 50 obit Sep 86

Streuli, Hans Apr 57

Stridsberg, Gustaf obit Dec 43

Strijdom, Johannes Gerhardus May 56 obit Nov 58

Strike, Clifford S. Nov 49

String Quartet Fishman, Jon see Phish

Stritch, Elaine Jun 88

Stritch, Samuel Apr 46 obit Sep 58

Stroessner, Alfredo Dec 58 Mar 81

Stroman, Susan Jul 2002

Strömberg, Leonard, Rev. obit Sep 41

Strong, Anna Louise Mar 49 obit May 70

Strong, Lee A. obit Jul 41

Strong, Maurice F. Dec 73

Strong, William McCreery obit May 41

Strossen, Nadine Oct 97

Strouse, Norman H. May 60 obit Mar 93

Strout, Richard L. Apr 80 obit Oct 90

Struble, Arthur D. Nov 51 obit Jul 83

Strughold, Hubertus Jul 66

Struther, Jan Jan 41 obit Oct 53

Struthers, Sally Jan 74

Struve, Otto Oct 49 obit Jun 63

Struzan, Drew Mar 2005

Stuart, Duane Reed obit Oct 41

Stuart, Gloria Apr 98

Stuart, J. Leighton Oct 46 obit Nov 62

Stuart, James Everett obit Feb 41

Stuart, Jesse Aug 40 obit Apr 84

Stuart, Kenneth Feb 44 obit Dec 45

Studebaker, John Ward May

42 obit Oct 89

Studebaker, Mabel Nov 48

Studer, Cheryl Apr 92

Stuhlinger, Ernst Nov 57

Stummvoll, Josef Jun 60

Stump, Felix B. Jan 53 obit Sep 72

Sturdee, V. A. H. Jul 42

Sture-Vasa, Mary Alsop *see* O'Hara, Mary

Sturges, Preston Apr 41 obit Oct 59

Sturgis, Samuel D., Jr. Jan 56 obit Sep 64

Sturzo, Luigi Feb 46 obit Nov 59

Stutz, Geraldine May 83 obit Yrbk 2005

Styne, Jule May 83 obit Nov 94

Styron, William Jul 68 Jun 86

Suárez González, Adolfo May 77

Subah, Abdullah al-Salim al, Sheikh *see* Abdullah, Al-Salim Al Sabah, Sheikh of Kuwait

Subandrio Mar 63 obit Apr 2005

Suchocka, Hanna Jan 94

Sucksdorff, Arne Apr 56 obit Sep 2001

Suenens, Léon Joseph, Cardinal May 65 obit Jul 96

Sues, Ralf May 44

Suesse, Dana May 40 obit Jan 88

Sueyro, Saba H. obit Sep 43

Sugar, Bert Randolph Nov 2002

Suggs, Louise Jan 62

Sugiyama, Hajime obit Oct 45

Sugrue, Thomas Jun 48 obit Feb 53

Suharto *see* Soeharto

Suhr, Otto Apr 55 obit Nov 57

Suhrawardy, H. S. Apr 57 obit Jan 64

Sui, Anna Jul 93

Suits, Chauncey Guy Feb 50

obit Oct 91

Sukarno Sep 47 obit Sep 70

Sukarnoputri, Megawati Sep 97

Sullavan, Margaret Jul 44 obit Feb 60

Sullivan, A. M. Dec 53 obit Aug 80

Sullivan, Brian Dec 57

Sullivan, Daniel Feb 2003

Sullivan, Ed Sep 52 obit Nov 74

Sullivan, Francis L. Jun 55 obit Jan 57

Sullivan, Gael May 47 obit Jan 57

Sullivan, Harry Joseph *see* Sullivan, Brian

Sullivan, Harry Stack Nov 42 obit Feb 49

Sullivan, Henry J. Jun 58

Sullivan, John L. Sep 48 obit Oct 82

Sullivan, Leon H. Mar 69 obit Sep 2001

Sullivan, Leonore Kretzer Dec 54 obit Oct 88

Sullivan, Louis Wade Jul 89

Sullivan, Mrs. John B. *see* Sullivan, Leonore Kretzer

Sullivan, Walter Sep 80 obit Jun 96

Sullivan, William H. Aug 79

Sulloway, Frank J. Sep 97

Sultan of Brunei *see* Bolkiah, Muda Hassanal

Sultan, Daniel I. Jan 45 obit Feb 47

Sulzberger, Arthur Hays Mar 43 obit Feb 69

Sulzberger, Arthur O., Jr. Jan 97

Sulzberger, Arthur Ochs Nov 66

Sulzberger, C. L. May 44 obit Nov 93

Sulzer, William obit Jan 42

Sumac, Yma Dec 55

Summer, Donna Jul 79

Summerfield, Arthur E. Sep

52 obit Jun 72

Summers, Lawrence H. Jul 2002

Summerskill, Edith Clara Apr 43 Jul 63 obit Apr 80

Summerville, Slim obit Feb 46

Summitt, Pat Jun 2005

Sumner, Cid Ricketts (WLB) Yrbk 54

Sumner, James B. Jan 47 obit Oct 55

Sumner, Jessie Jan 45 obit Oct 94

Sumner, Mrs. G. Lynn *see* Picken, Mary Brooks

Sun Fo Oct 44 obit Dec 73

Sun Myung Moon *see* Moon, Sun Myung

Sun Wen Apr 2001

Sun Yat-Sen Apr 44 obit Jul 81

Sun, Chingling *see* Sun Yat-Sen

Sunay, Cevdet Mar 69 obit Aug 82

Sunderland, Thomas E. Apr 62 obit May 91

Suner, Ramon Serrano *see* Serrano Suner, Ramon

Sung Tzu-wen *see* Soong, T.V.

Sununu, John H. May 89

Surles, Alexander D. Nov 45 obit Dec 47

Susann, Jacqueline May 72 obit Nov 74

Suslov, Mikhail A. Feb 57 obit Mar 82

Susskind, David May 60 obit Apr 87

Sutherland, Donald Feb 81

Sutherland, George obit Sep 42

Sutherland, Graham Jan 55 obit Apr 80

Sutherland, Joan Dec 60

Sutherland, Kiefer Mar 2002

Sutton, George P. Jul 58

Sutton, Percy Mar 73

Suvero, Mark Di *see* Di Suvero, Mark

Suydam, Edward Howard obit Feb 41

Suyin, Han *see* Han Suyin

Suzman, Helen Nov 68

Suzman, Janet May 76

Suzuki, Chiyoko *see* Suzuki, Pat

Suzuki, Daisetsu Teitaro Oct 58 obit Nov 66

Suzuki, David T. Jul 95

Suzuki, Ichiro Jul 2002

Suzuki, Kantaro, Baron Aug 45 obit May 48

Suzuki, Pat Jan 60

Suzuki, Umetaro obit Nov 43

Suzuki, Zenko Jan 81 obit Yrbk 2004

Svanholm, Set Dec 56 obit Dec 64

Sveda, Michael Dec 54 obit Nov 99

Svinhufvud, Pehr Evind obit Apr 44

Swados, Elizabeth Feb 79

Swaggart, Jimmy Oct 87

Swallow, Alan Feb 63 obit Jan 67

Swank, Hilary Sep 2000

Swann, Donald Jan 70 obit May 94

Swann, W. F. G. Feb 41 Dec 60 obit Mar 62

Swanson, Gloria Sep 50 obit May 83

Swart, Charles R. Jun 60

Swarthout, Gladys Mar 44 obit Sep 69

Swartwout, Egerton obit Apr 43

Swayze, Patrick Mar 91

Swearingen, John E. Jan 79

Sweeney, Anne Jun 2003

Sweeney, James Johnson Mar 55 obit Jul 86

Sweeney, John J. Jun 96

Sweet, William Ellery obit Jul 42

Swenson, Alfred G. obit May 41

Swidler, Joseph C. Mar 64

obit Jul 97

Swift, Ernest John obit Dec 41

Swift, Gustavus F. obit Dec 43

Swift, Harold H. Feb 50 obit Sep 62

Swigert, Ernest G. Oct 57 obit Feb 87

Swing, Joseph M. Apr 59 obit Feb 85

Swing, Raymond Jan 40 obit Feb 69

Swings, Paul *see* Swings, Pol

Swings, Pol Dec 54

Swinton, Tilda Nov 2001

Swirbul, Leon A. Apr 53 obit Sep 60

Switzer, George obit Yrbk 40

Switzer, Mary E. Jan 62 obit Dec 71

Swoopes, Sheryl Jul 96

Swope, Gerard Sep 41 obit Feb 58

Swope, Herbert Bayard Nov 44 obit Sep 58

Syal, Meera Feb 2001

Syberberg, Hans Jürgen Apr 83

Sydney, Mrs. Basil *see* Keane, Doris

Sydow, Max Von Apr 67

Sykes, Charles H. obit Feb 43

Sykes, Eugene Octave obit Jul 45

Sykes, Richard Eddy, Rev. obit Nov 42

Syme, John P. Mar 57

Symes, James M. Dec 55 obit Sep 76

Symington, James W. Jun 68

Symington, Stuart Sep 45 Jul 56 obit Feb 89

Symons, Arthur obit Mar 45

Synge, Richard Lawrence Millington Nov 53

Syran, Arthur George Mar 50

Szasz, Thomas Stephen Jan 75

Szell, George Jun 45 obit Oct 70

Szent-Györgyi, Albert Jan 55

obit Jan 87

Szeryng, Henryk Jan 68 obit Apr 88

Szigeti, Joseph May 40 Mar 58 obit Apr 73

Szilard, Leo Jan 47 obit Jul 64

Szold, Henrietta Jan 40 obit Apr 45

Szyk, Arthur Nov 46 obit Oct 51

T'ien Keng-hsin *see* Tien, Thomas

Tabb, Mary Decker *see* Decker, Mary

Taber, Gladys (WLB) Yrbk 52 obit May 80

Taber, John Feb 48 obit Jan 66

Taber, Louis J. Jun 42 obit Dec 60

Tabouis, Genevieve Jan 40

Tae Woo, Roh *see* Roh Tae Woo

Tafawa Balewa, Abubakar *see* Balewa, Abubakar Tafawa

Tafel, Richard L. Feb 2000

Taffin de Givenchy, Hubert *see* Givenchy, Hubert De

Taft, Charles P. Jul 45 obit Aug 83

Taft, Helen obit Jul 43

Taft, Horace D. obit Mar 43

Taft, Mrs. William Howard *see* Taft, Helen

Taft, Robert A. May 40 Apr 48 obit Oct 53

Taft, Robert, Jr. Oct 67 obit Feb 94

Tagliabue, Paul Oct 92

Tagliavini, Ferruccio Jun 47 obit Apr 95

Tagore, Rabindranath obit Oct 41

Tainter, Charles Sumner obit May 40

Taintor, Anne Jun 2005

Tajiri, Satoshi Nov 2001

Takeshita, Noboru May 88 obit Nov 2000

Talal Jan 52 obit Sep 72

Talbert, Billy Mar 57 obit Jun

obit Jan 99

Taylor, Robert May 52 obit Jul 69

Taylor, Susan L. Feb 97

Taylor, Telford Dec 48 obit Aug 98

Taylor, Theodore B. Apr 76 obit Feb 2005

Taymor, Julie Feb 98

Tchelitchew, Pavel Mar 43 obit Oct 57

Tcherkassky, Marianna Nov 85

Tchernichovsky, Saul obit Dec 43

Te Kanawa, Kiri Nov 78

Tead, Ordway May 42 obit Jan 74

Teagle, Walter C. Jun 42 obit Feb 62

Teague, Olin E. Mar 52 obit Apr 81

Teague, Walter Dorwin May 42 obit Jan 61

Teale, Edwin Way Dec 61 obit Jan 81

Tebaldi, Renata Apr 55 obit Apr 2005

Tebbel, John (WLB) Yrbk 53 obit Mar 2005

Tebbit, Norman Nov 87

Tedder, Arthur William Tedder, 1st Baron Jan 43 obit Oct 67

Teitgen, Pierre-Henri Jan 53

Teixeira-Gomes, Manuel obit Dec 41

Tejada, Miguel Jun 2003

Teleki, Paul, Count obit May 41

Telkes, Maria Nov 50 obit Oct 96

Teller Jun 2000 [Penn and Teller]

Teller, Edward Dec 54 Nov 83 obit Sep 2004

Tello, Manuel Dec 59 obit Jan 72

Tempest, Marie obit Dec 42

Temple, Shirley see Black,

Shirley Temple

Temple, William Apr 42 obit Dec 44

Temple, William, Archbishop of Canterbury see Temple, William

Templer, Gerald Jul 52 obit Jan 80

Templeton, Alec Mar 40 obit May 63

Templewood, Samuel John Gurney Hoare, 1st Viscount see Hoare, Samuel John Gurney

Tempski, Armine Von obit Jan 44

Tenby of Bulford, Gwilym Lloyd George, Viscount see Lloyd-George, Gwilym

Tener, John Kinley obit Jun 46

Tenet, George J. Aug 99

Teng Hsiao-ping see Deng Xiaoping

Teng Hsi-hsien see Deng Xiaoping

Teng Wen-pin see Deng Xiaoping

Tennant, William George Feb 45 obit Sep 63

Tennenbaum, Irving see Stone, Irving

Tennent, David Hilt obit Mar 41

Tennstedt, Klaus Sep 83 obit Mar 98

Tenzing Norkey Oct 54 [Hunt, John; Hillary, Edmund; and Tenzing Norkey] obit Jul 86

Ter Poorten, Hein Mar 42

Ter-Arutunian, Rouben Jun 63 obit Jan 93

Terboven, Josef Nov 41 obit Jun 45

Teresa, Mother Sep 73 obit Nov 97

Tereshkova, Valentina Dec 63

Terhorst, Jerald F. Feb 75

Terhune, Albert Payson obit

Apr 42

Terkel, Studs Nov 74

Terra, Daniel J. Nov 87 obit Sep 96

Terra, Gabriel obit Nov 42

Terrell, Daniel V. Apr 54

Terrell, Mary Church Jun 42 obit Oct 54

Terrell, St. John Feb 66 obit Jan 99

Terry, C. V. see Slaughter, Frank G.

Terry, Luther L. Oct 61 obit May 85

Terry, Randall A. Jan 94

Terry-Thomas Mar 61 obit Mar 90

Tertz, Abram see Sinyavsky, Andrei D.

Terzian, Harutyun G. obit Oct 41

Tesich, Steve Aug 91 obit Sep 96

Tesla, Nikola obit Feb 43

Tetley, Glen Jun 73

Tetrazzini, Luisa obit Jan 40

Tevfik Rushdi Bey see Aras, Tevfik Rüstü

Tewson, Vincent Feb 52

Teyte, Maggie Dec 45 obit Jul 76

Thach, John Smith Dec 60

Thackrey, Dorothy S. see Schiff, Dorothy

Thadden-Trieglaff, Reinold Von Jul 59

Thain, John A. May 2004

Thaler, William J. Feb 60 obit Yrbk 2005

Thant, U Feb 62 obit Jan 75

Tharp, Louise Hall (WLB) Yrbk 55

Tharp, Twyla Oct 75

Thatcher, Margaret Jul 75 Nov 89

Thayer, Ernest Lawrence obit Oct 40

Thebom, Blanche Oct 48

Theiler, Max Jan 52 obit Oct 72

Thekaekara, Matthew P. May

Sep 64

Thorkelson, Jacob obit Jan 46

Thorn, James Dec 49

Thornburgh, Dick *see* Thornburgh, Richard L.

Thornburgh, Richard L. Oct 88

Thorndike, Edward L. Sep 41 obit Oct 49

Thorndike, Sybil Dec 53 obit Aug 76

Thorneycroft, Peter Dec 52 obit Aug 94

Thornhill, Arthur H. Apr 58 obit Mar 70

Thornton, Charles B. Feb 70 obit Jan 82

Thornton, Dan Feb 54

Thorp, Willard L. Jul 47 obit Jul 92

Thorpe, James Francis *see* Thorpe, Jim

Thorpe, Jeremy Oct 74

Thorpe, Jim Nov 50 obit May 53

Throckmorton, Cleon Sep 43 obit Dec 65

Thurber, James Mar 40 Oct 60 obit Jan 62

Thurman, Howard Jun 55 obit Jun 81

Thurman, Robert A. F. Sep 97

Thurman, Uma Aug 96

Thurmond, Strom Sep 48 Nov 92 obit Nov 2003

Thurow, Lester C. Nov 90

Thurso, Archibald Henry Sinclair Macdonald, 1st Viscount *see* Sinclair, Archibald

Thye, Edward J. Oct 51 obit Nov 69

Thyssen, Fritz May 40 obit Mar 51

Thyssen-Bornemisza De Kaszon, Hans Heinrich Feb 89 obit Yrbk 2002

Tiant, Luis Jun 77

Tibbett, Lawrence Feb 45 obit

Oct 60

Tice, George A. Nov 2003

Tice, Merton B. Jun 55

Ticker, Reuben *see* Tucker, Richard

Tiegs, Cheryl Nov 82

Tien, Thomas May 46 obit Oct 67

Tierney, John Aug 2005

Tietjens, Eunice obit Nov 44

Tiger, Lionel Jan 81

Tigerman, Stanley Feb 2001

Tijerina, Reies Lopez Jul 71

Tikhonov, Valentin *see* Payne, Robert

Tilberis, Elizabeth *see* Tilberis, Liz

Tilberis, Liz Nov 98 obit Jul 99

Tillich, Paul Mar 54 obit Dec 65

Tillinghast, Charles C. Feb 62 obit Oct 98

Tillstrom, Burr May 51 obit Feb 86

Tilson Thomas, Michael May 71 Jun 96

Tilzer, Harry Von *see* Von Tilzer, Harry

Timbaland Mar 2003

Timberlake, Charles B. obit Jul 41

Timberlake, Clare H. Jan 61

Timberlake, Justin *see* 'N Sync

Timerman, Jacobo Nov 81 obit Jan 2000

Timmerman, George Bell, Jr. Jan 57 obit Feb 95

Timoshenko, Semyon Aug 41 obit May 70

Tinbergen, Niko Nov 75 obit Feb 89

Tindemans, Leo Mar 78

Tinguely, Jean Jan 66 obit Oct 91

Tinker, Clarence L. Jun 42

Tinker, Grant A. Mar 82

Tinkham, George H. Apr 42

obit Oct 56

Tinney, Cal Feb 43

Tinney, Frank obit Jan 41

Tippett, Michael Sep 74 obit Mar 98

Tipton, Jennifer Jul 97

Tipton, Stuart G. Mar 67

Tisch, Laurence A. Feb 87 obit Yrbk 2004

Tisdel, Alton P. obit Jul 45

Tiselius, Arne Apr 49 obit Dec 71

Tishler, Max Mar 52 obit May 89

Tiso, Joseph Mar 43 obit May 47

Tisserant, Eugene Apr 63 obit Apr 72

Titov, Gherman Dec 62 obit Jan 2001

Titterton, Lewis H. Sep 43

Tittle, Y. A. Mar 64

Titulescu, Nicolas obit May 41

Tizard, Henry Jan 49 obit Dec 59

Tjarda *see* Starkenborgh Stachouwer, A. W. L., Tjarda Van

Tobe *see* Davis, Tobé Coller

Tobey, Charles W. Jun 41 Jul 51 obit Oct 53

Tobey, Mark Mar 57 obit Jun 76

Tobias, Channing H. Jul 45 obit Jan 62

Tobin, Daniel J. Nov 45 obit Jan 56

Tobin, Harold J. obit Aug 42

Tobin, James Oct 84 obit May 2002

Tobin, Maurice J. Jun 46 obit Oct 53

Tobin, Richard L. Nov 44 obit Nov 95

Toch, Maximilian obit Jun 46

Todd, Alexander Mar 58 obit Mar 97

Todd, Lord *see* Todd, Alexander

Todd, Mike Dec 55 obit Jun

58

Todd, Richard [actor] Dec 55

Todd, Richard [football player] May 82

Todt, Fritz obit Apr 42

Toffler, Alvin Apr 75

Togliatti, Palmiro Nov 47 obit Oct 64

Tojo, Eiki *see* Tojo, Hideki

Tojo, Hideki Dec 41 obit Jan 49

Tokugawa, Iyesato, Prince obit Jul 40

Toland, Edmund M. obit Jul 42

Toland, Gregg Jul 41 obit Nov 48

Tolbert, William R., Jr. Mar 74 obit Jun 80

Tolbukhin, Fedor I. May 45 obit Dec 49

Toledano, Ralph De Dec 62

Toledano, Vicente Lombardo *see* Lombardo Toledano, Vicente

Toledo, Alejandro Nov 2001

Toles, Thomas G. *see* Toles, Tom

Toles, Tom Nov 2002

Tolischus, Otto David Jan 40 obit Apr 67

Tolkien, J. R. R. (WLB) Yrbk 57 Oct 67 obit Nov 73

Tolle, Eckhart Feb 2005

Tollefson, Thor C. Feb 63

Tolstoi, Aleksei Nikolaevich, Count obit Apr 45

Tolstoy, Alexandra Apr 53 obit Nov 79

Tomás, Américo Deus Rodrigues Dec 58 obit Nov 87

Tomasi, Mari May 41

Tomasson, Helgi Apr 82

Tomba, Alberto May 93

Tomlin, Lily Sep 73

Tomorrow, Tom Apr 2000

Tompkins, Ewell *see* Ewell, Tom

Tone, Franchot May 40 obit Nov 68

Tong, Hollington K. Dec 56

obit Feb 71

Tooker, George Mar 58

Toon, Malcolm Jul 78

Tope, John Feb 50

Topping, Norman Feb 59 obit Jan 98

Tormé, Mel Mar 83 obit Aug 99

Torn, Elmore, Jr. *see* Torn, Rip

Torn, Rip Apr 77

Torp, Oscar Dec 52 obit Jul 58

Torre, Joe May 72 May 97

Torre, Victor Raul Haya de la *see* Haya De La Torre, Víctor Raúl

Torre-Bueno, Lillian de la *see* De La Torre, Lillian

Torrence, Gwen Jul 96

Torres Bodet, Jamie *see* Bodet, Jaime Torres

Torrey, E. Fuller Jul 98

Torrey, George Burroughs obit Jun 42

Torrijos Herrera, Omar Jul 73 obit Sep 81

Tors, Ivan Feb 69 obit Aug 83

Torvalds, Linus Jul 99

Toscani, Oliviero Sep 97

Toscanini, Arturo Jun 42 May 54 obit Mar 57

Totenberg, Nina Mar 96

Totty, Charles H. Jan 40

Touré, Ahmed Sekou Jun 59 obit May 84

Tourel, Jennie Feb 47 obit Jan 74

Tournier, Michel Apr 90

Toussaint, Jeanne Feb 55

Tovey, Donald Francis obit Sep 40

Tower, John G. Dec 62 obit Jun 91

Towers, Graham F. Feb 52

Towers, J. H. Oct 41 obit Jun 55

Towle, Katherine A. Jan 49 obit May 86

Towne, Robert Jun 89

Townes, Charles H. Mar 63

Townsend, Edward Water-

man obit May 42

Townsend, Harry E. obit Oct 41

Townsend, Lynn A. Sep 66 obit Yrbk 2000

Townsend, Robert [actor] May 94

Townsend, Robert [executive] Nov 70 obit Mar 98

Townsend, Willard S. Jan 48

Townshend, Pete Aug 83

Toy, Henry, Jr. May 52

Toynbee, Arnold Joseph Jul 47 obit Jan 76

Tozzi, Giorgio Oct 61

Trabert, Marion Anthony *see* Trabert, Tony

Trabert, Tony Jul 54

Tracy, Spencer Apr 43 obit Oct 67

Train, Arthur obit Feb 46

Train, Russell E. Oct 70

Trammell, Niles Sep 40 obit May 73

Trampler, Walter Nov 71 obit Jan 98

Traphagen, Ethel Dec 48 obit Jun 63

Trapp, Maria Augusta May 68 obit Jun 87

Trask, James D. obit Jul 42

Traubel, Helen Jan 40 Feb 52 obit Oct 72

Trautman, George M. Oct 51 obit Sep 63

Travell, Janet G. Dec 61 obit Oct 97

Travers, P. L. May 96 obit Jun 96

Travis, Randy Sep 89

Travolta, John Oct 78 May 96

Tre Cool *see* Green Day

Treanor, Tom obit Oct 44

Tree, Marietta Dec 61 obit Oct 91

Tree, Mrs. Ronald *see* Tree, Marietta

Trefflich, Henry Jan 53 obit Sep 78

Tregaskis, Richard Aug 43

obit Oct 73

Tremonti, Mark *see* Creed

Trenet, Charles Feb 89 obit Sep 2001

Trenkler, Freddie Jun 71 obit Yrbk 2001

Tresca, Carlo obit Mar 43

Trevino, Lee Nov 71

Trevor, William Sep 84

Trevor-Roper, H. R. Sep 83 obit Jul 2003

Tribe, Laurence H. Jul 88

Tridish, Pete Apr 2004

Trigère, Pauline Feb 60 obit Jul 2002

Trigg, Ralph S. Nov 50

Trillin, Calvin Jun 90

Trilling, Diana May 79 obit Jan 97

Trimble, David Jul 2000

Trimble, Vance H. Dec 60

Trinidad, Felix Feb 2000

Trintignant, Jean-Louis Jul 88

Trippe, Juan T. Aug 42 Feb 55 obit May 81

Tritt, Travis Feb 2004

Troost, Laurens Jan 53

Trotsky, Leon obit Oct 40

Trotta, Margarethe Von Nov 88

Trotter, Frank Butler obit Apr 40

Trotter, Lloyd Jul 2005

Trottier, Bryan Jun 85

Troubetzkoy, Amelie obit Jul 45

Trout, Robert Oct 65 obit Jan 2001

Troutt Powell, Eve May 2004

Trowbridge, Alexander B. Mar 68

Troyanos, Tatiana Aug 79 obit Oct 93

Troyat, Henri Mar 92

Trudeau, Arthur Gilbert Apr 58 obit Aug 91

Trudeau, Garry Aug 75

Trudeau, Pierre Elliott Nov 68 obit Jan 2001

True, Rodney Howard obit

May 40

Trueba, Andrés Martínez *see* Martínez Trueba, Andrés

Trueblood, D. Elton Jan 64 obit Mar 95

Truex, Ernest Jan 41 obit Sep 73

Truffaut, François Jan 69 obit Jan 85

Truitt, Paul T. Sep 48

Trujillo Molina, Rafael Leónidas Jul 41 obit Oct 61

Trulock, Mrs. Guy Percy Jan 57

Truman, Bess Feb 47 obit Jan 83

Truman, David B. Jan 72 obit Yrbk 2004

Truman, Harry S. Jan 42 Apr 45 obit Feb 73

Truman, Margaret Jun 50 Jun 87

Truman, Mrs. Harry S. *see* Truman, Bess

Trumbo, Dalton May 41 obit Oct 76

Trumka, Richard L. Apr 86

Trump, Donald J. Feb 84

Truscott, Lucian K. May 45 obit Nov 65

Trussell, C. P. Jul 49 obit Dec 68

Trussell, Ray E. Jan 71 obit Feb 2000

Trygger, Ernst obit Nov 43

Tryon, George Clement Tryon, 1st Baron obit Jan 41

Tryon, Thomas Jan 77 obit Nov 91

Tsai Yuan-pei *see* Cai Yuan-pei

Tsaldaris, Constantin Nov 46 obit Jan 71

Tsarapkin, Semyon K. Jun 60 obit Nov 84

Tschirky, Oscar Jan 47 obit Dec 50

Tshombe, Moise Dec 61 obit Sep 69

Tsiang, T. F. Jun 48 obit Dec

65

Tsongas, Paul E. Jul 81 obit Mar 97

Tsui Hark Oct 2001

Tsung-Hsi, Pai *see* Pai Tsung-Hsi

Tsung-Jen, Li *see* Li Tsung-Jen

Tubb, Ernest Oct 83 obit Oct 84

Tubman, William V. S. Jan 55 obit Sep 71

Tuchman, Barbara W. Dec 63 obit Mar 89

Tuck, William M. Dec 46 obit Aug 83

Tucker, B. Fain Dec 57

Tucker, Henry St. George Sep 43 obit Nov 59

Tucker, Richard Mar 56 obit Feb 75

Tucker, Sophie Apr 45 obit Mar 66

Tuckwell, Barry Jul 79

Tudjman, Franjo Sep 97 obit May 2000

Tudor, Antony Nov 45 obit Jun 87

Tufts, James Hayden obit Sep 42

Tugwell, Rexford G. Sep 41 Jan 63 obit Sep 79

Tull, Tanya Nov 2004

Tully, Alice Jan 84 obit Feb 94

Tune, Tommy Jan 83

Tung, Hsien-kuang *see* Tong, Hollington K.

Tunnard, Christopher Jun 59 obit May 79

Tunney, Gene Sep 40 obit Jan 79

Tunney, John V. Jun 71

Tuomioja, Sakari Mar 54 obit Nov 64

Tupolev, Andrei N. Jan 57

Tupou IV, Taufa'ahau *see* Taufa'ahau Tupou IV

Turabi, Hassan al- Jan 99

Turbay Ayala, Julio César Jul

obit Aug 81

Urrutia, Francisco Jun 58

Usery, W. J., Jr. Jun 76

Usher, Elizabeth R. May 67

Usman Ali, Nizam of Hyderabad Oct 48 obit Apr 67

Ustinov, Peter Dec 55 obit
Aug 2004

Utley, Freda Dec 58 obit Mar
78

Utley, George B. obit Nov 46

Utrillo, Maurice Sep 53 obit
Jan 56

Utterback, Hubert obit Jul 42

Vadim, Roger Jan 84 obit Aug
2000

Vagnozzi, Egidio Cardinal
Mar 67 obit Feb 81

Vail, Robert W. G. Feb 45
obit Jul 66

Vaizey, John Jan 64

Vajpayee, Atal Behari Aug
2000

Valente, Benita Mar 88

Valenti, Jack Jan 68

Valentina Dec 46 obit Nov 89

Valentine, Alan Dec 50 obit
Sep 80

Valentine, Bobby Jul 2001

Valentine, Lewis J. Jun 46
obit Feb 47

Valentine, Stephen see Allen,
Steve

Valentino Nov 73

Valenzuela, Fernando Oct 82

Valera, Eamon de see De Valera, Eamon

Valery, Paul Ambrose obit
Aug 45

Vallee, Rudy Jun 47 Apr 63
obit Aug 86

Valletta, Vittorio Jul 67 obit
Jul 67

Valtin, Jan Apr 41 obit Jan 51

Van Acker, Achille see Acker, Achille Van

Van Allen, James A. Jan 59

Van Arsdale, Harry May 69
obit Apr 86

Van Buren, Abigail May 60

Van Damme, Jean-Claude

Mar 99

Van Den Haag, Ernest Oct 83
obit Jul 2002

Van Devanter, Willis obit Mar
41

Van Doren, Harold Living-
ston May 40 obit Apr 57

Van Doren, Irita Sep 41 obit
Feb 67

Van Doren, Mark Jan 40 obit
Feb 73

Van Druten, John Feb 44 obit
Feb 58

Van Dusen, Henry P. Dec 50
obit Apr 75

Van Duyn, Mona Jan 98 obit
Nov 2005

Van Dyke, Dick Mar 63

Van Dyke, W. S., 2d obit Apr
43

Van Exel, Nick Mar 2002

Van Fleet, James A. Apr 48
obit Nov 92

Van Gundy, Jeff May 2001

Van Hamel, Martine Sep 79

Van Heusen, Jimmy Jun 70
obit Apr 90

Van Heuven Goedhart, G. J.
see Heuven Goedhart, G. J.
Van

Van Horne, Harriet Dec 54
obit Mar 98

Van Houtte, Jean see Houtte,
Jean Van

Van Karnebeek, Herman
Adriaan obit May 42

Van Kleffens, Eelco (Nico-
laas) see Kleffens, Eelco
Van

Van Konijnenburg, Willem
Adriaan see Konijnenburg,
Willem Adriaan Van

Van Loen, Alfred Feb 61

Van Loon, Hendrik Willem
obit Apr 44

Van Mook, Hubertus J. Apr
42 obit Jul 65

Van Nuys, Frederick obit Mar
44

Van Paassen, Pierre Oct 42

obit Mar 68

Van Peebles, Mario Nov 93

Van Pelt, John V. Dec 46 obit
Sep 62

Van Royen, Jan Herman see
Royen, Jan Herman Van

Van Sant, Gus Mar 92

Van Schmus, W. G. obit Mar
42

Van Slyke, Donald D. Jan 43
obit Jul 71

Van Starkenborgh Stachouw-
er, Alidius Warmoldus
Lambertus Tjarda see
Starkenborgh Stachouwer,
A. W. L., Tjarda Van

Van Volkenburg, J. L. Jan 55
obit Jul 63

Van Wagoner, Murray D.
Nov 41 obit Aug 86

Van Waters, Miriam Mar 63
obit Apr 74

Van Zandt, James E. Nov 50
obit Mar 86

Van Zeeland, Paul see
Zeeland, Paul Van

Vanbrugh, Violet obit Jan 43

Vance, Cyrus R. Dec 62 Nov
77 obit Apr 2002

Vance, Harold S. May 49 obit
Nov 59

Vance, John T. obit May 43

Vance, Marguerite (WLB)
Yrbk 51 obit Jul 65

Vance, William Reynolds obit
Yrbk 40

Vandegrift, Alexander Archer
Jan 43 obit Jun 73

Vandenberg, Arthur H. Nov
40 Jun 48 obit May 51

Vandenberg, Hoyt S. Mar 45
obit May 54

Vanderbilt, Amy Feb 54 obit
Feb 75

Vanderbilt, Arthur T. Feb 47
obit Oct 57

Vanderbilt, Cornelius, III obit
Apr 42

Vanderbilt, Gloria Jul 72

Vanderbilt, William K. obit

Feb 44

Vandercook, John W. Apr 42 obit Feb 63

Vandiver, S. Ernest Jul 62 obit Yrbk 2005

Vandivert, William Mar 63

Vandross, Luther Sep 91 obit Yrbk 2005

Vane, John R. May 86 obit Yrbk 2005

Vaness, Carol Sep 86

Vanier, George Philias Jan 60 obit May 67

Vann, Robert Lee obit Yrbk 40

Vanocur, Sander Jan 63

Vansittart, Robert Jul 41 obit Apr 57

Varda, Agnès Jul 70

Vardaman, James K., Jr. Apr 51

Vargas Llosa, Mario Feb 76

Vargas, Getúlio Dornelles Aug 40 May 51 obit Oct 54

Varian, Dorothy Jan 43

Varmus, Harold E. Nov 96

Varnay, Astrid May 51

Varnedoe, Kirk Feb 91 obit Yrbk 2003

Vasarely, Victor Feb 71 obit May 97

Vasilevsky, Alexander M. Oct 43 obit Mar 78

Vassallo, Ernesto obit Jan 40

Vatutin, Nikolai F. Feb 44

Vaughan Williams, Ralph Dec 53 obit Nov 58

Vaughan, Guy W. Dec 48 obit Jan 67

Vaughan, Harry H. Mar 49 obit Jul 81

Vaughan, Sarah Nov 57 Apr 80 obit May 90

Vaughn, Jack H. Apr 66

Vaughn, Robert Sep 67

Veeck, Bill Nov 48 obit Feb 86

Veeck, William Louis, Jr. *see*

Veeck, Bill

Vega, Suzanne Aug 94

Veidt, Conrad obit May 43

Veil, Simone May 80

Veiller, Bayard obit Aug 43

Vejjabul, Pierra Mar 64

Veksler, Vladimir I. Jan 65 obit Nov 66

Velasco Alvarado, Juan Jun 70 obit Mar 78

Velasco Ibarra, José María Nov 52 obit May 79

Velázquez, Nydia M. Jul 99

Velde, Harold H. Mar 53 obit Jan 86

Velez, Lupe obit Feb 45

Velikovsky, Immanuel May 57 obit Jan 80

Vendler, Helen May 86

Venizelos, Sophocles Dec 50 obit Mar 64

Venter, J. Craig Feb 95

Ventris, Michael Jan 57

Ventura, Jesse May 99

Venturi, Ken Apr 66

Venturi, Robert Jul 75

Vera-Ellen Feb 59 obit Oct 81

Verdier, Jean, Cardinal obit May 40

Verdi-Fletcher, Mary Jan 97

Verdon, Gwen Oct 60 obit Jan 2001

Verdy, Violette Dec 69 Oct 80

Vereen, Ben Apr 78

Verity, C. William, Jr. May 88

Vermeij, Geerat J. Jun 95

Vermilye, William Moorhead obit Oct 44

Vernon, Grenville obit Jan 42

Vernon, Lillian Mar 96

Veronese, Vittorino Jun 59

Verrett, Shirley Apr 67

Verrett-Carter, Shirley *see* Verrett, Shirley

Versace, Donatella Jun 98

Versace, Gianni Apr 93 obit Sep 97

Vertès, Marcel Apr 61 obit Jan 62

Verwoerd, H. F. Mar 59 obit

Nov 66

Vezin, Charles obit May 42

Vian, Philip Aug 44 obit Sep 68

Vick, Michael Nov 2003

Vickers, Jon Mar 61

Vickery, H. L. Dec 43 obit May 46

Vickrey, Dan *see* Counting Crows

Victor Emmanuel III, King of Italy Jul 43 obit Jan 48

Victor, Sally Apr 54 obit Jul 77

Vidal, Gore Feb 65 Jun 83

Videla, Gabriel González *see* Gonzalez Videla, Gabriel

Videla, Jorge Rafaél Apr 78

Vidor, King Feb 57 obit Jan 83

Vieira Da Silva, Maria Helena Dec 58 obit May 92

Vieira, Meredith Apr 2002

Vienot, Pierre obit Oct 44

Viereck, George Sylvester Nov 40 obit May 62

Viereck, Peter Apr 43

Vigneaud, Vincent du *see* Du Vigneaud, Vincent

Viguerie, Richard A. Jan 83

Vila, George R. Mar 63 obit Aug 87

Vilar, Jean Apr 62 obit Sep 71

Vilas, Guillermo Apr 78

Villain- Marais, Jean *see* Marais, Jean

Villa-Lobos, Heitor Apr 45 obit Jan 60

Villard, Oswald Garrison Aug 40 obit Nov 49

Villella, Edward Mar 65

Villemure, Gilles Apr 74

Villon, Jacques Jan 56 obit Jul 63

Vinatieri, Adam Sep 2004

Vincent, Fay May 91

Vincent, Francis Thomas, Jr. *see* Vincent, Fay

Vincent, George Edgar obit

Mar 41

Vincent, Leon H. obit Apr 41

Vine, Barbara *see* Rendell, Ruth

Vinson, Carl Apr 42 obit Jul 81

Vinson, Fred M. Aug 43 obit Nov 53

Vinton, Bobby Jul 77

Vinton, Stanley Robert, Jr. *see* Vinton, Bobby

Viola, Bill May 98

Vip *see* Partch, Virgil Franklin

Virilio, Paul Jul 2005

Viscardi, Henry, Jr. Jan 54 Dec 66 obit Yrbk 2004

Visconti, Luchino Jan 65 obit May 76

Vishinskii, Andrei May 44 obit Jan 55

Vishnevskaya, Galina Jul 66

Vishniac, Roman Feb 67 obit Mar 90

Visser 't Hooft, Willem Adolph May 49 obit Aug 85

Vitale, Dick Jan 2005

Vo Nguyen Giap Feb 69

Vogel, Hans Jochen Jan 84

Vogel, Herbert D. Dec 54

Vogel, Paula Jul 98

Vogelstein, Bert Jan 96

Vogt, William Mar 53 obit Sep 68

Voight, Jon Apr 74

Voigt, Deborah Jan 99

Voinovich, George V. May 97

Volcker, Paul A. Jul 73

Vollenweider, Andreas May 87

Volpe, John A. Feb 62 obit Jan 95

Volterra, Vito obit Yrbk 40

Von Arco, Georg Wilhelm Alexander Hans, Graf *see* Arco, Georg Wilhelm Alexander Hans Graf Von

Von Aroldingen, Karin *see* Aroldingen, Karin Von

Von Békésy, Georg *see*

Békésy, Georg von

Von Bock, Fedor *see* Bock, Fedor Von

Von Brauchitsch, Heinrich Alfred Hermann Walther *see* Brauchitsch, Heinrich Alfred Hermann Walther Von

Von Braun, Wernher Jan 52 obit Aug 77

Von Brentano, Heinrich *see* Brentano, Heinrich Von

Von Däniken, Erich May 76

Von Dardel, Nils *see* Dardel, Nils Von

Von Einem, Gottfried *see* Einem, Gottfried Von

Von Frisch, Karl *see* Frisch, Karl Von

Von Fürstenberg, Diane Sep 76

Von Galen, Clemens August *see* Galen, Clemens August Von

Von Hagen, Victor Wolfgang Mar 42

Von Hammerstein-Equord, Kurt *see* Hammerstein-Equord, Kurt Von

Von Hassel, Kai-Uwe *see* Hassel, Kai-Uwe Von

Von Hayek, Friederich A. *see* Hayek, Friedrich A. Von

Von Heidenstam, Karl Gustaf Verner *see* Heidenstam, Verner Von

Von Heidenstam, Rolf *see* Heidenstam, Rolf Von

Von Kallay, Nicolas *see* Kallay, Nicholas De

Von Karajan, Herbert *see* Karajan, Herbert von

Von Kármán, Theodore May 55 obit Jun 63

Von KleinSmid, Rufus B. *see* Kleinsmid, Rufus B. Von

Von Kleist, Paul Ludwig *see* Kleist, Paul Ludwig Von

Von Klenze, Camillo *see* Klenze, Camillo Von

Von Mannerheim, Carl

Gustaf Emil, Baron *see* Carl Gustaf Emil

Von Manstein, Fritz Erich *see* Manstein, Fritz Erich Von

Von Neumann, John Jul 55 obit Apr 57

Von Otter, Anne Sofie *see* Otter, Anne Sofie von

Von Paassen, Pierre *see* Van Paassen, Pierre

Von Papen, Franz *see* Papen, Franz Von

Von Parseval, August *see* Parseval, August Von

Von Reichenau, Walter *see* Reichenau, Walter Von

Von Ribbentrop, Joachim *see* Ribbentrop, Joachim Von

Von Rundstedt, Karl *see* Rundstedt, Karl Von

Von Sauer, Emil *see* Sauer, Emil Von

Von Seyss-Inquart, Artur *see* Seyss-Inquart, Artur Von

Von Stade, Frederica Aug 77

Von Stauss, Emil Georg *see* Stauss, Emil Georg Von

Von Sydow, Max *see* Sydow, Max Von

Von Szent-Györgyi, Albert *see* Szent-Györgyi, Albert

Von Tempski, Armine *see* Tempski, Armine Von

Von Thadden-Trieglaff, Reinold *see* Thadden-Trieglaff, Reinold Von

Von Tilzer, Harry obit Mar 46

Von Trapp, Maria Augusta *see* Trapp, Maria Augusta

Von Wagner-Jauregg, Julius *see* Wagner-Jauregg, Julius Von

Von Weingartner, Felix *see* Weingartner, Felix

Von Wicht, John Jan 63 obit Mar 70

Von Zell, Harry Jun 44 obit Jan 82

Von Zemlinsky, Alexander *see* Zemlinsky, Alexander

obit Jan 51

Walker, Waurine Feb 55

Wall, Art Dec 59 obit Feb 2002

Wall, Evander Berry obit Jan 40

Wallace, Ben Apr 2004

Wallace, Clayton M. Sep 48

Wallace, Dewitt Apr 44 [Wallace, Dewitt; and Wallace, Lila Acheson] May 56 obit May 81

Wallace, Euan obit Apr 41

Wallace, George C. Dec 63 obit Nov 98

Wallace, Henry A. Aug 40 Jan 47 obit Jan 66

Wallace, Irving Mar 79 obit Sep 90

Wallace, Lila Acheson May 56 [Wallace, Dewitt; and Wallace, Lila Acheson] obit Jul 84

Wallace, Lurleen B. Sep 67 obit Jul 68

Wallace, Mike Jul 57 Nov 77

Wallace, Myron Leon *see* Wallace, Mike

Wallace, Ruby Ann *see* Dee, Ruby

Wallace, Thomas W. obit Sep 43

Wallach, Eli May 59

Wallenstein, Alfred May 40 Apr 52 obit Mar 83

Waller, Fats Apr 42 obit Feb 44

Waller, Fred Feb 53 obit Jul 54

Waller, Robert James May 94

Waller, Thomas Wright *see* Waller, Fats

Wallerstein, Judith S. Nov 96

Wallgren, Mon C. Nov 48 obit Nov 61

Wallis, Jim Jul 2005

Wallop, Douglass (WLB) Yrbk 56 obit Jun 85

Waln, Nora Jan-Feb 40 obit

Nov 64

Walpole, Hugh obit Jul 41

Walsh, Bill Nov 89

Walsh, Chad Feb 62 obit Mar 91

Walsh, George Ethelbert obit Apr 41

Walsh, J. Raymond Nov 46

Walsh, James J. obit Apr 42

Walsh, John Jul 2001

Walsh, Joseph obit Mar 46

Walsh, Lawrence E. Oct 91

Walsh, Mrs. Richard J. *see* Buck, Pearl

Walsh, William B. May 62 obit Mar 97

Walsh, William Henry obit May 41

Walsh, William Thomas Jul 41 obit Mar 49

Waltari, Mika Feb 50 obit Oct 79

Walter, Bruno Nov 42 obit Apr 62

Walter, Eugene obit Nov 41

Walter, Francis E. Jun 52 obit Jul 63

Walter, Wilmer obit Oct 41

Walters, Barbara Feb 71 Feb 2003

Walters, Vernon A. Feb 88 obit Jul 2002

Walton, Bill Mar 77

Walton, Ernest T. S. Mar 52 obit Sep 95

Walton, Sam Mar 92 obit Mar 92

Walton, William Mar 40 obit May 83

Walworth, Arthur Dec 59 obit Yrbk 2005

Wambaugh, Eugene obit Sep 40

Wambaugh, Joseph Mar 80

Wambaugh, Sarah Apr 46 obit Jan 56

Wampler, Cloud Dec 52

Wan, Prince Jun 54

Wanamaker, Pearl A. Sep 46

Wang Chao-ming *see* Wang

Ching-Wei

Wang Ching-Wei May 40 obit Jan 45

Wang Shih-Chieh Sep 45 obit Jun 81

Wang, An Jan 87 obit May 90

Wang, Ping-Nan Dec 58

Wangchuk, Jigme Dorji, Druk Gyalpo of Bhutan Oct 56 obit Sep 72

Wanger, Walter Jun 47 obit Jan 69

Wank, Roland Dec 43 obit Jul 70

Wapner, Joseph A. Sep 89

Warburg, James P. Apr 48 obit Jul 69

Warburton, Herbert B. Nov 51

Ward, Barbara Jan 50 Jan 77 obit Jul 81

Ward, Benjamin Aug 88 obit Yrbk 2002

Ward, Christopher L. obit Apr 43

Ward, Donovan F. Mar 65

Ward, Douglas Turner Sep 76

Ward, Lem obit Jan 43

Ward, Maisie Jan 66 obit Mar 75

Ward, Mary Jane Jun 46

Ward, Paul L. Mar 62

Ward, Robert Jul 63

Ward, William E. Nov 2005

Ware, David S. Sep 2003

Ware, Wallace *see* Karp, David

Warhol, Andy Feb 68 Jul 86 obit Apr 87

Waring, Fred Sep 40 obit Sep 84

Waring, George J., Mgr. obit Apr 43

Waring, J. Waties Dec 48 obit Mar 68

Waring, Roane Dec 43 obit Dec 58

Warne, William E. Nov 52 obit May 96

Warnecke, John Carl Jul 68

Warner, Albert Jan 45 [Warner, Albert; Warner, Harry M; and Warner, Jack L.] obit Jan 68

Warner, Edward P. Oct 49 obit Sep 58

Warner, Harry M. Jan 45 [Warner, Albert; Warner, Harry M; and Warner, Jack L.] obit Oct 58

Warner, Jack L. Jan 45 [Warner, Albert; Warner, Harry M; and Warner, Jack L.] obit Nov 78

Warner, John Christian Oct 50 obit Jul 89

Warner, John W. Nov 76

Warner, Milo J. Nov 41

Warner, Ty Nov 98

Warner, W. Lloyd Dec 59 obit Jul 70

Warnke, Paul C. Aug 77 obit Feb 2002

Warren, Althea Feb 42 obit Feb 60

Warren, Avra M. Feb 55 obit Mar 57

Warren, Diane Jun 2000

Warren, Earl Jan 44 Jan 54 obit Sep 74

Warren, Edgar L. Jul 47

Warren, Fletcher Jul 60 obit Mar 92

Warren, Fuller Dec 49

Warren, Harry Jun 43 obit Nov 81

Warren, Harry Marsh, Rev. obit Feb 41

Warren, Leonard Dec 53 obit Apr 60

Warren, Lindsay C. Nov 49

Warren, Robert Penn Jun 70 obit Nov 89

Warren, Shields Jun 50 obit Sep 80

Warren, Whitney obit Mar 43

Warren, William C. Jan 60 obit Yrbk 2000

Warwick, Dionne Feb 69

Wash, Carlyle H. obit Mar 43

Washburn, Bradford Jun 66

Washburn, Gordon Bailey

Dec 55

Washington, Alonzo May 99

Washington, Denzel Jul 92

Washington, Harold Feb 84 obit Jan 88

Washington, Walter E. Jul 68 obit Yrbk 2004

Wasilewska, Wanda Jul 44 obit Oct 64

Wason, Betty Aug 43

Wason, Edward H. obit Apr 41

Wason, Robert R. Jan 46 obit Sep 50

Wasserburg, Gerald J. Mar 86

Wasserman, Lew R. May 91 obit Yrbk 2002

Wasserstein, Wendy Jul 89

Waste, William Harrison obit Jul 40

Waterlow, Sydney P. obit Jan 45

Waterman, Alan T. Jun 51 obit Feb 68

Waters, Alice Jan 2004

Waters, Ethel Apr 41 Mar 51 obit Oct 77

Waters, James R. obit Jan 46

Waters, John Jun 90

Waters, Maxine Nov 92

Waters, Muddy May 81 obit Jun 83

Waterston, Sam Sep 85

Watkins, Arthur V. Jul 50 obit Dec 73

Watkins, Donald Jan 2003

Watkins, Gloria see Hooks, Bell

Watkins, James D. Mar 89

Watkins, Levi Jr. Mar 2003

Watkins, Shirley (WLB) Yrbk 58

Watkinson, Harold Mar 60

Watrous, George Dutton obit Yrbk 40

Watrous, Harry Willson obit Jan 40

Watson, Arthel Lane see Watson, Doc

Watson, Arthur K. Sep 71 obit

Oct 74

Watson, Burl S. Apr 57

Watson, Clarence Wayland obit Jul 40

Watson, Doc Feb 2003

Watson, Edwin M. obit Apr 45

Watson, Jack H., Jr. Nov 80

Watson, James D. Apr 63 Oct 90

Watson, John B. Oct 42 obit Dec 58

Watson, Lucile Dec 53 obit Sep 62

Watson, Mark S. Nov 46 obit Apr 66

Watson, Pearl Yvonne see Burke, Yvonne Brathwaite

Watson, Samuel Newell, Rev. obit May 42

Watson, Thomas J., Jr. Feb 56 obit Mar 94

Watson, Thomas J., Sr. Nov 40 Jul 50 obit Sep 56

Watson, Tom Jul 79

Watson-Watt, Robert Sep 45 obit Jan 74

Watt, Donald Jan 58

Watt, James G. Jan 82

Watt, Robert J. Mar 45 obit Sep 47

Wattenberg, Ben J. Jun 85

Wattleton, Faye Jan 90

Watts, Alan Mar 62 obit Jan 74

Watts, André May 68

Watts, Heather May 83

Watts, J. C. Jr. Mar 99

Watts, Julius Caesar see Watts, J. C. Jr.

Watts, Lyle F. Oct 46

Waugh, Auberon May 90 obit May 2001

Waugh, Frederick Judd obit Oct 40

Waugh, Samuel C. Dec 55 obit Oct 70

Waugh, Sidney Jul 48 obit Sep 63

Wavell, Archibald, 1st Earl

Mar 41 obit Jul 50

Waverley, John Anderson, 1st Viscount *see* Anderson, John

Waxman, Henry A. Jul 92

Wayans, Damon Nov 99

Wayans, Keenen Ivory Feb 95

Wayans, Marlon *see* Wayans, Shawn and Marlon

Wayans, Shawn and Marlon May 2001

Waymack, W. W. Mar 47 obit Jan 61

Wayne, David Jun 56 obit Apr 95

Wayne, John Feb 51 Jul 72 obit Aug 79

Weafer, Elizabeth Jan 58

Weafer, Mrs. Eugene C. *see* Weafer, Elizabeth

Weagant, Roy A. obit Oct 42

Weaver, Affie obit Jan 41

Weaver, Arthur J. obit Nov 45

Weaver, Dennis Nov 77

Weaver, Earl Feb 83

Weaver, Fritz Jan 66

Weaver, Pat Jan 55 obit Yrbk 2002

Weaver, Robert Clifton Apr 61 obit Oct 97

Weaver, Sigourney Mar 89

Weaver, Sylvester L., Jr. Jan 55

Weaver, Sylvester *see* Weaver, Pat

Weaver, Walter Reed obit Dec 44

Weaver, Warren Apr 52 obit Feb 79

Webb, Aileen O. Dec 58 obit Oct 79

Webb, Beatrice obit Jun 43

Webb, Clifton Mar 43 obit Dec 66

Webb, Jack May 55 obit Mar 83

Webb, James E. Oct 46 May 62 obit May 92

Webb, James H., Jr. Aug 87

Webb, Karrie Aug 2001

Webb, Loretta *see* Lynn, Lor-

etta

Webb, Maurice May 50 obit Sep 56

Webb, Mrs. Vanderbilt *see* Webb, Aileen O.

Webb, Walter Loring obit Mar 41

Webb, Wellington E. Aug 99

Webb, William Flood Dec 48

Webber, Andrew Lloyd *see* Lloyd Webber, Andrew

Webber, Chris May 2003

Weber, Dick Jun 70 obit Yrbk 2005

Weber, Joseph M. obit Jul 42

Weber, Louis Lawrence obit Mar 40

Weber, Max Jun 41 obit Dec 61

Webster, H. T. Mar 45 obit Nov 52

Webster, Margaret May 40 Sep 50 obit Jan 73

Webster, William H. Aug 78

Webster, William May 50 obit Jul 72

Wechsberg, Joseph Apr 55 obit Jun 83

Wecter, Dixon Nov 44 obit Sep 50

Wedel, Cynthia Clark Mar 70 obit Oct 86

Wedemeyer, Albert C. Jan 45 obit Feb 90

Wedgwood of Barlaston, Josiah Clement Wedgwood, 1st Baron *see* Wedgwood, Josiah C.

Wedgwood, C. V. Jan 57 obit May 97

Wedgwood, Josiah C. Apr 42 obit Sep 43

Weede, Robert Feb 57 obit Sep 72

Weeks, Edward Dec 47 obit May 89

Weeks, Sinclair Mar 53 obit Mar 72

Wegman, William May 92

Wegner, Nicholas H. Dec 49

obit May 76

Wei Jingsheng Sep 97

Wei Tao-Ming Dec 42

Weicker, Lowell P., Jr. Jan 74 May 93

Weidenbaum, Murray L. Mar 82

Weider, Joe Jan 98

Weidlein, Edward R. Jul 48 obit Nov 83

Weidman, Charles Apr 42 [Humphrey, Doris; and Weidman, Charles] obit Sep 75

Weidman, Jerome Aug 42 obit Jan 99

Weigle, Luther Allan Mar 46 obit Oct 76

Weil, Andrew Aug 96

Weil, Frank L. Feb 49 obit Jan 58

Weil, Lisl Jan 58

Weil, Richard, Jr. Jul 51 obit Jul 58

Weill, Kurt Dec 41 obit May 50

Weill, Sanford I. Jul 99

Wein, George Oct 85

Weinberg, Alvin M. Sep 66

Weinberg, Robert A. Jun 83

Weinberger, Caspar W. Jun 73

Weingartner, Felix obit Jun 42

Weinrig, Gary Lee *see* Rush

Weinstein, Bob Mar 97 [Weinstein, Harvey; and Weinstein, Bob]

Weinstein, Harvey Mar 97 [Weinstein, Harvey; and Weinstein, Bob]

Weir, Ernest T. Jun 41 obit Oct 57

Weir, Peter Aug 84

Weis, Jessica McCullough Dec 59 [Weis, Jessica McCullough] obit Jun 63

Weis, Mrs. Charles W(illiam), Jr. *see* Weis, Jessica McCullough

Weisen, Jim *see* Palmer, Jim

Weisgal, Meyer W. Oct 72

May 83

Westcott, John Howell obit Jul 42

Westheimer, Ruth Jan 87

Westin, Av Aug 75

Westley, Helen obit Feb 43

Westminster, Archbishop of *see* Hinsley, Arthur

Westmore, Perc Oct 45 obit Nov 70

Westmoreland, William C. Jun 61 obit Nov 2005

Weston, Brett Feb 82 obit Mar 93

Westwood, Vivienne Jul 97

Wetmore, Alexander Feb 48 obit Mar 79

Wetter, Ernst Feb 42

Wexler, Jacqueline Grennan Mar 70

Wexler, Jerry Jan 2001

Wexler, Nancy S. Aug 94

Wexner, Leslie Feb 94

Weyerhaeuser, Frederick E. obit Nov 45

Weyerhaeuser, George H. Jul 77

Weyerhaeuser, Rudolph M. obit Sep 46

Weygand, Maxime Jan-Jun 40 obit Mar 65

Weymouth, Frank E. obit Sep 41

Weyrich, Paul Feb 2005

Whalen, Grover A. Sep 44 obit Jun 62

Wharton, Clifton R. Jul 58 obit Jun 90

Wharton, Clifton R., Jr. Feb 87

Wheat, Alfred Adams obit Apr 43

Wheat, William Howard obit Apr 44

Wheaton, Anne Jan 58 obit May 77

Wheaton, Elizabeth Lee Jan 42

Wheeldon, Christopher Mar 2004

Wheeler, Burton K. Aug 40

obit Feb 75

Wheeler, Earle G. Nov 65 obit Feb 76

Wheeler, John Archibald Jan 70

Wheeler, Mortimer Mar 56 obit Sep 76

Wheeler, Mrs. Post *see* Rives, Hallie Erminie

Wheeler, Raymond A. Apr 57 obit Apr 74

Wheelock, Warren Mar 40 obit Oct 60

Wheelwright, Jere (WLB) Yrbk 52 obit Mar 61

Wheelwright, John B. obit Nov 40

Whelan, Wendy Oct 98

Wherry, Kenneth S. Apr 46 obit Jan 52

Whipple, Fred L. May 52 obit Yrbk 2005

Whipple, Maurine Mar 41

Whipple, Wayne obit Dec 42

Whitaker, Douglas Nov 51 obit Dec 73

Whitaker, Forest Feb 97

Whitaker, Mark Aug 2003

Whitcomb, Richard T. Dec 56

White Stripes Sep 2003

White, Alexander M. Jul 51 obit Jan 69

White, Betty Jun 87

White, Byron R. Dec 62 obit Jul 2002

White, Charles M. Jun 50 obit Mar 77

White, E. B. Oct 60 obit Nov 85

White, Edmund Jan 91

White, Edward H., 2d Nov 65 obit Mar 67

White, Francis W. Jan 54 obit Jun 57

White, Frank [broadcasting executive] Dec 50 obit Jan 80

White, Frank [governor] obit May 40

White, Gilbert F. Mar 53

White, Harry D. Sep 44 obit

Oct 48

White, Helen Constance Jul 45

White, Herbert S. May 68

White, Hugh L. Dec 55 obit Nov 65

White, I. D. Dec 58 obit Aug 90

White, Isaac Davis *see* White, I. D.

White, Jack *see* White Stripes

White, John F. Nov 67 obit Yrbk 2005

White, John R. Jan 56

White, Josh Aug 44 obit Nov 69

White, Katharine Elkus Feb 65 obit Jun 85

White, Kevin H. Dec 74

White, Margaret Bourke *see* Bourke-White, Margaret

White, Mark Aug 86

White, Meg *see* White Stripes

White, Michael R. Mar 99

White, Nelia Gardner (WLB) Yrbk 50 obit Oct 57

White, Patrick Jun 74 obit Nov 90

White, Paul Dudley Dec 55 obit Dec 73

White, Paul W. Mar 40 obit Oct 55

White, Portia Mar 45

White, Reggie Nov 95 obit Yrbk 2005

White, Robert E. May 84

White, Robert M. Mar 64

White, Robert M., 2d Mar 60

White, S. Harrison obit Feb 46

White, Stewart Edward obit Nov 46

White, Theodore H. Apr 55 Apr 76 obit Jul 86

White, Thomas D. Dec 57 obit Feb 66

White, Trumbull obit Feb 42

White, Vanna Jan 88

White, W. Wilson Jan 59 obit Jan 65

White, Wallace H., Jr. May 48

Wilder, Laura Ingalls

Wilder, Thornton Aug 43 Nov 71 obit Feb 76

Wildmon, Donald Jan 92

Wile, Frederic William obit Jun 41

Wile, Ira S. obit Nov 43

Wiles, Andrew J. Mar 96

Wiley, Alexander Apr 47 obit Jan 68

Wiley, Richard E. Mar 77

Wiley, William Foust obit Oct 44

Wilgress, Dana Jan 54 obit Oct 69

Wilgus, Sidney Dean obit Mar 40

Wilhelm, Hoyt Jul 71 obit Yrbk 2002

Wilhelmina Jun 40 obit Jan 63

Wilhelmina, Juliana Louise Emma Marie see Juliana, Queen of The Netherlands

Wilhelmina, Queen of the Netherlands see Wilhelmina

Wilkens, Lenny Jul 96

Wilkins, Dominique May 95

Wilkins, Hubert Jan 57 obit Feb 59

Wilkins, J. Ernest Dec 54 obit Mar 59

Wilkins, Maurice H. F. Jun 63 obit Yrbk 2005

Wilkins, Robert W. Jul 58 obit Yrbk 2003

Wilkins, Roger Aug 94

Wilkins, Roy Jun 50 Jan 64 obit Oct 81

Wilkins, T. Russell obit Feb 41

Wilkinson, Bud see Wilkinson, Charles

Wilkinson, Charles Apr 62 obit May 94

Wilkinson, Ellen Jul 41 obit

Mar 47

Will, George F. Sep 81

Willard, John obit Nov 42

Willes, Mark H. Mar 98

Willet, Anne Lee obit Mar 43

Willet, Henry Lee Mar 47

William II, Emperor see Hohenzollern, Friedrich Wilhelm Victor Albert

Williams of Barnburgh, Thomas Williams, Baron see Williams, Tom

Williams, Alford Joseph Jr. Oct 40

Williams, Andy Feb 60

Williams, Anthony A. Oct 99

Williams, Armstrong May 2004

Williams, Aubrey Willis May 40 obit Apr 65

Williams, Benjamin see Fairless, Benjamin F.

Williams, Betty Mar 79

Williams, Billy Dee Apr 84

Williams, Brian Jul 98

Williams, Camilla Jun 52

Williams, Cliff see AC/DC

Williams, Clyde E. Jul 47

Williams, Dick Dec 73

Williams, Doug Feb 99

Williams, Edward Bennett Jan 65 obit Sep 88

Williams, Edwin G. May 50

Williams, Emlyn Feb 41 Apr 52 obit Nov 87

Williams, Eric Feb 66 obit May 81

Williams, Errick see Williams, Ricky

Williams, Esther Feb 55

Williams, Francis, Baron see Francis-Williams

Williams, G. Mennen Apr 49 Jun 63 obit Mar 88

Williams, Gluyas Jun 46 obit Apr 82

Williams, Hank, Jr. Mar 98

Williams, Harrison A., Jr. Oct 60 obit Mar 2002

Williams, Jay (WLB) Yrbk 55

obit Sep 78

Williams, Jody Mar 98

Williams, Joe Apr 85 obit Jun 99

Williams, John [composer] Oct 80

Williams, John [guitarist] Jul 83

Williams, John A. Oct 94

Williams, John Bell Mar 64 obit May 83

Williams, John D. obit May 41

Williams, John H. Jan 60 obit May 66

Williams, John J. Jan 52 obit Apr 88

Williams, Joseph John, Father obit Yrbk 40

Williams, Lucinda Mar 99

Williams, Mary Lou Nov 66 obit Jul 81

Williams, Michelle see Destiny's Child

Williams, Myrna see Loy, Myrna

Williams, Paul Jun 83

Williams, Paul R. Mar 41 obit Mar 80

Williams, Pharrell see Neptunes

Williams, Ralph E. obit Jul 40

Williams, Ralph Vaughan see Vaughan Williams, Ralph

Williams, Ricky Aug 99

Williams, Robert R. Sep 51 obit Dec 65

Williams, Robin Jun 79 Jan 97

Williams, Roger J. Jul 57 obit Apr 88

Williams, Serena see Williams, Venus and Williams, Serena

Williams, Shirley Oct 76

Williams, Ted Apr 47 obit Oct 2002

Williams, Tennessee Jan 46 Apr 72 obit Apr 83

Williams, Theodore Samuel

Apr 72

Winchester, Alice Feb 54

Windsor, Duke of *see* Windsor, Edward

Windsor, Edward Sep 44 [Windsor, Edward, Duke of; and Windsor, Wallis, Duchess of] obit Jul 72

Windsor, Wallis Warfield Sep 44 [Windsor, Edward, Duke of; and Windsor, Wallis, Duchess of] obit Jun 86

Windust, Bretaigne Mar 43 obit May 60

Winfield, Dave Jan 84

Winfrey, Oprah Mar 87

Wingate, Orde Charles obit May 44

Winger, Debra Jul 84

Winiarski, Bohdan Feb 62

Winkler, Henry Sep 76

Winpisinger, William W. Feb 80 obit Feb 98

Winpisinger, Wimp *see* Winpisinger, William W.

Winslow, Anne Goodwin (WLB) Yrbk 48

Winsor, Frederick obit Jan 41

Winsor, Kathleen Dec 46 obit Yrbk 2003

Winster, Baron Feb 46

Winston, Harry Apr 65 obit Feb 79

Winston, Stan Jul 2002

Winter, Ella (WLB) Yrbk 46 obit Sep 80

Winter, Fritz Mar 58

Winter, George B. obit May 40

Winter, Paul Oct 87

Winters, Jonathan Mar 65

Winters, Shelley Apr 52

Winthrop, Beekman obit Yrbk 40

Wintour, Anna Jul 90

Wirth, Conrad L. Sep 52 obit Sep 93

Wirth, Timothy E. Mar 91

Wirtz, W. Willard Nov 46 Feb 63

Wise, James Decamp Apr 54

obit Apr 84

Wise, Robert Sep 89

Wise, Stephen S. Jul 41 obit May 49

Wiseman, Frederick Dec 74

Witherow, W. P. Apr 42 obit Mar 60

Witherspoon, Reese Jan 2004

Witos, Wincenty obit Dec 45

Witt, James Lee Mar 2000

Witt, Katarina Jul 88

Witte, Edwin E. Jul 46 obit Sep 60

Witten, Edward Jun 97

Wodehouse, P. G. Nov 71 obit Apr 75

Woese, Carl R. Jun 2003

Wofford, Harris Apr 92

Wohl, Louis De *see* De Wohl, Louis

Woiwode, Larry Mar 89

Wojciechowska, Maia Sep 76 obit Yrbk 2002

Wojtyla, Karol Jozef *see* John Paul II

Wolchok, Sam Oct 48 obit Mar 79

Wolcott, Jesse P. Dec 49 obit Apr 69

Wolf, Alfred, Rabbi Mar 58

Wolf, Naomi Nov 93

Wolfe, Art Jun 2005

Wolfe, Deborah Partridge Dec 62

Wolfe, George C. Mar 94

Wolfe, Hugh C. Feb 50

Wolfe, Humbert obit Jan 40

Wolfe, Julia Oct 2003

Wolfe, Tom Jan 71

Wolfenden, John Oct 70 obit Mar 85

Wolfenden, Lord *see* Wolfenden, John

Wolfensohn, James D. May 2000

Wolfert, Ira Apr 43 obit Feb 98

Wolff, Geoffrey Jan 97

Wolff, Maritta M. Jul 41 obit Yrbk 2002

Wolff, Mary Evaline *see*

Madeleva, Sister Mary

Wolfit, Donald Mar 65 obit Apr 68

Wolfowitz, Paul Feb 2003

Wolfram, Stephen Feb 2005

Woll, Matthew Jan 43 obit Sep 56

Wolman, Abel Feb 57 obit May 89

Wolman, Leo Sep 49 obit Dec 61

Wolper, David L. Oct 86

Woltman, Frederick Jul 47 obit Apr 70

Wonder, Stevie Mar 75

Wong Kar-Wai Apr 98

Wong Wen-Hao Nov 48

Wong-Staal, Flossie Apr 2001

Woo, John Feb 99

Wood, Charles Erskine Scott obit Mar 44

Wood, Edward Frederick Lindley, 3d Viscount H *see* Halifax, Edward Frederick Lindley Wood, 1st Earl of

Wood, Elijah Aug 2002

Wood, Grant Aug 40 obit Apr 42

Wood, Henry Joseph obit Oct 44

Wood, James Madison Feb 47 obit Dec 58

Wood, John Apr 83

Wood, John S. Jul 49 obit Nov 68

Wood, Kerry May 2005

Wood, Kingsley Nov 40

Wood, Louise A. Jul 61 obit Jul 88

Wood, Natalie Apr 62 obit Jan 82

Wood, Peggy Jul 42 Dec 53 obit May 78

Wood, Philip obit Mar 40

Wood, Robert D. Dec 74 obit Jul 86

Wood, Robert E. May 41 obit Dec 69

Wood, Sam Nov 43 obit Nov

49

Woodard, Alfre Feb 95

Woodard, Stacy obit Mar 42

Woodbridge, Frederick James Eugene obit Jul 40

Woodbury, Charles Herbert obit Jan 40

Woodcock, Charles Edward obit Mar 40

Woodcock, George Feb 64 obit Jan 80

Woodcock, Leonard Nov 70 obit Apr 2001

Wooden, John Jan 76

Woodham-Smith, Cecil Blanche Fitz gerald (WLB) Yrbk 55 obit Mar 77

Woodhouse, Barbara Feb 85 obit Aug 88

Woodhouse, Chase Going Mar 45 obit Apr 85

Woodley, Winifred see Hedden, Worth Tuttle

Woodlock, Thomas Francis obit Sep 45

Woodruff, Judy Sep 86

Woods, Bill M. May 66 obit Sep 74

Woods, Donald Feb 82 obit Nov 2001

Woods, Eldrick see Woods, Tiger

Woods, George D. Jul 65 obit Oct 82

Woods, James Nov 89

Woods, Mark Mar 46

Woods, Tiger Nov 97

Woods, Tighe E. Oct 48 obit Sep 74

Woodsmall, Ruth F. Jul 49 obit Jul 63

Woodson, Carter G. Feb 44 obit Yrbk 84 (died Apr 50)

Woodson, Rod Oct 2004

Woodsworth, J. S. obit May 42

Woodward, Arthur Smith obit Oct 44

Woodward, Bob Nov 76

Woodward, C. Vann May 86

obit Jun 2000

Woodward, Joanne Jun 58

Woodward, Patti see Darwell, Jane

Woodward, R. B. Feb 52 obit Sep 79

Woodward, Robert F. Dec 62 obit Yrbk 2001

Woodward, Stanley Jun 51 obit Oct 92

Wooldridge, Anna Marie see Lincoln, Abbey

Wooldridge, Dean E. Apr 58 [Ramo, Simon; and Wooldridge, Dean E.]

Woolf, Leonard Dec 65 obit Oct 69

Woolf, Virginia obit May 41

Woollcott, Alexander Jun 41 obit Mar 43

Woollen, Evans, Jr. Dec 48 obit Apr 59

Woolley, Edgar Montillion see Woolley, Monty

Woolley, Leonard Dec 54 obit Apr 60

Woolley, Mary E. Mar 42 obit Nov 47

Woolley, Monty Jul 40 obit Jun 63

Woolton, Frederick James Marquis, 1st Earl Oct 40 Oct 50 obit Feb 65

Woolwich, Bishop Suffragan of see Robinson, John

Wootton, Barbara, Baroness Wootton of Abinger Feb 64

Worcester, J. R. obit Jun 43

Worden, Edward Chauncey obit Nov 40

Work, Hubert obit Feb 43

Work, Martin H. May 51

Wörner, Manfred Oct 88 obit Oct 94

Worsham, Lew Jan 54 obit Jan 91

Worsley, Frank Arthur obit Mar 43

Worth, Irene May 68 obit Aug 2002

Worthington, Leslie B. Oct 60

obit Oct 98

Wouk, Herman (WLB) Yrbk 52

Wozniak, Stephen Jul 97

Wray, John Griffith obit May 40

Wren, Percival C. obit Jan 42

Wright, Anna Rose (WLB) Yrbk 52

Wright, Archibald Lee see Moore, Archie

Wright, Benjamin F. Jul 55 obit Mar 77

Wright, Berlin H. obit Jan 41

Wright, Fielding L. Sep 48 obit Jul 56

Wright, Frank Lloyd Jan 41 Nov 52 obit Jun 59

Wright, Harold Bell obit Jul 44

Wright, Helen Mar 56 obit Feb 98

Wright, Huntley obit Sep 41

Wright, Irving S. Oct 68 obit Mar 98

Wright, James Claud, Jr. see Wright, Jim

Wright, Jane C. May 68

Wright, Jeffrey May 2002

Wright, Jerauld Feb 55 obit Jul 95

Wright, Jim Apr 79

Wright, John J. Cardinal Feb 63 obit Oct 79

Wright, Louis B. Nov 50 obit Jun 84

Wright, Loyd Jul 55 obit Jan 75

Wright, Martha Feb 55

Wright, Michael Jul 61

Wright, Mickey Jan 65

Wright, Mrs. Donald McCloud see Meadowcroft, Enid

Wright, Orville Oct 46 obit Mar 48

Wright, Peter Feb 88 obit Jul 95

Wright, Quincy Oct 43 obit Dec 70

Wright, Richard Mar 40 obit

Jan 61

Wright, Robert Alderson Jul 45 obit Sep 64

Wright, Robert C. Jan 89

Wright, Ronald *see* Wright, Winky

Wright, Russel Sep 40 Dec 50 obit Mar 77

Wright, Steven May 2003

Wright, Teresa May 43 obit Yrbk 2005

Wright, Theodore P. Nov 45 obit Nov 70

Wright, Will Feb 2004

Wright, Winky Jul 2004

Wrigley, Philip K. Apr 75 obit Jun 77

Wrinch, Dorothy Jul 47

Wriston, Henry M. May 52 obit May 78

Wriston, Walter B. Nov 77 obit Aug 2005

Wrong, Hume Oct 50 obit Mar 54

Wrynn, Dylan *see* Tridish, Pete

Wu Yifang Aug 45 obit Jan 86

Wu, Chien-Shiung Oct 59 obit Apr 97

Wu, Gordon Sep 96

Wu, Harry Feb 96

Wu, K. C. *see* Wu, Kuo-Cheng

Wu, Kuo-Cheng Feb 53 obit Aug 84

Wu, Peter Hongda *see* Wu, Harry

Wuorinen, Charles Apr 72

Wurf, Jerry Jun 79 obit Feb 82

Wurster, William Wilson Nov 46 obit Nov 73

Wyatt, Jane May 57

Wyatt, John Whitlow Nov 41 obit Nov 99

Wyatt, Wilson W. Mar 46 obit Aug 96

Wyeth N. C. obit Nov 45

Wyeth, Andrew Apr 55 Nov 81

Wyeth, James Jan 77

Wylde, Zakk Oct 2004

Wyler, William Jan 51 obit Sep 81

Wylie, Max Jan-Feb 40 obit Nov 75

Wyman, Jane Mar 49

Wyman, Thomas Jun 83 obit Yrbk 2003

Wynder, Ernest L. Nov 74 obit Sep 99

Wynette, Tammy Jun 95 obit Jun 98

Wynkoop, Asa obit Dec 42

Wynn, Ed Jan 45 obit Jul 66

Wynonna May 96

Wyszynski, Stefan Cardinal Jan 58 obit Jul 81

Xenakis, Iannis Sep 94 obit Jul 2001

Xiaoping, Deng *see* Deng Xiaoping

Yadin, Yigael Feb 66 obit Aug 84

Yaffe, James (WLB) Yrbk 57

Yafi, Abdullah El- Jun 56

Yagudin, Alexei Feb 2004

Yahya Khan, A. M. Jan 71 obit Oct 80

Yalow, Rosalyn S. Jul 78

Yamaguchi, Kristi Jun 92

Yamamoto, Isoroko Feb 42 obit Jul 43

Yamamoto, Yohji Nov 2000

Yamanaka, Lois-Ann Jun 99

Yamani, Sheik Ahmed Zaki Sep 75

Yamasaki, Minoru Mar 62 obit Apr 86

Yamut, Nuri May 52

Yancey, Lewis Q. Alonzo obit Jan 40

Yang, Chen Ning Nov 58

Yang, Jerry Oct 97 [Yang, Jerry; and Filo, David]

Yang, You Chan Feb 53

Yankelovich, Daniel Mar 82

Yankovic, "Weird Al" Feb 99

Yankovic, Alfred *see* Yank-ovic, "Weird Al"

Yanks, Byron *see* Janis, Byron

Yaobang, Hu *see* Hu Yaobang

Yarborough, Cale Jan 87

Yarborough, Ralph W. Feb 60 obit Apr 96

Yard, Molly Nov 88

Yarmolinsky, Adam Mar 69 obit Jun 2000

Yaroslavsky, Emelyan obit Jan 44

Yarrow, William obit Jun 41

Yashin, Aleksei *see* Yashin, Alexei

Yashin, Alexei Jan 2003

Yassin, Ahmed Jul 98 obit Yrbk 2004

Yastrzemski, Carl May 68

Yates, Donald N. May 58

Yates, Elizabeth (WLB) Yrbk 48 obit Nov 2001

Yates, Herbert Jul 49 obit Mar 66

Yates, Sidney R. Aug 93 obit Jan 2001

Ybarra, Thomas Russell Jan 40

Ydígoras Fuentes, Miguel Nov 58

Yeager, Charles E. May 54

Yeager, Jeana May 87

Yeakley, Marjory Hall *see* Hall, Marjory

Yearwood, Trisha Jul 98

Yeats-Brown, Francis obit Feb 45

Yegorov, Boris Mar 68 obit Nov 94

Yeh Kung-chao *see* Yeh, George K. C.

Yeh, George K. C. Mar 53 obit Jan 82

Yellin, Samuel obit Nov 40

Yeltsin, Boris N. Jan 89

Yen, Y. C. James Jul 46 obit Mar 90

Yeoh Chu-Kheng *see* Yeoh, Michelle

Yeoh, Michelle Jan 98

Yepes, Narciso Oct 66 obit Jul

Carnegie, Hattie

Zanuck, Darryl F. Aug 41 Mar 54 obit Feb 80

Zapf, Hermann Jan 65

Zápotock, Antonín Jun 53 obit Jan 58

Zappa, Frank Feb 90 obit Feb 94

Zarb, Frank G. Sep 75

Zaroubin, Georgi N. Apr 53 obit Jan 59

Zatopek, Emil Apr 53 obit Feb 2001

Zeckendorf, William Mar 52 obit Nov 76

Zedillo Ponce De León, Ernesto Apr 96

Zeeland, Paul Van Mar 50

Zeeman, Pieter obit Dec 43

Zeffirelli, Franco Dec 64

Zeidler, Carl Frederick Jul 40 obit Feb 43

Zeineddine, Farid Feb 57

Zeisel, Hallie Burnett see Burnett, Hallie Southgate

Zellerbach, J. D. Dec 48 obit Nov 63

Zellweger, Renée Feb 2004

Zelomek, A. Wilbert Dec 56

Zemeckis, Robert Sep 97

Zemin, Jiang see Jiang Zemin

Zemlinsky, Alexander von obit May 42

Zenos, Andrew C. obit Mar 42

Zerbe, Karl Feb 59 obit Jan 73

Zerhouni, Elias Oct 2003

Zernike, Frits Feb 55 obit Apr 66

Zeta-Jones, Catherine Apr 2003

Zevin, Ben David Sep 43 obit Feb 85

Zhabotinskii, Vladimir Ev-genevich see Jabotinsky, Vladimir Evgenevich

Zhang Yimou Aug 92

Zhao Ziyang Jun 84 obit Yrbk 2005

Zhirinovsky, Vladimir Nov 95

Zhivkov, Todor Jan 76 obit Oct 98

Zhou Enlai see Chou En-Lai

Zhu Rongji Jul 2001

Zhukov, Georgi K. Feb 42 Apr 55 obit Sep 74

Zhukov, Georgy A. Oct 60

Zia Ul-Haq, Mohammad Jun 80 obit Sep 88

Ziegler, Karen Blanche see Black, Karen

Ziegler, Ronald L. Nov 71 obit Jul 2003

Ziemer, Gregor Apr 42

Ziff, William B. Oct 46 obit Feb 54

Zilboorg, Gregory Sep 41 obit Nov 59

Zim, Herbert S. Sep 56 obit Feb 95

Zimbalist, Efrem Mar 49 obit Apr 85

Zimbalist, Efrem, Jr. Feb 60

Zimmer, Hans Mar 2002

Zimmer, Henry obit May 43

Zimmerman, Alfred F. M. obit Jul 40

Zimmerman, M. M. Jul 57

Zimmerman, Robert see Dy-lan, Bob

Zindel, Paul Jun 73

Zinn, Howard Aug 99

Zinn, Walter H. Dec 55 obit Aug 2000

Zinnemann, Fred Mar 53 obit Jun 97

Zinni, Anthony C. May 2002

Zinsser, Hans obit Oct 40

Zirato, Bruno Dec 59 obit Jan 73

Ziskin, Laura Oct 97

Zito, Barry Jul 2004

Zivojinovich, Alex see Rush

Ziyang, Zhao see Zhao Ziy-ang

Zog I Aug 44 obit Jun 61

Zoli, Adone Mar 58 obit Apr 60

Zollar, Jawole Willa Jo Jul 2003

Zolotow, Maurice May 57

obit May 91

Zook, George F. Feb 46 obit Oct 51

Zorach, William Feb 43 Feb 63 obit Jan 67

Zorbaugh, Geraldine B. Dec 56 obit Sep 96

Zorin, Valerian A. Mar 53 obit Mar 86

Zorina, Vera Jan 41 obit Yrbk 2003

Zorlu, Fatin Rustu Dec 58 obit Nov 61

Zorn, John Aug 99

Zsigmond, Vilmos Oct 99

Zu Reventlow, Ernst, Graf see Reventlow, Ernst, Graf Zu

Zuazo, Hernán Siles see Siles Zuazo, Hernán

Zubiría, Alberto F. Dec 56

Zubrod, C. Gordon Jan 69 obit Jul 99

Zucker, Jeff Jan 2002

Zuckerman, Mortimer B. Jan 90

Zuckerman, Solly Jul 72 obit May 93

Zuckert, Eugene M. Apr 52 obit Yrbk 2000

Zukerman, Eugenia Jan 2004

Zukerman, Pinchas Nov 78

Zukor, Adolph Mar 50 obit Aug 76

Zulli, Floyd, Jr. Jan 58 obit Jan 81

Zuloaga, Ignacio obit Dec 45

Zumwalt, Bud see Zumwalt, Elmo R.

Zumwalt, Elmo R. Jun 71 obit Jun 2000

Zweig, Stefan obit Apr 42

Zwicky, Fritz Apr 53 obit Apr 74

Zwilich, Ellen Jan 86

Zworykin, Vladimir Kosma Dec 49 obit Sep 82

Zyuganov, Gennadi A. Oct 96